Architecture and Theology

For my parents,

Margaret and Alister Rae

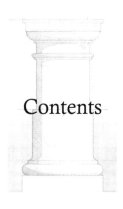

Contents

Preface   ix

1   New Ways of Seeing   1
    Doing Theology through the Spatial Arts

2   A Place to Dwell   11
    Construing the World through the Construction of Place

3   Freedom and Rule   37
    Conceiving the Law as a Realm of Freedom and Creativity

4   Making All Things New   75
    Transforming the World through Adaptation and Renewal

5   A Foretaste of Heaven   105
    Anticipating the New Jerusalem through the Civitas Terrena

6   Knowing and Dwelling   149
    Considering Epistemology through Habitation and Homelessness

7   Presence and Absence   181
    Discerning the Transcendent in the Realm of the Immanent

8   Places Full of Time   213
     Marking Time through the Medium of Place

9   Building from the Rubble   237
     Reaching for Redemption through Memory and Hope

Bibliography   257
Credits   273
Scripture Index   277
General Index   281

Preface

This book has been a long time in the making. I began thinking about theology and architecture when, as an architectural student at the University of Auckland in 1984, I wrote a dissertation on church architecture. Since that time, my awareness has grown that the fruitful interaction of theology and architecture extends well beyond buildings designed for worship. That awareness received considerable encouragement through the work of Jeremy Begbie, who in 1997 established Theology Through the Arts, a program of inquiry premised upon the conviction that theology has much to gain by engaging the arts in theological conversation. Jeremy himself has demonstrated how theological engagement with music can open up fresh lines of inquiry and generate new ways of articulating the subject matter of theology. The extraordinary fruitfulness of Jeremy's efforts extends also to the encouragement he has offered to artists and theologians to explore together how conversation between them might yield rich insight into the content of the Christian gospel.

Knowing of my own background in architecture, Jeremy approached me in 2001 and invited me, along with Alan Torrance, to establish a colloquium of theologians, architects, and other artists involved in shaping the built environment, who could extend the work of Theology Through the Arts into the arena of what we have called "the spatial arts." In pursuit of that goal, Jeremy approached John Witvliet, director of the Calvin Institute of Christian Worship at Calvin College in Grand Rapids, Michigan. John's enthusiasm for the project, and the generous support of the institute, led to the hosting of two international colloquia, in 2002 and 2004. To these three colleagues in the work of Christian theology, Jeremy Begbie, John Witvliet, and Alan Torrance, whom I greatly admire, I owe a huge debt of thanks.

Participants in the two colloquia were drawn from a range of disciplines including theology, architecture, philosophy, geography, and art history and included established academics, practitioners, and Ph.D. students working at the intersection of theology and the spatial arts. Our conversations were both stimulating and enjoyable, and I record my thanks to all those who took part. They were, in addition to Alan Torrance, Jeremy Begbie, and John Witvliet, Joyce Borger, Bill Dyrness, Trygve Johnson, Jack Kremers, David Ley, Henry Luttikhuizen, Graham Redding, Tiffany Robinson, Ben Suzuki, Duncan Stroik, Nicholas Wolterstorff, Douglas Farrow, Eric Jacobsen, Marga Jann, Jonathan Lee, Dino Marcantonio, Cherith Nordling, and Jo Ann Van Reeuwyk.

The explorations contained in this book received further stimulus from a two-day consultation in May 2016 with leading members of the Forum on Architecture, Culture, and Spirituality. The consultation was held at the Center of Theological Inquiry in Princeton, New Jersey and was hosted by the director of the center, Will Storrar. Will is extraordinarily adept at facilitating interdisciplinary engagement in service of the theological task and I thank him for his generous support and encouragement offered on that occasion and on many others. I am grateful, too, for the insight and convivial conversation shared with the other participants in that consultation, Will Storrar himself, Rebecca Krinke, Tom Barrie, Julio Bermudez, Douglas Duckworth, and Dominique Steiler. I am grateful, too, to Donald Strum, senior principal for design at the Michael Graves Architecture and Design Company, who, on the occasion of the consultation, hosted a visit to Michael Graves' own home in Princeton.

This book was further supported by two University of Otago research grants and by a research grant from the American Academy of Religion. I record my appreciation to both institutions, and particularly to the University of Otago, which allowed me two periods of research study leave during which I worked on this project. I spent the first of those periods of leave as a visiting scholar at Fuller Theological Seminary in Pasadena, California, where I had access to the seminary library and to the wonderful collection of books on architecture held at the Huntington Library in San Marino. I am grateful to Fuller Theological Seminary and to the Huntington Library for providing access to their literary resources.

At different stages of this project I benefitted from research assistance provided by two of my former Ph.D. students, Elizabeth Callender and Crystal Filep. Elizabeth assisted with bibliographic searches and Crystal with the images, including the beautifully rendered watercolor drawings that appear in chapter 3 and on the cover of the book. I am grateful to them both, and to graduate students and staff of the department of theology and religion at the University of Otago who have offered valuable feedback on several chapters that were presented in condensed form at the department's Postgraduate Seminars in Theology. Some of the material has also been tested at the GAPS Arts Series seminars in Auckland that were arranged by another former Ph.D. student, John Lewis. Feedback from the GAPS audience has provided further stimulus for my work. I record my thanks also to Kerry Crosland who assisted in editing many of the photographic images.

I gratefully acknowledge the editorial assistance received from the wonderful Jordan Rowan Fannin at Baylor University Press. Her enthusiasm for this project, her astute editorial judgment, and her efficiency in steering this book through the production phase are deeply appreciated. Jordan and the other staff at Baylor University Press who have assisted in bringing the book to press have been a joy to work with.

I wish to record, finally, my thanks to my family, to my wife, Jane, and to my parents, Alister and Margaret Rae, who with much patience and personal sacrifice have encouraged my interest in architecture and in theology. I am glad to dedicate this book to them.

1

New Ways of Seeing
Doing Theology through the Spatial Arts

Describing his formation as a pastor, the well-known author and pastoral theologian Eugene Peterson begins by reminding his readers of the importance of place. Places shape us; they contribute to our conception of the way things are in the world and they constitute the terrain upon which our lives unfold. Peterson writes:

> I have often had occasion while walking these hills or kayaking this lake to reflect on how important *place* is in the living of Christian faith. As I let the biblical revelation form my imagination, geography—this specifically Montana, Flathead geography—became as important to me in "the land of the living" as theology and the Bible did. I was becoming aware that every detail in the life of salvation that I was becoming familiar with in the scriptures took shape in named places that, with a good map, I can still locate: Ur and Haran, Bethel and Peniel, Sinai and Shiloh, Anathoth and Jerusalem, Nazareth and Bethlehem, Bethany and Emmaus . . . Soil and stone, latitude and longitude, lakes and mountains, towns and cities keep a life of faith grounded, rooted in *place*.[1]

Places are given, in the realm of nature, but they can also be made. From a humble shelter erected in a forest glade with materials found nearby, to such buildings as the Parthenon in Athens, Westminster Abbey in London,

---

[1] Eugene H. Peterson, *The Pastor* (New York: HarperCollins, 2011), 11.

the casinos of Las Vegas, or the Freedom Tower in New York, we construct places that speak of our values and aspirations and that determine in no small measure the ways we inhabit the world. As we inhabit them, they accrue meaning. They become repositories of memory, symbols of triumph or oppression, places of sorrow or joy. Peterson again observes: "Place gathers stories, relationships, memories."[2] Increasingly over time, places speak of who we are and of where we have come from. They both constrain and enable what we may yet do and become. The significance of architecture, suggests Alain de Botton, is "premised on the conviction that it is architecture's task to render vivid to us who we might ideally be."[3] Consideration of the impact upon us of place, of architecture, and of our built environment takes us, therefore, into realms of human memory, experience, and aspiration that are also of interest in theology.

Although the construction of our built environment relies heavily upon the calculations of science and the technical prowess of specialist fabricators, I am interested in the construction of our built environment as an artistic endeavor. I am interested, that is, in the ways in which our built environment exceeds the merely functional concern of providing suitable space and shelter for human activities of various kinds. Architecture is a poetic activity concerned with meaning and value. Indeed, all the arts that contribute to the shaping of our built environment—architecture, urban planning, sculpture, landscape design, and the like—share with the arts more broadly the capacity to open up new ways of seeing the world. They provide us with modes of discovery distinctly different from those employed in science or philosophy or indeed in the discipline of theology as it has customarily been practiced in the academy. Artists help us to see differently and to articulate things in ways inaccessible through other modes of inquiry.

Fascination with the different ways of seeing facilitated through art is the guiding interest of this book, specifically in relation to the subject matter of Christian theology. How might the art forms engaged in the formation of our built environment help us to explore, discover, and articulate the Christian faith today? What patterns and models might be found in our built environment that offer fresh ways of thinking about the subject matter of theology? What heuristic value might there be in a theological engagement with the built environment? The posing of such questions was not my own idea. They arose rather through conversations with Jeremy Begbie, who, through

---

[2] Peterson, *Pastor*, 13–14.
[3] Alain de Botton, *The Architecture of Happiness* (London: Penguin Books, 2006), 13.

the establishment of a program called Theology Through the Arts,[4] and in his own profound and very fruitful explorations in theology and music, has pioneered an engagement between theology and the arts that aspires not to offer a theology *of* the arts as has often been attempted, but rather to enter into conversation *with* the arts.[5] The purpose of the conversation is simply to explore what benefit there might be for theology in the different ways of seeing that artistic endeavor affords. What might be discovered, and what new modes of expression might emerge when theology avails itself of the insight generated through art? The attempt to explore the subject matter of theology *with* and *through* the arts requires a richer appreciation of the arts themselves than is common in our consumerist society. Midway through the twentieth century, Erich Fromm observed that

> contemporary man . . . is the eternal consumer. He takes in drinks, food, cigarettes, lectures, sights, books, films; everything is devoured, swallowed. The world has become one large object of his desire, one large bottle, one large breast. Man has become the eternally expectant and disappointed suckling.[6]

Art in the modern world is often subjected to the same consumerist impulse Fromm described. This project supposes, however, a less self-indulgent conception of the arts in which they help to extend our vision. Rather than assimilating art to a prior conceptuality so that it becomes merely a vehicle for expressing what we already know, the conversation attempted in this book is intended to open up new vistas, to seek new insight, and to draw attention to aspects of our human reality that we may have failed to see. Jeremy Begbie observes that "the 'heuristic' capacity of the arts has in the modern world frequently been downplayed or forgotten in favor of other functions of the arts

---

[4] The program was begun by Begbie at Ridley Hall in Cambridge during the 1990s, was then developed further in partnership with the Institute for Theology, Imagination and the Arts at St Andrews University, Scotland, and is continued now through Duke Initiatives in Theology and the Arts, based at Duke Divinity School in Durham, North Carolina, where Begbie is the Thomas A. Langford Research Professor of Theology.

[5] Begbie's published work on theology and music includes *Theology, Music and Time* (Cambridge: Cambridge University Press, 2000); *Resounding Truth: Christian Wisdom in the World of Music* (Grand Rapids: Baker, 2007); *Music, Modernity and God: Essays in Listening* (Oxford: Oxford University Press, 2013).

[6] Erich Fromm, *The Forgotten Language: An Introduction to the Understanding of Dreams, Fairy Tales and Myths* (New York: Rinehart, 1951). Cited without page reference in Christian Norberg-Schulz, *Architecture: Meaning and Place* (New York: Rizzoli, 1988), 18–19.

(e.g. self-expression, entertainment)."[7] Rowan Williams, also a participant in the Theology Through the Arts project, sheds further light on the capacity of the arts to be a vehicle of discovery.

> Art, whether Christian or not, can't properly begin with a message and then seek for a vehicle. Its roots lie, rather, in the single story or metaphor or configuration of sound or shape which *requires* attention and development from the artist. In the process of that development, *we find meaning we had not suspected*; but if we try to begin with the meanings, they will shrink to the scale of what we already understand: whereas the creative activity *opens up what we did not understand* and perhaps will not fully understand even when the actual work of creation is done.[8]

Williams' phrase captures well the goal of this project to "find meaning we had not suspected," particularly through attention to the spatial arts. As Begbie has put it, "Realities hitherto unnoticed come to meet me through art, call forth my attention, shift my outlook."[9]

In the case of architecture and urban planning, the realities that "come to meet us" are complex and multifaceted. Henri Lefebvre observes that "space has been shaped and moulded from historical and cultural elements, but this has been a political process. Space is political and ideological. It is a product literally filled with ideologies."[10] LeFebvre's cautionary tone is no doubt appropriate; the arrangement of space can be sinister and coercive, but not only so. It can also give rise to joy, celebration, and delight. It can speak of worthy goals and human aspirations, of God's self-disclosure, and of God's call upon us to live well in the midst of the created order.

In pursuit of "meaning we had not suspected," this book offers a series of conversations between theology and what I am calling the spatial arts: principally architecture, but also urban planning, landscape design, and sculpture. These arts give definition to the spaces we inhabit in our daily lives. They exert a substantial influence upon the unfolding of our daily activities, but we do not often pay attention to how they do that or to what they may reveal. This book is an attempt to direct attention to the built environment

---

 [7] Jeremy S. Begbie, "Theology through the Arts," oral presentation at the Theology and the Built Environment colloquium, Calvin College, Grand Rapids, September 2002.

 [8] Rowan Williams, "Making It Strange: Theology in Other(s') Words," in *Sounding the Depths: Theology through the Arts*, ed. Jeremy S. Begbie (London: SCM Press, 2002), 19–38, 28 (emphasis added).

 [9] Jeremy S. Begbie, Introduction to Begbie, *Sounding the Depths*, 1–13, 2.

 [10] Henri LeFebvre, "Reflections on the Politics of Space," trans. Michael J. Enders, *Antipode* 8 (1976): 30–36, 31.

and to engage in that attentiveness with an attitude of theological curiosity. The approach is not entirely new. Valuable explorations of the theological richness of the built environment have recently been undertaken by Timothy Gorringe,[11] Philip Sheldrake,[12] and Sigurd Bergmann, along with others who contributed to the collection of essays edited by Bergmann, *Theology in Built Environments*.[13] Within that work, Bergmann muses on whether it makes sense to develop a theology *of* the built environment, whether the built environment should itself be regarded *as* a form of theological expression, or whether we might think of doing theology *in* built environments. All of these are possible, I think, and legitimate. A theology *of* the built environment may consider the place of buildings in the working out of God's purposes and the flourishing of his creation. This, it seems to me, is the particular and very valuable contribution of Gorringe's work. Studies of the built environment *as* theology abound, particularly with respect to church architecture and in reflections on sacred space. Bergmann's own work, and that which he has gathered together in the collection of essays by a number of authors, is focused on doing theology "*in* and with regard to built environments."[14] My own approach combines some elements of the *as* and the *in*. I am interested in the ways in which theology may be developed and enriched through engagement with the built environment, and especially in the ways in which such engagement might prompt new ways of thinking about the subject matter of theology.

Each of the chapters of this book can be read on its own. There are thematic links between the chapters, but I make no attempt to develop an argument sequentially from one chapter to the next. Insofar as there is a logic to the arrangement of the chapters, it is roughly chronological. Beyond this introduction, the second chapter has as its principal focus the architecture of Abraham and his nomadic descendants. Taking the Roman architectural theorist Vitruvius Pollio as a conversation partner, and drawing upon the discussion of Vitruvius offered by Robert Dripps, I explore what is going on theologically in the building of altars as Abraham and his family journey

---

[11] T. J. Gorringe, *A Theology of the Built Environment: Justice, Empowerment, Redemption* (Cambridge: Cambridge University Press, 2002).

[12] See Philip Sheldrake, *Spaces for the Sacred: Place, Memory and Identity* (London: SCM Press, 2001); and *The Spiritual City: Theology, Spirituality, and the Urban* (Oxford: Wiley Blackwell, 2014).

[13] Sigurd Bergmann, ed., *Theology in Built Environments: Exploring Religion, Architecture, and Design* (New Brunswick: Transaction, 2009).

[14] Sigurd Bergmann, "God's Here and Now in Built Environments," in Bergmann, *Theology in Built Environments*, 9–22, 11 (emphasis added).

toward the promised land. Through subsequent chapters I consider the classical orders of architecture developed in ancient Greece and Rome, explore the destruction and rebuilding of Rome, dwell for a while in medieval and Renaissance Europe, find my way to the twentieth century through the *raumplan* theory of Adolf Loos and the architecture of Louis Kahn, visit a number of other modern architectural sites, and finally explore Daniel Libeskind's Jewish Museum in Berlin and his proposal for the rebuilding of Ground Zero in the wake of September 11, 2001.

In all of this, theology is the principal interest. There is, however, no single pattern of exploration. Sometimes the architecture plays the role of text. It "speaks" of particular theological commitments and aspirations and preserves a vision of human life before God that we are seldom attentive to. The vision of the heavenly Jerusalem, for instance, preserved in the architecture of late medieval and Renaissance cities offers a very concrete articulation of what the city should aspire to be. Although we are surrounded by architecture for much of our lives, a high level of architectural literacy is relatively rare. Many of us walk about our towns and cities oblivious to the ways in which architecture "speaks." Yet consideration of architecture as "text" is not novel. The idea that architecture can tell us something about what is going on in the world is as ancient as Scripture itself. In 1 Kings, for example, architecture becomes a medium of divine discourse, albeit in this case catastrophic. Speaking of the newly constructed temple, the Lord says to Solomon,

> This house will become a heap of ruins; everyone passing by it will be astonished, and will hiss; and they will say, "Why has the LORD done such a thing to this land and to this house?" Then they will say, "Because they have forsaken the LORD their God, who brought their ancestors out of the land of Egypt, and embraced other gods, worshipping them and serving them."
> (1 Kgs 1:8-9)

The temple could also be read as a text in its newly constructed state, before any threat of destruction had been realized. The temple architecture offered a theological vision of the cosmos flourishing according to God's good intent and of the whole world as a theatre of praise.[15] The narrative quality of religious architecture is perhaps commonly recognized, if not so readily understood, but nonreligious architecture is equally likely to convey through the built form particular narratives about the nature of the world and our place within it. Consider, for example, the National Mall in Washington, D.C.,

---

[15] On which, see, e.g., G. K. Beale, *The Temple and the Church's Mission: A Biblical Theology of the Dwelling Place of God* (Downers Grove, Ill.: InterVarsity, 2004).

FIGURE 1.1
The Mall, Washington, D.C.

Trafalgar Square in London, the Plaza de Mayo in Buenos Aires, the Avenue des Champs Élysées in Paris, or the avenue Unter den Linden in Berlin. These monumental streetscapes tell stories of national identity, of what their respective nations believe themselves to be. It is no accident that these places have been again and again the stages upon which historic moments in the nation's history have been enacted and memorialized.

Another form the conversation takes, other than reading the architecture as text, is to note patterns and relationships in architecture that suggest new ways of thinking about the subject matter of theology. In chapter 3, for instance, the relation between the strictly prescribed rules for the execution of the classical orders of architecture and the creativity and innovation expected of architects offers a model for thinking about the relation between law and freedom in Christian theology. In chapter 4, the reuse of materials from ancient ruins along with the remodeling and recommissioning of pagan buildings for Christian use prompts consideration of the relation between the old creation and the new in Christian theology and the proposal of a transformative rather than annihilationist eschatology. In chapter 7, the relation between presence and absence in architecture offers a model for thinking about the presence and the absence of God, and about the coming kingdom of God, which is commonly said to be inaugurated in and through Jesus but not yet present in its fullness.

In close alignment with Jeremy Begbie's vision for the Theology Through the Arts program, this book aspires to enrich theological conversation through conversation with the arts. I suggest three reasons why such a project may yield new insight and understanding. First, we live in a culture that is saturated with artistic expression. From the instantly accessible medium of music, through "tagging" or the more sophisticated graffiti art of Banksy, through film and theatre, public art installations, and on to the visual art with which we typically adorn our homes, art is a medium that is *virtually* omnipresent and frequently gives voice to public passions, interests, and concerns. "Spirituality," too, is commonly explored and expressed through the medium of art. As Begbie points out, "If part of theology's calling is to engage the main currencies of the cultural environment in which it finds itself, and if the late- or post-modern ethos is in many respects an artistic or aesthetic one (especially when broadly religious concerns are in view), then it is clear that those concerned to grow in wisdom about God cannot afford to ignore the arts."[16]

Second, the questions explored in theology and the mode of discourse adopted have often been shaped by theology's interactions with philosophy and with science. Fruitful though those conversations have been, a conversation with the arts promises a broadening of horizons and the opening up of new avenues of exploration. Such a conversation also makes possible an extension of theological inquiry beyond the narrow intellectualism in which it has often been confined. Art touches upon a broader range of human experience and, by means of what Begbie calls its "integrative power," facilitates an interrelation "of the intellect with other facets of our human makeup thus helping to nourish 'wise' theology and offset the kind of dichotomies which have plagued so much theology in the past."[17] There is obvious truth as well in the observation that not everything we know can be put into words. Art provides a means of articulating the truth of things, or of allowing us to see the truth of things, that is more capacious than the language commonly utilized in theology.

Third, it is arguable that the specific subject matter of theology itself invites, indeed compels, close contact with the spatial arts. So, for example, given the detailed attention that the biblical narrative gives to the material creation, to the land, to the building of altars and eventually a temple, and to an imagined heavenly city through which is represented a vision of human

---

[16] Jeremy S. Begbie, "Theology through the Arts" (unpublished Rationale Document for the Music and Theology colloquium, December 2001), 4.1.1.

[17] Begbie, "Theology through the Arts," 4.1.2.

life as it is intended to be by God, it would be curious if resources from the world of the spatial arts were not able to provide insight into these themes of theological reflection. That the spatial arts can indeed provide such resources is the assumption prompting this book. I hope that in the following pages, the legitimacy and the fruitfulness of that assumption will be demonstrated.[18]

[18] Readers who persevere to the end of this book will readily observe that I have left many relevant books unread and, of course, many interesting buildings unexplored. The observation will be correct. But my intention in this work is to open up a field of inquiry and to demonstrate its potential, not to exhaust it. The latter is impossible in any case. I will be content, therefore, if the book serves as a stimulus to further explorations of the field.

2

A Place to Dwell

Construing the World through the Construction of Place

The Christian theological tradition has had a great deal to say about the temporal dimension of human existence, about our historicity, about our being in time. But it has had little to say about spatiality.[1] This neglect is puzzling, for it is obvious that spatiality is as fundamental a characteristic of the created order as time. Space and time together constitute the divinely bestowed conditions of our creatureliness. It is surely as important theologically, therefore, to consider what it means to exist in space as it is to consider how we are to exist in time. My purpose in this book is to contribute to that task by drawing upon the way space and place are conceived and defined through the spatial arts, especially architecture.

Given that the meanings of both terms, "space" and "place," are contested, a comment about the definition of terms is appropriate to begin with. The contested nature of the terms reflects the multidisciplinary attention given to space and place. As Lineau Castello has recently pointed out, the concept of place (and equally of space) "has a *psychological* interpretation, an *architectural-urbanistic* interpretation, an *anthropological* interpretation, and

---

[1] Notable exceptions are to be found in the work of T. F. Torrance, Karl Heim, M. Spindler, and Harold Turner. More recently, John Inge, Timothy Gorringe, Sigurd Bergmann, and Philip Sheldrake have published monographs on the subject of space and place.

so on."[2] Each addresses the topic of place "according to an individual rationale inherent to each discipline."[3] It is not possible, nor would it be helpful,
to assimilate in a work such as this the full range of such interpretation. I will
employ, however, working definitions of space and place, somewhat along the
lines suggested by the Chinese geographer Yi-Fu Tuan. Tuan writes, " 'Space'
is more abstract than 'place.' What begins as undifferentiated space becomes
place as we get to know it better and endow it with value."[4] Theologically, we
might say that "space," along with "time," refers to the realm given by God
for habitation by his creatures. "Place," on the other hand, refers to concrete
locations within that realm that are endowed with value precisely because
they have become the site of particular experiences and encounters. Or, as
Jeff Malpas has it, place may be understood as "the open region in which
things are gathered and disclosed."[5] Malpas does not wish to conceive of the
meaning of "place" only in physicalist terms, but his suggestion that "the idea
of place [is] tied to a notion of gathering or 'focus' " serves well my purposes
here.[6] The same notion of place as imbued with significance of one kind or
another—a significance that is particular and infinitely variable according to
those who experience it—is also evident in Craig Bartholomew's theological
discussion of place in his 2011 book, *Where Mortals Dwell: A Christian View
of Place for Today*. Bartholomew writes:

> Place is the rich, African beauty of Rwanda and churches filled with human
> skulls from the genocide that still—how long?—indelibly marks the land-
> scape of that country. Place is an Amish farm, and the animal factory,
> "which, like the concentration camp, is a vision of Hell."[7] Place is the home
> one retreats to for rest and nourishment, and place is the "homes" that are
> the scene of abuse. Place is Mother Teresa's home for the dying in Calcutta—
> "something beautiful for God"—with its translucent light caught on camera
> by Malcolm Muggeridge, and also Birkenau and Auschwitz.[8]

    [2] Lineau Castello, *Rethinking the Meaning of Place: Conceiving Place in Architecture-
Urbanism* (Farnham: Ashgate, 2010), 27.
    [3] Castello, *Rethinking the Meaning of Place*, 27.
    [4] Yi-Fu Tuan, *Space and Place: The Perspective of Experience* (Minneapolis: University
of Minnesota Press, 1977), 6.
    [5] Jeff Malpas, *Heidegger's Topology: Being, Place, World* (Cambridge, Mass.: MIT Press,
2006), 31.
    [6] Malpas, *Heidegger's Topology*, 29.
    [7] Wendell Berry, *Way of Ignorance* (Emeryville, Calif.: Shoemaker & Hoard, 2005), 99.
    [8] Craig G. Bartholomew, *Where Mortals Dwell: A Christian View of Place for Today*
(Grand Rapids: Baker Academic, 2011), 1–2.

Very briefly put, for now, place is *significant* space. All that it takes for space to become significant is that it be recognized as the locus in which particular memorable and formative things have happened, are happening, or will happen. This conception of place will be worked out in more detail in what follows.

The Origins of Architecture

I take as my starting point the original text of architectural theory, *The Ten Books on Architecture*, written by the Roman architect Vitruvius Pollio in the first century B.C. Vitruvius offers detailed instruction on such matters as the measure and proportions of the classical orders of architecture, the requirements of dwellings, principles of town planning, acoustics, the use of materials, and so on. By way of introduction to book 2, however, he offers something rather different in character—an account of how architecture began. Vitruvius constructs a myth of origins, as it were, a story of urban humanity at its most primitive and basic level. As with all myths of origin, Vitruvius' story is not an archaeological project but seeks rather to reveal the fundamental conditions of human existence that now obtain in diverse historical and geographical circumstances. His basic thesis is that language, politics, and civilization are intimately bound up with humanity's sense of itself as existing in space; the advancement of human culture, furthermore, is both expressed in and facilitated by humanity's efforts to build a place to dwell.

"The men of old," Vitruvius begins, "were born like the wild beasts, in woods, caves and groves and lived on savage fare."[9] Notable here is that human beings, to begin with, are enclosed—by woods, caves, and groves. There is no sky and no horizon, no view to anywhere beyond the immediate vicinity. The inference Vitruvius draws here is that human beings, to begin with, have no sense of themselves as spatial beings. They are not conscious of their location in space, of existing here and not there. Their lives are consumed and their construal of the world is exhausted by their pursuit of "savage fare."

> As time went on, the thickly crowded trees in a certain place, tossed by storms and winds, and rubbing their branches against one another, caught fire, and so the inhabitants of that place were put to flight, being terrified by the furious flame. After it subsided, they drew near, and observing that they

---

[9] Vitruvius, *The Ten Books on Architecture*, trans. Morris Hicky Morgan (New York: Dover, 1960), 2.1.1 (38). Citations are from this translation unless otherwise noted.

were very comfortable standing before the warm fire, they put on logs and, while thus keeping it alive, brought up other people to it, showing them by signs how much comfort they got from it. In that gathering of men, at a time when utterance of sound was purely individual, from daily habits they fixed upon articulate words just as these had happened to come; then from indicating by name things in common use, the result was that in this chance way they began to talk, and thus originated conversation with one another.[10]

It was a chance outbreak of fire, according to this myth of origins, that occasioned the first gathering together of human beings and prompted the development of language. But the fire also produced another result equally central to the development of human culture and civilization. The fire formed a clearing. Humanity was no longer enclosed and introverted; the open space that now obtained awakened in primitive human beings a sense of their location in space, and it prompted in them the desire to define their own location through the building of shelters—the desire, that is, to make a place for themselves.[11] Vitruvius explains:

Finding themselves naturally gifted beyond the other animals in not being obliged to walk with faces to the ground, but upright and gazing upon the splendour of the starry firmament, and also in being able to do with ease whatever they chose with their hands and fingers, they began in that first assembly to construct shelters.[12]

That human beings do not walk with their faces to the ground is, according to Vitruvius, the first condition of their spatial awareness. Their upright stance enables, "in contrast to the crawling position, with its horizontal connection to the ground"[13] an orientation to a larger world. It enables human beings to look away from their immediate vicinity and to gaze "upon the splendour of the starry firmament." Central to Vitruvius' account is the impulse toward order that is engendered by the clearing in the forest. Humanity begins to contemplate the world, which is experienced for the first time not as random chaos but rather as a cosmos. The firmament above is suggestive of an overarching structure within which the things of the world have their place. Now there is something of which we can make sense, and

---

[10] Vitruvius, *Architecture*, 2.1.1 (38).

[11] Yi-Fu Tuan's distinction between space and place (noted above) comes into play here.

[12] Vitruvius, *Architecture*, 2.1.2 (38).

[13] I take the point from R. D. Dripps, whose study of Vitruvius is the basis for the ideas I am developing here. See R. D. Dripps, *The First House: Myth, Paradigm and the Task of Architecture* (Cambridge, Mass.: MIT Press, 1997), 17.

so language evolves, architecture begins, and civilization gets underway. The key point for our purposes is the dependence of this process upon the awakening in human beings of a sense of their location in space.

One might dispute particular details of Vitruvius' myth, but there is sufficient resonance in his account with the sentiments of Psalm 8 for us to pursue a theological consideration of his ideas. The Psalmist writes,

> When I look at your heavens, the work of your fingers,
> the moon and the stars that you have established;
> what are human beings that you are mindful of them,
> mortals that you care for them?
> Yet you have made them a little lower than God,
> and crowned them with glory and honor.
> You have given them dominion over the works of your hands;
> you have put all things under their feet. (Ps 8:3-6)

Here, too, contemplation of the heavens prompts wonder and inquiry concerning humanity's own place in the cosmos.[14] Architecture, according to Vitruvius, is one of the primary means by which that place is acknowledged and brought to expression. According to the Psalmist, worship is another. We shall see, in due course, how these two are brought together in creating a theology that makes something of space and place.

Meanwhile, however, we will consider further the architectural expression of this order. Dripps observes that the structure of the cosmos "has its counterpart in the orderly system that underlies the building of the first dwelling."[15] There is an attempt to replicate the perceived order in the cosmos. This is certainly the case in the architecture of classical Greek and Roman temples, which belonged to the era of Vitruvius himself. Order, symmetry and proportion are clearly the cardinal principles of the architecture that he commends.[16] Vitruvius explains:

> The design of a temple depends on symmetry, the principles of which must be most carefully observed by the architect. They are due to proportion, in

---

[14] Mircea Eliade offers evidence of the widespread occurrence across the cultures and religions of the world of the relation between humanity's sense of self and the contemplation of the heavens. See his book *The Sacred and the Profane: The Nature of Religion*, trans. Willard R. Trask (New York: Harcourt, Brace & World, 1959), chap. 1.

[15] Dripps, *First House*, 16.

[16] It would be left to the architectural theorists of the Renaissance, especially Sebastiano Serlio, to "sanctify" the orders and to present them as the invariable embodiment of all architectural virtue. See John Summerson, *The Classical Language of Architecture* (London: Thames & Hudson, 1980), 10–13.

Greek, *analogia*. Proportion is a correspondence among the measures of the members of an entire work, and of the whole to a certain part selected as standard. From this result the principles of symmetry. Without symmetry and proportion there can be no principles in the design of any temple.[17]

The order and symmetry on which Vitruvius insists for the temple are representative of the order revealed in the cosmos itself.[18] The effort to replicate, or testify to, this perceived cosmic order has been a common feature of sacred architecture throughout humanity's history.[19] Typically too, the architecture encourages a repeat of the "heavenward gaze" that awakens consideration of humanity's place in the world. In churches belonging to the tradition of Byzantine basilicas, for example, the firmament is represented in the vaults and domes, and the worshipper, gazing heavenward, finds depicted there Christ the Pantocrator surrounded by angels and saints, and sovereign over all. St Paul's Cathedral in London is a notable example of this form. The same motif was later adopted in libraries of the baroque period, as, for example, in the library of Admont Abbey in Austria. The collected scriptures of human learning were often housed under domed representations of the heavenly firmament; both products of human culture, the architecture and the books, testified to the order and intelligibility of the cosmos.[20]

More fundamentally, however, Vitruvius holds that all architecture, beginning with the rough shelters of primitive humanity, is to be understood as a means by which humanity simultaneously discovers and testifies to the order and intelligibility of the world. Architecture is not merely functional; it does more than provide shelter for human activity. It contributes also to the shaping of a paradigm or a conceptual framework for the habitation of our world. Christian Norberg-Schulz puts the matter thus: "We can . . . say that the idea of inhabiting a place consists of orientation and identification. We have to find out where we are and who we are in order for our existence to acquire some kind of meaning."[21] The definition of place and

---

[17] Vitruvius, *Architecture*, 3.1.1 (72).

[18] Such order is thought by Vitruvius to be revealed in the proportions of the human body; it is the proportions of the body that he takes as definitive for the Doric, Ionic, and Corinthian orders.

[19] This phenomenon has been well documented. See, e.g., Harold W. Turner, *From Temple to Meeting House* (The Hague: Mouton, 1979); and Eliade, *Sacred and the Profane*.

[20] The Admont Abbey library was designed by architect Gotthard Hayberger.

[21] Christian Norberg-Schulz, *L'abitare: L'insediamento, lo spazio urbano, la casa* (Milan: Electa, 1995), 7; cited by Maria Antonietta Crippa, "A Dwelling for Man within the Harmony of the Cosmos," in *Living Gaudí: The Architect's Complete Vision*, ed. Maria Antonietta Crippa (New York: Rizzoli, 2006), 13–38, 25.

FIGURE 2.1
St Paul's Cathedral

FIGURE 2.2
Library of Admont Abbey

the development of architecture are means by which human beings come to terms with what it is to live in the world, to distinguish their place within it, and to orient themselves according to its given order.

The Construction of Paradigms

The need of human beings to orient themselves to the given order of the world is widely recognized and has been variously described. In order for human life to have some direction, coherence, and meaning, we have need of what I refer to as a "worldview," a "plausibility structure," or a "paradigm for living." These conceptual and existential frameworks, formed and developed over time, enable us to see the world as a coherent and intelligible whole, and provide us with "the reliable and predictable grounding necessary for human action to unfold within this world."[22] Dripps identifies several features of paradigms that are worth noting before we proceed to a consideration of the ways in which particular places, sometimes articulated architecturally, can contribute to the formation and to the expression of theological paradigms.

The Public Character of Paradigms

One of the conditions under which humans inhabit the world is a degree of public agreement about the "reliable and predictable grounding" for human action. Architecture certainly contributes to such agreement (or compliance!), for it sets in stone, at least for a time, certain conceptions about the way the world is to be organized and human life is to be lived within it.[23] Dripps writes:

> The order that architecture must establish is a public order, yet accessible to each individual. This is not the world of the solitary individual in the forest, described by Vitruvius as incapable of making architecture until joined with others in the clearing: architecture is derived as a consequence of the initiation of discourse enabled by the gathering. Here also, the nascent political body determines the structure of institutions that will endure beyond each individual life and will ultimately shape the relationships among these people and between them and the earth.[24]

---

[22] Dripps, *First House*, 21.

[23] It is one of the tensions of architecture that it frequently endures long after the paradigms that it embodies have lost their public acceptance. The church buildings we inhabit are a notable case in point.

[24] Dripps, *First House*, 21.

Such institutions come about in a whole host of different ways, of course, ranging between democratic evolution and despotic imposition. That matter, however, is not my concern here. To be noted, rather, is the way the architectural definition of space and place contributes to the shaping of a people. It is a means for human orientation in and habitation of the world and can serve, as we shall see, their theological orientation as well.

Tradition

A corollary of the public nature of paradigms is the development of a tradition through which paradigms are handed on, enriched, and reshaped. The paradigm is by no means a static construct; it will have a fundamental structure that endures over time, but that structure is continuously accumulating articulate responses to the received world.[25] Vitruvius describes the process among primitive builders thus: "And since they were of an imitative and teachable nature, they would daily point out to each other the results of their building, boasting of the novelties in it; and thus, with their natural gifts sharpened by emulation, their standards improved daily."[26] Innovation and "handing over" are characteristics of the community's habitation of a paradigm, but both processes are undertaken for the sake of preserving something valuable. It is not merely the techniques of building that are preserved, however but also, along with them, a mode of dwelling in the world. "The patterns of an ordered existence that are at the foundation of this now purposeful settlement . . . derive their authority from their capacity to give tangible structure to the world . . . [and] coincide," Dripps argues, "with the structures fundamental to dwelling."[27]

The Evolution of Paradigms

Paradigms for construing the world take shape, according to Dripps, as the human subject recognizes a degree of discordance or discontinuity between the understood world and that which is beyond it. The paradigm is evolved in the space created by this discontinuity as a construct of critical reconciliation or judgement. In a manner similar to the advancement of scientific knowledge, as described by Thomas Kuhn, aspects of human experience or observation that appear anomalous within an established paradigm prompt

---

[25] Dripps, *First House*, 28.
[26] Vitruvius, *Architecture*, 2.1.3 (39).
[27] Dripps, *First House*, 31–32.

adaptations of the paradigm or, in some cases, a revolution in understanding.[28] Paradigms are thus developed in responsive dependence upon that which is given or revealed.

Freedom

It is an important feature of paradigms that they "establish the constraint that is the basis for any creative freedom."[29] This may be illustrated by the paradigmatic structures of a language. The rules of grammar establish the constraints that are the basis of free speech.[30] The language of classical architecture likewise provides a means for creative expression that has been turned to all manner of architectural endeavors, and its rules of proportion, based as they are upon the proportions of the human body, remain in play even when classical *style* has been left behind. "How is it," Dripps asks, "that the paradigm, a pattern held in common by a culture, can be responsive to the creative will of an individual?" Paradigms are not, he goes on, "monolithic cultural dinosaurs but are multifarious constructs, offering particular points of access to particular individuals." The creative possibilities available to individuals are revealed thus as "potentials within a more simple and overarching story."[31] Anticipating the eventual theological development of Dripps' discussion of paradigms in architecture, it is worth noting here the open character of paradigms and the freedom and creativity that is potentially afforded by them. Openness and freedom are not inevitable, of course; a paradigm, a worldview, or a metanarrative can just as well be constricting and coercive as liberating, but it is not bound to be so. It is arguable that the habitation of a paradigm or the adoption of a metanarrative according to which the world is construed and understood, far from being necessarily oppressive, is in fact a *conditio sine qua non* for any free and responsible human action. Without a paradigm or an existential framework of some sort that gives meaning and purpose to human action, we cannot be free; we become slaves to our own base instincts. The degree of freedom made possible through one's habitation of a paradigm will depend, however, upon the extent to which the particular paradigm conforms to what is good and beautiful and true. That the Christian construal of the world, the paradigm of the gospel, if you like, is directed

---

[28] See Thomas Kuhn, *The Structure of Scientific Revolutions*, 2nd ed. (Chicago: University of Chicago Press, 1970), 52–53.

[29] Dripps, *First House*, 26.

[30] For further discussion of the syntax of architecture, see Roger Scruton, *The Aesthetics of Architecture* (London: Methuen, 1979), chap. 7.

[31] Dripps, *First House*, 27.

toward freedom is evident in Jesus' claim that "if you continue in my word, you are truly my disciples; and you will know the truth and the truth will make you free" (John 8:32).

The Heuristic Character of Paradigms

That there is both a conservative and an innovative dimension to the habitation of a paradigm indicates that paradigms are heuristic in character. They facilitate discovery precisely by providing an order in terms of which new discoveries are rendered intelligible. Architecturally, the heuristic functioning of a paradigm works in two ways. "Understanding rarely comes," Dripps writes, "in the absence of action. The making of an artifact or an idea is always accompanied by a significant degree of revelation or discovery, far surpassing that of the more passive reception of information."[32] Or, as Vitruvius puts it,

> As men made progress by becoming daily more expert in building, and as their industry was increased by their dexterity so that from habit they attained to considerable skill, *their intelligence was enlarged by their industry* until the more proficient adopted the trade of carpenters. . . . From these early beginnings . . . they next gradually advanced from the construction of buildings to the other arts and sciences, and so passed from a rude and barbarous mode of life to civilization and refinement.[33]

Representation

A final feature of paradigms, according to Dripps, is their power to represent the world. "Represent" is a multivalent term, of course. It can mean to make present, or it can mean to stand in for something that is not there. The first meaning suggests the power to reveal something that has been unknown or obscure, to render it visible and intelligible. A scientific paradigm, for example—say that of Newtonian cosmology—renders the world present through mathematical representation in a way not previously possible. It enables us, that is, to see what is there. Representation as "making present," Dripps observes, is especially well suited to architecture. A house, for instance, represents a way of habitation in the world—whether Le Corbusier's mass-produced "machine for living in,"[34] Heidegger's farmhouse in

---

[32] Dripps, *First House*, 32.
[33] Vitruvius, *Architecture*, 2.1.6 (40) (emphasis added).
[34] Le Corbusier, *Towards an Architecture*, 2nd ed. (1928; repr., London: Frances Lincoln, 2008), 87.

the Black Forest,[35] or Antonio Gaudí's organic conception of the house in continuity with nature and as witness, thus, to the glory of God,[36] to name but three variants along a broad spectrum—while at the same time making present the respective modes of habitation.

"Represent" can also mean to stand in for something that is not there. In this case "stand in" testifies to what is not there and may act on its behalf. It functions as a witness or sign. Although architecture more typically seeks to make present, it can also be a means of testimony to that which is not present or at least not visible. Monuments provide an obvious example, especially those erected to testify to the deeds of those now departed. Such artifacts again serve the purpose of connecting us to the world and of inviting us to construe it in particular ways.

"A third meaning of representation," Dripps points out, "refers to the typical: 'to represent' is to typify a class of objects or ideas."[37] Typicality implies a degree of sameness between distinct entities that entitles us to expect a degree of consistency in the way such entities behave. That consistency enables us to plan ahead and to engage in projects under the reasonable assumption that our past experience can serve as a reliable guide to the future. The value of the typical comes from the hypothesis we must make that the reality at hand belongs to a coherent pattern of things and events. Such hypothesizing is yet one more means by which human beings take a stand in order to construe the world.[38] Representation, in all three forms, both depends upon and helps to configure a paradigmatic structure that in turn facilitates discovery, understanding, and habitation of our world.

The Construction of Theology

Having considered these resources of architectural history, we will now turn more explicitly to theology and develop a theological account of our being in space. We begin with the book of Genesis and with the stories told there, first, of the divinely established suitability of the world for creaturely habitation, in Genesis 1; and second, of two human beings *placed* in a garden, in chapter 2. With respect to creaturely habitation of the world, the obvious is worth stating: human beings, along with all of God's other creatures, need

---

[35] Martin Heidegger, "Building, Dwelling, Thinking," in Heidegger, *Poetry, Language, Thought*, trans. Albert Hofstadter (New York: Harper & Row, 1971), 145–61, 160.

[36] On which see Crippa, "Dwelling for Man," 37.

[37] Dripps, *First House*, 33.

[38] See Dripps, *First House*, 35.

a place to be, precisely because they are bodily creatures. The point needs to be stressed because it has proven to be a troublesome one within many of the world's great intellectual traditions. Our embodiment has often been thought incidental to our true identity as human beings; it has been treated as a temporary expedient that will have no part in the full and final realization of our identity. Dualistic conceptions of the world in which spirit is good and matter is bad are prominent across many human cultures and have left unfortunate traces in the tradition of Christian theology, too. Here in the Bible's opening chapters, however, materiality is a given and is declared to be good by the one who has made it (Gen 1:31). *Emplacement*, accordingly, is regarded as a good and necessary condition of God's gift of life to the creature. As the story unfolds, we learn that *displacement* threatens the life of the creature. Of particular interest here is the connection made in Genesis between spatial location and theological orientation. The placement of Adam and Eve in the garden of Eden places them within the realm of God's provision and of God's presence (2:16 and 3:8). Their defiance of God, conversely, leads to their displacement and eventually to their alienation from God.

Still within the realm of mythical origins, we are told in Genesis 4:17 that human beings begin to build. The first builder of a city was Cain, but as Jacques Ellul explains, the circumstances are far from auspicious.[39] After he had murdered his brother, Cain was summoned by God and cursed: "When you till the ground, it will no longer yield to you its strength; you will be a fugitive and a wanderer on the earth" (4:12). Despite the Lord offering Cain his protection, however, "Cain went away from the presence of the LORD, and settled in the land of Nod, east of Eden" (4:16). It is in Nod that Cain builds a city.[40] But there is an irony here, for "Nod" means "wandering." Cain has "gone away from the presence of the Lord" and attempts to fashion a world of his own. It is clear that human beings need a place to dwell, but there is no promise in this place that Cain makes, away from the presence of the Lord. Cain's attempts to settle, therefore, will not overcome his displacement from God.

Creation and fall both have to do, in this Genesis account, with humanity's location. By the hand of the Creator humankind is placed in Eden,

---

[39] See Jacques Ellul, *The Meaning of the City*, trans. Dennis Pardee (Grand Rapids: Eerdmans, 1970), 1–7.

[40] Craig Bartholomew advises that the Hebrew is unclear at this point. It is likely, he suggests, that it was Cain's son Enoch who built the first city. See Bartholomew, *Where Mortals Dwell*, 35. My point about the unpromising nature of this enterprise when undertaken apart from God remains valid, however.

but, following their disobedience, humans find themselves displaced. We noted above that the purpose of Vitruvius' myth of origins was to reveal the fundamental conditions of human existence that now obtain in diverse historical and geographical circumstances. Likewise here, the Genesis account offers a particular interpretation of who and where we are now. A striking echo of this Genesis account can be heard in the letters of Václav Havel, who writes:

> I believe that with the loss of God, man has lost a kind of absolute and universal system of coordinates, to which he could always relate anything, chiefly himself. His world and his personality gradually began to break up into separate, incoherent fragments corresponding to different, relative coordinates.[41]

Edward S. Casey likewise comments upon the loss. "By late modern times," Casey writes, "the world had become increasingly placeless, a matter of mere sites instead of lived places, of sudden displacements rather than of pervading implacements."[42] Because human fallenness is manifest in displacement or a loss of coordinates, it is significant that the history of redemption begins with God's promise of a new place to dwell. "The LORD said to Abram, 'Go from your country and your kindred and your father's house to the land that I will show you'" (Gen 12:1). Thus begins also the story of God's people, Israel, and of a particular, theological way of construing the world. The stories of Genesis 1–11 are a retrospective; they are the later products of a theology that properly begins with the call of Abraham, with the promise to him of a new place of dwelling and a new way of construing and living in the world.

In the discussion of Vitruvius above, we noted his contention that, having gazed upon the starry firmament, humanity began to build. Architecture is thus set forth as one of the primary means by which humanity's place in the world is acknowledged and expressed. The evidence of Psalm 8, we also noted, suggests that worship is another. These two, architecture and worship, are given together in the practice Abraham begins of building altars to the Lord. The altars constructed by Abraham—and in due course by his offspring—mark out the places of encounter between God and his people, and establish a set of coordinates in reference to which the people of Israel

---

[41] Václav Havel, "It Always Makes Sense to Tell the Truth" in *Open Letters: Selected Writings, 1965–1990*, ed. Paul Wilson (London: Faber & Faber, 1991), 84–101, 94–95.

[42] Edward S. Casey, *Getting Back into Place: Toward a Renewed Understanding of the Place-World* (Bloomington: Indiana University Press, 1993), xv.

learn to construe the world. The word "construct" derives from the Latin *construere*, which means to heap together, to pile up, or to fit together. The construction of altars may be seen, then, as the fitting together or construal of a theological paradigm, the key coordinates of which are established in response to the initiative and self-disclosure of God.

Abraham built his first altar in response to God's promise: on Abraham's arrival in Canaan, the Lord appeared to him and said, "to your offspring, I will give this land" (Gen 12:7). The altar is a marker of the covenant relationality into which Abraham has entered with the Lord. It establishes a point of orientation and will henceforth provide evidence of the order and coherence of the world. The altar is a marker along the way by which Abraham's world is being pieced together and rendered intelligible under the promise and the guidance of God.

Our earlier discussion of representation may be recalled here. To represent is first of all to make present. The altars constructed by Abraham and his descendants represent the covenant relationality between God and his people by demarcating the place where that relationality will be worked out. They are also memorials—representations, that is, of a particular encounter with God that is now in the past. And third, they function typically; that is to say, each single altar is a representation of the hypothesis—the faith, we might also say—that the encounter with God here memorialized belongs to a coherent pattern of divine agency in the world. The theological paradigm of covenant and promise is represented architecturally by the marking out of particular places where God has made himself known.

Distinguishing the notion of place from the vast expanse of space in general, Walter Brueggemann writes:

> Place is space which has historical meanings, where some things have happened which are now remembered and which provide continuity and identity across generations. Place is space in which important words have been spoken which have established identity, defined vocation and envisioned destiny. Place is space in which vows have been exchanged, promises have been made, and demands have been issued. Place is indeed a protest against the unpromising pursuit of space. It is a declaration that our humanness cannot be found in escape, detachment, absence of commitment, and undefined freedom.[43]

---

[43] Walter Brueggemann, *The Land: Place as Gift, Promise and Challenge in Biblical Faith* (London: SPCK, 1978), 5.

The Old Testament is rife with this deeply textured account of place, wherein

> being human, as biblical faith promises it, will be found in belonging to and
> referring to that particular place in which the historicity of a community
> has been experienced and to which recourse is made for purposes of orien-
> tation, assurance and empowerment.[44]

Throughout the biblical narrative, the building of altars forms this understanding of humanity's being in the world and functions in service to it.

The link between spatial orientation and moral orientation forms a crucial piece of Charles Taylor's important book *Sources of the Self.* "We know
where we are through a mixture of recognition of landmarks before us and
a sense of how we have travelled to get there."[45] For Taylor's "moral orientation" we may substitute "theological orientation." I am suggesting, furthermore, that in Israel's case at least, the link between theological and spatial
orientation is not merely analogous but intrinsic.

Evident, too, in Abraham's practice of altar building is the heuristic
functioning of the altars and of the paradigm that they help to demarcate.
Although Abraham set out without knowing whither he was going, the altars
he builds indicate key moments of discovery along the way and plot the
coordinates of an emergent pattern according to which he may go on. The
practice of altar building thus signifies an evolving relationship between God
and his people and gives a measure of permanence and durability to the
emergent theological and cosmological paradigm. Abraham, however, does
not conceive of this permanence and durability in static terms. The building
of an altar does not signify that God is present only in that particular place—
rather, that God is with him in all places. Thus it is that Abraham builds the
altar and moves on—he does not feel obliged to settle there. The covenant
relationality in which he finds himself is not expressed by remaining in the
place where God once revealed himself. His freedom to journey on is not

---

[44] John Inge, *A Christian Theology of Place* (Aldershot: Ashgate, 2003), 36. Here, Inge
is in fact following Brueggemann. Harold Turner notes that this is a phenomenon common
to many religions and cultures. "All space is organized and oriented by the sacred place, itself
regarded as the centre of man's life, the point of reference around which his world is built,
or, as it is vividly put in a number of traditions, the navel of the earth. From this point, men
take their bearings and establish some system and meaning in human existence; at the sacred
place life finds its centre of unity and ceases to be merely a chaotic flow of experiences."
Turner, *From Temple to Meeting House*, 9–10; cf. 19.

[45] Charles Taylor, *Sources of the Self: The Making of Modern Identity* (Cambridge, Mass.:
Harvard University Press, 1989), 48.

diminished but rather is enhanced by the confirmation in this place of God's presence and guidance.

In many of the world's religions, sacred places serve as points of orientation that ontologically found the world; however, it is a mistake, at least in Abraham's case, to draw too sharp a distinction between sacred and profane space and to suggest, as Eliade does, that sacred space is "the only *real* and *real-ly* existing space."[46] There are occasions in Israel's story when sacred space is demarcated, as in Exodus 3:5 when the Lord says to Moses, "Come no closer! Remove the sandals from your feet, for the place on which you are standing is holy ground." Similarly in the temple, Israel has its holy of holies that is not to be entered except on one day a year by the chosen priest. But these sacred spaces operate on the same principle by which the representative action of the priest is effective for all in Israel who do not enter the sacred place. The particular relates to the universal by way of effective representation.[47] The sacred place surrounding the burning bush or in the midst of the temple similarly indicates God's claim upon the whole earth and sets it all in relationship to him. It is not true in biblical theology, as Eliade contends, that the manifestation of the sacred in a particular location is the "revelation of an absolute reality, opposed to the nonreality of the vast surrounding expanse."[48]

As Abraham's story continues, more markers are set up, at Bethel; by the oaks of Mamre in Hebron, where the birth of Isaac is announced; and at Mount Moriah, where Abraham responds to God's command to sacrifice Isaac. At Mount Moriah the discordance between the understood world and that which lies beyond it becomes especially acute. The paradigm is under great strain here, and yet Abraham goes on; he builds the altar nevertheless, thus testifying to his faith that the world has a coherence known to God if not yet understood by Abraham himself. The account in Genesis 22 of an altar built at Mount Moriah remains to this day a coordinate in biblical theology that warns against the domestication and the confinement of God.

---

[46] See Eliade, *Sacred and the Profane*, 20–21.

[47] Paul appeals to the same principle when he says that if the first fruits are holy then the whole batch is holy (Rom 11:16).

[48] Eliade, *Sacred and the Profane*, 21. Helen Oppenheimer likewise disputes the view put forward by Eliade: "Sundays and churches are not nearer to God or more excellent; they are fractions, set apart to represent the truth that all time and space are God's. The part is consecrated, not instead of the whole, but on behalf of the whole." Oppenheimer, "Making God Findable," in *The Parish Church: Explorations in the Relationship of the Church and the World*, ed. Giles Ecclestone, 65–78 (London: Mowbray, 1988), 72.

Isaac himself and eventually Jacob continue the Abrahamic tradition, building altars at Beersheba, at Shechem, and then at Bethel; the name of the last means "the house of God." All of these altars mark places of an encounter with Yahweh and so become references both to the unfolding of a relationship and to the divinely bestowed order and intelligibility of the world. By this architectural means a theological paradigm is being constructed by the patriarchs, and a framework for the living of their lives is being established.[49] We recall the argument that "architecture . . . provides evidence of an ordered world. This evidence of order provides the reliable and predictable grounding necessary for human action to unfold within the world."[50]

We should note, of course, that architecture can also give expression to a false orientation. The building of the Tower of Babel, for instance, is a manifestation of the tendency of humans to foist upon the world an order of their own making. The patriarchs, by contrast, build altars in response to God's disclosure of himself. They are acts of worship rather than of hubris.

The places of encounter with God in Israel's story are not always marked by human constructions. Often the natural environment offers its own landmarks that, in consequence of God's presence there, become markers of God's dealings with his people and the coordinates of an increasingly rich theological paradigm. Mountains, for instance, frequently serve in this way. The paradigmatic significance of Mount Moriah has already been noted. Sinai and Zion are similarly prominent in the unfolding of Israel's story, the latter becoming, of course, the site of Israel's temple, said to have been chosen by Yahweh himself (Ps 132:13; Exod 15:17). Solomon's temple, the first to be built on Mount Zion, was not unique in Israel, there being other examples at Hebron, Bethel, and elsewhere,[51] but it would become more and more identified as the *exclusive* dwelling place of Yahweh, a pagan conception that gave rise to tension within Judaism itself.

The most radical opposition to the temple comes from Nathan, who, having initially approved of David's plan to build a temple, learns in a dream that Yahweh is unimpressed with David's desire to build a house for the Lord.

---

[49] John Inge recognizes the same dynamic at work in the construction of Christian shrines. He writes, the shrine is "a place which witnesses (like *martyria*) to the fact that God *has* acted in history in Christ and in those who have followed him faithfully in the past; that God *is* acting in the world in and through the lives of those who dedicate themselves to his will and whose witness is encouraged by sacramental encounters and the witness of holy places; and that God *will* act in history to consummate all places in Christ." *Christian Theology of Place*, 103 (emphasis in original).

[50] Dripps, *First House*, 21.

[51] Turner, *From Temple to Meeting House*, 51.

> Go and tell my servant David: Thus says the LORD: Are you the one to build me a house to live in? I have not lived in a house since the day I brought up the people of Israel from Egypt to this day, but I have been moving about in a tent and a tabernacle. Wherever I have moved about among all the people of Israel, did I ever speak a word with any of the tribal leaders of Israel, whom I commanded to shepherd my people Israel, saying, "Why have you not built me a house of cedar?" (2 Sam 7:5-7)

Jewish commentators on this text have offered varying accounts of Nathan's opposition; most wish to endorse the validity of the opposition *for that time*, while still approving the eventual construction of the temple by Solomon, David's son. The essence of Nathan's opposition, however, lies, as Harold Turner explains,

> in his contrast between the proposed temple and the tabernacle or tent sanctuary of the earlier period. It is possible to see [Nathan] as a genuine conservative theologically convinced that the peculiar characteristics of Israel's religion and the freedom of Yahweh himself were better served by the simplicity of the tabernacle than by the Canaanite luxuries of the proposed temple under royal patronage.[52]

The freedom of Yahweh is especially significant, I suggest. However we might understand the sanctification of place in biblical thought, it is a mistake to suppose that God's encounter with his people in particular places entails that God is to be *housed* in such places or that he is otherwise confined by them. We have commented already on Abraham's avoidance of any such conception.

Harold Turner contends, on the basis of 2 Samuel 7, that Yahweh is concerned not with a sacred place but rather with a holy people. That view is undoubtedly correct and receives support elsewhere in the Hebrew Scriptures (e.g., Ps 22:3; Isa 37:15; 66:1-2), but this does not mean (and Turner does not intend) that space and place should be considered theologically irrelevant. Such dismissal of place can derive from a disparagement of creation as the place and time given to human beings for the working out of their covenant relationship with God. My purpose, in agreement with recent theological

---

[52] Turner, *From Temple to Meeting House*, 74. Turner himself contends on the basis of 2 Samuel 7, that Yahweh is concerned not with a sacred place but rather with a holy people (75). That view is undoubtedly correct, but this does not mean that space becomes theologically irrelevant.

attention to the goodness of the created order,[53] is to recognize the fact and the theological importance of the spatial mediation of that relationality.

The Place of Christ

It has long been recognized that the Christian confession that the eternal Word of God has become flesh—has become a subject within the creaturely conditions of space and time—constitutes a profound affirmation of the goodness of the created order against those religions and philosophies that count the physical world of space and time, the *cosmos aisthētos*, as somehow less real than the world of spirit or mind, the *cosmos noētos*. It has commonly been argued, however—with respect to space and place—that the incarnate Word himself is ambivalent about the sacred places of Israel and shows little interest in buildings.[54] To be sure, he decries the desecration of the Temple in Jerusalem, but elsewhere he contemplates its impending destruction without apparent concern.

> As he came out of the temple, one of his disciples said to him, "Look, Teacher, what large stones and what large buildings!" Then Jesus asked him, "Do you see these great buildings? Not one stone will be left here upon another; all will be thrown down." (Mark 13:2)

The end of cultic sacrifice brought about by Christ's own redeeming work was taken to imply, understandably enough, that the temple had no enduring value as a means for mediating the relationship between God and his people. In similar vein, Peter appears to have been mistaken in supposing that the building of dwellings would be an appropriate response to the transfiguration (Matt 17:4; Mark 9:5-6; Luke 9:33).

Although Christians have built many thousands of churches in which to worship God, it is commonly argued, citing Jesus' own example, that buildings are not essential to Christian worship and mission, and that they constitute a somewhat incongruous response to the one who "has nowhere to lay his head" and who invites us to follow him. Although he is an advocate of church building, the architect E. A. Sovik acknowledges that "the New

---

[53] Colin Gunton's work on the doctrine of creation is a notable case in point. See his *The Triune Creator: A Historical and Systematic Study* (Edinburgh: Edinburgh University Press, 1998) and *Christ and Creation* (Carlisle, UK: Paternoster, 1992).

[54] Craig Bartholomew notes, but goes on to contest, the common assumption "that with the new era instituted by Jesus the importance of land and place recedes into insignificance." *Where Mortals Dwell*, 90.

Testament gives no hint that the Christians of the apostolic age built, or wanted to build, places of worship, or that they designated specific places exclusively for cultic use."[55] Paul's rhetorical challenge to the Corinthians, "Do you not know that you are God's temple and that God's Spirit dwells in you?" (1 Cor 3:16) might be taken as evidence of Paul's indifference to buildings and surely supports Turner's claim seen earlier that God is more interested in a holy people than in sacred space. A century after the apostolic period, Clement of Alexandria maintains the indifference: "For it is not now the place, but the assemblage of the elect, that I call the Church."[56] A little later Hippolytus of Rome wrote: "It is not a place that is called 'church,' nor a house made of stones or earth. . . . What then is the church? It is the holy assembly of those who live in righteousness."[57]

Despite the clear view in the New Testament that the locus of God's revelatory and reconciling work is now focussed on a person rather than on a place,[58] it is my contention that this christological focus does not entail that particular places, or indeed buildings, are no longer of any account in the mediation of God's relationship with his people. I take as my starting point for this view the advice given by the risen Christ (in Matthew, or by "a young man dressed in white" in Mark) to the women who encountered him beside the empty tomb: "Then Jesus said to them, 'Do not be afraid; go and tell my brothers to go to Galilee; there they will see me'" (Matt 28:10; cf. Mark 16:7). The proposed return to Galilee when the disciples, and Jesus himself, were already present in Jerusalem seems to be a great deal of trouble to go to if the place of divine encounter was no longer of any importance. Yet, in Matthew's Gospel, Jesus is very particular about it. Prior to his death, Jesus had counselled the disciples, saying, "After I am raised up, I will go ahead of you to Galilee" (Matt 26:32). Why should Jesus be so insistent on meeting them there? The surrounding verses hint at an answer. In Matthew 26 we read, "Then Jesus said to them, 'You will all become deserters because of me this night; for it is written, "I will strike the shepherd, and the sheep

---

[55] E. A. Sovik, *Architecture for Worship* (Minneapolis: Augsburg, 1973), 13.

[56] Clement of Alexandria, *Stromateis* 7.5 (*ANF* 2:530).

[57] Cited in John G. Davies, *The Secular Use of Church Buildings* (London: SCM Press, 1968), 4. The reference provided by Davies is "St. *Daniel* I.17.6, 7."

[58] T. F. Torrance thus writes that the "relation established between God and man in Jesus Christ constitutes Him as *the place* in all space and time where God meets with man in the actualities of human existence, and man meets with God and knows Him in his own divine Being." Torrance, *Space, Time and Incarnation* (Oxford: Oxford University Press, 1969), 75.

of the flock will be scattered." But after I am raised up, I will go ahead of you to Galilee.' "

The scattering of the sheep—their dislocation—is indicative here of a theological catastrophe. The world as the disciples had construed it is reduced to rubble by the death of Jesus. The paradigm built up as they followed him around Galilee disintegrates under the impact of his death. So Jesus takes them back to Galilee, "to the mountain to which he directed them" (Matt 28:16) precisely in order to set in place again the theological framework that he had erected during the three years of his ministry there. Jesus' rebuilding of the theological paradigm—incorporating now, to be sure, what happened at Jerusalem and Golgotha—is accomplished by retracing his steps, as it were, by revisiting the place where he had first established his messianic credentials. Disoriented by all that had gone on in Jerusalem, the disciples are directed to return to Galilee where they will be helped to find their bearings again.

A close reading of the Gospels of Matthew and of Mark reveals that references to Galilee, and indeed to places in general, are seldom incidental. Both evangelists establish a clear opposition between Galilee and Jerusalem, for example. Galilee is on the margins, "a circle of heathens" according to southern prejudice,[59] while Jerusalem is the center of Jewish life and faith. This explains Nathanael's incredulity, portrayed in John's Gospel, that the Messiah should come from Nazareth (John 1:46) and also the Pharisees' confident assertion that "no prophet is to arise from Galilee" (John 7:52).

It is, however, in Galilee that the Messiah appears, prompting R. H. Lightfoot to say that Galilee is the place of revelation and Jerusalem of judgement.[60] The negative portrayal of Jerusalem is evident as early as Matthew's infancy narrative. Matthew tells the story of Jesus' birth in Bethlehem. That geographical marker, too, is significant, for it was to be from Bethlehem, the city of David, that a ruler to be the shepherd of God's people would come (Matt 2:1-7). In the same passage, Matthew foreshadows the ominous part that Jerusalem will play in the career of Jesus: when Herod heard the news of Jesus' birth, "he was frightened, *and all Jerusalem with him*" (Matt 2:3). Already the contrast is made between all the people in Jerusalem, including Herod, whose desire to go and pay homage in Bethlehem is a terrible pretense, and those who offered true worship, the magi from the East.

---

[59] Galilee means "the circle." See Orlando E. Costas, *Liberating News: A Theology of Contextual Evangelization* (Grand Rapids: Eerdmans, 1989), 51.

[60] R. H. Lightfoot, *Locality and Doctrine in the Gospels* (London: Hodder & Stoughton, 1938), cited by Costas, *Liberating News*, 167n18.

Then follows the flight to Egypt, a device by which Matthew links the story of Jesus to that of Israel and makes clear that God's deliverance of his people from bondage in Egypt is the paradigm according to which we should view what is happening again now in the story of Jesus. The mention of Egypt sets us within a theological paradigm that has at its core the saving work of God. That episode is concluded when Joseph learns in a dream that he is to return with his family to Israel. Still, however, he avoids Judea, and, again being warned in a dream, he goes away to the district of Galilee.

The favoring of Galilee over Judea and Jerusalem continues through the next episode of Matthew's Gospel, the baptism of Jesus in the river Jordan. John the Baptist, we are told, is preaching in the wilderness, the place, we may recall, where Israel was first named as God's son (Exod 4:22), the place where God prepared his people to enter the promised land, the place where Elijah is strengthened for his role as prophet in Israel, and the place where God now, through baptism and trial, prepares his Son to be the Savior of the world.

The story of John the Baptist continues: "And people *from the whole Judean countryside and all the people of Jerusalem* were going out to him and were baptized" (Mark 1:5; cf. Matt 3:6). But "in those days *Jesus came from Galilee* and was baptized by John in the Jordan" (Mark 1:9; Matt 1:13). Not from the whole Judean countryside, nor from among "all the people of Jerusalem" is the true Son of God to be found. "Only the one from Galilee," William Lane observes, "proves to be the unique Son who genuinely responds to the prophetic call."[61] Orlando Costas sees in this opposition between Galilee at the periphery and Jerusalem at the center an indication that God's purpose of salvation involves the seeking out of the marginalized and the lost and a confrontation with the principalities and powers. He further suggests that Galilee, on the margins of Judaism, constitutes a bridge to the whole world. That Christ determines to meet the disciples there after the resurrection and to send them forth from there in mission is an indication of the universal scope of the gospel.

> The disciples met Jesus in the same place as they had been called—a "final demonstration" of what Jesus had repeatedly taught them—namely that he had come "to give himself for the many." Likewise, it was a reminder of the servant character of the evangelization they were to undertake in his name throughout the world.[62]

[61] William Lane, *The Gospel of Mark* (Grand Rapids: Eerdmans, 1974), 55.
[62] Costas, *Liberating News*, 61.

The relocation to Galilee is no incidental detail in the gospel account but serves to restore and dramatically extend the theological framework that had been so severely shaken by the trauma of the crucifixion. Functioning in much the same way as the conversation on the road to Emmaus in Luke's Gospel (Luke 24:13-27), the return to Galilee, in Matthew and Mark,

> was neither an exercise of nostalgia nor a return to the everyday of [the disciples'] past lives, but a recalling of the mission and ministry that had challenged them initially in Galilee, and that was now about to make new and dangerous demands if they were to be true to the call of the rejected servant whom they believed had been exalted by God.[63]

The disciples may have harbored hopes of sitting at their Lord's right hand, enthroned at the center of things in Jerusalem, but the meeting of the risen and glorified Christ in Galilee gives rise to another theology altogether. The synagogues and mountains and lakesides of Galilee on the margins are crucial coordinates in this new construal of the world.

The favor shown to Galilee in the gospel accounts of Jesus' ministry does not mean that Jerusalem is ignored. Jesus must go there, too. The reshaping of Israel's theological paradigm cannot ignore the place that had become the center of Israel's faith. That, indeed, is where the most dramatic reconfiguring will take place but, poignantly again, "outside the city gate" (Heb 13:12). The new temple that is raised up is raised up away from the center, replacing the old temple as the place of meeting with God. The demise of the temple in Jerusalem should not be taken as overturning the view that topography is theologically important. Precisely the opposite is true. A particular conception of place involving the notion that God is confined to the temple, or that his presence is concentrated exclusively in that place, is certainly done away with, but that particular construal of the world is replaced by a christocentric paradigm that takes its bearings from Bethlehem and Egypt, from Galilee and Golgotha, and most especially from the empty tomb.

The theme I have been exploring here could be traced in much more detail through the gospel accounts of Jesus' ministry. The places referred to in the Gospels become the coordinates of a new theological paradigm in which Jesus is shown to be the Messiah of Israel and also the Savior of the world. Matthew and Mark, we have seen, lay emphasis on the various

---

[63] Sean Freyne, *Jesus, a Jewish Galilean: A New Reading of the Jesus Story* (London: T&T Clark, 2004), 174; cited in Bartholomew, *Where Mortals Dwell*, 95.

places of Jesus' ministry because they contribute to our understanding of who Jesus is.

That shrines and churches should subsequently be built in these locations and that they should become places of pilgrimage has a certain legitimacy, not because these places are more holy than any others, much less because God is housed or confined there, but rather because they are coordinates of a new theology, showing the manner in which God is present to all the world. To visit such places, on pilgrimage especially, is one way of dwelling within that theological construal of the world.

It is clear from the biblical record that certain attitudes to place and certain modes of dwelling are mistaken. Expulsion from the garden and the story of the Tower of Babel provide early testament to this. So, too, do the misgivings about the temple by some of Israel's prophets and the ambivalence toward the temple shown by Jesus himself. We are not, therefore, to suppose of any religious building or place that God is confined there. A tent that could be moved was for long enough considered to be an appropriate place for the holy ark of God. As the people bearing the ark moved on, however, they left a trail of altars to mark where they had come from and what God had done for them along the way. Thus was a theology built up, a theology that did not disparage the created realities of space and time, but that saw in them the conditions under which God has encountered and will continue to encounter and guide his people.

Conclusion

The purpose of this chapter has simply been to demonstrate that the demarcation and habitation of space is a vitally important element in humanity's efforts to make sense of the world and to inhabit it successfully. Extensive confirmation of this insight through the course of the biblical story suggests that humanity's engagement with space and place deserves careful theological attention. I have suggested further, in agreement with the tradition of architectural theory set in train by Vitruvius Pollio, that the definition of particular places through building is one of the means by which human beings piece together and give expression to their various understandings of what it is to be human and to live well in this world. Architecture turns out to be, therefore, a fertile object of theological inquiry. In the following chapters, I will attempt to demonstrate the fruitfulness for theology of attending to what architects do.

3

Freedom and Rule
Conceiving the Law as a Realm of Freedom and Creativity

One of the defining characteristics of Modernity, the culture that emerged in the West in the wake of the Enlightenment, is its commitment to freedom. The Enlightenment itself was, in large part, a bid for freedom. Among the freedoms claimed were freedom of speech, freedom of association, freedom to decide upon one's own moral course, freedom of inquiry. The right to such freedoms entailed that one should not be bound in any way by traditional authorities, or by the rules of thought and action deriving from these authorities. The Bible, the church, and the cumulative wisdom of former generations in science, in art, in ethics, and so on, all may be consulted, but each of these authorities is subordinated to the new and superior authority of the individual.

There is no doubt that the Enlightenment has yielded much good fruit, and yet at its heart lies a deeply problematic conception of what true freedom consists in. Charles Taylor explains that the

> modern notion of subjectivity has spawned a number of conceptions of freedom which see it as something men win through to by setting aside obstacles or breaking loose from external impediments, ties or entanglements. To be free is to be untrammelled, to depend in one's action only on oneself. Moreover, this conception of freedom has not been a mere footnote, but one of the central ideas by which the modern notion of the subject has been defined, as is evident in the fact that freedom is one of the values most appealed to in modern times. At the very outset, the new identity

as self-defining subject was won by breaking free of the larger matrix of a cosmic order and its claim.[1]

In agreement with Taylor's analysis, John Webster observes that "modern understandings of freedom . . . define freedom as the absence of any necessary order or nature shaping the self."[2] But as Richard Bauckham has shown in his book *God and the Crisis of Freedom*, it is by no means clear that this idea of freedom, much less its exercise, yields the benefits that such freedom is supposed to secure.[3] That is because freedom so understood is barely distinguishable from selfishness and wholly indistinguishable from self-centeredness. The following espousal of such freedom, offered by John Stuart Mill, reveals the problem:

> The only freedom which deserves the name is that of pursuing our own good in our own way, so long as we do not attempt to deprive others of theirs, or impede their efforts to obtain it. Each is the proper guardian of his own health, whether bodily, or mental or spiritual. Mankind are greater gainers by suffering each other to live as seems good to themselves, than by compelling each to live as seems good to the rest.[4]

If it should be the case, as is argued in Christian theology, that human beings are irreducibly relational beings whose well-being is realized in relations of love with God and with neighbor, then there is something fundamentally wrong with the individualistic construal of freedom seen here in Mill and widely upheld in contemporary culture. Although Mill himself acknowledged that some socially agreed order and accompanying legal structure was necessary to safeguard individual freedom and to protect individuals from any harm that might be done to them by others, any social form that imposed obligations upon its citizens, beyond the obligation to refrain from harming others or inhibiting their freedoms, constituted a form of tyranny. Society, Mill contended, is a means of imposing the will of some upon the life of others—through law, but also through convention and custom, and so its power must be very strictly circumscribed. Constrained only by the

---

[1]   Charles Taylor, *Hegel and Modern Society* (Cambridge: Cambridge University Press, 1979), 155.

[2]   John Webster, *Barth's Moral Theology* (Edinburgh: T&T Clark, 1985), 122.

[3]   See Richard Bauckham, *God and the Crisis of Freedom* (Louisville, Ky.: Westminster John Knox, 2002).

[4]   John Stuart Mill, "On Liberty," in *Three Essays: "On Liberty"; "Representative Government"; "The Subjection of Women"* (Oxford: Oxford University Press, 1975), 18.

obligation to avoid inflicting harm on others, individuals should be left to chart their own course.

Among numerous problems with this modern view is a tragic failure to recognize the relational nature of our humanity. We are not isolated and independent individuals bound to be self-made men and women. Rather, our knowing and understanding of the world, our well-being, our flourishing, and our very humanity depend crucially upon the nature of our relationships with others—with God, with neighbor, and, as has now become obvious again, with the rest of the created order.[5] We will return to these matters in our discussion of the city in the following chapter. My purpose in the present chapter, however, is to explore the relation between freedom and law, or between freedom and rule. Taking a lead from architectural history, I propose to develop an account of that relation in which the existence of law or of rule is understood not as a threat but as a necessary condition of human freedom.

Rule in Architecture

We have considered the account given of the origins of building by the Roman architectural theorist Vitruvius Pollio. As primitive men and women became aware of their location in a cosmos, in an ordered world, they began also to fashion for themselves a place to dwell. Along with that architectural endeavor, they developed language, technology, culture, particular social arrangements, and an increasingly sophisticated conception of their place in the cosmos. According to Vitruvius their emerging view of the world was expressed in their architecture. Particular patterns of social life, varied conceptions of what human life amounts to and of what constitutes a life well lived, religious sensibilities, and cultural endeavors of various kinds all found expression in the forms and arrangement of their buildings. Their architecture both represented and contributed to their understanding of the order and coherence of the world.

---

[5] The supposition that nature was to be mastered and exploited was another tragic feature of Modernity that, contrary to Lynn White's deeply misleading but influential argument, does not derive principally from the Christian tradition but, in the West at least, from the peculiarly modern assertion of humanity's capacity and prerogative to be master of all. See Lynn White, "The Historical Roots of Our Ecological Crisis," *Science* 155, no. 3767 (1967): 1203–12; for a careful critique of White's argument on historical and theological grounds, see Selwyn Yeoman, "Is Anyone in Charge Here? A Christological Evaluation of the Idea of Human Dominion over Creation" (Ph.D. diss., University of Otago, 2011).

Vitruvius' speculations about the development of primitive architecture were a retrospective extrapolation derived from what architecture had become in the Greek and Roman world of his own time. Supported by the very highly developed technical skills of the craftsmen and builders of his day, Vitruvius and his fellow architects were guided in their vocation by a sophisticated aesthetic regime based, so Vitruvius contends, upon the order of nature itself, an order seen also in the form and proportions of the human body.[6] "Architecture," he writes, "depends on Order (in Greek τάξις), Arrangement (in Greek διάθεσις), Eurythmy, Symmetry, Propriety and Economy (in Greek οἰκονομία)."[7] In books 3 and 4 of his treatise, Vitruvius explains how these principles are to be executed through what are commonly known as the "classical orders" of architecture. Vitruvius describes in detail three of the five orders—the Doric, the Ionic, and the Corinthian—while in chapter 7 of book 2, he offers a few notes on the Tuscan. The fifth order, the Composite, is not mentioned. Although the Composite was utilized in Vitruvius' time, it may not have been regarded as a distinct order until much later, when the architectural theorists of the Renaissance distinguished it as such.[8]

The classical orders evolved as increasingly ornate and precisely calculated expressions of the trabeated form, in which a beam or lintel is laid horizontally across two posts, thus forming a basic structural element in two dimensions which, when extended through a third dimension, provides the framework for walls and a roof. Rafters that are pitched up from beams running the length of the structure on either side and forming an apex at their central meeting point provide a solution to the problem of keeping rain out of the building and form a gable or pediment at each end of the building. When this basic framework is set upon a foundational platform that serves also as a floor, one has in place all the essential structural elements of a classical Greek building. The classical "orders" are means by which these structural elements may be arranged and decorated to serve well the purpose for which a particular building is constructed and, by virtue of the building's conformity to an order, to ensure that the resulting structure provides an appropriate impression of its significance and is pleasing to the eye.

---

[6] Leonardo Da Vinci's well-known image of a human figure with arms outstretched and legs apart, inscribed simultaneously within a square and a circle, is intended to demonstrate the mathematically precise proportions of the human body and is based on Vitruvius' account of the matter. Da Vinci's drawing is called "Vitruvian Man."

[7] Vitruvius, *Architecture*, 1.2.1 (13).

[8] John Summerson reports that it was the Renaissance humanist Leon Battista Alberti "who added from observation a fifth order—the Composite—which combines features of the Corinthian with those of the Ionic." Summerson, *Classical Language of Architecture*, 9.

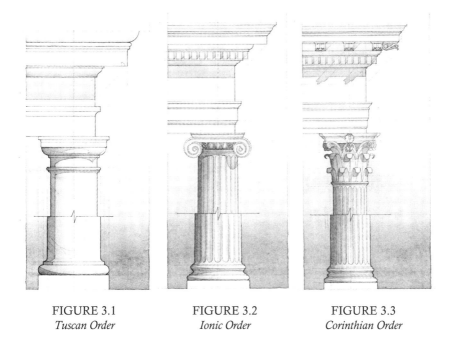

FIGURE 3.1   FIGURE 3.2   FIGURE 3.3
Tuscan Order   *Ionic Order*   *Corinthian Order*

The Tuscan is the simplest of the orders. Its columns are plain rather than fluted and it has no decoration apart from the moldings. Its sturdy appearance renders it suitable, according to theorists later than Vitruvius, for military architecture and fortifications. The Italian architect and theorist Sebastiano Serlio (1475–1554), for example, found it "suitable for fortified places such as city gates, fortresses, castles, treasuries, or where artillery and ammunition are kept, prisons, seaports, and other similar structures used in war."[9]

Next in the sequence is the Doric order, used, for example, in the Temple of Apollo at Delos. The triglyphs, the vertically grooved ornamental elements ranged across the frieze, are a distinguishing feature of the Doric order. The spaces between each pair of triglyphs are called metopes and were often embellished with sculptural decoration. The triangular tympanum on the gable end could also be decorated with elaborate sculptures and reliefs,

---

[9]   Sebastiano Serlio, *Tutte l'opere d'architettura et prospettiva di Sebastiano Serlio Bolognese* (Venice, 1619), bk. 4. Serlio's work was first published in successive volumes during the 1540s. English translation cited in James S. Ackerman, "The Tuscan/Rustic Order: A Study in the Metaphorical Language of Architecture," *Journal of the Society of Architectural Historians* 42, no. 1 (1983): 15–34, 15.

FIGURE 3.4
Doric Temple

typically depicting scenes from Greek or Roman mythology. Pedimental sculptures of this kind once adorned the Temple of Zeus at Olympia and the Parthenon in Athens. Vitruvius explains that the Doric is a masculine order suitable for temples dedicated to Minerva, Mars, and Hercules.[10] In specifying this, Vitruvius spoke against such temples being embellished with decoration. The avoidance of decoration is a principle that has not been observed, however, by many who have subsequently employed the Doric order. Recognizing its masculine character, Serlio advised that the Doric order should be used for churches dedicated to the likes of Christ the Redemptor, Saint Paul, or Saint George, each of whom, it was claimed, possessed the same kind of virility as his ancient predecessors.[11]

The Ionic order dispenses with triglyphs, leaving the frieze free for a continuous sculpture, sometimes restricted to one or both ends of the building but often running the full length of the perimeter. The most obvious distinguishing feature of the Ionic style, however, is the volutes at the top of the columns. These are often accompanied by further decoration, typically an egg-and-dart pattern. Palmettes and lotuses are sometimes used for additional decoration around the neck of the column. The Ionic column is more slender than the Doric. The height of the column is usually eight or nine times the diameter and may be more, whereas the the Doric column is six or seven times the diameter. Thinking the order suitable for temples to

[10] See Vitruvius, *Architecture*, 1.2.5 (15).

[11] I take the point from Alexander Tzonis and Liane Lefaivre, *Classical Architecture: The Poetics of Order* (Cambridge, Mass.: MIT Press, 1986), 38. Their source is Serlio, *Tutte l'opere d'architettura*, bk. 4, chap. 6.

Juno, Diana, and Father Bacchus, Vitruvius advises that "Ionic temples will be in keeping with the middle position which they hold; for the building of such will be an appropriate combination of the severity of the Doric and the delicacy of the Corinthian."[12]

The Corinthian column gains its softer appearance largely through the adornment of its capital with acanthus leaves and scrolls. Vitruvius explains that "in temples to Venus, Flora, Proserpine, Spring-Water and the Nymphs, the Corinthian order will be found to have peculiar significance, because they are delicate divinities and so its rather slender outlines, its flowers, leaves and ornamental volutes will lend propriety where it is due."[13]

I have provided here only a brief sketch of the classical orders. Vitruvius himself provides lengthy descriptions and specifies in precise mathematical detail how the constitutive elements of each of the orders are to be proportioned. Symmetry and proportion, along with purity of style, are cardinal virtues of the classical orders so described. Vitruvius writes, "If dentils be carved in the cornice of the Doric entablature or triglyphs represented in the Ionic entablature over the cushion-shaped capitals of the columns, the effect will be spoiled by the transfer of the peculiarities of the one order of building to the other, the usage in each class having been fixed long ago."[14] What Vitruvius calls "fitness" in architecture is achieved by the architect who knows the rules, who has the orders written on her heart, we might say, and who knows how to practice her art in conformity with them.

We noted earlier Vitruvius' claim that architecture consists of order, of arrangement, of eurythmy and symmetry, of propriety and economy. Order, he further explains, "gives due measure to the members of a work considered separately, and symmetrical agreement to the proportions of the whole. Arrangement includes the putting of things in their proper places and the elegance of effect which is due to adjustments appropriate to the character of the work. . . . Eurythmy is beauty and fitness in the adjustments of the members. . . . Symmetry is a proper agreement between the members of the work itself, and relation between the different parts and the whole general scheme, in accordance with a certain part selected as standard." Propriety, Vitruvius continues, "is that perfection of style which comes when a work is authoritatively constructed on approved principles. It arises from prescription . . . , from usage, or from nature." Economy, finally, "denotes the proper

---

[12] Vitruvius, *Architecture*, 1.2.5 (15).
[13] Vitruvius, *Architecture*, 1.2.5 (15).
[14] Vitruvius, *Architecture*, 1.2.6 (15).

management of materials and of site, as well as a thrifty balancing of cost and common sense in the construction of the works."[15]

A strong impression is given here of a long tradition, of an accumulated wisdom in which the architect is schooled and within which the architect goes about his or her work. The work of the architect is not a *creatio ex nihilo*. Architects do not begin with a blank slate but draw upon resources of wisdom yielding a sure knowledge of what in architecture is fitting and beautiful, and of how their work may be conformed to an order not of their own making but *given* in the nature of things. All of this contrasts markedly with the proclivities of our own age, in which tradition is conceived sometimes as an unwelcome constraint upon our freedom and creativity, or else as a kind of smorgasbord of ideas and practices from which we can pick or choose, and which we can adapt, ignore or discard at will. Sometimes the wisdom of the past is suspected of being merely an expression of the interests of those who held power. Not only in architecture do we find these proclivities. They are characteristic of Western culture in general and are apparent also in the church. It is not uncommon, for instance, to find services of worship that include a selection of liturgical elements that are traditional but assembled in ways that show no awareness of the liturgical grammar that provides Christian worship with its narrative direction and theological coherence. Freedom in liturgy is not the problem here; the problem rather is a lack of familiarity with the liturgical "rules" that give liturgy some coherence and ensure that it makes theological sense.

It is true that a cursory reading of Vitruvius may give rise to the impression that the classical orders leave no room for innovation and creativity by the architect. The precise mathematical specification of the details and proportions of the orders might suggest that the creation of architecture is simply a matter of following the formulae. Taking this view, John Ruskin once alleged that classicism is "utterly devoid of life." It is "an architecture invented, as it seems, to make plagiarists of its architects, slaves of its workmen, and sybarites of its inhabitants; an architecture in which intellect is idle, invention impossible, but in which all luxury is gratified, and all insolence fortified." Ruskin continues his tirade at some length, finally concluding, "whatever betrays the smallest respect for Vitruvian laws, or conformity with Palladian work,—that we are to endure no more."[16] Ruskin's is an extreme view, to be sure, but the suspicion that adherence to the rule stifles all creativity is shared

[15] These features of architecture are all set out in Vitruvius, *Architecture*, 1.2 (13–16).

[16] John Ruskin, *The Stones of Venice*, vol. 3, *The Fall*, 4th ed. (Orpington, UK: George Allen, 1886), 194.

by others. Thomas Gordon Smith, an advocate of classicism, acknowledges the widespread perception:

> For some, Vitruvius's name conjures visions of overdependence on rule; they fear that this force inhibits creativity and spontaneity. Conversely, others depend on the false hope that a canon contains formulae which, once plugged in, automatically solve challenging architectural problems. Vitruvius invites this expectation when he writes that the architect ". . . may find the proportions stated by which he can construct correct and faultless examples of temples in the Doric fashion."[17]

The expectation Smith notices is countered, however, by Vitruvius' appreciation elsewhere of the virtues of imagination and invention. "Imagination" he writes, "rests upon the attention directed with minute and observant fervour to the charming effect proposed," while invention "is the solving of intricate problems and the discovery of new principles by means of brilliancy and versatility."[18] Despite the meticulous attention to detail in Vitruvius' descriptions of the orders, much is left unsaid, as those have found who have tried to create exact models of the temples he describes. Vitruvius leaves much to the imagination and invention of the architect. Comparison can usefully be made here with the invention required of musicians as they interpret a score. Bruce Benson observes that composers are simply not able to define, in ways that leave no room for creative interpretation, precisely how a score is to be played.

> In regard to musical scores, musicologists often refer to this lack of precision as "underdetermination." That is, scores do not provide enough information to actually perform the work. One must know what to do with the notes on the page, and that knowledge comes only by being steeped in a performance practice or tradition.[19]

Genuine artistic accomplishment always depends upon a thorough awareness of and respect for the rules, or the "grammar," pertaining to particular spheres of artistic endeavor, but it can never be attained through mere obedience to the rules. In relation to architecture again, John Summerson explains that

---

[17] Thomas Gordon Smith, *Classical Architecture: Rule and Invention* (Layton, Utah: Gibbs M. Smith, 1988), 61. The citation of Vitruvius comes from *Architecture*, 4.3.2.

[18] Vitruvius, *Architecture*, 1.2.2 (14).

[19] Bruce Ellis Benson, "Improvising Texts, Improvising Communities," in *Resonant Witness: Conversations between Music and Theology*, ed. Jeremy S. Begbie and Steven R. Guthrie (Grand Rapids: Eerdmans, 2011), 295–322, 298.

it is a mistake ever to think of the "five orders of architecture" as a sort of child's box of bricks which architects have used to save themselves the trouble of inventing. It is much better to think of them as grammatical expressions imposing a formidable discipline but a discipline within which personal sensibility always has a certain play—a discipline, moreover, which can sometimes be burst asunder by a flight of poetic genius.[20]

While "a complaint may be made," suggests Mary Emerson, "that all Greek temples are the same . . . to the interested eye, each temple is unique. Even Doric temples, though said to conform to strict rules, all differ. As in any field of interest, what seems uniform to outsiders is—on inspection—full of nuance, innovation and individuality."[21] That is certainly true of the most well known of Doric temples, the Parthenon in Athens. It is overwhelmingly a Doric temple, and yet many things about it are Ionic.[22]

The inventiveness and creativity of its designers are apparent also in the skilled use of "refinements." Refinements are ingenious deviations from strict mathematical regularity employed to ensure that a building looks gracious. Strict adherence to mathematical proportions would not achieve that end. So, for example, the stylobate or stepped platform from which the columns rise is not flat but very slightly convex. A flat stylobate in a temple the size of the Parthenon would look sunken. The same is true for the architrave and cornices of the pediment. The Parthenon's columns also deviate from prescribed proportions; none of them are straight. They are of course tapered, narrowing at the top, but they are also made to swell slightly at the center, a technique called entasis. Entasis is utilized—again, to please the eye—to avoid the appearance of flimsiness in the columns, as if they might buckle under the weight of the structure above them. All of the columns are tilted slightly inward, and the corner columns are tilted inward in two planes so as to align with both front and flank. The corner columns are also slightly thicker not because of any structural need but to avoid the appearance of weakness at the corners. The width between columns, furthermore, is narrowed at the corners. Because the Doric order demands that the frieze be terminated with a triglyph on the corner, the corner column would protrude well beyond the corner if, like all the other columns, it were centered under the triglyph that is above it. Accordingly, there is often a slight contraction

---

[20] Summerson, *Classical Language of Architecture*, 11.

[21] Mary Emerson, *Greek Sanctuaries: An Introduction* (London: Bristol Classical Press, 2007), 1.

[22] I am indebted to Mary Emerson for her detailed account of the combination of Doric and Ionic elements in the Parthenon. See Emerson, *Greek Sanctuaries*, chap. 8 (82–99).

of the intercolumniation to accommodate the corner triglyph, and this also assists in giving the corners the appearance of strength.[23]

In the course of his discussion about the refinements required when utilizing the classical orders, Vitruvius explains: "For the eye is always in search of beauty, and if we do not gratify its desire for pleasure by a proportionate enlargement in these measures, and thus make compensation for ocular deception, a clumsy and awkward appearance will be presented to the beholder."[24] Strict adherence to geometrical rule would render the building ugly and ungainly. The rule is therefore to be engaged with a degree of flexibility and again, *inventiveness*. Although the Greeks prized mathematical order and precision, there is, we might say, a gracious accommodation of our human capacities in these temples erected to be places of encounter between the human and the divine. It is important also to observe that the "rule" set out by Vitruvius is fulfilled precisely as it is taken up by architects and applied *inventively* to a particular context. Slavish adherence to Vitruvius' instructions will not achieve the goal to which the rule is directed. It takes wisdom, creativity, and, one might say, inspiration to attain in any particular building the telos toward which the rule is directed. What Vitruvius calls "fitness" in architecture is achieved by architects who know the rules, who have the orders written on their hearts, but who know how to apply these rules with creativity and imagination.

Much later in the history of Western architecture, during the Renaissance, the classical orders, which had fallen out of fashion during the Middle Ages, were taken up again, as was much else from the classical era. It was the architects and theorists of the Renaissance who bestowed upon the classical orders a high canonical status and who published treatises in which they set out with more extensive precision than did Vitruvius himself how the details of each order were to be calculated and how they conformed to an order deeply engraved in the cosmos. We have referred already to Leon Battista Alberti (1404–1472) and Sebastiano Serlio (1475–1554). Others who contributed to this recovery and development were Andrea Palladio in Italy (1508–1580) and Claude Perrault in France (1613–1688). Summerson writes that it was Sebastian Serlio "who really started the orders . . . on their long career of canonical, almost legendary authority. . . . The orders came to be regarded as the very touch-stone of architecture, as instruments of the

---

[23] See Emerson, *Greek Sanctuaries*, 86–87 for further description of the refinements used in the Parthenon.

[24] Vitruvius, *Architecture*, 3.3.13 (86).

greatest possible subtlety, embodying all the ancient wisdom of mankind in the building art—almost, in fact, as products of nature herself."[25]

One might expect that the more exacting specification of details and the heightened canonical authority bestowed upon the orders during the Renaissance would engender greater rigidity in their use. It might be supposed that a more intense following of the rule would leave much less room for the imagination and invention that Vitruvius clearly thought essential in the making of good architecture. In general, however, the canonization of the orders had precisely the opposite effect. The meticulous attention of Renaissance architects to the rule inspired in them a freedom and creativity in the use of the orders far exceeding that of the architects of ancient Greece and Rome. It is fascinating to note that the Renaissance architects did not appeal only to the powers of human reason in their discernment of truth, order, and beauty in architecture, nor simply to their observations of nature. They appealed also to divine grace. Joseph Rykwert suggests that

> the architecture of the sixteenth century could not simply make its appeal to nature and reason, or base its procedure on the operations of reason prompted by philosophy; in the sixteenth century rules which had to be invoked constantly, such as those of the orders, had to have the sanction of grace, had to be derived from, guaranteed by divine revelation; although revelation did not in any way contradict the operations of reason, but rather sanctified, elevated them.[26]

We may take as an example of the expansive creativity and inventiveness of Renaissance architects the Tempietto of Donato Bramante, built around 1502 and now considered to be a masterpiece of the High Renaissance. Thomas Smith describes the Tempietto as "the first fully classical building of the Roman Renaissance."[27] The Tempietto is located in the cloister of San Pietro in Montorio, Rome, and is built on a site supposed to have been the exact spot of St. Peter's martyrdom. Bramante employed the Doric order "traditionally ascribed to Hercules, to convey Peter's heroic status"[28] but in a daring experiment, he topped the Vitruvian circular temple with a Renaissance dome.

---

[25] Summerson, *Classical Language of Architecture*, 9–10.

[26] Joseph Rykwert, *On Adam's House in Paradise: The Idea of the Primitive Hut in Architectural History*, 2nd ed. (Cambridge, Mass.: MIT Press, 1981), 120.

[27] Smith, *Classical Architecture*, 28.

[28] Smith, *Classical Architecture*, 28.

FIGURE 3.5
The Tempietto

Throughout the monument, in its form and in its decoration, Bramante adapted pagan elements to Christian use. The round form of temple was used in the classical era for temples to Diana (or the moon) and to Vesta and Hercules (or Mercury). According to Palladio, the temple of Vesta, the symbolic divinity of the Earth, was round in order to resemble the earth, by which the human race is sustained.[29] Eager to represent St. Peter as the guardian of the church and drawing upon Christ's designation of Peter as the rock upon which the church is founded, Bramante adopted the round form to signify the global scope of St. Peter's authority and significance.

For the decoration of the metopes, Bramante employed the symbols of Christ's sacrifice: the chalice, the eucharistic bread, and the incense boat, thus replacing with Christian symbols the sculpted skull of an ox, or *boukranion*, used in the Doric order to indicate the

blood sacrifice of pagan worship. I have provided here just a small sample of the extensive symbolism used in the building, much of it drawn from the classical era but always adapted to Christian use.[30] Arnaldo Bruschi makes well the point I wish to emphasize here: that rule and inventiveness are combined in Bramante's Tempietto in ways that show the necessity of both in the making of great architecture. Bruschi writes:

FIGURE 3.6
Metopes of the Tempietto

[29] The explanation here is drawn from Arnaldo Bruschi, *Bramante* (London: Thames & Hudson, 1973), 129.
[30] An extensive discussion of the Tempietto can be found in Bruschi, *Bramante*, 128–44.

> Bramante felt that he had so firm a grasp of the method, of the basic "principles" which according to the theorists were fundamental to a "modern" architecture which aimed at reviving that of the ancients, that it was unnecessary for him to follow any exact model or even Vitruvius's pedantic advice about the "peripteral temple." . . . Renewed study of the Antique enabled him to clarify, to a greater degree than had ever been done before, the precise meaning of the Classical language of architecture.[31]

Though modest in scale, the Tempietto provides a striking demonstration of the genius by which Bramante "brought to the making of architecture the fertile, freely associative inspiration born of a saturated memory."[32] This statement by David Mayernik captures the point exactly. Invention, creativity, and freedom are made possible, not by eradicating all rules or traditions but precisely by remembering and applying them well. Remembering well the rules that gave shape to the endeavors of our forebears is quite different, be it noted, from slavish repetition. Memory grants to us, rather, an understanding of what can be done with resources and a wisdom richer and more extensive than our own. It frees us precisely by locating us within a community and tradition that expands the range of purposes to which our own skills, wisdom, and industry may contribute, and thus opens up possibilities beyond the limits that would inevitably be imposed if we were required to begin everything anew and by ourselves alone. Memory also plays a key role in the practices of faith. For people of biblical faith, remembrance of the Lord your God who brought you out of the land of Egypt, or remembrance of the person of Christ as he took bread, gave thanks, broke it, and gave of himself, are remembrances of the conditions that gave rise to our freedom and of the gestures we are invited to make our own if freedom is to be exercised faithfully.

Of course, the exercise of freedom and invention involves risk. It involves striking out in new directions beyond the bounds of what has been attempted or understood before. It may not always be successful. In 1753 the French architectural theorist and Jesuit priest Marc-Antoine Laugier (1713–1769) published his *Essay on Architecture* in which he attempted to restore "order" to the classical orders and correct what he considered to be the faults of some aspects of Renaissance and post-Renaissance architectural practice. After first celebrating the recovery in France of the "virility" and "elegance" of

---

[31] Bruschi, *Bramante*, 136.

[32] David Mayernik, *Timeless Cities: An Architect's Reflections on Renaissance Italy* (Boulder, Colo.: Westview Press, 2003), 46.

classical Greek architecture, Laugier laments: "But at the very moment when we were approaching perfection, as if barbarism had not lost all its claim on us, we fall back into a low and faulty taste. Everything now seems to threaten us with a complete decadence."[33]

Disagreement about the maintenance of order is to be expected. Not only in architecture but in all the endeavors of humankind, invention is rightly balanced by conservatism and critiqued by others working in the field. Laugier's concern was that the inventiveness of Renaissance architects had in some instances destroyed the essential character of the classical orders. Nevertheless, freedom and invention are indispensable if the challenges of a new site and a new context are to be met. Thomas Smith offers an example of successful invention:

FIGURE 3.7
San Carlo alle Quattro Fontane

The composite capital, designed by Francesco Borromini in 1667 at the church of San Carlo alle Quattro Fontane, provides a historical model that sets a standard for preserving integrity while radically reinterpreting the canonical forms. . . . The Borromini capital conveys a sense of calm, not chaos, and its variations are made to support the meaning of this church built for the Trinitarian order. The Trinitarian emblem—the Greek cross—replaces the fleuron typically located at the centre of the abacus. The cross is framed by a laurel wreath, a symbol of victory. . . . Borromini substitutes Christian symbols for the elements used in antiquity to give vitality to the ancient language of classical architecture.[34]

It is not always agreed among observers of architecture, however, whether in a given instance integrity has been preserved. Smith elsewhere complains that

---

[33] Marc-Antoine Laugier, *An Essay on Architecture*, trans. Wolfgang Hermann and Annie Hermann (Los Angeles: Hennessey & Ingalls, 1977), 9. The "barbarism" that Laugier so despises refers to the Gothic style. See p. 8.

[34] Smith, *Classical Architecture*, 13–14.

radical changes in the Doric generally indicate misunderstanding instead of invention. A Doric capital and entablature from the Baths of Diocletian is decadent because acanthus leaves cover the echinus, and dentils, a distinctly Ionic feature, support the cornice. A decorative handling of all elements contradicts the character of the Doric as well.[35]

The Great Hall of the Baths of Diocletian is regarded by others, however, as a crowning achievement of Roman architectural innovation.[36] Disputes over the integrity of particular instances of classical form are not unprecedented. Vitruvius himself would have been no stranger to architectural controversy. The freedom and invention employed by architects in the classical period itself sometimes stretched the bounds of coherence and intelligibility. The Erechtheion, for example, one of the buildings atop the Acropolis in Athens, famously flouts the rules commended by Vitruvius. The most obvious point of controversy is the lack of symmetry in any of its aspects—in plan or in any of its four elevations. This is likely to have troubled Vitruvius, who repeatedly stressed the importance of symmetry.

FIGURE 3.8
The Erechtheion

[35] Smith, *Classical Architecture*, 65.

[36] See, e.g., Bruce Allsop, *A History of Classical Architecture* (London: Sir Isaac Pitman & Sons, 1965), 135. The Great Hall of the Baths of Diocletian was dedicated in Rome in 306 and was later converted to be the Church of Santa Maria degli Angeli.

The irregularity of the Erechtheion stands in marked contrast to its closest neighbor, the resolutely symmetrical Parthenon. Alexandra Lesk notes in her extensive study of the Erechtheion and its reception history that "this example of Classical architecture has evoked a wide range of reactions from all echelons of society, from locals to foreigners, from architects to scholars. To them, the Erechtheion is 'lopsided,' 'the epitome of elegance,' 'weighty,' 'transverse,' and 'preposterous.'"[37]

Scholars have often presumed that there must have been an original, symmetrical plan, and have devoted a great deal of energy both to recovering what that plan may have been and to explaining how the building turned out so differently.[38] Lesk observes, "This search for a symmetrical, original plan may be attributable to the early presumption that the acutely rational Greeks could never have designed a building like the Erechtheion on purpose."[39] Henry Inwood, on the other hand, whose design for St. Pancras Church in London is modeled on the Erechtheion, regarded the Erechtheion itself as an achievement illustrating "the nearer approaches, or even perfection of the art."[40]

We do not need to explore further the debate over the Erechtheion. The point is simply to note that alongside each other at the Acropolis sit two buildings, the Parthenon and the Erechtheion, that both exhibit a great deal of novelty and inventiveness in their use of the classical orders; but, while one engenders nothing but admiration for its mastery of style, the other raises the question of whether the inventiveness of its designers has transgressed the limits of what is fitting.

We learn from these disputes about authenticity and about the exercise of freedom that the classical orders described by Vitruvius are not to be conceived as rigid prescriptions determining, without regard for context, the precise form and appearance of particular buildings. Vitruvius is clear that architecture combines science with art, technology with craftsmanship, and rule with invention. Specification of the orders is only in part a specification of constraints; it is in equal part a specification of possibilities. It is

---

[37] Alexandra L. Lesk, "A Diachronic Examination of the Erechtheion and Its Reception" (Ph.D. diss., University of Cincinnati, 2004), 8–9. Mary Emerson supports the point, noting that some critics view the Erechtheion as "a triumph while for others it is a product of compromise and incompetence." Emerson, *Greek Sanctuaries*, 120–21.

[38] For details of these efforts, see Lesk, "Diachronic Examination," 50–63.

[39] Lesk, "Diachronic Examination." Comprehensive lists of the Erechtheion's many "peculiarities" are provided on pp. 54–55 of Lesk's dissertation.

[40] Henry William Inwood, *The Erechtheion at Athens* (London: James Carpenter & Son, 1827), 91.

in the proper balancing of rule and invention that an appropriate integrity will be preserved. The point of such concerns, Vitruvius explains, is to create buildings that "correspond to the grandeur of our history, and will be a memorial to future ages."[41] Correspondence to our history and the provision of a memorial or testimony are important considerations, I shall argue, in building the community of faith.

Order, Freedom, and Identity in Theology

The relationships we have seen between freedom and rule in classical architecture provide a model, I suggest, for understanding the relation between freedom and law in the Jewish and Christian traditions. It is instructive to begin with the Torah in Israel's understanding, for while the Torah finds expression in part in specific rules or laws, notably the commandments, it cannot be reduced to law. The Torah is an expansive concept, beginning at its most specific level with the five books of Moses telling of Israel's historical beginnings and expanding to include the whole content of Jewish teaching.[42] The Columbus Platform, a widely regarded statement of the principles of (Reform) Judaism, states that "the Torah, both written and oral, enshrines Israel's ever-growing consciousness of God and of the moral law. It preserves the historical precedents, sanctions and norms of Jewish life, and seeks to mould it in the patterns of goodness and holiness."[43] In the evening service the following prayer is recited:

> Torah and commandments, statutes and judgments have you taught us. Therefore, O Lord our God, on lying down and rising we shall think about your statutes and rejoice in the words of your Torah and your commandments for ever and ever. For they are our life and the length of our days.[44]

It is evident here that the Torah is something *given* to Israel. While there is no doubt that the people themselves have been involved in its production, the

---

[41] Vitruvius, *Architecture*, bk. 1, pref., 3. The translation used here is that of Frank Granger: Vitruvius, *On Architecture*, 2 vols. Loeb Classical Library (London: William Heinemann, 1931), 1:5.

[42] This point is explained in Nicholas de Lange, *Judaism* (Oxford: Oxford University Press, 1986), 24–25. See also Howard R. Greenstein, *Judaism—an Eternal Covenant* (Philadelphia: Fortress, 1983), 22.

[43] Cited in de Lange, *Judaism*, 32. The Columbus Platform is a Declaration of Principles adopted by the (Reform) Central Conference of American Rabbis at its meeting in Columbus, Ohio in 1937. See de Lange, *Judaism*, 7.

[44] Cited in de Lange, *Judaism*, 67.

Torah is understood, nevertheless, as revelation. "The teachings in question have a claim to authority which is based on their having been revealed by God."[45]

The prayer from the evening service indicates that the Torah in general and the commandments in particular are thought to be life giving. While the commandments include prohibitions, and thus constraints, they establish, in fact, the conditions under which life may be lived well. Just as the classical orders of architecture embody the accumulated wisdom of a long tradition and set out the means by which a noble and gracious architecture may be realized, so in Judaism obedience to the laws contained in the Torah is the means by which the freedom given to those called out of bondage in Egypt may be realized in its fullness.[46] Covenant relationship is the broader framework and purpose within which the law has its place. Nicholas de Lange thus explains, "Judaism without law would possibly not be Judaism . . . , but a Judaism which is nothing but law would be a travesty of Judaism."[47]

De Lange explains further that Jewish law, or *Halakah*, must be understood as a living tradition. "It responds to the changing needs of the people."[48] As with the orders of architecture, once again, faithfulness to the "rule" is required in order to achieve the desired end, but faithfulness does not preclude freedom and invention; indeed, freedom and invention are required if the rule is to be interpreted and adapted to particular contexts. The Columbus Platform thus states:

> Being products of historical processes, certain of [the Torah's] laws have lost their binding force with the passing of the conditions which called them forth. But as a depository of permanent spiritual ideals, the Torah remains the dynamic source of the life of Israel. Each age has the obligation to adapt the teachings of the Torah to its basic needs in consonance with the genius of Judaism.[49]

Reference to the "genius of Judaism" suggests that there is a principle lying at the heart of Judaism upon which the Torah is founded, and that must be safeguarded in all adaptations of the Torah to the new conditions in which Israel finds itself. That foundational principle is identified by Jesus as the

[45] De Lange, *Judaism*, 25.
[46] See Abraham Heschel, "Religion and Law," in *Between God and Man: An Interpretation of Judaism: From the Writings of Abraham J. Heschel*, ed. Fritz A. Rothschild (New York: Harper & Brothers, 1959), 155–61, 155.
[47] De Lange, *Judaism*, 67.
[48] De Lange, *Judaism*, 69.
[49] Cited in de Lange, *Judaism*, 32.

command to "love the Lord your God with all your heart, and with all your soul, and with all your mind. This is the greatest and first commandment. And a second is like it: 'You shall love your neighbor as yourself'" (Matt 22:37-39). "On these two commandments," Jesus continues, "hang all the law and the prophets" (Matt 22:40). The creativity needed in the application of the law is always directed, therefore, to the fulfilment of this command to love both God and neighbor.

> The law, stiff with formality, is *a cry for creativity*; a call for nobility concealed in the form of commandments. It is not designed to be a yoke, a curb, a strait jacket for human action. Above all, the Torah asks for *love: thou shalt love thy God; thou shalt love thy neighbour*. All observance is training in the art of love. . . . The end of our readiness to obey is the ability to love. The law is given to be cherished, not merely to be complied with.[50]

We noted above the importance of tradition in the classical orders of architecture. The importance of inventiveness notwithstanding, the architect is a participant in a tradition and is never expected to start from scratch. Her inventiveness is never a *creatio ex nihilo*. Enshrined in the rule is a tradition of accumulated wisdom that extends the possibilities open to any single architect far beyond what he or she is capable of alone. One of the benefits of well-formulated law, accordingly, is to convey that wisdom. Yet this function of law frequently offends the individualistic and autonomous sensibilities of contemporary Western culture. Both in Kant's insistence that obedience to any command originating outside the rational deliberations of one's own intellect is an abdication of moral responsibility, and in the petulant retort, "no one tells me what to do," we encounter the presumption that the individual is the final and sufficient moral authority. In his defense of the importance of law in Jewish tradition, Abraham Heschel observes,

> There are those who are ready to discard the message of the divine commands and call upon us to rely on our conscience. Man, we are told, is only under obligation to act in conformity with his reason and conscience, and must not be subjected to any laws except those which he imposes upon himself. Moral laws are attainable by reason and conscience, and there is no need for a law-giver. God is necessary [in the case of Kant] merely as a guarantee for the ultimate triumph of the moral effort.[51]

---

[50] Abraham Heschel, "Law and Life," in Rothschild, *Between God and Man*, 161–64, 162 (emphasis in original).

[51] Heschel, "Religion and Law," in Rothschild, *Between God and Man*, 157.

The example of classical architecture, however, enables us to see that adherence to a rule need not subvert one's freedom and creativity but may be instead the very condition under which freedom and creativity are allowed to flourish. Alain de Botton observes, also with reference to architecture, that the problem with unrestricted choice "is that it tends not to lie so far from outright chaos."[52] For Kant, of course, the choice he exhorts us to make is not unrestricted. It is disciplined by reason. It is, however, a profoundly impoverished reason that refuses to be nourished and guided by the wisdom of others.[53] Heschel writes,

> The individual's insight alone is unable to cope with all the problems of living. It is the guidance of tradition on which we must rely, and whose norms we must learn to interpret and to apply. . . . Judaism calls upon us to listen *not only* to the voice of the conscience but also to the norms of a heteronomous law.[54]

There is a further reason, a theological one, to avail ourselves of the wisdom enshrined in law, Heschel argues. It is that "those who call upon us to rely on our inner voice fail to realize that there is more than one voice within us, that the power of selfishness may easily subdue the pangs of conscience."[55] Put otherwise, they fail to take sufficient cognizance of human sinfulness. Kant, of course, realized that we have a propensity for sin, but he did not recognize the negative impact of that propensity on the very faculty he thought could save us from it—namely, our reason. Judaism, by contrast, does not regard the rational capacity of the individual as a sufficient authority for the moral life, much less for a life lived in faithfulness to the covenant. The will of God, expressed in the Torah and in its laws, stands higher than the carefully reasoned insights of any individual.

Appreciation of the role of law in Judaism requires that the individual commandments be understood in relation to the whole. Just as in architecture there are many elements that contribute to the overall beauty and coherence of, for example, the Ionic order, so too in Jewish law, Heschel explains,

> It is impossible to understand the significance of single acts, detached from the total character of a life in which they are set. Acts are components of a

---

[52] de Botton, *Architecture of Happiness*, 44.

[53] It is interesting to note that after listing all the disciplines pertinent to the practice of architecture, Vitruvius acknowledges that the architect cannot be expert in all of them and so must rely on the expertise of others. See Vitruvius, *Architecture* 1.1.11–18.

[54] Heschel, "Religion and Law," in Rothschild, *Between God and Man*, 158.

[55] Heschel, "Religion and Law," in Rothschild, *Between God and Man*, 158.

whole and derive their character from the structure of the whole . . . just as the parts are determined by the whole, the whole is determined by the parts. Consequently the amputation of one part may affect the integrity of the entire structure, unless that part has outlived its vital role in the organic body of the whole.[56]

We may again see a parallel here with the debates that took place especially in the wake of the Renaissance, but also among contemporary scholars, about the Erechtheion—for example, over the arrangement of parts necessary to maintain the integrity of each of the classical orders of architecture and to achieve the desired end. This reveals an essential feature of law. Its specific details and provisions are directed toward the maintenance of a larger entity. In the case of Judaism, that larger entity is the covenant relationality God has established with Israel as described and developed in the Torah and passed down through liturgical enactment and through the patterns of everyday life. Heschel calls this "the order of Jewish living" and writes:

> What we must try to avoid is not only the failure to observe a single mitzvah, but the loss of the whole, the loss of belonging to the spiritual order of Jewish living. The order of Jewish living is meant to be, not a set of rituals but an order of all man's existence, shaping all his traits, interests and dispositions; not so much the performance of single acts, the taking of a step now and then, as the pursuit of a way, being on the way; not so much the acts of fulfilling as the state of being committed to the task, the belonging to an order in which single deeds, aggregates of religious feeling, sporadic sentiments, moral episodes become part of a complete pattern.[57]

We can see here that the law is not an end in itself; it is one among several means by which "the order of Jewish living" is maintained. It serves, therefore, to preserve the integrity of Judaism as a complete pattern of life lived in covenant relationality with Yahweh.[58] Its observance is a means by which Yahweh's chosen people can be identified as such. That is the purpose of

---

[56] Heschel, "Religion and Law," in Rothschild, *Between God and Man*, 159.

[57] Heschel, "Religion and Law," in Rothschild, *Between God and Man*, 160.

[58] When we speak of the law in this aspect, the term is better represented by the Hebrew term *torah* than by the Greek term *nomos* used to translate it in the Septuagint. This widely accepted point was made, for instance, by H. J. Schoeps in his study *Paul: The Theology of the Apostle in the Light of Jewish Religious History* (Philadelphia: Westminster, 1961), 29. I am persuaded, however, by Stephen Westerholm's contention that the term *nomos* used later by Paul usually refers in Paul's own writings to the Sinaitic legislation rather than to the full scope of the Torah. See Stephen Westerholm, *Israel's Law and the Church's Faith: Paul and His Recent Interpreters* (Grand Rapids: Eerdmans, 1988), 108–9.

circumcision, for example, but it is equally the purpose of the commandments to have no other gods before me, to love the Lord your God with all your heart and strength and mind, and to love your neighbor as yourself. It is in the observance of these laws especially, and in the observance of all the commandments taken together, that the distinctiveness of Israel is established and the divine calling of Israel to be a light to the nations is answered.

The law functions in Israel to demarcate the center and scope of a particular order of living. Its center, and the law's first commandment, is the worship of Yahweh, and its scope is indicated by the spelling out of what faithfulness to Yahweh entails in all areas of life—in economics, in family life, in obligations to one's neighbors, and so on. The law sets out what life should look like among those who have been delivered from bondage and who are called now to live in covenant relationship with God, with neighbors, and with the whole of the created order.

Thus, while Luther is correct that the law, Christianly conceived, is not to be conceived as a condition to be met before God justifies and forgives and establishes his people—compliance is not the basis of justification—it seems probable that the law was not understood in this contractual way in early Judaism either.[59] Contrary to Luther's view of how the law functioned in Judaism, it is not to be understood as a "mighty hammer"[60] convicting us of sin and preparing us for grace.[61] Its purpose, rather, coming 430 years after the promise (Gal 3:17), is to delineate the form of life appropriate for a people set free from bondage and established as God's covenant people. As my former teacher, Alan Torrance, often puts it, "The indicatives of grace precede the imperatives of the law."[62] Observance of the law, furthermore, including the law's own provisions for atonement and reconciliation when Israel fails in its calling, becomes, for Israel, a means by which the people of God are identifiable precisely as God's people, a witness both to his grace and to his loving purpose for the world.

---

[59] This is the important conclusion of E. P. Sanders' seminal work, *Paul and Palestinian Judaism* (Philadelphia: Fortress, 1977).

[60] See Luther's "Lectures on Galatians," in *Luther's Works*, vol. 26, ed. Jaroslav Pelikan (Saint Louis: Concordia, 1963), 336.

[61] Luther, "Lectures on Galatians," 314.

[62] Alan Torrance, in lectures delivered at the University of Otago, 1988–1990.

Law and Rule in Christian Faith

I have attempted to develop an analogy between the application of rules in the classical orders of architecture and the function of law in the order of Jewish living. But what of Christian faith? Do the categories of rule and law remain applicable in the context of Paul's declaration in Romans 10:4 that Christ is the end of the law? Does not Christian freedom consist, in part, in freedom from the law? If that is so, what becomes of those aspects of the law apparently endorsed by Jesus himself?[63] Has God's righteous will, expressed, for example, in the Decalogue, now been abrogated? Wolfhart Pannenberg suggests that these are questions that have still not been settled in the history of Christian theology.[64] I do not presume to have settled them in what follows, but some progress may be made, I suggest, by taking a lead from Vitruvius. While in classical architecture, on Vitruvius' account, adherence to the rules of the respective orders is not a sufficient condition for the creation of buildings well fitted to their purpose, when combined with careful attention to context and an inventive response to that context, adherence to the rules will preserve the integrity of each of the orders and show forth "the grandeur of our [Roman] history and be a memorial for future ages."[65] So too in Christian existence, I suggest, adherence to an accumulated wisdom expressible in the form of rules or laws, combined with an inventive response to particular contexts, will serve to preserve the integrity of the gospel, show forth the ways in which God has been active in "our" history, and offer a memorial or testimony to future ages as well as our own of the grace and the love of God made present for us in Christ. There are two strands to the following argument. I will attempt first to show the enduring validity of the law in the context of Christ's fulfillment of it before then considering how the application of a rule in the classical orders of architecture might shed light on the role in Christian life of the "Rule of Faith." I will also attend to the characteristically modern concern that adherence to law or to a rule, particularly to a law given by God, is incompatible with the exercise of human freedom.

In the Old Testament the law demarcates the center and scope of Israel's life in covenant relationality with God. In the New Testament, however, and in the proclamation of the early church, Jesus Christ is proclaimed to be the center not just of Israel's relation to Yahweh but of the whole creation as it is

---

[63] See, e.g., Matt 22:34-40, 23:27; Mark 17:19.

[64] Wolfhart Pannenberg, *Systematic Theology*, vol. 3, trans. Geoffrey W. Bromiley (Grand Rapids: Eerdmans, 1998), 60.

[65] Vitruvius, *Architecture*, bk. 1, pref., 3 (Granger trans.), 1:5.

ordered to the divine purpose. He is the one through whom all things came to be and in whom all things hold together (Col 1:15-17); he is the one who presents his people holy and blameless to the Father (Col 1:22), and in him God was pleased to reconcile all things to himself (Col 1:20). By virtue of Christ's being and doing these things, Paul declares that he is the telos of the law (Rom 10:4); he is the end to which the law is directed and the one in whom it is fulfilled. Not only Jews but Gentiles, too, are now enabled to participate in the reality to which the law is directed, precisely through faith in Christ—through participation, that is, in his life of perfect obedience to and faithful worship of the Father.

Only in the sense of its now having been fulfilled should it be said that the law is at an end. It is not appropriate to say that the power of the law to effect salvation has also ended, because according to Paul at Romans 3:20—and, I suggest, according to Jewish understanding as well—the law never had that power. The law delineates how covenant relationality is to be worked out, not how it is to be established. That Christ is the *end* of the law does not mean, moreover, that the law is annulled. To be sure, the Gentiles who are enabled now, in Christ, to participate in covenant relationality with God are not required to become Jews and so need not observe those laws that served principally to identify Israel in particular as God's chosen people. Hence Paul declares, for example, that the Gentiles who participate in the new covenant in Christ need not be circumcised. Ethnicity and the religious observances of a particular ethnic group are no longer signs of God's election, as once they were, for in Christ there is neither Jew nor Greek. The identity of Christians as a people reconciled to God is established by virtue of their participation through the Spirit in the life of him who has fulfilled the law and who has thus secured, once and for all, the telos delineated by the law's commands; namely, life in reconciled relationship with God and with all that God has made. It is not true, however, that those freed from the provisions of the law identifying Israel in particular as God's people may now have other gods before Yahweh or that they may worship idols, or kill, or covet. To that idea Paul responds emphatically: "Do we then overthrow the law by this faith? By no means [*me genoito*]! On the contrary, we uphold the law" (Rom 3:31, cf. Rom 6:15; Gal 3:21).

As the rabbis of Israel have themselves allowed, "Certain of [the Torah's] laws have lost their binding force with the passing of the conditions which called them forth"[66] but this does not annul the abiding capacity of the law

---

[66] Columbus Platform, cited in de Lange, *Judaism*, 32.

in general to specify the form that the life of God's people should take in light of their deliverance by God from bondage. It remains true that the worship of other gods, or the resumption of killing or of covetousness, or the bearing of false witness would plunge Jew and Gentile alike back into the bondage from which they have been liberated. The parable Jesus tells of an unforgiving servant makes precisely this point (Matt 18:23-35). The enduring validity of the law lies in its purpose of reminding Jews and Gentiles alike of what life should look like among those who have been saved. Far from constraining or denying our freedom, the law delineates what free life looks like. It is a life free from bondage to idols and free from the vortices of covetousness, falsehood, adultery and so on. The law is a constraint not upon freedom, but upon chaos.

In the mode of inventive adaptation and *in the light of Christ*, Paul, who has shortly beforehand declared Christ to be the end of the law, does not hold back from setting out in some detail in Romans 12–15, for example, a rule of life that he expects his readers to embrace now that God has set them free. What is more, Paul several times draws upon the authority of the Torah in support of his exhortations, cites the Decalogue explicitly, and then makes the standard rabbinic point that love is the fulfilling of the law (Rom 13:9-10).[67] Christ's fulfillment of the law clearly does not mean for Paul that the law is annulled. Its fulfillment by Christ certainly entails that salvation is achieved for us in spite of our persistent failure to fulfill the law's command, but it does not entail that the commands contained in the Decalogue, for supreme instance, no longer have any binding force.

That the law has enduring significance for Christians is borne out, I suggest, by Jesus' own application of the law to the situations in which he finds himself. He displays, with respect to the law, the freedom and inventiveness that are necessary if the purpose of the law is to be fulfilled. He is not bound by it as a slave is bound to his or her master but exhibits a mastery of it in the same sense that the architects of the Parthenon, for instance, exhibited a mastery of the classical orders, adapting, extending and refining them to execute a building of great beauty and grandeur, well suited to its purpose. While it is necessary to acknowledge the limits of this analogy, limits pertaining to the fact that Christ's *author*ity over the law is a function of his *author*ship of it, there is benefit nevertheless in exploring the analogy further. Noteworthy

---

[67] See also Rom 12:19, 20; 13:9; 14:11; 15:3, 11, 12, 21. For a brief outline of the importance attached to love of neighbor in rabbinic literature, see Samuel S. Cohon, *Essays in Jewish Theology* (Cincinnati: Hebrew Union College Press, 1987), 201–18.

in particular is the inventiveness, the creativity, and the refinement exhibited in Jesus' fulfillment of the law.

Respect for the law is a prominent theme in Matthew's Gospel. Indeed Matthew styles Jesus as a new Moses, not overturning but fulfilling and renewing the law once given to Moses. In the Sermon on the Mount, clearly a complement to the deliverance of the law at Sinai, Jesus declares: "Do not think that I have come to abolish the law or the prophets; I have come not to abolish but to fulfill. For truly I tell you, until heaven and earth pass away, not one letter, not one stroke of a letter, will pass from the law until all is accomplished" (Matt 5:17-18). Jesus continues in the sermon, however, to exhibit a relation to the law not of subservience but of mastery. The several sayings beginning, "You have heard that it was said, but I say to you . . ." indicate that Jesus' authority exceeds that of the law; yet the qualification he offers in each case does not contradict but intensifies the demand of the law. The command, "you shall not murder," for instance, is intensified so that being angry with one's brother or sister, or accusing him or her of being a fool is treated with the same seriousness as murder itself.[68] That pattern continues through the remainder of Matthew 5 as Jesus intensifies the demands of the law and makes them a great deal more challenging.[69] It also becomes clear, however, as the gospel narrative unfolds, that Jesus is not concerned here with the letter of the law but with its spirit. In Matthew 12 he flouts the letter of the law by allowing his disciples to pluck grain on the Sabbath. For the sake of the indignant Pharisees, he cites by way of justification the example of David, who once did the same (Matt 12:2). Immediately following this incident, Jesus again transgresses the letter of the law by healing on the Sabbath a man with a withered hand (Matt 12:9-14). While Jesus has violated the letter of the law by his action, he again counters the Pharisees' indignation by drawing attention to the compassionate nature of the healing and by insisting that "it is lawful to do good on the sabbath" (v. 12). Because the strictures of the law are directed toward righteousness, toward the doing of good, the law is not flouted but rather fulfilled through the healing of a man on the Sabbath. It is important to recognize here that "doing good" should not be understood in narrowly moralistic terms but rather as the realization of that goodness bestowed upon the creation by God. The provision for rest

---

[68] See Matt 5:21-22.

[69] Matt 5:43-44 is a partial exception to this rule, because the quoted precept in verse 43 is not found in Israel's law. It is likely, however, to have been a precept that was well known to his audience and generally accepted as sage advice. In this case Jesus counters the instruction and commends a different course of action altogether.

on the Sabbath may certainly be regarded as an instance of that goodness, but the realization of that goodness is accomplished, in this particular case, by the removal of suffering and by the gift of freedom and rest to one whose ill health had been both bondage and tribulation. The Markan gloss, "The sabbath was made for humankind, and not humankind for the sabbath" (Mark 2:27), confirms the point that the law is not to be conceived as an end in itself but as guidance for the realization of some greater telos.

Here the analogy with the rules pertaining to the classical orders of architecture proves instructive, for it helps us to see the law not in the pejorative terms in which it is often regarded but rather as a set of specifications delineating the essential characteristics of some noble end—in this case, a life lived in accordance with God's good purposes for the world.

In the Renaissance the architectural specifications set out by Vitruvius were reworked and intensified by Alberti, Serlio, Palladio, and others, but the intensification of the law's demands by these theorists was guided by a profound understanding of its spirit. Far from constraining them, therefore, the higher degree of specification became the basis for a great deal more freedom and invention in architecture than had been exhibited by their forbears in the classical era itself. Some, like Laugier, worried that the creativity of some Renaissance architects in France constituted a violation of the law governing the classical orders rather than its fulfillment, but because the spirit rather than the letter is of utmost importance in such disputes, they cannot be settled by legal wrangling. The authority of one who has mastered the law, and who therefore lives according to its spirit, is its own witness. This authority is recognized by its difference from those who teach and act like "scribes."[70]

Freedom and invention were not the preserve of the Renaissance architects, of course. We have seen that these were in play during the classical period as well. The architects of the Parthenon, for instance, Callicrates and Ictinus, along with the master sculptor Pheidias, who probably had overall charge of the building process, knew the rules of the Doric and Ionic orders so well that they were able to adapt them through use of refinements to achieve an end that would not have been achieved had they followed the letter of strict mathematical symmetry and proportion. Something similar, I suggest, is apparent in Jesus' readiness to heal on the Sabbath. Strict adherence to the letter of the law is set aside in order that its spirit might be fulfilled. We have to reckon, of course, with Jesus' insistence that "until heaven and earth pass away, not one letter, not one stroke of a letter, will pass

---

[70] Cf. Matt 7:28-29.

from the law until it is accomplished" (Matt 5:18), but the meaning of this saying is surely illuminated by Jesus' own practice. Jesus freely interprets, adapts, and refines the law, yet Scripture is treated with great respect and its authority is upheld. The written law still serves well as a record of the wisdom accumulated through Israel's encounters with God and is not to be done away with. The phrase "It is written . . ." is justification enough, both in Jesus' teaching and throughout the New Testament, to command assent for what is now being proclaimed anew, reinterpreted, and applied to the circumstances of the present age. Adaptation, inventiveness, and refinement, rather than annulment, characterize Jesus' engagement with the law. These are in fact the conditions by which the law may be fulfilled, its goal realized. Thomas Smith recognizes this in his treatise on the relation between rule and invention in architecture. "All classical buildings," he writes,

> are ordered, and order depends upon rule. The narrow definition of rule limits it to the value of a dictionary. Abstract, inviolable rules establish canonical orders and types of buildings. These rules objectively indicate a single way of drawing a column, for example, and are authoritarian standards. Like the dictionary, they define it, provide spelling, and offer limited advice for its usage. This notion of rule isolates the column from practical application and gives little information about fitting it into the context of a building or using it poetically.[71]

The wisdom needed to apply the rule in a given context we might call inspiration. Such inspiration is certainly required in the theological case where guidance and empowerment by the Spirit are needed if we are to live according to the law of God as Jesus did and thus participate in the order of life to which Scripture testifies.

One further consequence of inspired, Christ-like observance of the law is that those who do observe the way of life inaugurated by and fulfilled in Christ are identifiable as Christians. Just as in architecture, observance of the rules, inventively and with appropriate refinement, allowed particular buildings to be identified as Doric or Ionic or Tuscan, for example, and just as adherence to the law, albeit falteringly, identified Israel as the people of God, so too adherence to a particular way of life renders Christians recognizable in the world. That way of life is centered around worship and is manifest above all in love of God and neighbor, a love that is itself described as the sum of the law (Matt 22:40).

---

[71] Smith, *Classical Architecture*, 58.

The Rule of Faith

The positive conception of the relation between rule and freedom that we have seen in the orders of architecture may be applied as well to the theological notion of the Rule of Faith. In an age committed to autonomy and self-determination, the idea of a Rule of Faith is commonly interpreted in pejorative terms. A rule is understood as something imposed, restrictive, authoritarian, and in conflict with the prerogative we each hold to determine for ourselves the "truth" by which we will live. Emancipation from rules and from traditional authorities is regularly hailed as one of the great achievements of the Enlightenment, an "achievement" given impetus, it must be acknowledged, by Luther's earlier stand in favor of the individual's prerogative to read and interpret Scripture against traditional ecclesiastical authority. Tradition, rule, and authority are typically construed, in the modern world, as a threat to freedom. The matter is conceived as a zero-sum game: the more rule, the less freedom. Rules are thought to constrain and inhibit rather than facilitate the development of culture and the flourishing of human life.

Again, however, the classical orders of architecture, executed according to precisely defined rules, provide evidence of an altogether different relationship between freedom and rule. Familiarity with the rules equipped classical and Renaissance architects with the resources to create buildings of grandeur and beauty that remain among humanity's highest architectural achievements. Successful utilization of the rules, far from inhibiting creativity, adaptation, and invention, required exactly that: an artistic and innovative sensibility that successfully adapted and refined the received tradition in ways suited to the requirements and aspirations of each new architectural project.

The Rule of Faith ought to be understood, I suggest, in similar terms. In varying formulations,[72] the Rule of Faith sets out the essential elements of the gospel of grace according to which God has established the conditions necessary for the flourishing and fulfillment of all creation. The Rule of Faith typically takes narrative form, or, at minimum, it identifies the defining features of the narrative's plot. The narrative begins with the work of God in creation, recalls the testimony in life and utterance of the patriarchs and prophets,

---

[72] There is no single definitive expression of the Rule of Faith. Classical examples outlining the key elements of the apostolic faith may be found, however, in the works of Ignatius, Polycarp, Irenaeus, and Tertullian, among others. For a good summary of the content and purpose of the Rule of Faith, see Kathryn Greene-McCreight, "Rule of Faith," in *Dictionary for Theological Interpretation of the Bible*, ed. Kevin J. Vanhoozer (Grand Rapids: Baker Academic, 2005), 703–4.

and centers upon the incarnation of the Son and the giving of his life for our salvation. It tells of his resurrection from the dead, his ascension, and his continuing intercession for the world. It tells also of the instructive and enabling work of the Spirit and of the formation of the community of Christ's people, commissioned to tell the story and to participate in the unfolding drama of God's purposes for the world. Finally, the Rule of Faith typically concludes by recalling the promise that in God's time all things will be completed and God's purpose will be fulfilled.

Its narrative form notwithstanding, the Rule of Faith implies some rules about what it means to speak and live gospel. For instance: to speak truthfully of God, we must speak of the triune life of the Father, the Son, and the Spirit; to speak truthfully of the basis and nature of salvation, we must speak of what has been done for us in and through the life, death, and resurrection of Jesus and of what is being done for us through the continuing intercession of Son and Spirit; to speak truthfully of the scope of salvation, we must speak of the whole creation ordered to God's good purpose; to speak truthfully of what it is to be human, we must speak of the one who became flesh and dwelt among us, who took upon himself our humanity, and who reconciled us to the Father. To live within and to enjoy the freedom of a life reconciled to God, we must keep company with the risen Christ, and thus also with the community called Church that he establishes as his body and of which he is the Head and so on.

These rules have a very important feature: while they do indeed constrain—they define some limits to what may truthfully be said of God—it is important nonetheless to recognize that they are permissive. The rules set out the particular conditions under which *we are enabled* to speak truthfully of God; they set out the basis upon which *we are liberated* to walk free from the bondage of sin and death; they describe the conditions through which *we are equipped* to live as beloved children of God and to participate in the working out of God's good purposes for the world. To put it otherwise, the limitations set upon faithful Christian witness by the Rule of Faith *specify* rather than *hem in* the possibilities of life and speech that are facilitated by the gospel.[73] The Rule of Faith "sets the stage," as Paul Blowers puts it, "for what a 'faithful' hearing and interpretive performance of [Scripture's story]

---

[73] I have adapted here an insight of John Webster, who, in *Barth's Moral Theology*, writes of the limitations of creatureliness: "limitation *specifies* rather than *hems in* the creature" (115) (emphasis in original).

will be"[74] and presents in brief, summary form the confessional resources with which the Church is enabled to speak and live the good news.

Referring again to the function of the rule in classical architecture, Thomas Smith writes, "We may sometimes fear that rule will overwhelm our independence, but this does not take its real function into account. Rule exists to maintain the basic form, meaning and character of the order, and it has accomplished this with remarkable continuity."[75] The rule serves in part, therefore, to establish and maintain the distinct identity of, for example, the Doric, the Ionic, or the Corinthian order. A similar purpose attended the development of the Rule of Faith in the early church. Much has been written about the need to establish and maintain the identity of the Christian faith and Church over against the rival claims of Gnosticism, Marcionism, and so on. Irenaeus' *Adversus Haereses*, in which appears an early formulation of the *regula fidei* (Rule of Faith), is certainly concerned to distinguish authentic Christian witness, a witness "received from the apostles and their disciples,"[76] from the "lying words"[77] of the Valentinians, among others. But the development of the Rule was not simply reactionary. It was also an attempt to set forth, as Paul Blowers again has put it, "the basic 'dramatic' structure of a Christian vision of the world."[78] The point of the Rule of Faith being a "dramatic" structure is that Christian faith is identified principally by a set of dogmatic propositions to be believed but rather by its witness to an unfolding drama, the drama of God's creative and redemptive purposes for the world, conveyed through the promise made to Israel and fulfilled among us through the work of Christ and the Spirit. In articulating the rudiments of this drama, the Rule of Faith secures the distinctiveness of Christian identity and identifies the space within which Christian life is to be lived. Blowers observes that the most basic issue motivating transmission of the Rule of Faith is "that of Christian *identity*, identification with and in a particular story that transcends all *local* particularities and aspires to universal significance."[79] And further: "The Rule in effect offers the believer a place in the story by commending a way of life framed by the narrative of creation, redemption in Jesus Christ, and new life in the Spirit."[80] The point again to

---

[74] Paul M. Blowers, "The *Regula Fidei* and the Narrative Character of Early Christian Faith," *Pro Ecclesia* 6, no. 2 (1998): 199–228, 210.

[75] Smith, *Classical Architecture*, 62.

[76] Irenaeus, *Against the Heresies*, 1.10.1 (*ANF* 1:330).

[77] Irenaeus, *Against the Heresies*, pref., 1 (*ANF* 1:315).

[78] Blowers, "*Regula Fidei*," 202.

[79] Blowers, "*Regula Fidei*," 214.

[80] Blowers, "*Regula Fidei*," 214.

be made here is that the Rule opens up new possibilities—redemption in Christ and new life in the Spirit—rather than constrains. It offers testimony to the expansive purpose of God to set us free from bondage and establish on earth the freedom and the fullness of life for which we were made.

Participation in a drama involves, of course, the performance of particular actions. For all his conviction that the orders of architecture reflected and were derived from the universal principles of cosmic order, Vitruvius' purpose in setting them out was intensely practical. The end in view was not mere knowledge but the realization of these principles in wood and stone, in the concrete reality of particular buildings. So too the Rule of Faith envisages a particular form of life. According to Tertullian, the Rule of Faith "has a law"; that is, its observance consists in a set of practices.[81] Similarly, Gregory Nazianzen prefaces his setting out of the Rule of Faith by describing it as a new Decalogue.[82] For the most part, the Rule does not prescribe any particular actions. Instead, as we have noted, it takes narrative form; it recalls the story of God's action and invites participation in the drama so described. In this dramatic quality it is, admittedly, not like the Vitruvian rule in architecture, but the Rule of Faith does call forth the inventiveness, adaptation, and refinement required also by Vitruvius. The Rule of Faith, if it is to be observed, requires us to consider what human actions are "fitting" in light of God's action in and for the world.

In the course of his Rule of Faith, set out in *Adversus Haereses*, Irenaeus does commend one action: worship. In the light of what God has done, "every knee should bow of things in heaven and things in earth, and things under the earth, and that every tongue should confess to Him."[83] Christian life and faith is founded, nurtured, inspired, and renewed at its doxological center when the people of God are gathered to hear the Word and receive the sacraments. The hearing of the Word is, first and foremost, a retelling of the story summarized in the Rule of Faith, and then also the commissioning, preparation, and equipping of the Church to go into all the world as bearers and proclaimers of the good news. Celebration of baptism and of the Eucharist is likewise a remembrance of the drama through which sin is overcome and the new creation is brought to birth. The freedom of the children of God, celebrated in baptism, is achieved through atonement and the forgiveness of sins, but as Colin Gunton has pointed out, it is not a shapeless freedom. It is

---

[81] Tertullian, *The Prescription against Heretics*, 14 (*ANF* 3:250). This, and the following reference to Gregory Nazianzen, I owe to Paul Blowers.

[82] Gregory Nazianzen, *Orations*, 40.45 (*NPNF*, 7:376).

[83] Irenaeus, *Against the Heresies*, 1.10.1 (*ANF*, 1:330).

not freedom in a vacuum. "Just as sin takes shape, as the opening chapters of Genesis show, in a range of personal and social dislocations, so salvation takes shape in a matrix of new and reconciled patterns of relations."[84] The monastic communities established in the Middle Ages formalized this matrix of relations into a pattern of life they, too, called a rule. The monastic rule served well to maintain a form of life in the monastic communities that was centered in worship and issued in missional service to the world. Only a remnant now remains of the great monastic tradition, and so the church has to discover anew how to maintain in its life together a fitting witness to the transformative work of God. Now in a very different world, it faces the challenge of making itself identifiable again as the body of Christ. And yet, lessons may still be learned from the past. In an era characterized by individualism and acquisitive consumerism, the adherence of Christian communities to some contemporary successor of the monastic rule, suitably adapted and refined, may well be an important step. It may assist also in freeing Christians from the various forms of captivity—consumerism, careerism, individualism, and the like—that are widespread in contemporary Western society.

Just as baptism celebrates the commencement of a new order of life, so too does the Eucharist. The eucharistic liturgy repeats the narrative of God's creative and redemptive work in the world and at its high point we hear the words, "do this in memory of me." But what exactly is the Christian community to do? It has often been supposed that participation in the sacrament itself—participation in the ritual—is the necessary and sufficient response to Christ's instruction, but the gestures we are called to imitate are those *represented* in the breaking of bread and the pouring of wine—namely, the total giving of one's life—after the pattern of Christ himself, in accordance with the purposes of God. What that means in practice has to be worked out by the church in every concrete situation. The gestures of Christ himself, represented in the Eucharist, make clear that compliance with the eucharistic rule—"do this"—will involve unconditional love, sacrifice, compassion, forgiveness, obedience to the Father's will, and so on. The church has a long tradition in which these gestures of faith have been made—not always unerringly, of course but, by God's grace, sufficiently well for those who come after to have seen and heard the witness of faith and so to be gathered themselves into the drama of God's new creation. They, too, in turn, are called to apply the Rule of Faith, creatively, inventively, and with adaptations and

---

[84] Colin E. Gunton, "God, Grace and Freedom," in *God and Freedom: Essays in Historical and Systematic Theology*, ed. Colin E. Gunton (Edinburgh: T&T Clark, 1995), 119–33, 131.

refinements suitable to the challenges of their own context, but always intent on the faithful continuation of the story articulated in the Rule.

It must be noted that the inventiveness, adaptation, and refinement that I am proposing do not refer to the creation of a different gospel from that which has been handed down through the apostles. Irenaeus makes clear, following his articulation of the Rule of Faith, that while there is need for further exploration,

> it does not follow because men are endowed with greater and less degrees of intelligence, that they should therefore change the subject-matter [of the faith] itself, and should conceive of some other God beside Him who is the Framer, Maker, and Preserver of this universe, (as if He were not sufficient for them), or of another Christ, or another Only-begotten.[85]

Inventiveness, adaptation, and refinement refer to the kind of creative yet faithful and radical response to the challenges of the age evident, for example, in the stand taken by early Christians against killing and against participation in the imperial army; in the Nicene confession that the Son is *homoousios to patri*; in Luther's declaration that the righteousness of God is a gift given through Christ rather than something earned; in the stand taken by William Wilberforce, Abraham Lincoln, Frederick Douglass, Sojourner Truth, and others against the practice of slavery; in the peaceful resistance to colonial oppression shown by the Māori people of Parihaka in New Zealand under the leadership of Te Whiti o Rongomai and Tohu Kākahi; in Rosa Parks' polite refusal to give up her seat on a bus in Birmingham, Alabama; in Dorothy Day's establishment of the Catholic Worker Movement, and so on. None of these actions are prescribed in the Rule of Faith but they each constitute, I suggest, a faithful execution of the Rule. The invention and creativity represented here is of the kind commended by the classical rhetoricians for whom *inventio* was "both a repetition and a transformation, for it is the art of taking that which already exists and developing or elaborating upon it. As such, it involves *imitatio* but it goes beyond simple imitation."[86]

Of course, it is fundamental to the story itself that we are not left to our own devices when developing and elaborating upon the Rule of Faith. The central plotline of the narrative summarized in the Rule of Faith is that God is at work through his Word and Spirit, gathering, inspiring, and equipping a people and sending them forth to be a herald and foretaste of the coming

---

[85] Irenaeus, *Against the Heresies*, 1.10.3 (*ANF* 1:331).

[86] I take the point from Benson, "Improvising Texts, Improvising Communities," in Begbie and Guthrie, eds., *Resonant Witness*, 300.

kingdom of God. The inventive adaptation and refinement of the Rule by successive generations of Christians is best understood, therefore, as a responsive participation, enabled by the Spirit, in the continuing work of God.

The question arises, of course, whether the church can go astray, whether in its sincere efforts to respond to the challenges of the times or because of the continuing effects of human sin, attempts at inventive adaptation and refinement can result in distortions and betrayals of the narrative articulated in the Rule of Faith. The answer to this question, as history abundantly testifies, is certainly yes. And so the further question presents itself: what can be done to identify and to avoid, as far as possible, such distortions and betrayals? There are no guarantees against error, but, trusting prayerfully in the guidance of the Holy Spirit, the church must be ever attentive to the Word of God; it must return again and again to listen anew to the self-presentation of God in Jesus, in Scripture and in the tradition of Christian proclamation and theological reflection throughout the ages. The church's commitment to such attentiveness, however, is a necessary but not sufficient safeguard against error.

We may appeal also to what is called, somewhat loosely, "the test of time." This is a test applied in many fields of human endeavor including, as we have seen, the practice of architecture.[87] The inventiveness, adaptations, and refinements of every age are reviewed, assessed, and taken as instructive, one hopes, by the generations that follow. The modern university is an institution (founded by the church for this purpose) that has a particular but by no means exclusive responsibility to safeguard and promote the search for truth and understanding in human endeavor. Both within and beyond the university, the church through its teachers and councils and through others gifted in theological discernment—including every local congregation as it meets for study and prayer—makes an assessment over time of the legitimacy of each particular expression of the endeavor in which it is engaged. A judgement thereby evolves, informed by the wisdom of the community of saints and profiting from the benefit of hindsight, about the fittingness of particular expressions of the divine drama narrated in the Rule of Faith. The almost universal allegiance of the worldwide church to the Nicene Creed, the stand taken by Martin Luther against the practice of indulgences, and the more recent condemnation by the World Alliance of Reformed Churches of theological justifications of apartheid, provide instances of how the church has

---

[87] Recall the debates about the legitimacy of the Erechtheion as an expression of the classical orders, or Laugier's concern in the Rennaissance about what he perceived to be the distortion of classical form in some contemporary architecture.

assessed particular expressions and adaptations of the Rule of Faith as faithful or not. The judgements of the wider Christian community, given time to assess carefully and prayerfully the efforts of particular, localized Christian communities to speak and enact the gospel, provide, again, a necessary but not sufficient safeguard against error.

These necessary safeguards against error—the commitment to prayerful attentiveness and the testing by the wider community of faith—are themselves subordinate to the one, *sufficient* safeguard against error; namely, the providence of God. Unable itself to offer any infallible guarantee against error,[88] the church trusts that God will not leave himself without a witness (Acts 14:17). The church goes its way in faith, ever refining and creatively adapting what it has heard and understood in order to meet the challenges of each new era, while trusting prayerfully that God himself will see to it that the truth of the gospel is preserved.

Conclusion

By drawing upon the example of classical architecture, I have attempted to demonstrate in this chapter the possibility of a positive construal of the relation between law and freedom, rule and invention. I have suggested, against the predilections of our age, that the discipline and constraint of the law in the biblical narrative, and of the Rule of Faith in the Christian tradition, far from being a threat to human freedom, provide, instead, complementary accounts of what free life consists in, and of its basis. The biblical law, beginning with the reminder that God is the one who delivered his people from bondage, and the Rule of Faith, climaxing in its declaration of Christ's victory over sin and death, tell of God's gift of freedom to humankind. These declarations of freedom call forth and make possible a truly free and truly human life that is centered in worship, corresponds to God's creative and redemptive purposes for the world, and serves thus as a witness to God's glory.

---

[88] In this, of course, the churches of the Reformation hold a different view from that of the Roman Catholic Church.

4

Making All Things New
Transforming the World through Adaptation and Renewal

Shortly after his victory at the Milvian Bridge and alleged conversion to Christian faith in A.D. 312, the Emperor Constantine gifted land in the Lateran quarter of Rome to the bishop of Rome, Pope Miltiades, whose short term of office extended from 311 to 314. Herbert Kessler and Johanna Zacharias explain that "to make space on the site for a grand church to be dedicated to the Savior, Constantine levelled the cavalry barracks—that is, those of the very troops he had routed in 312 in the battle of the Milvian Bridge against his rival Maxentius (306–312). The demolished barracks walls provided the church's foundations."[1] The church built there, now known as St John Lateran, became the cathedral of the bishop of Rome. Alongside it a palace was built for the bishop that served as the papal residence until the fourteenth century. This took place in a city that had been portrayed two centuries earlier in the biblical book of Revelation as a city of evil and corruption. Chapter 18 of Revelation opens with John's vision of an angel descending from heaven and crying out against a city, called Babylon by the angel, but identified in the previous chapter as Rome, "built on seven hills (17:9). . . . She is 'Babylon the great, mother of whores.'"[2] Babylon was the ancient city

---

[1] Herbert L. Kessler and Johanna Zacharias, *Rome 1300: On the Path of a Pilgrim* (New Haven: Yale University Press, 2000), 13–14.

[2] Richard Bauckham, *The Theology of the Book of Revelation* (Cambridge: Cambridge University Press, 1993), 126.

representing oppression, exile, corruption, and evil in Israel's story, but at the time of John's vision, Rome was perceived as the principal oppressor of the fledgling Christian community. In a thinly veiled reference to Rome, then, the angel looks to the future and declares:

> It has become a dwelling place of demons,
> a haunt for every foul spirit,
>   a haunt of every foul bird,
>   a haunt of every foul and hated beast.
> For all the nations have drunk
>   of the wine of the wrath of her fornication,
> and the kings of the earth have committed fornication with her,
>   and the merchants of the earth have grown rich from the power of
>   her luxury.
> Then I heard another voice from heaven saying,
> "Come out of her, my people,
>   so that you do not take part in her sins,
> and so that you do not share in her plagues;
> for her sins are heaped high as heaven
>   and God has remembered her iniquities." (Rev 18:2-5)

"Babylon" is used here as a cipher for the corrupt and depraved city. While a number of cities have been identified as "Babylon" among interpreters of Revelation, dominating the reception history is the understanding of Babylon as the Beast of Rome.[3] Whatever the particular city, however, "Babylon's defilement contaminated those who lived within. The only recourse was to flee its immorality into the haven of pure Christian communion."[4]

Annihilation or Renewal?

John goes on to contrast this earthly city with "the holy city, the new Jerusalem, coming down out of heaven from God" (Rev 21:2). The new city takes its place within "a new heaven and a new earth; for the first heaven and the first earth had passed away" (21:1). That the present reality will somehow be replaced is attested clearly enough in John's vision, but whether or not there will be some continuity between the old creation and the new remains a

---

[3] See Judith Kovacs and Christopher Rowland, *Revelation: The Apocalypse of Jesus Christ*, Blackwell Bible Commentaries (Oxford: Blackwell, 2004), 178.

[4] Renate Viveen Hood, "Pure or Defiled? A Sociological Analysis of John's Apocalypse," in *Essays on Revelation: Appropriating Yesterday's Apocalypse in Today's World*, ed. Gerald L. Stevens (Eugene, Oreg.: Wipf & Stock, 2010), 87–99, 97.

matter of debate. In a recent study of whether biblical eschatology portrays an annihilationist or transformative future for the created order, Mark Stephens poses the question thus:

> With regard to the nonhuman material world, does John the Seer envisage an eschatological annihilation of the cosmos, and its replacement with something else, or does he instead envisage an eschatological renewal of the present cosmos, which despite its significant experience of transformation, stands in some kind of material continuity with the present order of things[?][5]

Stephens himself observes that "the presence of radically different conclusions remains apparent."[6] Scholarly opinion during the twentieth century generally held that apocalyptic literature in Judaism from the first century B.C., and then in Christianity, presents an annihilationist view. According to Robert Charles, for example, "The older doctrine in the O.T. was the eternity of the present order of things. This was the received view down to the second century B.C." However, "From the 1st century B.C. onward in Judaism and Christianity, the transitoriness of the present heaven and earth was universally accepted."[7] Rudolf Bultmann agrees: "The end is not the completion of history but its breaking off, it is, so to speak, the death of the world due to its age. The old world will be replaced by a new creation, and there is no continuity between the two Aeons."[8]

Despite Charles' claim of "universal acceptance," however, others have argued just as stridently that the book of Revelation in particular offers hope of a "material continuity" between the new creation and the old.[9] According to James Cate, for example, the relation between the old cosmos and the new is to be understood as a transition, as a transformation of the old rather than its extinction and replacement.

> Revelation does describe a catastrophic moment that ushers in the transition of the ages. That moment, however, is not the destruction of the earth; that transition is described as the fall of the bloated urban monstrosity of

---

[5] Mark B. Stephens, *Annihilation or Renewal? The Meaning and Function of New Creation in the Book of Revelation* (Tübingen: Mohr Siebeck, 2011), 1–2.

[6] Stephens, *Annihilation or Renewal*, 5.

[7] Robert H. Charles, *A Critical and Exegetical Commentary on the Revelation of St. John*, International Critical Commentary (Edinburgh: T&T Clark, 1920), 2:193.

[8] Rudolf Bultmann, *The Presence of Eternity: History and Eschatology* (New York: Harper, 1957), 30. Cited in Stephens, *Annihilation or Renewal*, 3.

[9] See Stephens, *Annihilation or Renewal*, 3–4.

ancient Rome symbolized as Babylon (18:1-24). The scattered debris are not the skeletal remains of all creatures great and small, but the smoldering trash of a city's once treasured merchandise, the broken pieces of its crass consumerism now a desolate wasteland (18:11-13).[10]

While acknowledging that there is room for debate on the matter, Stephens himself argues in favor of a transformational view. Commenting, for example, upon the visions in Revelation 4 and 5 of the whole creation gathered in praise of the Creator and the Lamb, Stephens writes:

> Such portrayals suggest, but do not demand, that a model of creational renewal is being envisaged, in which God's coming to the earth brings liberating transformation as opposed to cosmic annihilation. In simple terms, the idea of a "replacement" creation (*creatio de novo*) appears less coherent, for what is acclaimed is the actualization of creation-wide worship, such that the heavens are glad and the earth rejoices at the coming of God.[11]

These opening visions in which creation as a whole is gathered in praise of the Creator anticipate the final outcome of God's work even though an intermediate stage of judgement and destruction will ensue. "This is important," Stephens explains,

> because if one were to read, in isolation, the cumulative visions of destruction that follow, such visions could potentially be construed as evincing an annihilationist attitude towards creation. But with their being preceded by this opening vision of the heavenly court, John creates an undercurrent of cosmic renewal to the surface imagery of cosmic destruction.[12]

It is important to notice also the reference to a rainbow encircling God's throne in chapter 4, verse 3. The rainbow recalls the covenant made with Noah through which God promises never again to destroy the earth (Gen 9:11). The presence of the rainbow thus provides another hint that although judgement and destruction are in store, annihilation of the earth is not in view.[13]

---

[10] James Jeffrey Cate, "How Green Was John's World? Ecology and Revelation," in *Essays on Revelation: Appropriating Yesterday's Apocalypse in Today's World*, ed. Gerald L. Stevens (Eugene, Oreg.: Wipf & Stock, 2010), 145–55, 151–52.

[11] Stephens, *Annihilation or Renewal*, 190.

[12] Stephens, *Annihilation or Renewal*, 191. Stephens attributes the insight to David M. Russell, *The "New Heavens and the New Earth": Hope for the Creation in Jewish Apocalyptic and the New Testament*, Studies in Biblical Apocalyptic Literature 1 (Philadelphia: Visionary Press, 1996), 200.

[13] See Stephens, *Annihilation or Renewal*, 175–76.

The Rebuilding of Rome

As we have noted above, the chapters that follow in the book of Revelation tell of an especially severe judgement upon the city of Rome, but if the eschatological future of the created order involves transformation rather than annihilation, might it be that God will show mercy in the end even to Rome? Might it be that Rome, a city like the old Jerusalem that "kills the prophets and stones those who are sent to it" (Matt 23:37) will, like the New Jerusalem, be taken up into the divine economy of redemption and transformation? The conversion of Constantine, coming two hundred years after John's vision in which Rome is condemned as the "great mother of whores," prompted in Christian imagination a vision of Rome redeemed, of Rome sanctified by the newfound faith of its emperor, and, more importantly, by the martyrs who had suffered there. To be sure, Constantine would soon move the capital of the Roman Empire away from "the eternal city" to the ancient city of Byzantium, and less than a century later Rome itself would suffer defeat at the hands of the Goths and fall into decay. But these events could be interpreted later as necessary stages in Rome's redemption. As time progressed, and especially as Rome assumed renewed importance as the center of Christendom, the architecture of imperial Rome was reinterpreted and reshaped according to a Christian narrative about the earthly city anticipating the city yet to come. David Mayernik observes that despite its fall into decay and the plundering of its urban fabric for building projects elsewhere, Rome emerged "with perhaps the richest palimpsest of a coherent story possible." Mayernik continues:

> The dream of what Rome could be, and the memory of what it once had been, guided a process that the architectural historian Joseph Connors has called *incremental urbanism*: Establish a piazza here, design a new façade there, place a door to align with a street, straighten a street or bend it toward a monument. Those urban projects that blossomed out of localized building activity also left traces of grander visions on their immediate context.[14]

The grander vision to which Rome's city builders aspired through the course of the Middle Ages was essentially a biblical one; it was a vision of the "holy city" portrayed in the Bible as the fulfillment of God's purpose to dwell with his people and to establish on earth the harmonious coexistence of all that he has made. If Rome could not itself be that paradise, then it

---

[14] Mayernik, *Timeless Cities*, 2–3.

could at least provide a foretaste of the promised New Jerusalem. It could, in the meantime, show forth what the New Jerusalem would be like. That such an understanding of Rome's significance came to be widely accepted throughout Christendom can be seen, for example, in the instructions given for the painting of an altarpiece to be placed in the church of the Carthusians in Villeneuve-les-Avignon.[15] The commissioned painter, Enguerrand Quarton (1410–1466), is instructed to show the form of paradise in which will be depicted the Trinity, Mary, the angels, the apostles, and various other saints. Beneath this paradise the heavens should appear and then the world "in which should be shown part of the city of Rome," including the church of St. Peter, the Ponte Sant'Angelo, part of the walls of Rome, "houses and shops of all types," the Castel Sant'Angelo, and "a bridge over the river Tiber which goes into the city of Rome." The inclusion of various churches around Rome is then specified. From Rome a river should be shown flowing down to the sea, on the other side of which Jerusalem should be depicted. Farther afield various other biblical scenes were to be shown, including especially scenes involving Moses. The arrangement described gives pride of place among all the things of earth to the city of Rome. It is portrayed as the terrestrial city closest to paradise. The instructions given to the artist reveal the belief, found well beyond Rome itself, that the city had indeed become a foretaste of the New Jerusalem.

In this and the following chapter I intend to explore the theological convictions that guided the transformation of ancient Rome from the city portrayed in John's apocalypse as the epitome of evil to the "holy city" of the medieval world. I will be concerned in particular with the ways in which the architecture of the ancient imperial city built, according to Vitruvius, to "correspond to the grandeur of our history, and [as] a memorial to future ages"[16] came to tell the very different story of Christian redemption under Christ's kingly rule.

In the year 313, with the construction of the church dedicated to St. John in Rome's Lateran quarter, there begins a narrative in stone testifying to the possibility of divine mercy and renewal. The church itself, as noted above, was built at the behest of Constantine on the site of a military barracks. Although Constantine himself may not have recognized the symbolism, the replacement of a military barracks with a sanctuary for Christian worship

---

[15] See "Contract for Painting an Altarpiece for Dominus Jean de Montagnac, Priest," in *A Documentary History of Art*, vol. 1, *The Middle Ages and the Renaissance*, ed. Elizabeth Gilmore Holt (Princeton: Princeton University Press, 1947), 298–302.

[16] Vitruvius, *Architecture*, bk. 1, pref., 3 (Granger trans.), 1:5.

could be seen by Christians, traditionally resistant to military service, as a partial realization of the eschatological promise that the nations "shall beat their swords into ploughshares, and their spears into pruning hooks" (Mic 4:3). While Christian opposition to military service and to war eroded very quickly as Christianity's alliance with and assumption of political power developed, other aspects of the Bible's eschatological promise continued to find expression in the architecture of Christianized Rome and throughout Europe. "When, in 324, [Constantine] founded Constantinople—a 'new Rome' at the site of the Greek city of Byzantium on the Bosphorus—[he] left a vacuum of temporal governance in the old city that popes gradually filled."[17] Through the course of the Middle Ages, "old Rome," now subject to ecclesiastical governance, increasingly styled itself as the New Jerusalem and became a place of pilgrimage for Christians. We will explore further in the following chapter the architectural content and form of the New Jerusalem as it was conceived in the Middle Ages but, in keeping with this chapter's theme of the eschatological *transformation* and *renewal* of creation, our principal focus for the moment will be upon the architectural transformation of the city's fabric. The theological end in view is an exploration of the relation and continuity between the old creation and the new.

The Basilica

Prior to Constantine's construction of the church dedicated to the Savior in the Lateran quarter, Christians in Rome—a small minority of the population—had worshipped in private houses called *tituli*, according to the names of their owners. The church that Constantine commissioned, therefore, was the first built in Rome specifically for use as a place of Christian worship. The architectural form adopted for the church was the basilica, a specifically Roman adaptation of classical style created for the Roman forum in the second century B.C.[18] The selection of this form for a church dedicated to Christ served to distinguish the building from the classical pagan temple but introduced into church architecture an unmistakable connection to political power. More positively, given that the term "basilica" is derived from the Greek *basileus* (king) and means a royal hall, it might be argued that the basilica built for worship of the "king of kings" was turned for the first time to its most fitting purpose. In fulfillment, so it seemed, of the declaration in

---

[17] Kessler and Zacharias, *Rome 1300*, 14.
[18] See Stefan Grundmann, ed., *The Architecture of Rome* (Stuttgart: Axel Menges, 1998), 33.

Revelation 11:15 that "the kingdom of the world has become the kingdom of our Lord and of his Messiah, and he will reign for ever and ever," the adoption of the basilica as a place of Christian worship signified that the rule of Christ had replaced the "pretentious sovereignty"[19] of ancient Rome.

As the basilica form was adapted for Christian use, transepts were added to form a cross, thus establishing the cruciform plan as the norm for church architecture and linking Christ's kingship to his suffering and death. "The tower, which became a characteristic feature of Christian churches, was probably added late in the fourth century or early in the fifth," initially to symbolize Jerusalem.[20] In the adaptation of the basilica form, this product of human culture is put to theological use; namely, the praise of the Savior, and a hint is given of the old creation being transformed into the new. One of the key marks of the new creation is that all things in heaven and earth are properly ordered to Christ, the one in and through whom all things came to be. Appropriation of the basilica form for Christian use may signify, therefore, the transfer of cosmic sovereignty that is anticipated in the book of Revelation. This transfer is indicated in Revelation 11:15 and in 21:2, and is reiterated in 22:1: "where the throne of God which was previously in heaven is now located upon the earth."[21] The basilica church foreshadows this eschatological reality.

The Use of *Spolia*

The redeployment of the pagan city's built heritage is seen also in the baptistery that stands alongside the Lateran basilica's main entrance. Baptism is itself, of course, the sacrament of regeneration and new life. That is signified in the octagonal form of the building, the number eight representing the first day of a new creation. The unadorned brick exterior of the building presents a plain face to the outside world, but among the riches to be found within the building are porphyry columns purloined from ancient buildings and reused in the construction of the baptistery.[22] Porphyry was a highly sought after stone obtainable at great expense only from a quarry in Egypt. It became a signifier of regal status.

---

[19] I take the phrase from Stephens, *Annihilation or Renewal*, 248.
[20] John Cloag, *The Architectural Interpretation of History* (London: A&C Black, 1975), 115–16.
[21] Stephens, *Annihilation or Renewal*, 248.
[22] Kessler and Zacharias, *Rome 1300*, 17.

The reuse of *spolia* from ancient buildings became common practice during the reign of Constantine and continued thereafter. Originally referring to the spoils of war, *spolia* is a term now used in archaeological and architectural discourse to identify "fragments reused in a context different from the original one."[23] Precisely what motivated this practice is highly contested. While some scholars see an ideological element in the plunder and reuse of architectural elements from an era now supposed to have been surpassed, others prefer a much more pragmatic explanation centered on the ready availability of materials from buildings that had fallen into disuse. Among ideological explanations there are conservative and progressive possibilities, the former being concerned with the reclamation of past glories; the latter, consonant with the practice of returning home with the spoils of war, suggests a victory of the new era over the old. Thus the use of *spolia* from pagan architecture in a church built by Constantine as an ex-voto to Christ might indicate a conservative admiration for the rich artistic heritage of ancient Rome, but it is also possible to view the practice as an expression of the theme of regeneration and the ushering in of the new creation.[24] Indeed these two possibilities are not mutually exclusive. It may be argued that the rich fruits of human culture once dedicated to pagan ends, but highly valued for their artistic merit, are consciously ordered to a new purpose. They serve now as a witness to the redemptive work of Christ the Savior, to whom, as we have seen, the building was dedicated.

Renewed interest in the use of *spolia* came about through the publication in 1969 of an essay by Arnold Esch, who "shifted the emphasis from the afterlife of classical antiquity (with its implication of death) to reuse as a form of new life, with different modalities and myriad inventive outcomes."[25] Theologically conceived, of course, death and new life are not separable entities but successive stages in the redemptive work of God. The use of *spolia*

---

[23] Paolo Liverani, "Reading *Spolia* in Late Antiquity and Contemporary Perception," in *Reuse Value: Spolia and Appropriation in Art and Architecture from Constantine to Sherrie Levine*, ed. Richard Brilliant and Dale Kinney (Farnham: Ashgate, 2011), 33–51, 45.

[24] Beat Brenk argues that the use made of *spolia* by Constantine is likely to have been motivated by aesthetic concerns and that it inaugurated a tradition among subsequent emperors of preserving the glories of ancient Rome. He does not consider whether there might also have been a theological motivation. See Beat Brenk, "Spolia from Constantine to Charlemagne: Aesthetics versus Ideology," *Dumbarton Oaks Papers* 41 [*Studies on Art and Archeology in Honor of Ernst Kitzinger on His Seventy-Fifth Birthday*] (1987): 103–9, 104–5.

[25] Dale Kinney, Introduction to Brilliant and Kinney, *Reuse Value*, 1–11, 1. The essay by Arnold Esch to which Kinney refers is "Spolien: Zur Wiederverwendung antiker Baustücke und Skulpturen in mittelalterlichen Italien," *Archiv für Kulturgeschichte* 51 (1969): 1–64.

FIGURE 4.1
Porphyry Columns in the Baptistery of St. John Lateran, Rome

in the building of churches, hospitals, almshouses, and the like, whether intended as such or not, may be read in theological terms as an instance of the creation being transformed and of the material realities of human life being redeployed for service in the coming kingdom of God. While some scholars, as we have noted, deny such ideological interpretations,[26] there is

[26] Hugo Brandenburg, e.g., while acknowledging that the use of *spolia* has commonly been regarded both as a means of political legitimation for a new emperor in his own building programs and as "the manifestation of the victory of Christianity over paganism," himself contends that a simple pragmatic explanation is to be preferred. The use of *spolia* simply indicates the ready availability of materials either from buildings now abandoned or from workshops that produced standard architectural ornaments for general use. Brandenburg concludes that "it is utterly inappropriate to interpret the acquisition of older building materials from stocks in public depots for use on public buildings and important church foundations as constituting acts of 'appropriation,' or to attribute to it any ideological significance." See Brandenburg, "The Use of Older Elements in the Architecture of Fourth- and Fifth-Century Rome: A Contribution to the Evaluation of Spolia," in Brilliant and Kinney, *Reuse Value*, 53–73, 53, 70. In the same volume, however, Arnold Esch is much more sympathetic to ideological interpretations of the reuse of *spolia*. See his essay, "On the Reuse of Antiquity: The Perspectives of the Archaeologist and the Historian," 13–31.

no doubt that the citizens of Rome were beginning to see the architectural fabric of their city transformed and rededicated to the service of Christ. That transformation continued apace throughout the Middle Ages, not just in Rome but wherever Christianity took hold.

The positive portrayal of the use of *spolia* that I am proposing here must be tempered somewhat by the claim often made that the use of *spolia* necessarily involves violence.[27] Certainly the original use of the term to name the spoils of war invites an enduring association with violence. It must be admitted, moreover, that the association seems valid in instances where otherwise intact buildings are defaced through the removal of parts of their fabric. Where the spoliate materials have been salvaged from buildings that have by other means fallen into ruin or disrepair, however, their preservation and reuse can be viewed more positively.[28] The refashioning of Rome's built environment at the hands of Christians is a mixed story with regard to the way spoliate materials were acquired. Certainly, as the Middle Ages progressed, building materials from ancient buildings like the Colosseum were indeed plundered for use elsewhere. It should also be noted, however, that much of the initial destruction of Rome's great imperial buildings took place at the hands of the Visigoths during the sack of Rome in A.D. 410 and through a further invasion by the Vandals in 455. The subsequent salvage and redeployment of carved stone and other materials from the ruins ensured, in these cases, the preservation of the classical heritage and secured a new use and purpose for what had been laid to waste. In a similar manner, the reclamation of whole buildings and their redeployment—as churches, for example—ensured their survival. Without such redeployment they would likely have fallen into decay. In cases where ancient buildings or monuments were defaced or destroyed simply for the sake of plundering their architectural treasures, the allegation of violence has some merit. From a Christian perspective, two responses may be offered. The first is simply to acknowledge the validity of the charge.[29] The pursuit of Christian ends, in this case the construction of churches, hospitals, and other buildings serving the cause

---

[27] See, e.g., chaps. 9 and 10 in Brilliant and Kinney, *Reuse Value*.

[28] So contends Brandenburg in "Use of Older Elements," in Brilliant and Kinney, *Reuse Value*.

[29] In "A Report to Pope Leo X on Ancient Rome," the unknown author holds the "barbarians" to be principally responsible for much of the destruction of Rome's architectural heritage, but he acknowledges that successive popes have also played their unfortunate part. Some evidence suggests that the author may have been Baldassare Castiglione (1478–1529), possibly working in collaboration with Raphael. The text, along with an introductory note about authorship, can be found in Holt, *Documentary History of Art*, 1:289–96.

of Christian worship and compassionate service, has sometimes engaged unchristian means. That is a cause for regret and reveals the continuing moral ambiguity that attends so much human action.

Sometimes, however, the destruction considered violent may be defended. The dismantling of the architecture of Germany's Third Reich, for example, even where some artistic merit might be claimed for it, could be viewed with some justification, not as a violation of the cultural artifact but as the eradication of an architecture that glorified an evil regime. Such destruction raises the question whether the progress of good requires that the paraphernalia as well as the practices of evil be destroyed. Certainly, the biblical portrayal of divine judgement sometimes employs violent imagery. While mercy and transformation are predominant themes in the Bible, there are occasions when the biblical writers supposed that evil and its material symbols must be cleared away and destroyed in order that good might prevail. The destruction may be conceived as a necessary means to a good end, comparable perhaps to the surgical removal of a malignant tumor. Employing such a principle, John Goldingay contends that within the Hebrew Bible "thinking about the interim end is dominated by the notion of calamity, but thinking about the ultimate End is dominated by the theme of restoration, renewal and the fulfilment of that creation project."[30] In support of the point, Mark Stephens says of the destruction imagery in the book of Revelation that it "depicts part of the process by which the present world order is judged and evil powers removed, in order that creation might be taken to its eschatological goal."[31] He notes further, however, that "the undercurrents of renewal established by the wider frame, combined with crucial programmatic statements such as [Rev] 11:18, enable the audience to see that this surface imagery of destruction is not to be interpreted as the systematic annihilation of creation."[32] Though I do not wish to defend all the destruction that went on in the city of ancient Rome, there were, unquestionably, aspects of imperial Roman culture and society that on account of their immoral quality needed to be brought to an end. It is arguable that the architecture that housed and embodied practices that were deeply immoral should therefore be destroyed, even while much else in the imperial city could be restored and renewed. The assumption that pagan architecture ought to be destroyed is evident in the description of Rome given in the widely read fourteenth-century text,

---

[30] John Goldingay, *Old Testament Theology*, vol. 2, *Israel's Faith* (Downers Grove, Ill.: InterVarsity, 2006), 505, cited in Stephens, *Annihilation or Renewal*, 43.

[31] Stephens, *Annihilation or Renewal*, 258.

[32] Stephens, *Annihilation or Renewal*, 258.

the *Metrical Version of Mandeville's Travels*. Working under the mistaken assumption that the Colosseum was once the "moost mervailous temple of alle," the poet contends that it had to be demolished both because its glories could deflect the attention of the Christian pilgrim and because of the presumptuous claim to earthly predominance embodied in the giant statue of the sun ("that riche mamette") that, again mistakenly, was presumed to have stood in the Colosseum. The poet tells us that Pope Sylvester "distroyed that temple of lim and stone / And other temples ful many oone" and in their place built churches that testify to more enduring Christian riches.[33] Although the poet cited here knew little, apparently, of the Colosseum's former use, he represents an attitude held by some that the architecture of Rome's pagan past ought to be destroyed in order to make way for a Christian *urbs*. David Benson explains that "in many medieval descriptions of Rome . . . pagan monuments are shown to have to 'die' in order that the new religion might live." As will be considered further below, however, specifically in relation to the remains of the Colosseum, some portion of the architecture supporting morally dubious regimes might usefully be retained in memorial to the victims and as a cautionary reminder of the depths to which humankind may sometimes descend.

While the destructive features of the use of *spolia* must be acknowledged, a positive appraisal may also be warranted. Theologically speaking, we must recognize that the products of human culture are often fraught with moral ambiguity, but they may be pressed into the service of the divine economy and bear witness nevertheless—perhaps especially in their imperfect state—to the redemptive and merciful purposes of God. Accordingly, the changing face of Europe's urban landscape and redeployment of the elements of ancient Roman architecture can be seen to portray a Christian vision of God's reordering of creation.

We have so far considered physical examples of *spolia*, but the term has been applied as well to intellectual property. Richard Brilliant distinguishes between *spolia in se* (referring to material objects) and *spolia in re*, which refers to verbal and visual motifs, ideas, and the like.[34] Ideas and images are

---

[33] M. C. Seymour, ed., *The Metrical Version of Mandeville's Travels*, Early English Society, o.s. 269 (London: Oxford University Press, 1973). I take the point along with the citations from C. David Benson, "The Dead and the Living: Some Medieval Descriptions of the Ruins and Relics of Rome Known to the English," in *Urban Space in the Middle Ages and Early Modern Age*, ed. Albrecht Classen and Marilyn Sandidge (Berlin: Walter de Gruyter, 2009), 147–82, 158.

[34] See again Kinney, Introduction to Brilliant and Kinney, *Reuse Value*, 2

commonly taken up, interpreted, adapted, and redeployed in what is called their "reception history." This process, too, is evident in the changing face of Rome's architecture. In the church of Santa Pudenziana, for instance, built in Rome toward the end of the fourth century, a mosaic portrays Christ wearing a golden toga with purple trim, a sign of imperial authority, and surrounded by his apostles, who wear senatorial togas. Christ is pictured as an emperor surrounded by his senate. Above them, amid the clouds, the heavenly Jerusalem is depicted in the architectural style of ancient Rome. Gerard O'Daly observes that "'Rome' and 'Roman' were quickly and irresistibly coming to mean something new, but the striking feature was the redeployment of the old idiom in a new context, not its total replacement."[35]

FIGURE 4.2
Apse Mosaic, Santa Pudenziana

Of course, this redeployment is risky. According to John's Gospel, Jesus insisted that his kingdom was not of this world (John 18:36), and he resisted the temptation to style himself as a political leader. Depicting Christ as an emperor and his apostles as his senate runs the risk, therefore, of confusing the kingdom of God with the kingdoms of this world. Regrettably, and with disastrous results, the church has sometimes succumbed to the theologically erroneous view that Christ or his disciples should take over Caesar's throne.

---

[35] Gerard O'Daly, *Augustine's "City of God": A Reader's Guide* (Oxford: Clarendon, 1999), 16.

On the other hand, Jesus is rightly called King and Lord. His apostles were indeed guilty of the accusation brought against them that they were "acting contrary to the decrees of the emperor, saying that there is another king named Jesus" (Acts 17:7; cf. John 19:12). C. Kavin Rowe has argued in a recent monograph that it was Caesar rather than Christ who was guilty of pretense, for, theologically speaking, Caesar had no rightful claim to the throne in the first place.[36] The Kingship of Christ exposes the fraudulent nature of Caesar's claims, and indeed of all human claims to absolute authority. Redeployment of the old imperial idiom, and of the architectural heritage of ancient Rome, is therefore charged with powerful theological significance. The reality of God's kingdom ushered in by Jesus is not "otherworldly." It is not a "merely spiritual" reality requiring a language, an architecture, or a culture wholly discontinuous with the old. It requires, rather, the radical transformation of our present earthly reality and the restoration of creation to the purpose originally intended for it by God.

The Conversion of Buildings

We have considered so far three forms of architectural transformation that took place in Rome: the building of the Lateran basilica on the foundations of a razed military barracks, the use of spolia both in the church itself and in the neighboring baptistery, and the reuse of old idioms to portray the Lordship of Christ. A fourth form of transformation was the simple appropriation of secular or pagan religious buildings for Christian use. The first examples of this practice occur in the sixth century and include the reconsecration of an audience hall and small temple in the Roman Forum as the Church of Santi Cosma e Damiano, the erection of Santa Maria Antiqua in palace buildings at the foot of the Palatine, and the conversion of the Curia into the Church of Sant'Adriano.[37] Lewis Mumford tells us that "by the fourteenth century nearly half of the thousand or more churches of Rome still indicated, by their name or their visible structure, their pagan origin."[38]

The conversion of buildings in the Roman Forum to a church honoring the Syrian brothers Cosma and Damiano, both of whom were medical doctors, was undertaken during the pontificate of Felix IV (526–530). The

[36] See C. Kavin Rowe, *World Upside Down: Reading Acts in the Graeco-Roman Age* (Oxford: Oxford University Press, 2009), 112.

[37] These examples are noted in Grundmann, *Architecture of Rome*, 35–36, 69, 80–81.

[38] Lewis Mumford, *The City in History: Its Origins, Its Transformations, and Its Prospects* (New York: Harcourt, Brace & World, 1961), 244.

only alteration made to the building prior to its consecration was the addition of liturgical furnishings and the decoration of the existing apse and its surrounding arch with extraordinarily beautiful mosaics. Amid resplendent representations of the eschatological imagery found in the book of Revelation, the apse mosaic depicts the apostles Peter and Paul presenting the brothers Cosma and Damiano, with their crowns of martyrdom, to Christ. An inscription explaining the significance of the mosaic reads:

AULA DEI CLARIS RADIAT SPECIOSA METALLIS
IN QUA PLUS FIDEI LUX PRETIOSA MICAT
MARTYRIBUS MEDICIS POPULO SPES CERTA SALUTIS
VENIT ET EX SACRO CREVIT HONORE LOCUS . . .

This hall of God shines brightly with beautiful metals,
In which the precious light of faith gleams even more.
From the martyred doctors a certain hope of salvation comes to the people
and this sacred place has increased in honor . . .[39]

Of particular note for our purposes here is the claim that this sacred place increases in honor through its dedication to the martyrs Cosma and Damiano. Incrementally, as Rome's rich stock of secular and pagan buildings is converted to Christian use, the city itself is being sanctified, not through the annihilation of Rome's heritage but through its transformation and renewal.[40]

Among the most notable examples of the conversion of ancient Roman buildings to Christian churches are the Pantheon and the Baths of Diocletian. The Pantheon is especially striking not only because of the magnificence of the building but also because of its original dedication to pagan religious practices. Although the Pantheon continued to be used as a pagan temple for some time after the conversion of Constantine, it was closed in the fifth century. Then, at the beginning of the seventh century, the Byzantine Emperor Phocas gave the Pantheon to Pope Boniface IV, who reopened it as a place of Christian worship and consecrated it to St. Mary of All Martyrs in 609 or 610.[41]

Considering whether Catholicism represents "the destruction or the redemption of pagan religion," Tina Beattie reflects on this rededication of the Pantheon:

---

[39] My translation.

[40] An illustrated account of the mosaics in the Church of Santi Cosma e Damiano can be found in Kessler and Zacharias, *Rome 1300*, 96–101.

[41] Tina Beattie, *Eve's Pilgrimage: A Woman's Quest for the City of God* (London: Burns & Oates, 2002), 68.

If Christ is the redeemer of the cosmos in whom all things are reconciled and made new, then his saving grace should encompass every dream of heaven, every experience of the divine, suffusing all that is with the peace and love of God so that it becomes transformed in the incarnation.[42]

FIGURE 4.3
The Pantheon

While there are grounds in the New Testament on which to affirm the reconciliation of "all things" (see especially Col 1:20), the point must be stated carefully. The redemptive activity of Christ does not leave things as they were. Redemption involves both judgement and transformation; it involves both the laying bare of evil and the making new of all things (Rev 21:5).

While there is some uncertainty about the purpose for which the Pantheon was originally built, whether for the worship of pagan gods or for the imperial cult,[43] Christians of the early medieval period would certainly have regarded either use as incompatible with Christian faith. Yet Christians in Rome, acting under papal direction, had no qualms, apparently, about the conversion of such a building to Christian use. The reuse of the building, especially as a place for Christian worship, constitutes a positive appraisal of the fruits of human culture. Even those works of human hands designed for contrary purposes need not be excluded from God's intention that all things should be reconciled to him. Such is the work of grace.

A rather different example of the fabric of pagan religious architecture taking on a new role in service of a Christian vision of true worship occurs in the church of San Clemente. The church now standing dates from the twelfth century, but a flight of stone steps leading down from an annex now used as a souvenir shop takes the visitor back some 1,600 years. The church at street level stands on top of a much earlier one built in the late fourth

---

[42] Beattie, *Eve's Pilgrimage*, 68.
[43] This uncertainty is noted by Grundmann in *Architecture of Rome*, 51.

century. Yet beneath the nave of this ancient church there is still a further layer of architectural history. Archaeologists have discovered a house and the rooms of an official building of first-century Rome, included among which is a well-preserved Mithraeum, or temple to Mithras, a pagan god of wisdom and light.[44] Evidently, the fourth-century builders of the first Christian church on the site did not consider it necessary to destroy the pagan temple but used it to provide foundations for their own architectural enterprise. It is hardly conceivable that this constructional expedient did not also involve a theological judgement about the propriety of building a Christian church using an intact pagan temple as a foundation. It must have been decided by some Christians that, like meat sacrificed to idols (cf. 1 Cor 8:4-10), there is no inherent harm in the material accompaniments to pagan religion and that their redeployment for Christian use could be construed as one more way in which the things of earth, fallen and bearing the marks of human sin, are enabled to participate in the praise of God's glory.[45] The decision to retain the pagan temple as the foundation for a church might also signal the obedience of those Christian builders to the parable told by Jesus of the wheat and the tares (Matt 13:24-30). Contrary to our human inclination to root out what we perceive to be unworthy of participation in the kingdom of heaven or a threat to the realization of God's purposes, the parable counsels against our presumption to take up the role of final judge and urges caution in our efforts to sort good from evil. It is a notable feature of Augustine's treatment of the two cities, the *civitas Dei* and the *civitas terrena*, that, while concerned with the characteristics of each, he does not presume to be the judge in this world of who or what belongs to each city. Rather, the earthly and the heavenly cities are "in this present world mixed together and, in a certain sense, entangled with one another."[46] Evident not only in the Pantheon or in the church of San Clemente but in the city of Rome generally, the growing conviction that this earthly city could represent and bear witness to the New Jerusalem did not require the annihilation of all that had gone before and that had contributed to Rome's dubious renown.

---

[44] A fuller description of the pagan shrine, from which I take these details, can be found in P. D. Smith, *City: A Guidebook for the Urban Age* (London: Bloomsbury, 2012), 102–3.

[45] Not surprisingly, this attitude did not always prevail. With encouragement first from Constantine and then from Constantius II, Christians did vandalize pagan temples and strip them of their idols.

[46] Augustine, *The City of God against the Pagans*, trans. R. W. Dyson (Cambridge: Cambridge University Press, 1998), 11.1 (450). Citations throughout the present work are taken from Dyson's translation. References to the book number and chapter of *City of God* will be followed, as here, with the page number of this edition in parentheses.

Rome's Pagan Past

That the architectural heritage of pagan Rome could be redeployed in service of a Christian vision of the heavenly city was dependent on God's sanctification of the city. This sanctification came about in part, it was believed, through the blood of the martyrs. Indeed, the celebration of martyrs and the veneration of their relics became central to the new identity that Rome forged for itself as the Middle Ages progressed. Numerous sarcophagi, frescoes, mosaics, statues, and reliquaries throughout the city attest to this.[47] We take just one instance as exemplary. In frescoes of the Sancta Sanctorum, the papal chapel in the Lateran, the martyrdoms of Saints Peter and Paul are depicted. Both are presented as taking place in Rome. In the background of the scene of Peter's crucifixion are two notable Roman buildings: the pyramid of Romulus, which was demolished in the late fifteenth century as part of the remodeling of the Borgo area undertaken by Pope Alexander VI, and the Castel Sant'Angelo, which is still standing today.[48] The very same architectural elements are depicted again in the portrayal of Peter's crucifixion on a panel in the bronze doors of St. Peter's Basilica. The first building, the pyramid of Romulus, recalls the legendary beginnings of Rome and so gathers up the full stretch of Roman history into the drama of redemption and sanctification, while the Castel Sant'Angelo, built as a mausoleum for the emperor Hadrian and once the tallest building in Rome, was a prominent reminder of Rome's imperial past. The appearance of these ancient Roman buildings in a fresco portraying Peter's crucifixion serves both as a reminder of the political power responsible for his martyrdom and as an indication that through the blood shed by apostles and saints, the city as a whole has been sanctified and redeemed.

While the blood of the martyrs, alleged to have been shed in Rome, was believed to contribute to the sanctification of the ancient city, more important still was the presence of Christ himself. During the Middle Ages the dwelling of Christ with his people, itself a feature of the New Jerusalem (see Rev 21:3), was represented especially through the *Acheropita*, an icon of Christ that according to legend was begun by St. Luke and completed

---

[47] Consider also the Church of Santa Prassede, built during the papacy of Paschal I (817–824). It was built to rehouse relics from the catacombs and the bodies of saints and martyrs formerly buried in cemeteries outside the city walls. A plaque in the church itself lists 2,300 in all. Kessler and Zacharias, *Rome 1300*, 109.

[48] See further details in Kessler and Zacharias, *Rome 1300*, 46–48.

by angels. The icon was carried in procession through the streets of Rome during the Feast of the Assumption.

> Borne before the *Lupa*, the great bronze equestrian, and the other trophies of the ancient empire assembled at the papal palace, the *Acheropita* vividly reminds the faithful that Christ is now ruler of Rome and that his vicar, the pope, governs a capital city made sacred by the Savior's presence.[49]

The symbolic portrayal of Christ's sanctification of the city continued as the icon was carried through the city streets and as it passed by and through ancient monuments like the Arches of Constantine and of Titus, the Imperial Fora and the Colosseum.

The Colosseum, however, presented a considerable challenge to the narrative of redemption. Although gladiatorial contests at the Colosseum and the pitting of humans against wild beasts did not include, as tradition has it, numerous Christian martyrdoms, the building represents, nevertheless, the worst of Rome's imperial history and remains a symbol of persecution and human brutality. How was this cultural monstrosity to be dealt with in the process of turning Rome into a Christian city? The Colosseum continued to be used for contests until the sixth century, although gladiatorial contests are thought to have ceased in the mid-fifth century. Shortly thereafter it was utilized for residential accommodation and workshops, and at least one chapel was constructed within its walls. Later, the Colosseum also served as a quarry. Stone was taken from it to build palaces, churches, and hospitals. In 1397, for example, the confraternity of the Raccomandati del Salvatore ad Sancta Sanctorum was given one-third of the Colosseum to assist in the confraternity's charitable activities, prominent among which was the building of hospitals.[50] At the same time Pope Innocent VIII authorized the use of the Colosseum for dramatic reenactments of the passion of Christ. These Christian uses of the Colosseum, along with the redeployment of its architectural remains could conceivably be seen as a work of redemptive transformation as the architecture supporting Rome's brutal history was progressively turned to a Christian purpose.

In the sixteenth and seventeenth centuries, the church sought a productive use for what remained of the Colosseum itself. Bernini developed a scheme to

---

[49] Kessler and Zacharias, *Rome 1300*, 65.

[50] Kirstin Noreen, "Sacred Memory and Confraternal Space: The Insignia of the Confraternity of the Santissimo Salvatore (Rome)," in *Roma Felix: Formation and Reflections of Medieval Rome*, ed. Éamonn Ó Carragain and Carol Neuman de Vegvar (Aldershot: Ashgate, 2007), 159–87, 168.

turn it into an elaborate church, but a lack of funds prevented the realization of his plans; Pope Sixtus V thought to convert it into a wool factory to provide employment for Rome's prostitutes. This plan, too, was never realized. The interest in "Christianizing" the Colosseum in some fashion continued throughout the late Middle Ages and into the Renaissance. A painting still partially visible today on one of the arches of the Colosseum depicts the city of Jerusalem, including the crucifixion of Jesus outside the city walls. The painting by an unknown artist is likely to have coincided with the consecration of the monument to Christ and the Christian martyrs in 1675 during the pontificate of Clement X. In 1769 Pope Benedict XIV endorsed the mistaken view that the Colosseum had been a site where Christians had been martyred. He again consecrated the site and installed stations of the cross in the amphitheater, thus making it a site of Christian devotion. Still today the Pope leads a procession on Good Friday around the stations of the cross. For visitors at other times, though, a plain wooden cross standing on the spot of the emperor's podium provides testimony, for those who have eyes to see, to the need for penitence in the face of human brutality and to the hope that Christ's victory over violence and death will finally be completed.

FIGURE 4.4
The Colosseum

FIGURE 4.5
The Colosseum Cross

A further contemporary use of the Colosseum reinforces that hope. Following a series of demonstrations against the death penalty staged at the Colosseum in 2000, the building became a symbol in the international campaign against capital punishment. The illumination of the building at night was changed from white to gold whenever a person condemned to death anywhere in the world had his or her sentence commuted or was released, and again when any jurisdiction anywhere in the world abolished the death penalty.[51] Architecture has, in this instance, become a symbol of transformation; the Colosseum offers a poignant reminder of sinfulness as its original use is recalled, while its plain cross and changing illumination testify that the forces of evil can be overcome.

Preservation of the Colosseum as a reminder of human sinfulness may yield a further theological lesson. The book of Revelation promises a heavenly city in which sin will have no place, in which every tear will be wiped from our eyes and in which death will be no more, but it is doubtful that the annihilation or obliteration of all the manifestations of human sin will serve well God's purpose of reconciling all things to himself. According to Scripture, the overcoming of sin—its forgiveness, that is—involves God's "not remembering" our sin.[52] As Søren Kierkegaard explains, drawing upon Isaiah 38:17, not remembering sin means putting it behind one's back so that it no longer holds one's attention and no longer determines how one will relate to the sinner—with hatred, perhaps, or with the desire to seek revenge.[53] Nevertheless, Kierkegaard insists, "sin cannot be taken away as nothing. It is bought at too high a price for that."[54] Forgiveness removes the heavy burden of sin, but the one who is forgiven shoulders a light burden in its place, "the recollection that everything is forgiven him!"[55] Forgiveness and the wiping away of every tear notwithstanding, the state of reconciliation does not obliterate all memory of sin. A memorial enables recollection of what has been forgiven, not for the purpose of retaining the burden of guilt—that is to be put behind

---

[51] See Gayle Young, "On Italy's Passionate Opposition to Death Penalty," CNN.com, February 4, 2000. The website "Death Penalty Information Centre," accessed March 20, 2013, cites another instance in which the Colosseum's illumination was changed to honor Connecticut's repeal of the death penalty; see the post "Roman Colosseum Lit to Mark Connecticut's Abolition of Death Penalty."

[52] See, e.g., Isa 43:35; Heb 8:12; 10:17.

[53] See Søren Kierkegaard, *Works of Love*, ed. and trans. Howard V. Hong and Edna H. Hong (Princeton: Princeton University Press, 1995), 295.

[54] Søren Kierkegaard, *Upbuilding Discourses in Various Spirits*, ed. and trans. Howard V. Hong and Edna H. Hong (Princeton: Princeton University Press, 1993), 247.

[55] Kierkegaard, *Upbuilding Discourses*, 247.

us—but so that there may be a true appreciation of its overcoming. Augustine in *The City of God* makes the same point:

> In the Heavenly City, then, there will be freedom of will: one freedom for all, and indivisible in each. That city will be redeemed from all evil and filled with every good thing; constant in its enjoyment of the happiness of eternal rejoicing; forgetting offences and forgetting punishments. *Yet it will not forget its own redemption, nor will it be ungrateful to its Redeemer.* As a matter of rational knowledge, therefore, it will remember even its past evils, even while entirely forgetting the sensual experience of them. . . .
>
> So also, there are two ways of forgetting evil; for the man who has knowledge and understanding of it forgets it in one way, whereas one who has suffered it in his own experience does so in another: the former by disregarding what he knows, and the latter by escaping what he has suffered. According to the second kind of forgetfulness, the saints will have no memory of past evils. They will be set free from them all, and they will be completely deleted from their feelings. Yet the power of knowledge will be so great in the saints that they will be aware not only of their own past suffering, but also of the everlasting misery of the damned. For if they were not to know that they had been miserable, how could they, as the psalm says, for ever sing the mercies of God?[56]

That the Colosseum was only partially dismantled, then, serves to remind us of progress made toward redemption, and of the mercy through which the world's trespasses are not counted against it (2 Cor 5:19). It exposes history,[57] reminds us of principalities and powers overcome, and thus gives cause for gratitude and joy. Of course, there is much progress yet to be made toward the elimination of evil and the defeat of the powers that war against God, but the ruins of the Colosseum along with the plain cross that now stands in their midst may point us to a need not for the present age only but also in the heavenly city, for some memorial of that which will, by then, have been finally vanquished—a memorial showing forth the nature and scope of divine mercy and grace.

Classical Style

One final instance of the reappropriation of Roman (and Greek) architecture for Christian use does not involve the reuse of materials or buildings but consists, rather, in the adoption and adaptation of the techniques, the

---

[56] Augustine, *City of God*, 22.30 (1180–81) (emphasis added).
[57] I take the phrase from Kinney, Introduction to Brilliant and Kinney, *Reuse Value*, 3.

architectural forms, and the details of the classical tradition. We have discussed this development already in chapter 3 but with a different concern—namely, the relation between freedom and rule. The employment of classical architectural style deserves consideration again here, with a focus this time both on the propriety, theologically speaking, of reappropriating for Christian use the cultural heritage of pagan antiquity and on the role played by human cultural endeavor in the divine economy.

In contrast with an annihilationist conception of the new heavens and the new earth in which all trace of the present creation will be eradicated, a transformative eschatology allows that the fruits of human culture will be taken into the divine economy, there to be perfected and related to their true source. According to St. Basil, this is the Spirit's work. The Spirit is the perfecting cause of creation, the one who brings things to their true and proper end.[58] Here we find a crucial theological principle for the interpretation of Rome's regeneration at the hands of the medieval city builders. The city of Rome was increasingly viewed as a foretaste and anticipation of the New Jerusalem, but it could be so, if at all, only as the Spirit perfected and sanctified the work of human hands. The perfection of such work consists, according to St. Basil, in its being properly oriented to its true end, which is to show forth the glory of God. The employment of classical architecture to show forth, as Vitruvius hopes, "the grandeur of *our* history" involves, arguably, a mistaken conception of humanity's true end and of humanity's own glory. For the true telos and glory of humankind consists in its being made for fellowship with God. There is no doubt that the artistic and technical achievements of the architects of Greece and Rome were aesthetically magnificent, but so long as they were directed toward the worship of idols, the celebration of imperial power, and the exploitation of others of God's creatures, then even the most exquisitely executed examples of craft and design still bore the marks of sin.

That remains true of all the works of human hands, for though justified, we are yet sinners; but when the classical language of architecture, or any other architecture for that matter, is employed for the building of hospitals, orphanages, almshouses and places of worship, as it was in medieval and Renaissance Europe, it begins to show forth, however imperfectly, an entirely different grandeur, the grandeur of the divine economy in which the lame are healed, the blind see, the poor have good news preached to them. In such ways as this, the work of the creature is directed toward the praise of its Creator. Such work of human hands is, of course, imperfect and provisional. It is still

---

[58] Basil, *De Spiritu Sancto*, 9 (*NPNF₂* 8:16).

compromised by sin and awaits the final transformation promised and anticipated in the resurrection of Jesus from the dead, but in the regeneration of the
city of Rome during the Middle Ages, we may see the Spirit at work turning
hearts and minds to a future different from the past, a future represented in
John's vision in Revelation of a New Jerusalem in which God will dwell with
his people, and the pain and the anguish and the suffering of our present existence will have passed away, and all things will have been made new. That the
forms and details of classical architecture, developed without reference to the
biblical vision of God's coming kingdom, can nevertheless be turned to the
purpose of bearing witness to that kingdom is confirmed by Paul's affirmation
that all things are created through and for Christ and all things hold together
in him (Col 1:16-17). The significance of this Pauline teaching is that it brings
all things into the realm of the divine economy and envisages the perfection of
all things through their reconciliation to God (Col 1:20).

Conclusion

The theme guiding this chapter has been the reuse, reappropriation, and
reinterpretation in Christian Rome of Rome's pagan past and particularly its
architecture. The regeneration of Rome's built environment offers lessons, I
have suggested, in favor of an eschatological vision in which the things of
earth are renewed rather than destroyed. The biblical vision of the renewal and
perfection of creation is predicated upon God's declaration of the goodness
of creation, upon his making it suitable for the working out of his purposes.
God's admonition to Peter, "What God has made clean, you must not call
profane" (Acts 11:9), can be applied not only to the things made suitable for
human consumption but also to the goodness of created reality as a whole. In
accordance with this theological judgement, the builders of Christian Rome
saw no need, in general terms, to clear away what had been inherited from
Rome's past. It could be reappropriated, reused, and rededicated to serve the
purpose of establishing on earth a foretaste of the heavenly city. This reappropriation did not proceed without some purgation, however. The leveling of the
military barracks in the Lateran to make way for the Church of St. John, for
example, may be read as the elimination of things that have no place in the
coming kingdom of God, as a sifting of the wheat from the chaff.

The exploration of Rome's architectural heritage and transformation
prompts reflection on the way we conceive the continuity between the old
creation and the new, both at a cosmic level and in respect of the individual.
It also prompts consideration of the way in which identity is established, preserved, and transformed. Despite the divided opinion among scholars about

whether the book of Revelation presents an annihilationist or a transformative eschatology, Christian theologians have generally favored a transformative account of God's new creation in which the created order is preserved and renewed. Paul Althaus asserts of Catholic orthodoxy: "Transformation, not annihilation—that is the unanimously held doctrine from Irenaeus onwards, by way of Augustine and Gregory the Great, Aquinas and the whole of mediaeval theology, down to the present-day Catholic dogmatics."[59] Jürgen Moltmann finds an exception in seventeenth-century Lutheranism, particularly in the theology of Johann Gerhard, but he, too, contends that the predominant view has been the transformative one.[60] According to this view the present created order will be transformed, made new, and perfected in the age to come. It holds fast to the promise given to Noah: "I establish my covenant with you, that never again shall all flesh be cut off by the waters of the flood, and never again shall there be a flood to destroy the earth" (Gen 9:11), to the promise fulfilled in Christ: "through him God was pleased to reconcile to himself all things, whether on earth or in heaven, by making peace through the blood of his cross" (Eph 1:20), and to the promise declared once more in John's vision of the final end of all things: "See, I am making all things new" (Rev 21:5). The transformative view also finds support in creedal affirmations of the resurrection of the body. The resurrection body is conceived in material terms, albeit, as Paul says, in a form that is changed (1 Cor 15:51-53). In a recent comprehensive study of the relevant biblical material, J. Richard Middleton contends that "the Bible consistently anticipates the redemption of the entire created order, a motif that fits very well with the Christian hope of the resurrection, which Paul calls 'the redemption of our bodies' (Rom 8:23)."[61] The material creation is involved somehow in the transformation and renewal promised in the divine economy.

This indeed is the theological assumption that lies behind the city of Rome's transformation from the city of evil to a holy city. The city itself was sanctified, it was thought, through the blood of the martyrs and through the realization of God's promise to dwell with his people, and this sanctification was manifest in the renewal and transformation of its architectural fabric. The very same stones, and, in some cases, the very same buildings,

---

[59] Paul Althaus, *Die letzten Dinge: Entwurf einer christlichen Eschatologie*, 1st ed. (Gütersloh: C. Bertlesmann, 1922), 350. Cited in Jürgen Moltmann, *The Coming of God*, trans. Margaret Kohl (Minneapolis: Fortress, 1996), 268.

[60] See Moltmann, *Coming of God*, 268–69.

[61] J. Richard Middleton, *A New Heaven and a New Earth: Reclaiming Biblical Eschatology* (Grand Rapids: Baker, 2014), 14.

that testified once to the power and glory of pagan Rome were consecrated to Christian use and became a witness to and foretaste of the *civitas Dei*. The transformation took place variously. In some cases it occurred simply through the reuse of stones gathered from the ruins of ancient buildings or plundered from existing buildings. Elsewhere, architectural elements such as carved columns, capitals, lintels, and architraves were preserved and put to use in buildings that were otherwise new. Sometimes new churches were built on the foundations of ancient buildings. The architectural forms of ancient Rome, like the basilica or royal hall, were adapted for Christian use, notably through the addition of transepts to render cruciform the space now dedicated to Christ the King. Often, as we have seen, whole buildings were modified through the introduction of Christian ornamentation, particularly mosaics, furnishings and statuary.

In each case, though in varying measure, the material reality is preserved, and yet the identity of the fabric concerned is transformed. An audience hall and small temple in the Roman Forum becomes through reconsecration and the addition of exquisite mosaics a church dedicated to the worship of Christ.[62] Spoliate columns and pilasters salvaged, possibly, from an imperial palace now adorn the entrance to a Christian baptistery. Materially identical to the architectural elements they were when once they adorned an imperial palace, the columns and pilasters are now distinguished by their employment in the sacrament of redemption and new life. They signal the entrance to that sacrament's enactment. Albrecht Classen, commenting on the rebuilding of Rome, observes that for some medieval writers "dead Rome is the foundation for a new Rome, the future, heavenly Jerusalem."[63] Even the Colosseum, as magnificent in its form as it was brutal in its purpose, has taken on new identity as a memorial to a sinfulness overcome and as a beacon of hope in the face of killings still inflicted. There is in these transformations, imperfect and provisional though they remain, an intimation of the final transformation of God's creation and the reconciliation of all things to himself.

While human endeavor, along with the cultural products issuing from it, has often been directed toward sinful ends, the redeployment of those products in the transformation of the city of Rome betokens a distinctive characteristic of the divine economy—namely, its eschewing of waste. The

---

[62] While further additions have since been made to the basilica of Santi Cosma e Damiano, the original structure has been preserved.

[63] Albrecht Classen, "Urban Space in the Middle Ages and the Early Modern Age: Historical, Mental, Cultural and Social Economic Investigations," in Classen and Sandidge, *Urban Space*, 1–146, 110.

goodness of creation is confirmed by God's loving care for all that he has made and by his desire that all things should be gathered into reconciled communion with himself. The principle of careful reclamation, evident in the reuse of parts of Rome's architectural fabric, echoes the determination seen in Jesus' teaching and in his ministry to seek out and to save the lost. Jesus deliberately gathers up all that has been discarded and all that has been scarred by sin, for it is of such as these that his kingdom will be built. There is in this policy of reclamation a salutary reminder, and perhaps a judgement to be heard, concerning the throwaway culture we now inhabit, a culture that not only abandons the past but imperils the future, too.

A further important feature of the theme developed in this chapter is the place that the past will have in God's final reconciliation of all things to himself. It is a mistake, I think, to conceive the eschatological realm as an entirely new stretch of time in which all that has been is lost. We do better to think of it as the redemptive re-membering of all that has gone on in history, as the re-collection into reconciled relationship with God of all that has been. David Mayernik, in his study of the Renaissance cities of Italy, observes that "to the humanist mind cities needed continuity with their past, between buildings along a street or around a piazza, even across a river, to be harmonious like the universe and memorable like the cities of our imagination."[64] This contrasts with the modernist impulse to leave the past behind.[65] God, however, puts nothing behind him, except our sin.[66] His purpose is to gather up every sparrow that has fallen, all the glories and calamities of human history, every soul formed according to his plan, that they might find their proper place in a creation perfected and made new.

Having suggested in this chapter that the regeneration and "Christianization" of the urban fabric of Rome can be understood as a process coherent with God's final transformation and renewal of the created order, it is essential also to point out that there can be no simple equation of this work of human hands with the divine economy. Stephens advises with respect to the book of Revelation that

---

[64] Mayernik, *Timeless Cities*, 58.

[65] An extreme expression of that impulse can be seen in the musings of Le Corbusier: "Therefore my settled opinion, which is a quite dispassionate one, is that the centres of our great cities must be pulled down and rebuilt, and that the wretched existing belts of suburbs must be abolished and carried further out; on their sites we must constitute . . . a protected and open zone, which when the day comes will give us absolute liberty of action, and in the meantime will furnish us with a cheap investment." Le Corbusier, *The City of Tomorrow*, trans. F. Etchells (New York: Dover, 1987), 96.

[66] See the discussion above of Kierkegaard's reading of Isa 38:17.

John's . . . story of new creation ultimately undercuts any and every attempt to bring about a purely human-constructed utopia. John's language of the first heavens and first earth "passing away" (21:1) implies a belief on John's part that creation can only attain its eschatological goal by means of a final intervention from God. [67]

The nature of that divine intervention is apparent in Jesus, in his life, death, and resurrection and in his ascension to the right hand of the Father. In becoming flesh, the eternal Word of God and second person of the Trinity establishes and confirms creation as the terrain within which God's purposes will be worked out. Through the fortunes of this human life, formed from dust, conceived and enlivened by the Spirit, and made new through resurrection, the purpose of God for all flesh is revealed. Given, further, that the life, death, and resurrection of Jesus do not simply announce but also inaugurate the new creation, we should expect to see the signs of new creation apparent among us now. That expectation was conveyed to John the Baptist when he sent disciples to ask whether Jesus was the "one who is to come" and then received the reply: "Go and tell John what you hear and see: the blind receive their sight, the lame walk, the lepers are cleansed, the deaf hear, the dead are raised, and the poor have good news brought to them" (Matt 11:4; cf. Luke 7:22). The events to which Jesus refers are transformations of the created order. They concern the healing and flourishing of the things of this world. This vision of creation's renewal is anticipated by Trito-Isaiah, among other biblical witnesses, who writes of a future in which good news will be proclaimed to the oppressed and liberty will be announced to the captives (Isa 61:1). Especially striking is the inclusion in Isaiah's vision of a renewed urban fabric: "They shall build up the ancient ruins, they shall raise up the former devastations; they shall repair the ruined cities, the devastations of many generations" (Isa 61:4). Of Jerusalem in particular Isaiah writes that there the people "will build houses and inhabit them; they shall plant vineyards and eat their fruit" (Isa 65:21). Mark Stephens comments:

> What is so crucial to note is how "worldly" this entire vision is, how earthy and tangible. This is a divine oracle which speaks about life in the real world, a life of houses and gardens, of childbirth and prayer, rather than a life in a never-never land. This is a consummation of history, not a denial of it.[68]

---

[67] Stephens, *Annihilation or Renewal*, 262.
[68] Stephens, *Annihilation or Renewal*, 29.

The transformation of Rome, to take but one expression of this hope, may be seen as a shadow, a foretaste, an anticipation of that eschatological transformation through which God's purposes for creation will be fulfilled. It is merely that, of course—a shadow and foretaste in which the marks of human sin remain. As with all creation, this human city yet waits in travail for the final completion of God's redemptive work (cf. Rom 8:22-23). Despite being "merely" a foretaste, the transformations brought about in the city of Rome can provide, nevertheless, a glimpse of what may be hoped for on behalf of all creation: that it may be renewed, that it may provide eloquent testimony to the glory of God, that it may in the end be brought to its true purpose.[69]

[69] The point I have sought to make in this chapter echoes that of N. T. Wright, who contends that "the point of the present kingdom is that it is the first-fruits of the future kingdom; and the future kingdom involves the abolition, not of space, time, or the cosmos itself, but rather of that which threatens space, time and creation—namely, sin and death. The vision of 1 Corinthians 15 thus coheres neatly with that of Romans 8.18–27, and, for that matter, Revelation 21. The creation itself will experience its exodus, its return from exile, consequent upon the resurrection of the Messiah and his people." Wright, *Jesus and the Victory of God* (London: SPCK, 1996), 218.

5

A Foretaste of Heaven
Anticipating the New Jerusalem through the Civitas Terrena

Consideration of the relation between rule and freedom in chapter 3 led us to an understanding of human freedom centered upon the relational nature of human existence. Freedom is not to be conceived as the unencumbered prerogative of isolated individuals to do as they please but rather in terms of the expansive possibilities for human creativity and flourishing opened up by virtue of one's participation in a community. The community is extended in space and time and can draw, therefore, upon an accumulated wisdom and experience greater than any individual could possibly arrive at on his or her own. Life in community, I suggested, is essential to human flourishing and well-being. Yet the problem of how best to live in community with one another is a constant challenge. Whether we are concerned with personal relationships, families, churches, neighborhoods, cities, nation states, or with the relations between nations, the challenges of life in community are ever before us.

Our existence in relationship is the great theme of the Bible. The biblical drama begins with creation—with God's establishment of a place and time for creaturely existence. Day by day as the act of creation proceeds the multitude of living things is brought forth and given a place to dwell. Then, on the sixth day, God creates humankind: "In the image of God he created them; male and female he created them" (Gen 1:27). The second account of creation, in chapter 2, has God say, "It is not good that the man should be alone" (Gen 2:18). Human well-being depends crucially upon our living in relationship with others. In the beginning, the relations between the creatures are ordered well; they are ordered to God's good purpose. But soon we learn that the relations that God established have been thrown into chaos, precisely because of humanity's decision to go its own way, to defy the instruction of God. Disobedience yields disruption and disorder, alienation from God, enmity between the man and the woman and between their off-spring. The freedom given to humanity to live in harmonious relationship with God and with all that God had made is turned to disruptive ends. As we noted in chapter 2, freedom exercised as defiance yields suffering, toil, displacement, and bondage. And yet, the freedom exercised in humanity's defiance is limited. We do not have the freedom to uncreate ourselves, to make ourselves something other than a people created by God to live in covenant relationship with him and with one another. The Bible tells the story of divine persistence, of forgiveness, of grace. It tells of God's steadfast love (Lam 3:22; Ps 33), of the Creator who is set upon making all things new (Rev 21:5), and of the God who will not rest until the work of healing and of reconciliation is complete (John 5:2-17).

The City as Eschatological Image

Surprisingly, perhaps, given the negative portrayal of many biblical cities, the harmonious coexistence of all that God has made and toward which God's work is directed is represented several times in the Bible through the image of a city. Although the story begins in a garden, it concludes with the advent of a New Jerusalem, a city of peace where humanity will live in travail no more. The Lord will dwell with his people in that city, the glory of the Lord will shine forth from it, and the nations will walk in its light (Rev 21). Despite its prominence in biblical eschatology, and despite the claim often made that "the city is humankind's most sophisticated image of order"[1] or "the most precious collective invention of civilization,"[2] the city may seem in our own time to be an unlikely image for a perfected order of human life. Cities in the modern world have their glories, to be sure, but they are also associated with

---

[1] The claim is here articulated by Graham Ward in his *Cities of God* (London: Routledge, 2000), 2. Cf. Tina Beattie, who writes, "Ultimately the city is a work of redemption, wherein we transform the garden of creation into the history and the culture of our human becoming." Beattie, *Eve's Pilgrimage*, xi. Such positive appraisals of the city find eminent precedent in the *Politics* of Aristotle, and, in the Christian tradition, in theologians such as Abelard and Aquinas. For specific references see Gorringe, *Theology of the Built Environment*, 142.

[2] Mumford, *City in History*, 67.

crime, poverty, congestion, alienation, and, increasingly, the exploitation and destruction of nature. We have seen in the past century the rapid proliferation and expansion of built environments that are radically unsuitable for the long-term sustainability and well-being of human communities. Richard Rogers, the well-known English architect, thinks that we have lost sight of what a city should be. "We are witnessing," he says, "the destruction of the very idea of the city."[3] In similar vein, James Kunstler expresses a concern shared by many that we are failing in the modern world to build good cities:

> The result of Modernism, especially in America, is a crisis of the human habitat; cities ruined by corporate gigantism and abstract renewal schemes, public buildings and public spaces unworthy of human affection, vast sprawling suburbs that lack any sense of community, housing that the un-rich cannot afford to live in, a slavish obeisance to the needs of automobiles and their dependent industries at the expense of human needs, and a gathering ecological calamity that we have only begun to measure.[4]

Kunstler's anguish over the modern city would come as no surprise to Saint Augustine, who saw no good end for the earthly city. A city shaped by humanity's own desires and neglectful of God's purposes could have no future and was bound to be destroyed.[5] Augustine had the recent experience of Rome, sacked by the Goths in A.D. 410, as evidence for his view, and he could draw, as well, upon frequent biblical references to the vulnerability and fleeting glory of earthly cities. The prophet Isaiah, for example, writes:

> Desolation is left in the city,
>   the gates are battered into ruins.
> For thus it shall be on the earth
>   and among the nations,
> as when an olive tree is beaten,
>   as at the gleaning when the grape harvest is ended. (Isa 24:12-13)

Israel knew only too well the vulnerability of cities, even of Jerusalem, the holy city. Jerusalem was a city blessed by God, to be sure, but it fell prey to the marauding armies of Judah's neighbors, its temple was destroyed, and the city was reduced to rubble. The destruction of the earthly Jerusalem and

---

[3] Richard Rogers, *Cities for a Small Planet* (London: Faber & Faber, 1997); cited without a page reference in John Inge, *Christian Theology of Place*, 20.

[4] James Howard Kunstler, *The Rise and Decline of America's Man-Made Landscape* (New York: Touchstone, 1994), 59–60.

[5] See, e.g., Augustine, *City of God*, 19.28 (964).

the exile of its inhabitants brought great anguish to its people. Exile from the city meant for them estrangement from God. And so the psalmist's cry: "How could we sing the Lord's song in a foreign land?" (Ps 137:4). Their exile served, however, to increase their longing for a city established by God (Ps 87:5), a city that will endure forever (Ps 48:8). That longing is taken up elsewhere in Israel's scriptures, especially in Ezekiel 40–48 but also in the New Testament—in Hebrews, for example (Heb 11:10, 11:16, 12:22, 13:14), and, above all, in John's vision of the heavenly city in Revelation 21 and 22. In the New Testament, the advent of that city is thought to be assured on account of the victory of Christ over all that stands against the final realization of God's purposes.

That indeed is the principal theme of the book of Revelation. Despite appearances to the contrary—despite, in particular, the corruption, the persecution, and the tyrannical power that characterized the imperial city of Rome, the heavenly city promised by God will surely prevail in the end. In the meantime, John writes to reassure his readers of that promise. Richard Bauckham thus explains,

> Because their spiritual centre in the present is hidden and contradicted (11:1-2), while the splendour and power of Babylon dominate the world, including the life of their own cities, John's readers need the vision of a centre in the eschatological future towards which they may live. It has to be presented as the alternative to Babylon, and so the visions of the harlot city Babylon (17:1–19:10) and the Lamb's bride the New Jerusalem (21:9–22:9) form a structural pair in the latter part of the book. They both play on the ancient mythic ideal of the city as the place where human community lives in security and prosperity with the divine in its midst. Babylon represents the perversion of this ideal. . . . Conversely, the New Jerusalem represents the true fulfillment of the ideal of the city, a city truly worth belonging to. [6]

John's vision of the two cities throws into sharp relief the recurring biblical contrast between a world marred by sin and death and the world as it is destined to be according to the creative and redemptive purposes of God. And yet the image of the city used to portray the ideal community established by God has repeatedly inspired efforts to replicate or foreshadow in our earthly cities the heavenly city yet to come. It is the impulse behind such efforts that prompts the concern of this chapter: How might the architecture of the earthly city yield insight into the nature of the city yet to come? The question requires, to begin with, some clarifications. The first is terminological. In

---

[6] Bauckham, *Revelation*, 130.

English we use the word "city" to convey two concepts that were differentiated in Latin by the terms *urbs* and *civitas*. Isidore of Seville explains that, "*urbs* (also city) is the name for the actual buildings, while *civitas* is not the stones, but the inhabitants."[7] This distinction makes clear why Augustine in his extensive account of the *civitas Dei* shows no interest in the built form of the city. The *civitas Dei*, in his view, was a social and spiritual reality that had little to do with the built environment or *urbs*.[8] That view is widely repeated in the subsequent theological tradition, particularly in commentaries upon Revelation 21, and yet, as Philip Sheldrake rightly notes, there can be "no absolute separation between the 'city as buildings' and its social characteristics."[9] In further clarification of the question posed above, then, my interest lies in the way architecture—the *urbs*—may portray a particular understanding of the *civitas*, particularly of the *civitas Dei*. The end in view is theological; so, to repeat the question: How might the architecture of earthly cities lead us to an enriched understanding of the nature of the heavenly city? What might we learn by taking the city itself as text?[10] I will be concerned in the main with cities of the medieval and Renaissance periods, for in this era, called Christendom, cities were frequently shaped, at least in part, by an eschatological vision, a theological conception of what we might call the "end" or telos of human life. That is not to say—far from it—that medieval cities approximated more closely to the ideal than cities of any other era, but there is interest for my purposes in the way the architecture of medieval cities was shaped by theological concerns.

Before proceeding further it is necessary also to acknowledge that beyond the distinction made between *civitas* and *urbs*, there is further, largely unresolved, debate about what exactly constitutes a city.[11] Half a century of

---

[7] Isidore of Seville, *The Etymologies of Isidore of Seville*, trans. Stephen A. Barney, W. J. Lewis, J. A. Beach, and Oliver Berghof (Cambridge: Cambridge University Press, 2006), 15.2.1 (305).

[8] Some commentators wish to credit Augustine with a little more interest in the fate of the *urbs* than I have suggested here. See, for instance, Philip Sheldrake, "A Spiritual City: Urban Vision and the Christian Tradition," in Bergmann, *Theology in Built Environments*, 151–69, 156–57; also, Mayernik, *Timeless Cities*, 5–7.

[9] Philip Sheldrake, "A Spiritual City? Place, Memory and City Making," in *Architecture, Ethics, and the Personhood of Place*, ed. Gregory Caicco (Hanover, N.H.: University Press of New England, 2007), 50–68, 54.

[10] This has been a common strategy in recent study of the city, and of places more generally. See, e.g., Sheldrake, "Spiritual City?" in Caicco, *Architecture, Ethics, and the Personhood of Place*.

[11] Timothy Gorringe provides a brief account of the difficulty in finding a clear definition in *Theology of the Built Environment*, 138–40. Some writers have suggested that no

subsequent discussion has confirmed Lewis Mumford's claim, made in 1961, that "no single definition [of the city] will apply to all its manifestations and no single description will cover all its transformations."[12] The work of this chapter does not require, however, that we settle upon a definition of the city. It is sufficient to identify some features that apply to all cities even if those features are not sufficient on their own to distinguish cities from other settlements—towns, suburbs, or rural communities, for example. The most important of these features, for our purposes, is that the city is a social reality more or less well supported by the built environment in which the drama of social life takes place. Cities are a particular expression of the basic human need and obligation to live in relationship with others. "The term 'city,'" writes Robert Wilkin, "designates a community, a corporate and social entity, an ordered purposeful gathering of human beings."[13] Bruce Malina adds the necessary architectural and spatial qualification but supports the emphasis upon social form: "A city," says Malina, "is a bounded, centralized set of social relationships concerned with effective collective action and expressed spatially in terms of architecture and the arrangement of places."[14] It is these two features of cities—their centralized set of social relationships concerned with effective collective action, and the spatial expression of these relationships through architecture and the arrangement of places—that will concern us in what follows. It is through an examination of these features, starting with the architecture and arrangement of places, that I hope to offer some insight into what may be envisaged in the biblical employment of the city as a favored image for the completion and fulfillment of God's purposes.

Augustine's "City of God"

The first in the Christian tradition to explore the biblical image of the city at any length was St. Augustine, who, in an effort to make theological sense of the fall of the Roman Empire, took up the idea of the heavenly city in order to show that Christian hope is not invested in the *civitas terrena* but in the

---

single definition is possible. Rather, a bundle of criteria are needed to identify cities. See, for example, Edith Ennen, *The Medieval Town*, trans. Natalie Fryde, Europe in the Middle Ages (Amsterdam: North-Holland, 1979), 5.

[12] See Mumford, *City in History*, 3.

[13] Robert L. Wilken, "Augustine's City of God Today," in *The Two Cities of God*, ed. Carl E. Braaten and Robert W. Jenson (Grand Rapids: Eerdmans, 1997), 28–41, 30.

[14] Bruce J. Malina, *The New Jerusalem in the Revelation of John: The City as Symbol of Life with God* (Collegeville, Minn.: Liturgical Press, 1995), 40. Malina provides a list of social geographers and historians who have said more or less the same thing.

civitas Dei. That such a theological corrective was needed indicates the degree to which it had been assumed, following the conversion of Constantine, that Rome had thrown off its evil past as portrayed in Revelation and had found a new destiny as herald and forerunner of the kingdom of God. Eusebius, the "chief apologist" of Constantine's reign, compared Constantine to Christ and suggested that Constantine's "earthly empire replicates the heavenly kingdom."[15] While Constantine chose to establish his capital elsewhere and named it New Rome, this did not diminish, apparently, old Rome's sense of itself as the eternal city that was destined to lead and preside over the world's redemption. Evidence for this may be found in the writings of Prudentius, who wrote for Christian patrons in the late fourth and early fifth centuries, and whose poems celebrate Rome's rebirth as a Christian city. The ideology promoted by Prudentius in *Contra Orationem Symmachi*, for example, "depended on the assumed invulnerability of the city of Rome."[16] It is on account of this assumption, O'Daly explains, that "when Alaric besieged and occupied Rome in 410 the cultural shock outweighed the physical or political consequences of the event." The impact upon Roman sensibilities, including those of the Christians in Rome, is indicated by Jerome, who "compared Rome's fall with the Babylonian destruction of Jerusalem. . . . [A] threat to the Roman empire appeared to undermine the political and social basis upon which the Christian Church was presumed to be founded."[17]

Thus it was that Augustine felt it necessary to make clear that the fall of the city supposed to have been eternal presented no threat to the fulfillment of God's purpose to establish his kingdom, for the truly eternal and holy city is not built with human hands.[18] Indeed, it is not to be identified at all with any earthly conurbation, be it Jerusalem or Rome; it is instead the elect people of God gathered into spiritual communion with Christ. The citizens of the *civitas Dei* are "those who live according to the spirit."[19] They are the saints gathered from the long history of Israel and united together in the

---

[15] Eusebius promotes this view in a panegyric written in 336 to celebrate the thirtieth anniversary of Constantine's accession. This report of it is found in O'Daly, *Augustine's "City of God,"* 9.

[16] O'Daly, *Augustine's "City of God,"* 23.

[17] Jerome, "Letter 123," para. 16 (*NPNF₂* 6). The explanation is taken from O'Daly, *Augustine's "City of God,"* 28.

[18] The notion of Rome as the "eternal city"—represented in numerous sources and promoted by the Latin poets Tibullus, Ovid, and Virgil, e.g.—developed as the Roman Empire grew in size and in power. It seemed inconceivable during the centuries of Rome's imperial strength that the power and glory of Rome could ever be undone.

[19] Augustine, *City of God,* 14.1 (581).

Church with disciples of Christ in the present age, and in ages yet to come. Augustine's work traces the history of *two* cities, the earthly city divided by the enmity and sinfulness stemming from Adam's fall, and the heavenly city established by God to repair the damage wrought by human sin. Thomas Merton explains,

> It was in the "new Adam," Christ, that man was to be raised again to the friendship and vision of God—not indeed the contemplation Adam had enjoyed in Eden, still less the clear vision of beatitude: but heaven was to begin on earth in faith and charity. . . . The whole of history since the ascension of Jesus into heaven is concerned with one work only: the building and perfecting of the "City of God."[20]

The two cities, writes Augustine himself,

> have been created by two loves: that is, the earthly by love of self, extending even to contempt of God, and the heavenly by love of God extending to contempt of self. The one, therefore, glories in itself, the other in the Lord; the one seeks glory from men, the other finds its highest glory in God, the Witness of our conscience. The one lifts up its head in its own glory; the other says to its God, "Thou art my glory, and the lifter up of mine head" [Ps. 3.3]. In the Earthly City, princes are as much mastered by the lust for mastery as the nations which they subdue are by them; in the Heavenly, all serve one another in charity, rulers by their counsel and subjects by their obedience. The one city loves its own strength as displayed in its mighty men; the other says to its God, "I will love Thee, O Lord, my strength" [Ps. 18.1].[21]

Augustine here identifies several essential features of the city of God, notably the loving service its citizens offer to one another, and their love for and reliance upon God. He has much to say about the nature of the relationships in the heavenly city and we will consult him again as this chapter proceeds, but let us note at this point that the focus of his interest upon the gathering of the saints, and their constitution as the Church, yields an eschatological vision narrower than that of the Bible itself. There is little attention given in *The City of God* to the perfecting of creation, to the reconciliation of the *world* as a whole (2 Cor 5:19; cf. Col 1:20), or to the freeing of creation from its bondage (Rom 8:21). Augustine conceives his city of God almost entirely in

---

[20] Thomas Merton, Introduction to Augustine, *The City of God*, trans. Marcus Dods (New York: Random House, 1950), xv–xx, xii.
[21] Augustine, *City of God*, 14.28 (632).

spiritual terms and shows no interest at all in the architecture of the heavenly city. One might not think that remarkable, except that it contrasts sharply with Ezekiel 40–48 and Revelation 20–21, the two most extensive treatments of the heavenly city in the Bible, both of which portray in some considerable detail the architecture of the New Jerusalem.

With very few exceptions, theologians in the subsequent theological tradition have shared Augustine's lack of interest in the architecture of the heavenly city. The urban form of the New Jerusalem receives scant attention in theological eschatology. Philip Bess observes that

> much recent Christian reflection on [eschatology] has been highly political and highly abstract, positing—with some justice—the ultimate reign of God as the eternal presence of love, or peace, or justice, or liberation. In contrast, there is very little consideration of the reign of God in physical, spatial or sensual imagery.[22]

It was not so in the medieval and Renaissance eras. City building, at that time, was a theological concern. If it were not possible to realize in full the biblical vision of a heavenly city, the earthly city should be, at least, an anticipation of the city yet to come.

Anticipation of the Heavenly Jerusalem

In his book *Timeless Cities*, David Mayernik explores at length the lofty vision that inspired the city builders of the Renaissance. Before the Enlightenment, he writes, "cities to the European imagination . . . were more than simply Places, they were built Ideas suffused with cultural Memory."[23] He continues: "For city builders for more than a thousand years after Augustine the urban realm became a great memory theatre where our best aspirations were played out, the place where we said the most substantial things about who we are and what we long for."[24] The building of cities with some telos in view is not unique to the medieval and Renaissance periods, of course, but in the late Middle Ages and Renaissance, the church possessed, for better and for worse, both the resources and the power to implement that vision in ways unmatched in any other era. The cities of that time prove to be, therefore, a

---

[22] Philip Bess, *Till We Have Built Jerusalem: Architecture, Urbanism and the Sacred* (Wilmington, Del.: ISI Books, 2006), 94.
[23] Mayernik, *Timeless Cities*, 12–13.
[24] Mayernik, *Timeless Cities*, 13.

rich stimulus to the interpretation of those biblical visions in which the New Jerusalem is portrayed in architectural terms.

That Christianity had a significant impact upon the organization of the polis in the medieval era and beyond can hardly be doubted. Sheldon Wolin explains that

> the significance of Christian thought for the Western political tradition lies not so much in what it had to say about the political order, but primarily in what it had to say about the religious order. The attempt of Christians to understand their own group life provided a new and sorely needed source of ideas for Western political thought. Christianity succeeded where the Hellenistic and late classical philosophies had failed, because it put forward a new and powerful ideal of a community which recalled men to a life of meaningful participation.[25]

Like Augustine, Wolin was not much interested in architecture, but the meaningful participation in the life of the community of which he speaks was facilitated in no small measure by the architectural form of the medieval polis. Christianity's "powerful ideal" found expression in the piazzas and colonnades, in the churches and monuments, and in the monastic, residential, and civic buildings of medieval cities, all of them arranged, where possible, to facilitate meaningful participation in cities that were earthly, to be sure, but that offered testimony to a city yet to come, a heavenly city in which creation's telos, the harmonious coexistence of all that God has made, would at last be realized in full.

To be fair to Augustine, he did not discount entirely the possibility that cities built on earth might foreshadow in some measure the heavenly city. Referring to Jerusalem in particular, he writes:

> There was, indeed, a kind of shadow and prophetic image of this City of the Saints: an image which served not to represent it on earth, but to point towards that due time when it was to be revealed. This image, Jerusalem, was also called the Holy City, not as being the exact likeness of the truth which is yet to come, but by reason of its pointing towards that other City.[26]

Whereas Augustine himself seems to suggest that the need of such a city on earth has by his time already passed, medieval city builders, often working

---

[25] Sheldon Wolin, *Politics and Visions: Continuity and Innovation in Western Political Thought* (Boston: Little, Brown, 1960), 97.

[26] Augustine, *City of God*, 15.2 (636).

under papal direction, were in little doubt that the city on earth should be a witness to and foretaste of the heavenly Jerusalem.

The material expression of Christian faith in the architecture of European cities began evolving after the conversion of Constantine and the proclamation of the Edict of Milan in 313. "From that moment on Christian worship and the desire to teach and consolidate faith shaped the form, provided the content, and inspired the splendor of all things made for public use—churches, mostly, and the paintings, mosaics, carvings, and inscriptions that decorated them."[27] This was especially true of the city of Rome. It was once associated, as we have noted above, with Babylon, "the great whore," but, following an interim period of neglect and decay, the eternal city began to undergo a transformation in the theological imagination. It would become, in time, a representation no longer of invincible imperial power and earthly glory, but of the heavenly city, the new Jerusalem. As they built on and with the stones of Rome's pagan past, Christians of the medieval era imagined themselves participating in the work of the new creation, a work that involved political, social, spiritual, and also urban transformation. In his survey of the city through history, Lewis Mumford explains:

> By renouncing all that the pagan world had coveted and striven for, the Christian took the first steps toward building up a new fabric out of the wreckage. Christian Rome found a new capital, the Heavenly City; and a new civic bond, the communion of the saints. Here was the invisible prototype of the new city.[28]

It is this suggestion of Rome as prototype that prompts the concern of this chapter: What might be learned theologically of the city yet to come, from the efforts in the Middle Ages and Renaissance to provide in stone an image or foretaste of that city? Four themes present themselves for consideration: the first concerns the organization of public space. The privatization of faith is a peculiarly modern development quite unknown to the medieval world. It is accompanied by the selfish individualism that has impacted so negatively the design of contemporary towns and cities where public space has frequently been reduced to the space left over after private interests have been served. It was not so in Europe prior to the modern era. The care then taken over the public realm reflected the priority given to the well-being of the community and the assumption of a common cause. There is something to

---

[27] Kessler and Zacharias, *Rome 1300*, 3.
[28] Mumford, *City in History*, 243.

be learned here about the social life of the New Jerusalem. A second theme, closely related to the first, is the provisions made in the medieval city for the welfare of the widow, the orphan, and the stranger and for the overcoming of pain and suffering. Medieval practice in these matters undoubtedly fell far short of what the Bible calls for, but there are remarkable innovations in the architecture that express the biblical ideal. Third, one of the definitive features of the New Jerusalem in the book of Revelation is the immediate presence of God with his people: "See the home of God is among mortals. He will dwell with them; they will be his peoples and God himself will be with them" (Rev 21:3). This third theme, too, finds expression in the landscape of the medieval city. A fourth theme is worship. Again in Revelation, worship, particularly of the Lamb, is a central feature of life in the heavenly city. To the degree that the architecture reflects actual practice, this emphasis was a feature of life in the medieval city, too. While we will consider each of these themes in turn, it will become evident as we proceed that there is much overlap between them. That is to be expected given the close association in the Bible between true worship and the pursuit of justice for the oppressed, the widow, and the orphan (see, for instance, Isa 1:11-17).

Public Space

The suggestion that earthly cities in general and Rome in particular could be, even in some small measure, an anticipation and foretaste of the heavenly city found expression naturally enough in the thousands of churches built in Europe throughout the Middle Ages that became the focal point for the life of their surrounding communities. We will consider one or two such churches by way of example later in this chapter, but I am more interested in the ways in which the city as a whole was conceived as an anticipation of the heavenly Jerusalem. Crucial to this conception was the relation between private and public space. Christian faith was not regarded then, as it is now in the West, as a private matter. While there is a proper distinction to be made between public and private, the biblical account of God's purposes knows nothing of a salvation that does not involve the well-being of the community as a whole. The instructions given by Jeremiah to God's people living in exile in Babylon capture the biblical view that the individual's salvation is inseparably bound up with the welfare of the city:

> Thus says the LORD of hosts, the God of Israel, to all the exiles whom I have sent into exile from Jerusalem to Babylon: Build houses and live in them; plant gardens and eat what they produce. Take wives and have sons and

daughters; take wives for your sons and give your daughters in marriage, that they may bear sons and daughters; multiply there and do not decrease. But seek the welfare of the city where I have sent you into exile, and pray to the LORD on its behalf, for in its welfare you will find your welfare. (Jer 29:4-7)

That Christians in the Middle Ages took seriously the injunction to seek the welfare of the city is illustrated in a fifteenth-century Biccherna[29] panel by the artist Neroccio di Bartolomeo di Benedetto de' Landi titled *The Virgin Commends Siena to Jesus*. In a gesture signifying unity and concord, Mary draws a cord around a stylized model of the city and petitions a heavenly Jesus to ensure the city's well-being. The city itself is supported by three columns, each of a different hue: white, dark green, and dark red, the traditional colors of faith, hope and charity. These virtues, it is hoped, characterize the city as a whole and undergird Mary's plea for divine favor.[30] The image

FIGURE 5.1
The Virgin Commends Siena to Jesus,
by Neroccio di Bartolomeo

reflects the assumption, taken for granted in the premodern world, that humanity's relation to God is a corporate concern.

The builders of medieval cities shared the conviction that Christian existence encompassed the whole of life, both public and private, and public space was shaped accordingly. They sought in the built form of the city to give expression to the Christian hope and to provide a theatre for the continuing drama of Christian life. Given the prevalence of this view in the Middle Ages and its embodiment in urban form, Richard Sennett's contrary claim that "medieval builders sought to separate the life of the street from spiritual life, protecting the spirit

---

[29] The Biccherna was the Sienese magistrate or chancellery of finance during the thirteenth and fourteenth centuries. The records of the Biccherna's office were kept in books bound with painted leather covers.

[30] I have drawn my account of the image from Chiara Frugoni, *A Day in a Medieval City* (Chicago: University of Chicago Press, 2005), 22–23.

within church walls" is simply puzzling.[31] To be sure, medieval builders built places of sanctuary and retreat, but the public spaces of medieval cities served regularly as a setting for liturgical action and were often designed both to facilitate the ritual enactment of Christian devotion and to encourage public engagement in the drama of faithful Christian existence. With respect to the city of Rome, for instance, Joseph Dyer reports that against the backdrop of the city, "enhanced by the presence of numerous churches, palaces, and towers of the nobility, the religious processions of medieval Rome wended their way. Rome favored what Victor Saxer called 'essentiellement une liturgie de movement . . . une liturgie en plein air.'"[32] The processional liturgies were public events staged in "the open air."

Sennett's suggestion that Augustine is responsible for introducing a sharp disjunction between private and public, and rendering "inner" and "outer" as incommensurate dimensions, is equally unpersuasive.[33] Augustine's *Confessions* may justly be identified as the precursor of modern autobiography and as having introduced a particular religious focus upon the self, but this observation does not justify the conclusion that Augustine's conception of faithful Christian existence is essentially a matter of private, individual piety. Thomas Merton offers a salutary corrective:

> It may come as a surprise to some to learn that St. Augustine quite spontaneously regarded contemplation as a communal endeavor. Solitude may be necessary for certain degrees of contemplative prayer on earth, but in heaven contemplation is the beatitude not merely of separate individuals but of an entire city. That city is a living organism whose mind is the Truth of God and whose will is his Love and His Liberty.[34]

[31] Richard Sennett, *The Conscience of the Eye: The Design and Social Life of Cities* (New York: W. W. Norton, 1990), 21.

[32] Joseph Dyer, "Roman Processions of the Major Litany (*litaniae maiores*) from the Sixth to the Twelfth Century," in Ó Carragáin and Neuman de Vegvar, *Roma Felix*, 112–37, 113. The citation from Saxer is taken from Victor Saxer, "L'utilisation par le liturgie de l'éspace urbain et suburbain: L'exemple de Rome dans l'antiquité et le haut Moyen-Âge," in *Actes du XIe Congrès International d'Archéologie Chrétienne: Lyon, Vienne, Grenoble, Genève et Aoste (21–28 septembre 1986)*, Studi di Antichità Cristiana 41—Collection de l'École française de Rome 123 (Rome: École française de Rome, 1989), esp. 936–37.

[33] See Sennett, *Conscience of the Eye*, 9. Philip Sheldrake suggests that Sennett "misunderstands both Augustine and the role of 'the sacred' in the premodern city partly because he overlooks the fact that sacredness was not confined to churches but dispersed into a wider sacred landscape of the streets." Sheldrake, "Spiritual City?" in Caicco, *Architecture, Ethics, and the Personhood of Place*, 54.

[34] Merton, Introduction to Augustine, *City of God*, xv–xx, xi–xii.

Augustine himself writes, "The philosophers also consider that the life of the wise man is a social one; and this is a view of which we much more readily approve. For we now have in hand the nineteenth book of this work on the city of God; and how could that City have first arisen and progressed along its way, and how could it achieve its proper end, if the life of the saints were not social?"[35]

Although the disjunction between exteriority and interiority, between public and private, has more recent roots than Sennett alleges, there can be little doubt of his claim that modern Western culture is deeply afflicted by the privatization of faith and the consequent desacralization of the public realm. These twin afflictions have many symptoms and numerous deleterious effects that are frequently evident in modern cities. Sennett observes:

> What is characteristic of our city-building is to wall off the differences between people, assuming that these differences are more likely to be mutually threatening than mutually stimulating. What we make in the urban realm are therefore bland, neutralizing spaces, spaces which remove the threat of social contact: street walls faced in sheets of plate glass, highways that cut off poor neighbourhoods from the rest of the city, dormitory housing developments.[36]

The individual is left "in the helpless isolation of his unfreedom."[37] These characteristics of many modern cities militate against Jesus' injunction to love our neighbor and threaten to undermine the *koinonia* that is portrayed in the New Testament as one of the first fruits of Christian discipleship.[38] Although we cannot now build cities as they were built in the Middle Ages, and while the relative homogeneity of medieval communities is unlikely to be repeated, the theological convictions embodied in much medieval architecture still constitute a salutary critique of the individualistic and privatized faith to which Western Christians have commonly succumbed. The architecture of the medieval city was shaped by a communal vision of the life that was pleasing to God.

---

[35] Augustine, *City of God*, 19.5 (925).

[36] Sennett, *Conscience of the Eye*, xii.

[37] Raymond Unwin, cited in *The City Reader*, ed. Richard T. Le Gates and Frederic Stout (London: Routledge, 1996), 355. See further on this theme: Charles Taylor, *The Ethics of Authenticity* (Cambridge, Mass.: Harvard University Press, 1991), 1–12.

[38] See Acts 2:44.

One important manifestation of this vision was the public enactment of the Christian theological narrative not only in sanctuaries dedicated to that purpose but also in the streets and squares of the city. Lewis Mumford writes:

> Whatever the practical needs of the medieval town, it was above all things, in its busy turbulent life, a stage for the ceremonies of the Church. Therein lay its drama and its ideal consummation. . . . For the key to the visible city lies in the moving pageant or the procession; above all, in the great religious procession that winds about the streets and places before it finally debouches into the church or the cathedral for the great ceremony itself. Here is no static architecture.[39]

We may recall here the argument advanced in chapter 2 that the altars erected by Abraham and his progeny were set up to mark places of divine encounter. They were architectural markers of an emerging theology. In like manner, the liturgical processions of the medieval church made their way through the town or city, noting as they passed by or pausing for prayer at the places where God's continuing engagement with his people had been memorialized. In Rome, of course, the liturgical processions were often led by the pope, and they attracted pilgrims from throughout the Christian world. The elaborate processions "turned all of Rome into a dynamic theatre space where sacred and political dramas were regularly played out."[40] The earliest known ceremonial book outlining papal processional routes, written by Benedictus Canonicus in the mid-twelfth century, traces the route taken by popes as they made their way from the Church of St. John in the Lateran to their coronation in the Vatican.[41] Benedictus Canonicus also compiled the *Mirabilia Urbis Romae*, which provides a guide for the pilgrim to Rome's cityscape and narrates the Christian legends connected with many of the sites along the processional routes.

The expression in architecture of a publicly agreed narrative about the identity of its people and their participation in a particular history was characteristic not only of Rome but of medieval cities generally. Cities functioned as great civic classrooms, conveying in their architecture a particular account of the way history has unfolded, the purposes toward which history was thought to be directed, and the response humankind was expected to make to God's call upon them to be his people. The buildings of the

---

[39] Mumford, *City in History*, 277.

[40] Mayernik, *Timeless Cities*, 66. See also Sheldrake, "Spiritual City," in Bergmann, *Theology in Built Environments*, 159.

[41] See Mayernik, *Timeless Cities*, 66–74.

premodern period routinely contributed to a shared public narrative expressing the nature and purpose of humanity's participation in the cosmic order. Liturgical processions through the streets of medieval cities were a principal means of relating this narrative and were notable because they invited participation of all in the city, women and children included. Those not walking in the procession itself could line the processional routes and share in the work of decorating the houses and streets along the way. The *Possesso* was the procession from St. John Lateran to St. Peter's and back again, undertaken whenever a new pope made his way from his residence in the Lateran to be installed as pope at St. Peter's. The route was also a "memory path" that

> served a specific evocative function, represented essentially by the ceremonial roles of the two churches where the procession began and ended; but spots along the path itself evoked deliberate memories of the papacy's role in Rome (such as Castel Sant' Angelo, the via del Governo Vecchio, the Capitoline, the Colosseum, the arch of Constantine and so on). It was in fact a route that *recalled* ideas and events, each important locus along the way being recognizable, discrete and mnemonically "loaded."[42]

The *Possesso* was a relatively rare event, of course, but regular processions during Holy Week and on feast days such as the first day of Advent, Corpus Christi, Ascension, and Pentecost, utilized the built environment as the backdrop for the liturgical narrative and regularly drew the populations of medieval cities into the streets in corporate acts of celebration, devotion, thanksgiving, and supplication. Participants in the feast day processions would pause for contemplation and prayer at Santa Croce, the Church of the Holy Cross, where Christ's suffering and death would be recalled; at Santa Prassede, where the bones of martyrs lay buried, thus calling to mind the communion of saints and the path of suffering; and at Santa Maria Maggiore, where Mary's humility and obedience called forth thanksgiving and a commitment to imitate her willingness to serve the divine purpose. Churches dedicated to various saints—St. Paul, St. John, and of course St. Peter—provided further reminders of the path of faithful discipleship to which all are called. Inside the churches, finely crafted mosaics, relics, liturgical furnishings, and the architectural forms of the buildings themselves would tell further of the biblical story.

Herbert Kessler and Johanna Zacharias offer their account of Rome's architectural and artistic heritage from the perspective of a fourteenth-century

---

[42] Mayernik, *Timeless Cities*, 67.

pilgrim who arrives in the city from the southeast to take part in the procession for the Feast of the Assumption of the Virgin Mary. Their pilgrim enters the city at the Porta Praenestina, also known as the Porta Maggiore. Kessler and Zacharias have placed in her hands, as a guide to the city, the *Graphia Aureae Urbis Romae*, which identifies the Porta Maggiore as one of twelve gates to the city. Rome had more than twelve gates, in fact, but the naming of twelve is the first of many suggestions the pilgrim will encounter that her visit to Rome will draw her closer to the heavenly Jerusalem. Revelation 21:12-13 has it that twelve gates will provide access to the heavenly city.[43]

Whereas the heavenly city described in Revelation 21 has no temple, for its temple is the Lord (Rev 21:22), the city of Rome has hundreds of churches, commemorating the saints and martyrs who have gone before and reminding the pilgrim of her participation in the communion of saints extended in time and space. Kessler and Zacharias describe the cityscape revealed to their imaginary pilgrim thus:

> Even before passing under the Porta Maggiore, our pilgrim has parted ways with the many others who have detoured to pray at the church of St. Lawrence Outside the Walls (San Lorenzo fuori le mura). The bell tower at the Lateran church, which can be seen from inside the Porta Maggiore, serves as a beacon for the traveler who would stay on course for the papal precinct, for there one can witness the start of the Assumption Day procession that will begin this evening. . . . Although she is missing St. Lawrence's, the Lateran-bound pilgrim will have the opportunity to offer a prayer instead at the important church of the Holy Cross in Jerusalem (Sta. Croce in Gerusalemme) which stands virtually midway between the Porta Maggiore and the first major objective within the city, the Lateran.[44]

The Church of the Holy Cross was established to house relics of the cross on which Christ was crucified and which, according to legend, were brought back to Rome by the Empress Helena (ca. 255–ca. 330), who had discovered the true cross in the Holy Land. The availability in Rome of this central object of Christian devotion and symbol of God's reconciliation of sinful humanity to himself indicates that it is now in Rome, rather than in Jerusalem, that the pilgrim will experience the presence of God.

---

[43] The same strategy was employed by authorities in Florence. Philip Sheldrake reports that Florentine statutes of 1339 emphasize the existence of the sacred number of twelve gates even though, in fact, the city had by then extended to fifteen gates. See Sheldrake, "Spiritual City?" in Caicco, *Architecture, Ethics, and the Personhood of Place*, 56.

[44] Kessler and Zacharias, *Rome 1300*, 11.

It was not only the churches that provided explicit reference to the biblical story or supported Rome's conception of itself as the heavenly city. As the pilgrim participates in the feast-day procession through the streets of Rome, she will pass beneath the Arch of Titus, which depicts Titus' victory over Jerusalem and the destruction of the temple in A.D. 70. The soldiers are shown returning to Rome with the menorah and the table for the shewbread taken from the temple. They are, of course, pagan soldiers under the command of a pagan emperor, but the destruction of the temple in Jerusalem and transport of the temple furnishings to Rome reinforced the later medieval view that Rome was now the holy city, a foretaste of the New Jerusalem.[45]

FIGURE 5.2
The Arch of Titus

Processional enactments of particular aspects of the biblical narrative that utilized the architecture as mnemonic markers of key moments in the narrative served not only to educate those who took part, nor only to facilitate

---

[45] My purpose in drawing attention to the relief sculptures of the Arch of Titus and to their suggestion that Rome is the New Jerusalem is to endorse neither a supersessionist account of the relation between Judaism and Christianity nor the pillaging of Judaism's treasures, but rather to highlight a further instance of the way in which the built environment of Rome gave expression in the public realm to a particular understanding of how the city as a whole foreshadowed the coming city of God and played a key role in the realization of God's purposes.

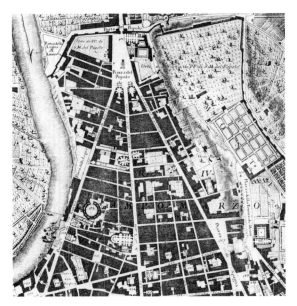

FIGURE 5.3
Trident Street Pattern, Rome

their participation in a life of Christian devotion, but also to establish the
urbs itself as an ever-present and enduring expression of a particular theological vision. Although the festal processions were occasional, the architectural
markers of the Christian narrative were present every day and so the city
became, quite literally, a place to inhabit the Christian story.

Devices of urban planning adopted in the Renaissance, inspired especially by Pope Nicholas V, whose papacy extended from 1447 to 1455, offered
further support to the suggestion that Rome's inhabitants, and those who
visited, were part of a city redeemed and sanctified by Christ. From the early
sixteenth century pilgrims arriving from the north entered through the Porta
Flaminia and immediately found themselves in the Piazza del Popolo, the
people's square. Radiating out from the piazza three streets provided three
routes for the pilgrim to travel deeper into the holy city itself. David Mayernik tells us that "this trident street pattern . . . had sacred Trinitarian connotations that were very much intentional and effectively mapped onto the
Roman urban fabric a *vestigium*, a trace or reflection, of the Trinity, invest-
ing the streets of Rome with symbols of sacred mystery."[46] Later still, in the

---

[46] Mayernik, *Timeless Cities*, 221.

seventeenth century, the twin churches of Santa Maria dei Miracoli and Santa Maria di Montesanto were built in the two V shapes created by the three streets, thus setting the church at the entrance to the triune mystery.

Renaissance pilgrims would find further theological imagery in the layout of streets as they passed through the Borgo district and approached St. Peter's Basilica. We know that Michelangelo conceived the dome of St. Peter's to represent the divine mind or head.[47] Bernini continued the imagery in his design of the colonnades surrounding Piazza San Pietro, which represent the embracing arms of Christ. The streets of the Borgo leading into the piazza, through which the Corpus Domini procession makes its way, were, then, arranged to complete the representation of the body of Christ.

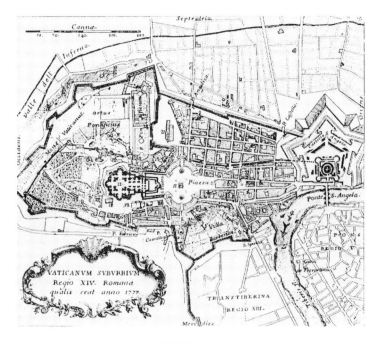

FIGURE 5.4
The Borgo District

What theological value is there in this urban representation of the Christian narrative? Above all, I suggest, it presents Christian discipleship as a form of life to be lived in the public realm. The form of Jesus' own life of obedience played out in the streets and synagogues, on the lakeshores and

[47] Mayernik, *Timeless Cities*, 77.

hillsides, and in the towns and cities of Palestine offers little encouragement to those who imagine Christian faith to be simply a matter of private devotion. It also provides a counter to those voices in the theological tradition that have conceived Christian life in purely spiritual terms. The life of the earthly city, though distinct from the heavenly city, is in all its facets a matter of theological concern. God is concerned with the sanctification not merely of souls but of the whole of our earthly existence, including the life of the polis. In his study *Cities of God*, Graham Ward reminds us that

> before the privatisation of Christian faith, Christianity was profoundly concerned with the body, with incarnation, with living as gendered human beings in physical bodies while simultaneously relating to the social and civic bodies and participating in the ecclesial and sacramental body of Christ. Christian theology will have to retell these traditional accounts—in Augustine, in Gregory of Nyssa, among others, and learn from them.[48]

Beyond the theological writings of Augustine and Gregory of Nyssa, we find preserved in the cityscape of Rome a further witness to the presence of Christ in the midst of our earthly existence. Representation of the Trinity and of the body of Christ in the streets of late medieval and Renaissance Rome reminds us that the place given for us to inhabit is a place sanctified in its entirety by divine presence. Just so, it is a place where there can be life. The life of the creature, that is to say, is predicated upon the divine economy in which God first makes space (and time) for the creature and then, since the creature is other than God, establishes fellowship with humanity by coming among us. To engage the vocabulary of John's Gospel, the divine economy creates a dwelling place for the creature "in Christ."

Representation of the Trinity and of the body of Christ in the streetscape of Rome could be seen as one more instance of humanity's sinful proclivity to domesticate God, to tether him to the limits of our own conceptual and technical prowess, and thus to deny the ontological otherness and the transcendence of God. That risk attends every human effort to "speak" of God, not only in architecture or in other art forms, but also in the theology expressed in words, be they scholarly, kerygmatic, or doxological. It is a risk we are bound to take, however, in virtue of the fact that God involves himself in our time and space and calls forth a witness to his presence. On account of God's self-presentation through Word and Spirit, the content of that witness is determined no longer by the limits of our own conceptual and technical

---

[48] Ward, *Cities of God*, 75–76.

prowess but by the constraints of revelation and inspiration. It is in that light that the streetscape of Rome may be read not as an idolatrous violation of divine otherness and transcendence but as an expression of consent to God's call upon us to dwell with and in him.

Another and more comprehensive account of God's call to dwell with him is found in the biblical report of the covenant that God establishes first with Israel but extends eventually, through its fulfilment in Christ, to "all the families of the earth" (Gen 12:3). Karl Barth contends that the covenant is the internal basis of creation—the internal basis, that is, of our having space and time in which to live.[49] The gift of space serves to differentiate the creature from God—God gives space for something other than himself to be—and creates a condition indispensable to relationship. As Barth again explains, precisely because there is distance between one thing and another, the possibility of relationship exists.[50] Space is given to God's creatures in order to facilitate relationship, both with God and with one another.

Here again the spatial arrangements of the medieval city correspond more effectively to this divine intent than many modern cities that, in their urban form, commonly resist the idea that we are created for community. Gated and high-security residential estates, streetscapes inhospitable to pedestrians, buildings clad in mirror glass that reflect their surroundings but contribute nothing themselves to the public realm, even locked churches: all of these reveal the extent to which contemporary Western culture has retreated from the biblical idea that human well-being is realized in communion with God and with neighbor. The architecture of modernity—not always, but frequently—is symptomatic of the triumph of private, individual interests over the public good. While it certainly must be admitted that the medieval city fell far short of the ideal society, its architecture was inspired, nevertheless, by a vision of community life far more closely aligned to the biblical ideal. According to the Bible, it is in the city—a corporate and social entity—rather than in solitude that humanity finds its true end. Drawing upon Psalm 147, Augustine teaches that the true end of humanity, realized in the city of God, is peace. Yet, as Robert Wilken explains, "Throughout his discussion, Augustine's language is social, not individualistic." He continues:

---

[49] Barth's exposition of this claim can be found in §41.3 of *Church Dogmatics*, III/1, ed. G. W. Bromiley and T. F. Torrance (Edinburgh: T&T Clark, 1958), 228–329.

[50] See Barth's discussion of divine omnipresence in §31.1 of *Church Dogmatics*, II/1, ed. G. W. Bromiley and T. F. Torrance (Edinburgh: T&T Clark, 1957), 440–90.

Peace does not simply mean union between an individual believer and God; it is a "perfectly ordered and harmonious fellowship in the enjoyment of God, and a mutual fellowship in God." Peace is an end that can only be fulfilled in community and enjoyed when all the members of the community share in that good.[51]

The persistence of that view throughout the Middle Ages is illustrated in Dante's *Divine Comedy*:

> And he continued: "Now tell me would it be worse
> for man on earth if he were not a social being?"
> "Yes," I agreed, "and here I ask no proof."
> (*Paradiso*, canto 8, lines 115–117)[52]

Aquinas, too, insists that "one man cannot live a self-sufficient life. It is therefore natural for man to live in fellowship with many others."[53]

In his imaginative account of life in the Middle Ages, Arsenio Frugoni, who held a chair in medieval history at the University of Rome, places particular emphasis on the social life of the city:

> All the citizens are like members of one big family, and they get to know one another as they make their way through the domestic streets. Suddenly we emerge into an open space, or a piazza, and find a public well. While the women wait their turn at the well they exchange a wealth of news about what is going on in the city and they carry it back with them, along with the water.[54]

The point of interest here is the support given to social life by the built environment. The domestic streets, a piazza, and a public well are places of social engagement and foster the development of familial bonds. The piazzas, especially, served as daily places of congregation for the conduct of business in open-air markets, for entertainment, for religious festivals, and so on; they became focal points for the life of the polis. The Piazza San Marco in Venice and the Piazza del Campo in Siena are particularly famous examples.

David Mayernik imagines the piazza in Venice "serving the role of a church nave, a vast outdoor container for the precious reliquary that is San

---

[51] Wilken, "Augustine's City of God Today," 32.

[52] Dante Alighieri, *Paradiso: A Verse Translation*, ed. and trans. Robert and Jean Hollander (New York: Doubleday, 2007).

[53] Thomas Aquinas, *The treatise "De regimine principum" or "De regno,"* in *Aquinas: Political Writings*, ed. R. W. Dyson (Cambridge: Cambridge University Press, 2002), bk. 1 (6).

[54] Arsenio Frugoni, Introduction to C. Frugoni, *Day in a Medieval City*, 1–13, 6.

Marco, which was positioned almost like an altar of this outdoor church."[55] Mayernik further supposes "that the architecture, as it was being conceived, must have foreseen its role as public stage and auditorium."[56] Michel de Montaigne, during his visit to Siena in the mid-sixteenth century, was similarly impressed by that city's Piazza del Campo:

> The square in Siena is the most beautiful that is to be seen in any city. Mass is said there every day in public, at an altar in view of all the houses and shops round about, so that the artisans and all these people can hear it without leaving their place and abandoning their work. And when the elevation [of the eucharistic body of Christ] takes place a trumpet sounds to give notice to all.[57]

In his impassioned plea for a recovery of what he calls "civic realism," architect Peter Rowe holds up the medieval city of Siena as an example: "The three civic values of *iustitia, libertas, et honor*—justice, freedom, and honor—were paramount in the lives of most Sienese."[58] Rowe commends Siena's "insistent institutional orientation away from individual aggrandizement and toward *bonum commune*—the common good," and he sees this embodied especially in the Piazza del Campo not only in its built form but in the statutes, originating in the thirteenth century, that indicate the manner in which the Piazza should be developed so as to serve well the public interest.[59] This it did abundantly, serving variously as an open-air hall or church where clergy like St. Bernardine would preach and conduct discussions, as a forum for political discussions and civic ceremonies of various kinds, as a market place, and

---

[55] Mayernik, *Timeless Cities*, 108.

[56] Mayernik, *Timeless Cities*, 100. Albrecht Classen likewise observes that many different religious plays staged in the public urban realm "provided a medium for communicating with the citizens regarding their religious values and morality." See Classen, "Urban Space in the Middle Ages," 89.

[57] Michel de Montaigne, *Travel Journal*, trans. Donald M. Frame (New York: North Point, 1983), 159. Cited in Mayernik, *Timeless Cities*, 175.

[58] Peter G. Rowe, *Civic Realism* (Cambridge, Mass.: MIT Press, 1997), 22.

[59] See Rowe, *Civic Realism*, 24–25. It is sometimes alleged that the corporate life of the medieval city was still exclusive of women, the poor, and so on. See, e.g., Malcolm Miles' criticism of Lewis Mumford's idealization of the medieval city in Miles, *Art, Space and the City: Public Art and Urban Futures* (London: Routledge, 1989), 28; or Gorringe, *Theology of the Built Environment*, 171. There can be no question that medieval society did not achieve the full participation of all as commended by the gospel, but recent scholarship has brought to light a higher degree of participation by women, for example, than has previously been recognized. See, for instance, Shennan Hunter, "Women, Men and Markets: The Gendering of Market Space in Late Medieval Ghent," in Classen and Sandidge, *Urban Space*, 409–31.

FIGURE 5.5
Piazza del Campo

routinely, of course, as a place of daily informal meetings among the citizens of Siena. The piazza was "large enough to accommodate Siena's entire population, which it did on occasions of severe duress, when the populace prayed together for deliverance."[60]

Similar examples from throughout Europe abound. The point to be made regarding such public spaces is that the vision of life together embodied in this architecture is based on theological convictions about the corporate nature of human well-being and of the city of God to which human history is directed. One of the first fruits of the pouring out of the Spirit following Peter's proclamation of the gospel, as reported in Acts 2, was *koinonia*, the establishment of a common life, not instead of privacy and retreat but blended with it: "day by day, as they spent much time together in the temple, they broke bread at home" (Acts 2:46). There is distinction, rather than division, here between the *res publica* and the *res privata*, between temple and home, while the call to community, to be together with God and with one another, appears as a distinctive feature and product of the gospel proclamation. Augustine contends, accordingly, that "the peace of the Heavenly City is a perfectly ordered and perfectly harmonious fellowship in the enjoyment of God, and of one another in God."[61] For Augustine, as John Burnaby

---

[60] Rowe, *Civic Realism*, 28.
[61] Augustine, *City of God*, 19.13 (938).

explains, "the *Summum Bonum* is by its very nature the *bonum commune*, a good that can be possessed only by being shared."[62]

The daily celebration of the Mass in the Piazza del Campo "in view of all the houses and shops around" and from which could be heard the trumpet sound that accompanied the elevation of the eucharistic body of Christ, served as reminder to the citizens of Siena that the *bonum commune*, disrupted by human sin, is restored only through Christ. It is for this reason, Kristen Deede Johnson explains, that "Augustine can conceive of no 'individual' life of faith separated from the church and its sacraments."[63] The sacramental remembrance and celebration of the reconciling work of Christ is therefore set at the heart of the city, in the midst of the *res publica*, precisely because through the life, death, and resurrection of Christ, a new community is brought into being, a community in Christ's body. The celebration of the Eucharist in the midst of the city serves also as an anticipation of the heavenly city in which, according to Augustine, "nothing will give more joy . . . than this song of the glory of the grace of Christ, by Whose blood we are redeemed."[64]

Welfare in the City

The recognition, in Christian Europe of the medieval era, that the welfare of the individual was bound up with the welfare of the city as a whole entailed that the welfare of all who lived in the city should be attended to. This concern, too, found expression in architecture. The commitment of the monasteries to caring for the sick, housing the orphan, and providing for the destitute spilled over into the cities where monasteries were located and became a central part of the efforts to replicate on earth, as far as possible, the ideal city of the kingdom of God. David Mayernik describes the scene in Florence:

> Florence's citizen-supported hospitals were a source of pride to the medieval and Renaissance city, and her system of lay confraternities and their charitable activities is a unique aspect of the city's sense of *civitas*. In providing a suitable home for one of these caretaking institutions Brunelleschi's *Ospedale* for orphans, or "Innocents" (*Innocenti*), brings in effect the architectural language of the monastic cloister, with its ordered rhythm of arcades, to the

---

[62] John Burnaby, *Amor Dei: A Study of the Religion of St. Augustine* (London: Hodder & Stoughton, 1938), 127.

[63] Kristen Deede Johnson, *Theology, Political Theory and Pluralism: Beyond Tolerance and Difference* (Cambridge: Cambridge University Press, 2006), 160.

[64] Augustine, *City of God*, 22.30 (1181).

public square. Monasteries were often the sole refuge of orphans; Brunelleschi therefore brought not only the physical form of the cloister but its associations to the res publica. This functionally and symbolically transformed the nature of public space into a more literal mirror of the *civitas dei* like that usually reserved for the monastery.[65]

This Florentine example is remarkable both because of the prominence of the Ospedale's location adjacent to the Church of the Annunciation and facing an elegant piazza, and because of the quality of architecture devoted to housing the orphans. The superbly executed loggia, the composite columns and ceramic roundels with reliefs of babies, the careful attention given to the tabernacle windows in the attic story, the beautiful internal cloister, and the proportional logic of the building all indicate the generous provision for the care of children left as orphans or abandoned by their parents.

FIGURE 5.6
Ospedale degli Innocenti

FIGURE 5.7
Roundels of the Ospedale degli Innocenti

Elaborate buildings providing for the needs of the widow, the orphan, and the stranger were also common in Rome. The Lateran quarter became

[65] Mayernik, *Timeless Cities*, 162.

famous not only for its papal residence and episcopal Church of St. John but also for its several hospitals.[66] A number of hospitals and other provisions both for the poor and for pilgrims appear to have been maintained under papal direction and with papal support. A papal bull of 1105 issued by Pope Paschal II refers to a *ptochium* in the Lateran quarter that Paschal II himself appears to have restored. A *ptochium* is a hostel for the poor, although the bull specifies that it is for the use of *peregrinorum ac pauperum*, the foreigner and the pauper.[67] Hospitals were founded with increasing frequency during the twelfth and thirteenth centuries, especially in Italy. They were commonly attached to churches and monasteries, and provided not only medical care but food for the hungry, respite care for widows and orphans, and alms for the poor.[68] Writing in the mid-fifteenth century, the renowned architect Leon Battista Alberti informs us that Tuscany is famous for its "tradition of religious piety" and boasts "splendid hospitals, built at vast expense, where foreigners as well as natives receive everything they need for treatment."[69] Lewis Mumford confirms the point:

> Hospitals, for the general care of the sick and ailing, were now provided on a remarkable scale. The sanatorium was no longer a health resort set apart from the city and catering mainly to those who could afford to travel, but a place in the heart of the city, near at hand, open to all who needed it, under the care of men and women willing to undertake all the repulsive offices demanded by sickness, wounds, and surgical operations. Both the hospital and the isolation ward were the direct contributions of the monastery; and with them came a more general kind of hospitality for the healthy, in need of overnight rest and food.[70]

The point of interest for our purposes here is that elaborate architecture was devoted to the care of the sick and the destitute. Mumford observes

---

[66] See Kessler and Zacharias, *Rome 1300*, 70.

[67] This and much more detail about provisions for the poor and the sick in the Lateran quarter can be found in Debra J. Birch, *Pilgrimage to Rome in the Middle Ages: Continuity and Change* (Woodbridge, UK: Boydell Press, 1998), 123–49.

[68] Numerous sources testify to the rapid expansion of hospital building in the late Middle Ages and Renaissance. See, e.g., Michael Mollat, *The Poor in the Middle Ages: An Essay in Social History*, trans. Arthur Goldhammer (New Haven: Yale University Press, 1986), 90–102, 146–53, 267–71, 281–90.

[69] Leon Battista Alberti, *L'architettura (De re aedificatoria)*, ed. and trans. G. Orlandi and P. Portoghesi, vol. 1 (Milan: Il Polifilo, 1966), 367–68, cited in K. Park and J. Henderson, "'The First Hospital among Christians': The Ospedale di Santa Maria Nuova in Early Sixteenth-Century Florence," *Medical History* 35, no. 2 (1991): 164–88, 169.

[70] Mumford, *City in History*, 267.

further that "not the least handsome buildings in the late medieval city were in fact the almshouses."[71] The grandeur of such buildings, along with the financial resources devoted to their construction, clearly indicated the seriousness with which medieval cities took the biblical injunction to care for the widow, the orphan, and the stranger. "Hospitals were among the earliest and the largest public buildings, other than churches, in medieval towns. They vied in size with market halls and the great halls built for justice or council by rulers or cities."[72] An account of a proposed hospital building by Filarete, the architect of the famed Ospedale Maggiore in Milan, indicates his concern that a hospital be "beautiful and capable of fulfilling the needs of infirm men and women."[73] The concern for beauty expressed here reflects not only the architect's own aesthetic ideals but a widespread view in late medieval society that attention to the needs of the sick and the destitute was a Christian duty, the importance of which should be reflected in the quality of the buildings in which such care was provided. No doubt it seemed appropriate also, given that care for the sick was certainly a spiritual affair, that the architecture for hospitals shared some of the characteristics of church and monastic architecture. All such buildings would include a chapel, of course, often as the building's central feature. As James Brodman explains, "hospitals in medieval and late medieval Europe were sacred places. . . . Hospital statutes from throughout medieval Europe always give priority to the spiritual over the secular well-being of sick inmates, to sacramental care over medical treatment."[74] Further evidence of the sacred importance of the hospitals is indicated by their entrances, many of which, according to Girouard, "were indistinguishable from cathedral portals." One of the portals of the Hôtel-Dieu in Paris, an institution that took in not only the sick but also pilgrims,

[71] Mumford, *City in History*, 267.

[72] Mark Girouard, *Cities and People: A Social and Architectural History* (New Haven: Yale University Press, 1985), 44.

[73] Cited in Renzo Baldasso, "Function and Epidemiology in Filarete's Ospedale Maggiore," in *The Medieval Hospital and Medical Practice*, ed. Barbara S. Bowers (Aldershot: Ashgate, 2007), 107–120, 115. Baldasso explains, "The standard edition of Filarete's architectural treatise from which the citation is drawn is edited by Maria Finoli and Liliana Grassi: *Antonio Averlino detto il Filarete, Trattato di architettura*, 2 vols. (Milan 1972) . . . The hospital is described in Book 11, 1:297–322. The Trattato has been translated into English by John R. Spenser, *Treatise on architecture: being the treatise by Antonio di Piero Averlino, known as Filarete*, 2 vols (New Haven, CT, 1965)" (1084).

[74] James W. Brodman, "Religion and Discipline in the Hospitals of Thirteenth-Century France," in Bowers, *Medieval Hospital*, 123–32, 123.

FIGURE 5.8
Hospital of the Holy Spirit

pregnant mothers, foundling children, and the aged, bore the words "Here is the House of God and the Door to Heaven."[75]

The Hospital of the Holy Spirit in Rome, founded in 727, reconstructed by Pope Innocent III in 1198, and rebuilt by Sixtus IV in 1473–1478 after a fire, features a great central hall accommodating up to three hundred beds. At the center of the hall and visible to all are a chapel and altar located under a domed tower. The dome rises from an octagonal drum in which twelve niches house statues of saints. The octagon, as noted in the preceding chapter, is a symbol of post-resurrection life, thus giving some hope to those whose illnesses were often terminal, while the altar and tower direct the thoughts and supplications of the sick and needy toward God. The statues, calling attention to the intercession of the saints, provide further evidence of the compassionate care in which the sick are held. In fulfillment of the need for all patients to be able to see the altar from their sickbed, hospitals commonly adopted a cross-shaped plan with four wards radiating out from a central crossing in which the altar and chapel were housed. Mark Girouard imagines that "the chapels, glowing with stained glass, gilding and painting, must have seemed like a glimpse of paradise to the inmates, lying in the stink of disease and death in the wards."[76]

[75] Girouard, *Cities and People*, 46.
[76] Girouard, *Cities and People*, 46.

Two points of theological importance may be drawn from this brief survey of the architecture of charity in the medieval world. The first concerns our humanity and what is necessary for human well-being. The cross-shaped hospital halls with their central chapels present a vision of human life in which material needs are integrated with the spiritual. Healing—or care for the dying, as the case may be—takes place in sight of the altar where the grace and mercy of God is proclaimed and enacted, and where hope in Christ's victory of life over death is proclaimed through the sharing of bread and wine. This is a long way from our present tendency to separate the science of medicine from the "consolations" of faith and much closer to the healing ministry of Jesus in which forgiveness and a new relationship with God appear as vital elements in the leper's cleansing, the blind person's sight, or the paralytic's restored capacity to walk. The modern world, repeating the errors of numerous earlier dualisms that have variously devalued either the spirit or the body, has torn asunder what God put together as constitutive features of our human being. Flesh and spirit are not separable elements of our humanity but are, *in combination*, essential features of created life made for fellowship with God. The architecture of charity in the Middle Ages allowed, accordingly, for the needs of body and soul to be attended to together.

If there is no dualism of body and soul, a second point follows—namely, that God's purpose to draw his creatures into reconciled relationship with himself involves matter as well as spirit. Not merely our souls but the created order in all its material reality is the object of God's creative and redemptive economy. Charles Cochrane observes that "from this point of view, the panorama of human history may be conceived as a record of the divine economy, the working of the Spirit in and through mankind, from the creation of the first conscious human being to its full and final revelation in the incarnate Word."[77] Or, as Colin Gunton puts it, "The incarnational interaction of God with material reality entailed an affirmation of the reality and importance of the latter."[78] Gunton himself suggests that medieval theology often lost sight of the goodness and value of the material world. The architecture of the medieval world tells a different story, however—and not just the architecture of charity that we have been discussing here but the efforts more generally to build on earth a city that approximated as nearly as possible the key features of the promised city of God. Indeed, there may have been more encouragement in Augustine than Gunton allows for the pursuit on earth of the

---

[77] Charles N. Cochrane, *Christianity and Classical Culture*, 2nd ed. (Oxford: Oxford University Press, 1944), 367–68.
[78] Gunton, *Triune Creator*, 103.

kingdom of God. We have acknowledged already that Augustine shows little interest in the architecture of the heavenly city and focuses especially on its spiritual quality, but his account of the *civitas Dei* is in fact linked explicitly to the goodness of creation. In book 11 of *The City of God* he writes:

> When it is said, "God saw that it was good," it is thereby sufficiently signified that God made what He made not from any necessity, nor because he had need of any benefit, but simply from his own goodness; that is, so that it might be good. And this was said after the created thing had been made, so that there might be no doubt that its existence was in harmony with the goodness for the sake of which it was made. And if this goodness is rightly understood to be the Holy Spirit, then the whole Trinity is revealed to us in the works of God. In this Trinity is the origin, the instruction and the blessedness of the holy City which is on high, among the holy angels. For if we ask, Whence comes it? God founded it; or Whence comes its wisdom? God enlightened it; or Where lies its happiness? In the enjoyment of God. It has its form by subsisting in Him; its enlightenment by contemplating Him; its joy by abiding in Him. It is; it sees; it loves. Its strength is in the eternity of God; its light is in God's truth; in God's goodness is its joy.[79]

The same goodness of God in which the heavenly city has its origin is also displayed in creation through the working of the Spirit. The architectural legacy of the medieval world reveals that its citizens viewed the work of the Spirit in creation not merely as something to be contemplated but as an economy into which their own creative energies were drawn. This was evident in the building of churches, of course, but equally throughout the city and especially, as we have considered here, in the buildings built to feed the hungry, to clothe the naked, to tend the sick, to welcome the stranger, and to house the widow and the orphan. Philip Sheldrake notes that a city's claim to holiness in the medieval era was often supported by the attention given to the feeding of the hungry, the welcoming of strangers, and the clothing of the naked.[80] Medieval Christians were inspired in their charitable work by the biblical injunctions to care for the least among them, but Augustine's influence is also worth noting. From his account of the city of God, they would have learned that "the city that is united in charity is the only one to possess true peace, because it is the only one that conforms to the true order of things, the order established by God."[81]

---

[79] Augustine, *City of God*, 11.24 (481–82).
[80] Sheldrake, "Spiritual City," in Bergmann, *Theology in Built Environments*, 159–60.
[81] Merton, Introduction to Augustine, *City of God*, xiii.

The Dwelling of God with His People

A central feature of the promise in Revelation of the coming New Jerusalem is the reality of God's presence with his people (Rev 21:3). Richard Bauckham points out that John's vision weaves together many strands of Old Testament tradition "into a coherent and richly evocative image of a place in which people live in the immediate presence of God."[82] Insofar, then, as Rome claimed to be the closest thing on earth to the New Jerusalem, it had also to claim that God's presence could be experienced there. There were several devices, architectural and otherwise, by which this claim was made. The first and most obvious was the presence in Rome of Peter's tomb and the long line of Peter's successors who, as Christ's vicars on earth, had likewise been entrusted with the keys of the kingdom. To be in Rome, therefore, was to draw close to the heavenly portal and so also to God himself. A second device was the presence in Rome of numerous relics associated with the life of Christ; the bones of hundreds of saints and martyrs housed in the city's churches further enhanced, it was supposed, the sacredness of the city. Cities and churches throughout Christendom laid claim to holy relics, of course, but they were present in Rome on such a scale as to render it the *caput urbium*, "the chief of cities."[83] Numerous churches, including the old St Peter's, which stood from the fourth to the sixteenth centuries before being replaced by its Renaissance successor, provided a home for the relics and were places where the citizens of Rome along with pilgrims to the holy city could meet with God. The city and the churches were sanctified by the presence of the relics and by the blood of the martyrs, thus making Rome a place where God's presence could be assured. Such was Rome's claim, but it is not one that can withstand serious theological scrutiny. The commercial production of "relics" for purchase by pilgrims eager to take home their own sacred souvenir and the sheer implausibility of many claims to authenticity even in respect of those relics that were genuinely old are themselves sufficient to discredit the industry. Nor is it possible to construct a credible theological argument in favor of the view that veneration of a saint's toenail or lock of hair either brings one closer to God or helps to solicit divine favor. And yet, there is in all this a genuine theological question to be considered. How is God present among us?

---

[82] Bauckham, *Revelation*, 132.

[83] I take the point from Alan Thacker, "Rome of the Martyrs: Saints, Cults and Relics, Fourth to Seventh Centuries," in Ó Carragáin and Neuman de Vegvar, *Roma Felix*, 13–49, 13. Rome's status as a pilgrimage city was well established, according to Thacker, by the late fourth century, especially through the efforts of Pope Damasus and the poet Prudentius.

A full treatment of that question requires much more space than we have here, but we may sketch the rudiments of an answer before turning to the question whether and how we may speak of God's presence in particular "sacred" places. The first and most important thing to say is that God is present through his Word and Spirit. "The Word became flesh *and dwelt among us*" (John 1:14). Through the enabling of the Spirit who gives eyes to see, ears to hear, and minds to apprehend, we are enabled to "see the glory" (John 1:14b) of the God who dwells among us. It is through Word and Spirit, furthermore, that God reveals himself as sovereign over all things. Precisely on account of his sovereignty, God is present to and with all things. There is nothing remote from him; there is nothing that exists or can exist apart from his creative, and redemptive, and loving presence.[84] The second thing to be said of God's presence, therefore, is that God is omnipresent.[85] As Barth puts it, God's omnipresence is a determination of his freedom.[86] God is neither confined to one place nor constrained in his capacity to be present to all things by the distance between one place and another. Neither is he limited in his capacity to be present in particular and specific ways in particular places and on particular occasions:

> There is no absence, no non-presence, of God in His creation. But this does not form any obstacle to a whole series of special presences, of concrete cases of God being here or there. . . . The reason for this is that we are dealing with the presence of the living God. And these special cases take place in the context of what God does as He reveals Himself and reconciles the world with Himself.[87]

Were he not free to be present in specific and particular ways, Barth avers, he would be lifeless and loveless. Instead, however, "God's true omnipresence, according to the testimony of Scripture, includes the possibility and actuality of His differentiated presence with himself, and with everything else, without any curtailment or weakness or diminution of Himself."[88]

It is in the light of God's freedom to be present in specific and particular ways that the possibility of our speaking of sacred space is raised. In chapter 2, I presented an account of the altars built by Abraham and his progeny, observing that the altars were built to mark places of divine encounter, to

---

[84] I take the point from Barth, *Church Dogmatics*, II/1, 461.
[85] As is confessed, for instance, in Ps 139:5-10 and in Romans 8:37-39.
[86] Barth, *Church Dogmatics*, II/1, 461.
[87] Barth, *Church Dogmatics*, II/1, 477.
[88] Barth, *Church Dogmatics*, II/1, 473.

memorialize particular moments in which God's presence and guidance were given in a special way. In a rather different episode, Moses encounters God through the sign of a burning bush and is told to remove his sandals for he walks on holy ground (Exod 3:5). In both instances, particular places were sanctified by God's special presence. Might the same be said of Rome, or of particular places in Rome? The question is prompted by Rome's reputation in the medieval world as a "holy" city, but Rome will serve here as an example of what can also be true elsewhere according to the sovereign freedom of God.

A short distance from the Colosseum in the direction of the Lateran is the small church of San Clemente to which I referred earlier. It is not one of the seven pilgrimage churches in Rome, but it is frequently visited, nevertheless, on account of the beauty of its interior, and it serves, more importantly, as a place of worship and devotion for Christians living in its vicinity. For the past 350 years the church has been tended by Irish Dominicans to whom it was granted after the expulsion of Roman Catholics from Ireland in 1667. Before them it had been served by an Augustinian order, the Ambrosians, and earlier still by Roman diocesan priests. As indicated in the preceding chapter, San Clemente is notable because of its construction in three layers. The lowest level is a Roman house that included a Mithraeum, a pagan temple; the intermediate layer is an early Christian church dating from the fourth century; and the third level, the only one above ground, is the present basilica, built in the twelfth century. It appears that Christians have worshipped on the site since the second century, originally in the Roman house and then, of course, in each of the subsequent church buildings.

Access to the church from the street is by way of an unassuming porch that is set within a two-storied gatehouse. The entrance opens onto a colonnaded atrium, enclosed on all four sides and so creating a place of sanctuary and withdrawal from the bustling streets outside. A fountain at the center of the courtyard, along with simple planting, recalls the biblical imagery of the garden and the water of life and anticipates the symbolism developed more fully inside the church. Yet the space remains relatively austere and humble in form. This is no grand entrance but a forecourt that encourages humility and quiet preparation as one makes one's way to the church ahead. As were Moses' sandals as he entered upon holy ground, cell phones and other such paraphernalia of modern life are out of place here; they are not needed as one prepares to meet with God. The paving pattern of the courtyard provides no direct route to the church door. Visitors are more likely to take a path to the right under the covered portico, where their journey will replicate that traditionally taken by monks walking around the cloister in prayer.

On entering the church, visitors may feel as though they have entered a different world. Completely cut off now from any visual connection to the world outside, they are surrounded instead by a space exquisitely decorated with a multicolored Cosmatesque[89] pavement that carpets the floor; granite and marble columns; walls; arches; liturgical furniture; paintings on the walls above the arches depicting scenes from the Bible and from the lives of saints; an elaborate coffered ceiling; and, drawing one's eye above all else, an apsidal semidome decorated with a splendid mosaic.[90] Setting aside, for present purposes, the convoluted story of clerical ambition, genuine piety, self-interested patronage, and all those other human complexities typically involved in the production of buildings like San Clemente, the basilica as it now stands has a single purpose: to surround the worshipper with the rich narrative of Christian doctrine and draw him or her into fellowship with God. This is a place where heaven and earth meet, a theme represented especially in the decoration of the apse.

FIGURE 5.9
San Clemente Atrium

FIGURE 5.10
San Clemente Interior

[89] Cosmatesque, or Cosmati, is a style of decorative stonework inlay developed in Italy in the Middle Ages.

[90] For a detailed description of the interior of San Clemente, see Kessler and Zacharias, *Rome 1300*, 72–89. The following description of the apse decoration relies heavily on the account in Kessler and Zacharias.

At floor level a semicircular bench is provided for clergy. Above the bench in fresco are Mary and the twelve apostles gathered around Christ: "standing on the banks of a river that is alive with fish and planted with flowers and palm trees, the saintly founders of God's Church inhabit paradise."[91] Rising farther above the cornice separating the earthly from the heavenly realm, we are taken into a shimmering world of brilliantly colored stone and glass set against a gold background. At the lowest level of the mosaic twelve lambs process from the gates of Bethlehem and Jerusalem to Christ the Lamb, depicted in the center. Above them an inscription refers to the vine of Christ that "the law makes wither but which the cross brings to life."[92] The inscription relates to the mosaic's principal theme, described here by Kessler and Zacharias:

> Stags, birds, a snail, a lizard, and two peacocks (the traditional birds of paradise), advance toward a river, which issues forth in four streams . . . the allusion here is to Genesis (2:9-10): "And in the middle of the garden [of Eden] he set the tree of life and the tree of the knowledge of good and evil. There was a river flowing from Eden to water the garden, and when it left the garden it branched into four streams." The profusion of life and nourishment visualized here refers also to the recapitulation at the end of the New Testament: "He showed me the river of the water of life, sparkling like crystal, flowing from the throne of God and of the Lamb down the middle of the city's street. On either side of the river stood a tree of life, which yields twelve crops of fruit, one for each month of the year; the leaves of the trees serve for the healing of the nations" (Rev. 22:1-2).[93]

The branches of the vine spiral outward and form fifty circular compartments that frame images of plants and animals creating a profusion of life; this is creation redeemed and enabled at last to flourish. The flourishing of creation takes place because of Christ and his sacrifice, depicted in the cross at the center of the mosaic. On the cross is the dying Christ with Mary and John at his side while the hand of the Father appears from above to award the victor's crown. Elsewhere in the mosaic, biblical figures, the evangelists, and saints from the patristic era are depicted, but so too are ordinary folk going about their daily business: a farm girl feeding poultry and a shepherd with his dog; the meeting of heaven and earth includes them. At the apex of the arch a portrait of Christ framed by a blue star-filled ring attests his presence in

---

[91] Kessler and Zacharias, *Rome 1300*, 81.
[92] Kessler and Zacharias, *Rome 1300*, 82.
[93] Kessler and Zacharias, *Rome 1300*, 83.

heaven. In his hand he holds the gospel; he, the Logos, gives himself through the Word of Scripture read in the church below.[94] Looking toward the heavenly figure of Christ, the prophet Isaiah unrolls a scroll inscribed with the words from Isaiah 6:1: "I saw the Lord sitting on a throne . . ." The words are sufficient to evoke the text that follows, repeated also in the celebration of the Eucharist:

> . . . high and lofty; and the hem of his robe filled the temple. Seraphs were in attendance above him; each had six wings with two they covered their feet and with two they flew. And one called to another and said:
> "Holy, holy, holy is the LORD of hosts;
> the whole earth is full of his glory." (Isa 6:1b-3)

The Isaiah text attests the presence of God in the temple and the shining of his glory throughout the earth. The appearance of the text in the church of San Clemente confirms the claim implicit in the architecture as a whole that this is the dwelling place of God. We can confirm, on good biblical and theological grounds, that as Christians have gathered in that place through almost two millennia to break bread as Christ instructed, to hear the Word read and proclaimed, and to offer up their prayers, that God has been with them. But can we speak of the space itself as sacred? Can it be true in any sense that God dwells here, within these four walls, in a way not true of all creation? Can particular architectural spaces be identified as the loci of God's special presence so that, on every occasion of our visiting them, we ought, figuratively speaking, to remove our sandals? Solomon, at the dedication of the temple in Jerusalem, offers a cautionary word: "But will God indeed dwell on the earth? Even heaven and the highest heaven cannot contain you, much less this house that I have built!" (1 Kgs 8:27). Yet, as Barth points out, "Solomon prays later that God will have His earthly place in this temple":[95]

> Regard your servant's prayer and his plea, O LORD my God, heeding the cry and the prayer that your servant prays to you today; that your eyes may be open night and day toward this house, the place of which you said, "My name shall be there," that you may heed the prayer that your servant prays toward this place. (1 Kgs 8:28-29)

Earlier in 1 Kings 8 we are told that during the dedication of the temple a cloud "filled the house of the LORD" (v. 10), and "the glory of the LORD filled the house" (v. 11). In response Solomon recalls the Lord's promise that

---

[94] Kessler and Zacharias, *Rome 1300*, 86.
[95] Barth, *Church Dogmatics*, II/1, 469.

he "would dwell in thick darkness" (v. 12) and so declares to the Lord, "I have built you an exalted house, a place for you to dwell in forever" (v. 13). Only later does Solomon check himself and, in humility, offer the prayer of verses 28-29.

Two things may be affirmed on the basis of this episode. First, Israel expects, on the basis of the divine promise, that the Lord will indeed dwell with his people, the impossibility of his being *contained* in the temple notwithstanding. Second, the special presence of God cannot be determined from the side of humanity. It is only something for which humans can pray. Put otherwise, we cannot build sacred space. There are no architectural specifications that will ensure that a particular space is sacred. But space may be sanctified by the Lord's presence. There is precedent for this claim, not only in the glory of the Lord that filled the temple but in the sanctification of human flesh wrought by the Spirit in Mary's womb and again in the sanctification of bread and wine as these are shared in remembrance of Christ. Just so, stones that are hewn from the hillsides around Rome and fashioned into a house for worship may be made holy by divine use. To be sure, God will not be confined there, nor will his special presence be apparent unless we approach in prayer, but for those who do come prayerfully, the space of San Clemente, as with all architecture dedicated to the glory of God, may both prompt and aid our attentiveness to the special presence of God. Neither sandals nor cell phones will be required.

Worship

The vision of the heavenly city present in the book of Revelation culminates in a scene of worship as the servants of God gather around the throne of God and the Lamb (Rev 22:3-6). In his account of the city of God, Augustine takes up and extends the theme:

> Nothing will give more joy to that City than this song of the glory of the grace of Christ, by Whose blood we are redeemed. Then shall these words be fulfilled: "Be still and know that I am God"; then shall be that great Sabbath which has no evening, which God celebrated among His first works, as it is written: "And God rested on the seventh day from all His works which He had made. And God blessed the seventh day, and sanctified it; because that in it He had rested from all His work which God began to make."

We ourselves shall become that seventh day, when we have been filled up and made new by His blessing and sanctification. Then shall we be still, and know that He is God.[96]

Although Rome styled itself as a prototype of the New Jerusalem, the proliferation of church buildings in that city constituted an admission that it could be, at best, only a prototype and not the heavenly city itself. For in the city described in Revelation, John saw no temple, "for its temple is the Lord God the Almighty and the Lamb" (Rev 21:22). In order, however, for Rome to foreshadow the heavenly city, worship should lie at its heart and pervade the life of the city. We have seen above the ways in which this doxological intent was expressed in the urban environment through the proliferation of churches, through the processions in which the city itself became a grand theatre for the liturgical enactment of the Christian story, through the representation of the Trinity in the streets radiating from the Piazza del Popolo and in the representation of the body of Christ in the Borgo area. Those who lived in Rome and those who visited on pilgrimage to the "holy city" were everywhere reminded of the invitation to worship, of the invitation to participate in the drama of God's meeting with humanity through the liturgical life of the church. The high point of this development was undoubtedly the Renaissance, and especially the alterations made to Rome's cityscape by Pope Sixtus V. Although his papacy was brief (1585–1590), Sixtus initiated dramatic changes to Rome's street system that allowed pilgrims to move easily among the seven pilgrimage churches; his desire "was to make the whole of Rome into 'a single holy shrine.' "[97] While the conception of Rome as a holy city in fact predated Sixtus V by several centuries, P. D. Smith captures well the papal intent when he says that Sixtus "transformed Rome from a city of narrow medieval streets into a triumphal capital city of squares and broad avenues. But the great achievement of Sixtus was also to create a holy city, one where the sacred became part of daily life."[98]

Although Rome laid claim to being the city most closely resembling the heavenly city yet to come, the attention it gave to worship was not unique. Lewis Mumford, writing of the European city in the fourteenth century, observes that "the main business of this community was not trade, however

---

[96] Augustine, *City of God*, 22.30 (866).

[97] Sigfried Giedion, *Space, Time and Architecture: The Growth of a New Tradition* (Cambridge, Mass.: Harvard University Press, 1967), 92. Giedion quotes Ludwig Freiherr von Pastor, *Sisto V: Il Creatore della Nuova Roma* (Rome: Tipografia Poliglotta Vaticana, 1922). No page number is given.

[98] Smith, *City*, 111.

eagerly the merchants might, as individuals, be concerned in amassing a fortune: its main business was the worship and glorification of God."[99] While some scholars prefer to argue that economic factors rather than religious ones gave the late medieval city its particular vitality,[100] for our purposes here we need only accept the uncontentious point that the architecture of the period reveals the very high value placed on the practices of Christian worship.

Conclusion

It may well be correct to say that

> Augustine sharply rejected any notion that a human group could be modelled on the heavenly City, or reflect it as an image reflects its original. The heavenly City was the eschatological orientation, what the Church will be at the end, when it is purified of its chaff on God's threshing floor; but that is a purification that may not be anticipated. That City is not a model, but an anchor, a direction, the fixed point at the far end of the Church's unending pilgrimage.[101]

However, is the view itself correct? Is it true to say that the heavenly city may not be anticipated on earth, however provisionally and imperfectly? Is it correct to conceive the heavenly city so completely as an otherworldly reality? The builders of medieval cities clearly thought not. The heavenly city served for them as a model that ought to shape the form of the earthly city, which then became, in turn, a witness to and foretaste of the city yet to come. We have traced in this chapter the ways in which that witness found expression in the architecture of the medieval world, especially in Rome, but also in cities throughout Europe. Christian theology has generally been sympathetic to the idea that the eschatological age has begun in Christ and we ought therefore to see the signs of the kingdom breaking into the present age. This view has its origins in the question asked of Jesus by the followers of John the Baptist: "Are you the one who is to come, or are we to wait for another?" To this, Jesus replies, "Go and tell John what you hear and see: the blind receive their sight, the lame walk, the lepers are cleansed, the deaf hear, the dead are raised, and the poor have good news brought to them" (Matt 11:4-5; Luke 7:22). These are signs of the coming kingdom indicating that the divine

---

[99] Mumford, *City in History*, 266.

[100] See, e.g., Henri Pirenne, *Medieval Cities* (Princeton: Princeton University Press, 1925).

[101] This account of Augustine belongs to the fine work of R. A. Markus, *The End of Ancient Christianity* (Cambridge: Cambridge University Press, 1990), 176.

work of bringing about a new creation has begun already in and through Jesus. The fabric of the present order has already begun to be transformed and so may be, as the Spirit renders it so, a testimony to and anticipation of the eschatological future. This role of eschatological forerunner is commonly assigned to the church. Wolfhart Pannenberg describes the church as "an anticipatory sign of God's coming rule and its salvation for all humanity,"[102] and John Zizioulas, representing the Orthodox view, regards the church in its celebration of the Eucharist as "the image of the eschaton."[103] While modern theologians like Zizioulas and Pannenberg are generally keen to avoid any triumphalistic claims about the church, the new creation inaugurated in the life, death, and resurrection of Jesus and the pouring out of the Spirit at Pentecost demand recognition as the irruption in history of the age to come. As Christiaan Mostert carefully puts it,

> The church may not arrogate to itself the finality and glory of the kingdom, but the reality of the kingdom is present in the sign of the church in an *anticipatory* way. . . . Already God's salvific future becomes a present reality in the church, albeit brokenly, as it proclaims the gospel, celebrates the sacraments, lives prayerfully and exercises a diaconal and pastoral ministry.[104]

Medieval Christians, continuing into the Renaissance, accepted this eschatological understanding of their present reality but saw it extending to the city as a whole. For all the "brokenness" of the medieval world, the architecture remaining from that era holds before us a vision of what the city ought to be: more noble and certainly more theologically commendable than the vision represented in contemporary cities, the planning of which has typically been surrendered to chance and to the economic ambitions of developers.

---

[102] Wolfhart Pannenberg, *Theology and the Kingdom of God*, ed. R. J. Neuhaus (Philadelphia: Westminster, 1969), 78.

[103] John Zizioulas, *Lectures in Christian Dogmatics*, ed. Douglas H. Knight (London: T&T Clark, 2008), 160.

[104] Christiaan Mostert, "The Kingdom Anticipated: The Church and Eschatology," *International Journal of Systematic Theology* 13, no. 1 (2011): 25–37, 35 (emphasis in original).

6

Knowing and Dwelling
*Considering Epistemology through Habitation
and Homelessness*

The Bible begins, in Genesis 1:1–2:4, with an account of creation, of how and to what purpose the world came to be. The principal concern of the biblical account is not to provide an explanation of the mechanics of the world's origins and development such as might constitute a rival to scientific explanations of the process but rather to articulate Israel's conviction that the world is the product of divine intent. The story of creation in Genesis 1 expresses the conviction that, sometimes despite appearances,[1] the world is upheld by God, that it has an order and coherence at least partially accessible to human understanding, and that it is a suitable place for the working out of God's good and loving purposes. That it is a suitable place for human habitation is emphasized by God's placement of human beings in a garden and by God's abundant provision for their needs. Their physical needs are satisfied by the flourishing of the garden itself (1:29), their social needs by the companionate relationship in which they have been set (1:27c; cf. Gen 2:18-25), and their need for a distinct identity and purpose as human creatures by their having been made in the image of God (1:27).

---

[1] Walter Brueggemann advises that Genesis 1 is usually "assigned to the Priestly tradition, which means that it is addressed to a community of exiles," to a community that had suffered severe disruption and had cause to doubt whether God really was the Creator and Lord of all that exists. See Walter Brueggemann, *Genesis*, Interpretation Commentary (Atlanta: John Knox, 1982), 22.

These affirmations about the nature of things are constituents of a faith generated by Israel's divine vocation. As the book of Genesis itself will soon tell, Israel is a people called by God to live in covenant relationship with him and to declare to all nations that they, too, are called to live within the realm of divine blessing and promise. To recognize that the claims articulated in Genesis 1 are affirmations of faith is to acknowledge that they are not self-evident. Indeed there is evidence to the contrary, evidence from which one might conclude that the world is not especially hospitable to human life that it does not always comply with our estimations of its order and coherence and that God, if God exists, is indifferent to our needs. The world exhibits signs of disorder that counter, it seems, the faith expressed in Genesis 1 that the world is the product of God's benevolent intent. And so we proceed, by way of a second creation account in Genesis 2 that is more anthropocentric in its focus, to Genesis 3, where the world's disorder is confronted and woven into the story. There is no denying—indeed the biblical story repeatedly acknowledges—that human life is not consistently easy or joyful or blessed. There is no shortage of evidence to support a view of the world contrary to that offered in Genesis 1. The reality of suffering and struggle in this world, not only among human beings but also among others of God's creatures, has to be acknowledged. Genesis 3 does that, but it also focuses on a particular aspect of the problem. It does not provide a comprehensive theodicy, an exhaustive account of why there should be any suffering in the world, but it does direct humanity's attention to our own culpability in the matter. The details of the familiar story—the temptation to eat from the tree of the knowledge of good and evil in contravention of God's instruction, the serpent's misrepresentation of that instruction, the disobedient act, and its dire consequences—need not be examined here. We recall instead the central point of the story that many of the problematic aspects of our habitation of the world can be attributed to our defiance of God's good ordering of things.[2] Rather than inhabiting the realm of divine blessing and constraint, human beings are persuaded that life will be better under their own rule. Acting upon that impulse, humanity defies God's instruction and takes for itself the prerogatives of sovereignty that belong to God alone.

The connection between two aspects of this story—namely, knowing and dwelling—leads us directly to the theme of this chapter. Note first that the fruit eaten in defiance of God's command was picked from the tree of

---

[2] Human exploitation and destruction of the natural environment is a telling case in point.

the knowledge of good and evil (Gen 2:17). Not content with the sufficiency of the knowledge already given them by God, humanity sought omniscience in addition to sovereignty. The point is confirmed by the serpent's suggestion to Eve that if she eats from the tree her "eyes will be opened and [she] will become like God, knowing good and evil" (3:5). The second detail of importance for this chapter is the displacement that ensues as a consequence of humanity's defiance. We have referred to the point already in chapter 2: in the face of Adam's bid for sovereignty, "the LORD God sent him forth from the garden of Eden" (3:23). Later in the story, Cain, the firstborn son of Adam and Eve, takes upon himself yet another divine prerogative—to end the life of another human being. "Cain rose up against his brother and killed him" (4:8). The consequence again is displacement and further alienation from the land which had been given as blessing to God's creatures: "The LORD said . . . 'When you till the ground, it will no longer yield to you its strength; you will be a fugitive and a wanderer on the earth'" (4:12). This is a tale of dislocation and of homelessness. It names with a spatial metaphor humanity's discontent, its restlessness, its sense that all is not well with the world as we now inhabit it.[3]

The metaphor of homelessness has often been employed to speak of human culture. In 1973, for example, Peter Berger, Brigitte Berger, and Hansfried Kellner offered a sociological analysis of modern consciousness under the title *The Homeless Mind*. Among the "discontents and counterformations engendered by the institutional structures of modernity" they describe the discontents that derive from "the pluralization of social life-worlds":

> The pluralistic structures of modern society have made the life of more and more individuals migratory, ever-changing, mobile. In everyday life the modern individual continuously alternates between highly discrepant and often contradictory social contexts. In terms of his biography, the individual migrates through a succession of widely divergent social worlds. Not only are an increasing number of individuals in a modern society uprooted from their social milieu, but in addition, no succeeding milieu succeeds in becoming truly "home" either.[4]

---

[3] For a more detailed exposition of Genesis 2–3 as a story first of emplacement and then of displacement, see Bartholomew, *Where Mortals Dwell*, 23–30.

[4] Peter Berger, Brigitte Berger, and Hansfried Kellner, *The Homeless Mind: Modernization and Consciousness* (New York: Random House, 1973), 181–84. More recently still, in 2008, the metaphor of homelessness has been used by Steven Bouma-Prediger and Brian Walsh to name a range of challenges prevalent in contemporary Western culture. See Bouma-Prediger and Walsh, *Beyond Homelessness: Christian Faith in a Culture of Displacement* (Grand Rapids: Eerdmans, 2008).

There are strong echoes here of the displacement that afflicts humanity when, after succumbing to the tempter's wiles, Adam and Eve find themselves alienated from God and from the place in which their well-being was assured. The experience of displacement is often a disorienting one; the loss of a dwelling place is accompanied by uncertainty and the disruption of one's worldview and of the conceptual framework that had given sense and meaning to the world. Berger and his coauthors observe: "What is truth in one context of the individual's social life may be error in another. What was considered right at one stage of the individual's social career becomes wrong in the next."[5] It is especially in the sphere of religion that the "homelessness" of modern social life finds its most devastating expression: "The age-old function of religion—to provide ultimate certainty amid the exigencies of the human condition—has been severely shaken. Because of the religious crisis in modern society, social homelessness has become metaphysical."[6] The suggestion that homelessness, in this metaphysical sense, is bound up with a loss of certainty is a commonly repeated theme in recent literature, as is the converse suggestion that "implacement," to use Edward Casey's term, is essential to the ways in which we make sense of the world.[7] Christian Norberg-Schulz contends, for instance, that "dwelling consists in orientation and identification. We have to know where we are and how we are, to experience existence as meaningful."[8]

The point of interest here is the connection between knowing and dwelling. Displacement gives rise to an epistemological crisis. Homelessness engenders uncertainty and leaves us less assured about what is true and trustworthy in the world. It is commonly suggested, therefore, that one of the tasks of architecture is to assist in ameliorating our homeless condition,[9] so to "provide us with a foothold in the realm of the real."[10] Some caution

---

[5] Berger et al., *Homeless Mind*, 184.

[6] Berger et al., *Homeless Mind*, 184–85.

[7] Casey, *Getting Back into Place*, 3.

[8] Christian Norberg-Schulz, *The Concept of Dwelling: On the Way to Figurative Architecture* (New York: Rizzoli, 1985), 7. A similar point is made by K. Dovey, who observes, "To be at home is to know where you are; it means to inhabit a secure centre and to be oriented in space." See Dovey, "Home and Homelessness," in *Home Environments*, ed. I. Altman and C. M. Werner, Human Behavior and Environment 8 (New York: Plenum, 1985), 33–64, 36.

[9] Thomas Barrie, "A Home in the World: The Ontological Significance of Home," in *Architecture, Culture and Spirituality*, ed. Thomas Barrie, Julio Bermudez, and Phillip James Tabb (Farnham: Ashgate, 2015), 93–108, 97.

[10] Juhani Pallasmaa, *The Embodied Image: Imagination and Imagery in Architecture* (Chichester: John Wiley & Sons, 2011), 123.

is needed regarding this idea, as Thomas Barrie notes: "The capacity of architecture to articulate the human condition and render it more comprehensible and meaningful, is limited at best (in part, because of the enormity of the task), and it does so problematically and inadequately." Yet, Barrie continues, "architecture may have the most promise of materializing and eliciting the collective aspects of the human condition, and of transcending the depressing and erroneous concept of separate individuality and human exceptionality." While at face value architecture might appear here as a rival to religion, whose function it has usually been to "articulate the human condition and render it more comprehensible and meaningful,"[11] I shall set aside any competitive construal of the matter and explore whether there may be some profit for religion, and more specifically for Christian theology, in exploring the ways in which architecture has sought to ameliorate our homeless condition. In what follows I will be concerned especially with the ways in which our efforts to know the world are closely entwined with our habitation of it.[12]

Retreat from the World

In the Vitruvian account, discussed earlier, of humanity's first efforts at constructing a place to dwell, habitation and construction are presumed to be modes of epistemic progress.[13] The spatial awareness occasioned by a fire in the forest that created a clearing and opened new vistas on the world brought with it, Vitruvius imagines, an inkling of order, a sense that the world was not merely random chaos but an ordered cosmos. That inkling of order generated within human beings a desire to discover the workings of the cosmos and to establish for themselves a place within it. This impulse, Vitruvius contends, is a condition required for the development of architecture, a condition, that is, of the human effort to express and to fashion a place for themselves within the cosmic order. For Vitruvius, however, this fashioning of a place for human habitation is not first a work of invention but requires, to begin with, attentiveness to an order that is already there. The principles of symmetry, order, and proportion essential to the making of good architecture are

---

[11] Barrie, "Home in the World," in Barrie, Bermudez, and Tabb, *Architecture, Culture and Spirituality*, 99.

[12] There is no prospect of my being able in this volume, let alone in this chapter, to exhaust the potential of such exploration, but, as indicated in the introduction to this work, I hope to do enough to demonstrate the fruitfulness of the endeavor.

[13] See chap. 2 above.

not human inventions, Vitruvius contends, but are given within the structure of the cosmos itself. The discernment of these properties of reality, and the effort to utilize them in architecture, are thus to be understood as means by which humanity comes to know the world.

Vitruvius continues his account through to the development of the classical orders in the architecture of Greece and Rome. He describes in great detail, as we have seen, the materials to be used and the proportions to be maintained in the construction of all manner of buildings, both public and domestic. The "orders" of architecture so described and the rules determining their use reflect an order found in nature itself, supremely, it was presumed, in the proportions of the human body. It was by employing the proportions of the body, Vitruvius writes, "that the famous painters and sculptors of antiquity attained to great and endless renown."[14]

The Vitruvian account of humanity's heuristic endeavors is essentially Aristotelian rather than Platonic. That is to be expected given architecture's essential concern with material realities. Architecture is not reducible merely to particular configurations of material elements, but it does not exist without bricks and mortar, stone, timber, and steel. No credible claim can be made that the concept in the mind of the architect is a more perfect and a more real instance of architecture than the building itself, fashioned from materials that nature makes available. Of particular interest, however, is Vitriuvius' conviction that human beings come to know the world through their exploratory habitation of it, rather than by withdrawing from it in Cartesian fashion to a realm of abstract and detached contemplation. We recall Vitruvius' contention that "as men made progress by becoming daily more expert in building, and as their industry was increased by their dexterity so that from habit they attained to considerable skill, *their intelligence was enlarged by their industry.*"[15] Vitruvius had no less confidence in universal principles than did Plato, but, in the manner of Aristotle, he considered that the universal principles of cosmic order were to be discovered by attending to and engaging with the particularities of nature. The proportions of the human body, as we have noted, were studied by Vitruvius and replicated in the classical proportions of the Doric, Ionic, and Corinthian orders. Quatremére de Quincy, who from 1788 to 1825 edited the *Dictionnaire d'Architecture*, noted approvingly that "it was by emulating nature through taking up the

---

[14] Vitruvius, *Architecture*, 3.1.3 (72).
[15] Vitruvius, *Architecture*, 2.1.6, as cited in chap. 2 above (emphasis added).

proportions of the human body that the primitive Greek builders raised their craft to the status of great art."[16]

The Aristotelian conception of epistemic progress has not been without rivals in Western culture. Indeed, the development of that culture is marked by a long and continuing dispute about the nature and basis of human knowing. Underlying that dispute, and closely related to it, is a further disagreement about the nature of reality itself. Are we to know the truth of things by attending to the ever-changing particularities of the material world, or are these liable to deceive us? Instead of seeking understanding through empirical observation, are we better off trusting the deliverances of abstract thought and reason? Are the material phenomena of space and time proper objects of knowledge, or are they a mere shadowy and approximate reflection of the eternal, singular, and purely rational order of things? Heraclitus is the usual exemplar of the first view in each pair of alternatives. Movement, flux, and the particularities of the material world were for him the constituents of reality itself, each instantiation of which was a modification of the fire that animated all things.[17] Parmenides, on the other hand, represents the view that the real is eternal and unchanging, and that it is accessible to our understanding not through the illusory world of sense experience but through the exercise of reason. According to Parmenides, truth is, *necessarily*, singular and unchanging. It could not reliably be represented, therefore, in the temporal and material world of flux and decay. Only through the exercise of pure reason, detached from mundane concerns, could humanity know the truth. It was by following Heraclitus rather than Parmenides, therefore, that Aristotle developed his empirical account of the knowing process, whereas Plato, his teacher, had sided with Parmenides' distrust of appearances and his conviction that true knowledge comes about through rational reflection upon the eternal and immaterial realities lying beyond the world of sense experience. Plato's disparagement of the *cosmos aisthētos*, of the world perceived through sense experience, is apparent in the *Timaeus*, in which Plato has Timaeus ask,

> What is that which is always real and has no becoming, and what is that which is always becoming and is never real? That which is apprehensible by thought with a rational account is the thing that is always unchangeably

---

[16] This paraphrase of Quincy's view is taken from Joseph Rykwert, *On Adam's House in Paradise*, 37.

[17] The exegesis of Heraclitus' fragmentary extant writings is a matter of considerable dispute. The point here, however, is not to provide a definitive interpretation of Heraclitus but to describe a type of philosophy of which Heraclitus is thought to be the generative exemplar.

real; whereas that which is the object of belief together with unreasoning
sensation is the thing that becomes and passes away, but never has real
being.[18]

On Plato's account, therefore, Vitruvius was mistaken in supposing that
humanity's knowledge could be advanced by attention to the particularities
of the natural world.

This ancient dispute remained unresolved when, at the dawn of Modernity, scientific endeavor was at once discovering the untrustworthiness of
sense experience (despite appearances, the sun does not revolve around the
earth) and learning that there was an order inherent in nature itself that
could be discovered through reasoned observation and calculation. Here we
come upon the key point of difference between Vitruvius and the modern
account. Whereas for Vitruvius, primitive men and women learned of the
world through their engagement with it, particularly in building—in their
fashioning of artifacts expressive of the order of the cosmos—modern men
and women learn best the orders of nature, so it is believed, when they adopt
the stance of an external and uninvolved observer. Disengagement, Charles
Taylor has argued, is one of the hallmarks of Modernity. "It is of the essence
of reason . . . that it push us to disengage." Taylor continues, "Knowledge
is no longer understood as our being attuned to the order of things we find
in the cosmos, but rather as our life being shaped by the orders which we
construct according to the demands of reason's dominance."[19] Colin Gunton
explains further:

> Disengagement means standing apart from each other and the world and
> treating the other as external, as mere object. The key is the word *instru-
> mental*: we use the other as an instrument, as the mere means for realizing
> our will, and not as in some way integral to our being. It has its heart in the
> technocratic attitude: the view that the world is there to do with exactly as
> we choose. Its other side—and I give an extreme view—is that we do not
> seek in the world for what is true and good and beautiful, but create our
> truth and our values for ourselves.[20]

Descartes is a primary example and forerunner here. In the preamble to his
Meditations he tells of the need to detach himself from the world of sense

[18] Plato, *Timaeus*, trans. Francis M. Cornford (Indianapolis: Liberal Arts, 1959), 27d–
28a (16).
[19] Taylor, *Sources of the Self*, 155.
[20] Colin E. Gunton, *The One, the Three and the Many: God, Creation and the Culture of
Modernity* (Cambridge: Cambridge University Press, 1993), 14.

experience, and to set aside all that he had come to know through external sources, through tradition and through the testimony of others. Apparently unaware of the impossibility of achieving such a goal, Descartes sought in the realm of his own "pure" thought a refuge from every external influence. The first of four rules of inquiry that Descartes proposes for himself is that "I should include in my judgements nothing more than what presented itself so clearly and so distinctly to my mind that I might have no occasion to place it in doubt."[21] Descartes elsewhere advises that the deliverances of the senses, along with the opinions and examples of others, cannot satisfy this requirement of clarity and distinction. The rational mind and essential human self exist apart from the machinations of nature and, from this point of detachment, are able to discern through rational calculation the truth of things as they really are. The question arises, however, whether this preference for abstract calculation yields knowledge of things as they really are or whether, instead, it forces the world to conform to an order of our own making. Gunton's suggestion above is that the latter is true.

Descartes' influence upon modern culture has been profound. His famous declaration of absolute confidence in the proposition "I think, therefore I am" set modern culture on a track toward radical individualism in which all claims to truth, goodness, and beauty are referenced, above all, to the self and to what seems plausible to the solitary individual. The "depressing and erroneous concept of separate individuality," lamented by Thomas Barrie above, has become rampant now. As we will see below, the Cartesian account of our knowledge of the world has had profound effects upon how we have sought to dwell within it.

The retreat in epistemology to the confines of individual judgement and rationality, and the accompanying disengagement from the world, has not gone unchallenged, of course. Johan von Goethe can be found among the protestant voices:

> From early on I have suspected that the so important sounding task "Know thyself" is a ruse of a cabal of priests. They are trying to seduce man from activity in the outside world, to distract him with impossible demands; they seek to draw him to a false inner contemplation. Man only knows himself insofar as he knows the world—the world which he only comes to know in himself and himself only in it.[22]

---

[21] René Descartes, "Discourse 2," in *"Discourse on Method" and "The Meditations,"* trans. F. E. Sutcliffe (Harmondsworth: Penguin Books, 1968), 41.

[22] The quotation from Goethe appears in Sennett, *Conscience of the Eye*, viii.

Vitruvius, de Quincy, and Goethe, among many others, testify to a mode of knowing that requires attentiveness before invention and a readiness to take cues from that which precedes and may be distinguished from the deliverances of our own intellect. Not only nature but also history and tradition may be our teachers. The Romantic defense of such a proposal was, however, a rearguard action, largely unsuccessful in its efforts to oppose or at least qualify both the rationalism and the individualism inherent in the Age of Reason. Modernity, and Postmodernity a fortiori, assert emancipation from the past and favor the reason and experience of the individual over the accrued wisdom of tradition. The hero of Modernity eschews reliance on the testimony of others and holds audaciously to a conception of reality forged, allegedly, entirely from what he has thought out for himself. No such hero exists, of course, for none of our thinking can be absolutely independent of the languages, conceptualities, and worldviews within which we have been reared. But the disparagement of tradition and the elevation of the self to be the sole judge of truth have, in Western culture, largely carried the day.

This story may be traced in architectural history as well. Architects, in their efforts to aid our understanding and our habitation of the world, have been no less prone to rationalistic excess than philosophers and theologians. Philip Bess has recently noted that "heroic individualism and a fetish for novelty are dominant themes of today's architectural culture."[23] Cultures are complex, of course, and so too are their genealogies. It is uncontroversial, however, to trace a lineage from classical Greek thought through to its recovery in the Renaissance and forward to the rationalistic spirit of the Enlightenment. But there are important distinctions to be made among these eras and among their respective assertions of human competence. Whereas the link between rationalism and individualism is apparent in the classical era—the Delphic oracle "know thyself" being an exemplary assertion of that link— that era was shaped also by Aristotle's conception of moral and intellectual virtues—virtues that, although cultivated by the individual's power of reason, were nevertheless dependent also upon the cultivation of friendship. Nor was Aristotle alone in holding this view; Plato and Socrates had thought the same. Intellectual and moral virtue were certainly not conceived as achievements of individuals working alone. The forum or Areopagus was the place of intellectual and moral advancement, a far cry from the isolation Descartes sought within the confines of his own room.[24]

---

[23] Bess, *Till We Have Built Jerusalem*, 193.
[24] Descartes, "Discourse 2," in Sutcliffe, *Discourse on Method*, 35.

The Renaissance, too, while undoubtedly providing nourishment for Cartesian rationalism, is distinguished nevertheless by its eagerness to learn from tradition, from those who had gone before and who had developed a wisdom whose value endured. Bess writes:

> The sense of obligation to both sacred order and historic standards of excellence . . . constrained Renaissance architects in a way that modernist progressive historiography by its own logic simply cannot. Modernism pledges allegiance to innovation, in the name of the future; but since the future is by definition unknowable except to God—a clue, perhaps, to the aspirations of modernists—and since past standards of architectural excellence bear no relationship to the present, it is easy to show how it has come to pass that the modernist hero is defined primarily by his or her disregard of constraints.[25]

Postmodern architecture, too, appears guilty at times of thumbing its nose at traditional constraints and of treating the past merely as a repository of images and ideas that can be deployed in our own age without regard for their original context or substance. It has often been remarked that Friedrich Nietzsche pioneered this modern and postmodern spirit. Alasdair MacIntyre writes of the Nietzschean hero who "finds his good nowhere in the social world to date, but only in that in himself which dictates his own new law and his own new table of the virtues."[26]

Rationalistic Excess in Architecture

It is time for us to investigate now the ways in which our estimations of how we know the world have impacted upon our efforts to find a home within it. I will consider first some unfortunate examples of rationalistic excess in architecture that are widely regarded as having accentuated rather than ameliorated our homeless condition. This section serves as a foil to later examples that offer more promising pointers for overcoming our homeless condition and return us to the biblical account of that crisis with which we began.

In 1925 Le Corbusier, a doyen among modernist architects, proposed a plan for a new city quarter in Paris that required the flattening of the medieval district of Marais, an area of two square miles north of the Seine. The Plan Voisin was a utopian vision for a new city form, requiring for its realization a

---

[25] Bess, *Till We Have Built Jerusalem*, 195.

[26] Alasdair MacIntyre, *After Virtue* (Notre Dame, Ind.: University of Notre Dame Press, 1981), 257.

flat topography devoid of all natural features, the eradication of all previous constructions on the site, and complete freedom from the constraints of client interest. Le Corbusier planned to build upon this "blank canvas" a series of X-shaped towers on a grid plan, each of them eight hundred feet high. The towers were to be mass produced, their replication through successive extensions of the grid being constrained only by the pace at which bulldozers could make the landscape ready.[27] A central feature of mechanistic production is the capacity to make all products the same. In this type of production, rigorous conformity to a universal standard is approached much more nearly than if production is left to the manual skills of individual laborers. Homogeneity is considered to be a virtue, and irregularities are eliminated as far as possible. It is thus one of the great paradoxes of Modernity, and of Postmodernity, too, that the celebration of individuality and human autonomy has been accompanied by a relentless drive toward uniformity, made possible by means of production and an ideological vision that would have everything conform to a universal design. In a culture utterly insistent upon the inviolability of individual freedom, particularity and difference are eroded more and more. The spirit of mass production and depersonalization is captured in Le Corbusier's now notorious declaration that "a house is a machine for living in."[28]

The dominance of the machine in the Plan Voisin is evident in other ways, too:

> Le Corbusier makes an extreme use of perspective in order to render the towers; the perspective on this city is drawn from someone in an airplane. While the architectural convention of looking down on a big built object to see it whole is commonplace, Le Corbusier has so stretched this convention, by positioning the viewer so high in the sky, that it is impossible to see much detail in the buildings; one notices more the way the X's look when mechanically repeated. There is thus a loss of historical relations and of concrete details in Le Corbusier's manifesto; the Plan Voisin is the very emblem of a disembodied neutral city.[29]

---

[27] It is salutary to note that when Descartes outlined his determination to doubt everything and to discount everything that he had learned hitherto, he employed the metaphor of a building that requires demolition so that not even the foundations are left, thus to make way for a completely new building established "by the plumb line of reason." See Descartes, "Discourse 2," in Sutcliffe, *Discourse on Method*, 37.

[28] Le Corbusier, *Towards an Architecture*, 87.

[29] Sennett, *Conscience of the Eye*, 171.

FIGURE 6.1
Plan Voisin

A disembodied city is surely one in which we have little prospect of finding a home. Fortunately, the Plan Voisin was never built, but imitations of
it were, especially in Britain and in the United States. The Cabrini-Green
housing development, for example, built in Chicago over a period of twenty
years from 1942 replicated Le Corbusier's vision of high-rise apartment living but, through the rapid onset of violent crime, poverty, the neglect of
maintenance, and the failure to provide basic services like rubbish collection, Cabrini-Green quickly became a symbol of the problems associated
with public housing in the United States. By 2008 most of the development
had been razed, its dehumanizing effects having attained a magnitude no
longer tolerable. Cabrini-Green, along with Le Corbusier's earlier vision of
a new urban environment, were projects in which conformity was coerced.
The mass production and replication of housing units undertaken in service
of a particular vision of human equality conveyed an irresistible message that
only one kind of human being could live here. Anyone not conforming to
type soon left, and Cabrini-Green quickly became a ghetto. The residents
were alienated from one another and from the wider world.

The Cabrini-Green housing development, following Le Corbusier's grand
Plan Voisin and replicated many times over around the world, is an architectural expression of the phenomenon of disengagement to which Charles
Taylor earlier drew our attention. Such disengagement typically renders us
blind to the order given in creation itself and drives us toward the imposition

of an order of our own devising. That is the impulse that led Le Corbusier to propose eliminating the "chaos" of the Marais in Paris, replacing it with a Cartesian grid and building upon that grid an architecture that was immediately comprehensible. The God's-eye view from on high presented by Le Corbusier is appropriate for an architecture in which nothing is hidden but everything is known.

The Cabrini-Green development gives one pause to wonder, however, whether the strict mathematical order sought after by Le Corbusier and by those who followed him was an order of humanity's own making rather than an order found in the world itself. The alienation and discomfort experienced by the residents of housing estates modeled after the Plan Voisin may best be understood as a consequence of the architectural overriding of what is given in the landscape. In the Plan Voisin, the value accumulated through centuries of human habitation in the Marais was also to be overidden. Such architectural projects, far from ameliorating our homeless condition, have revealed and exacerbated it.

Reason's quest for order and its prescription of how we ought to inhabit our world need not, however, take the form espoused by Descartes. Taylor observes, for instance, a stark difference between the functioning of reason in Descartes and its operations in Plato, the difference being the contrasting intent of Plato to discover an order that inhered in the cosmos itself. Cartesian disengagement, says Taylor,

> involves a very different concept of reason from Plato's. Just as correct knowledge doesn't come any more from opening ourselves to the order of (ontic) Ideas but from our constructing an order of (intra-mental) ideas according to the canons of *évidence*; so when the hegemony of reason becomes rational control, it is no longer understood as our being attuned to the order of things we find in the cosmos, but rather as our life being shaped by the orders we construct according to the demands of reason's dominance.[30]

Being attuned to an order of things we find in the cosmos is a matter to which I shall return below. First, however, let us consider further "the demands of reason's dominance." The Cartesian ethic and epistemology push us to disengage, says Taylor, from other people, from history and tradition, and from the realities of the material world. The relentless uniformity of the Plan Voisin is premised on the view that the needs of all residents are the same. The antecedent assumption is that all people are the same. Housing estates like

---

[30] Taylor, *Sources of the Self*, 155.

the Plan Voisin built elsewhere around the world have indicated, however, that the presumption of homogeneity violates the plurality and difference that is given in the world. The vision of equality and uniformity is realized only as the natural diversity of a community is eroded and the homogeneity of a ghetto is set in its place. The fact that diversity is a necessary feature of well-ordered human society is illustrated by the sharp rise in violent crime and other forms of antisocial behavior among those who are left in places like Cabrini-Green.[31] Cabrini-Green itself soon came to be known as "Little Hell."

Of course, a further form of disengagement from other people brought about by the "dominance of reason" is evident in Le Corbusier's willingness to disrupt the lives of those thousands of people who already lived in the two square miles of Paris north of the Seine. Le Corbusier's determination to establish a new order among them took no account of the order that already obtained. Rather,

> Le Corbusier set himself against the ways in which time is usually felt in urban space. The facades of old buildings and worn paving stones offer evidence that our own lives are no more and no less than an addition to the past. Le Corbusier rejected this evidence; he wanted modern architecture, which seeks for freedom of movement in a perfectly co-ordinated form, to expunge historical time from the city.[32]

Whereas disengagement from time and history is apparent in Le Corbusier's preparedness to eradicate all record of past habitation of the Marais quarter, disengagement from nature is evident in his proposal to set his utopian vision upon a grid plan that takes no account of the local environment and could, in principle, be set down anywhere the necessary earth-moving equipment was available. The grid is a concoction of abstract, mathematical reasoning. Rather than following a pattern of settlement that conforms in some measure to the topography of a particular location, cities based on a grid plan conform to a logic that obscures the natural features of the land.

---

[31] One of the lessons that may be taken from the story of the Tower of Babel is that God's scattering of the people, far from being an instance of divine curse or punishment, in fact marks the reestablishment of the proper diversity that God has bestowed upon humanity. For an exposition of this reading, see Allan Bell, "Interpreting the Bible on Language: Babel and Ricoeur's Interpretive Arc," in *Ears That Hear: Explorations in Theological Interpretation of the Bible*, ed. Joel B. Green and Tim Meadowcroft (Sheffield: Sheffield Phoenix Press, 2013), 70–93.

[32] Sennett, *Conscience of the Eye*, 170.

Referring to the painted grids that surfaced in twentieth-century cubist painting, Rosalind Kraus comments, "the grid announces, among other things, modern art's will to silence, its hostility to literature, to narrative, to discourse." And further: "Flattened, geometricized, ordered, it is antinatural, antimimetic, antireal. It is what art looks like when it turns its back on nature. . . . Insofar as its order is that of pure relationship, the grid is a way of abrogating the claims of natural objects to have an order particular to themselves."[33] Kraus contends that from the point of view of the exponents of such painting, artists like Mondrian and Malevich, "the grid is a staircase to the Universal, and they are not interested in what happens below in the Concrete."[34] The grid plan has obvious advantages, of course, in respect of simplicity of movement, but in Sennett's view it is also an expression of control and of detached neutrality.[35]

Hippodamus, the ancient Greek architect thought to have been responsible for the redesigning of Miletus after the Persian sack of 479 B.C. and for the planning of Piraeus, considered the grid to be an expression of the rationality of civilized life.[36] Though offering qualified approval of Hippodamus' introduction of regularly laid-out streets, Aristotle dismissed the architect's forays into political theory, implying that an obsession with symmetry was being taken too far.[37] The Romans used the grid plan for the laying out of military camps and then for the establishment of cities in territories brought under Roman rule. That the grid was not simply a pragmatic solution allowing for ease of movement and navigation is evidenced by the insistence of the ancient writer Hyginus Gromaticus that it was the task of the priests inaugurating a new Roman town to place the first axis, because "boundaries are never drawn without reference to the order of the universe, for the *decumani* are set in line with the course of the sun, while the *cardines* follow the axis of the sky."[38] But here we see again a difference between ancient and Modern thought. Whereas for the city planners of old, the grid was an attempt to replicate an order perceived to be inherent in the cosmos, Sennett contends

---

[33] Rosalind Kraus, "Grids," *October* 9 (1979): 50–64, 50.

[34] Kraus, "Grids," 52.

[35] See Sennett, *Conscience of the Eye*, 48.

[36] Sennett, *Conscience of the Eye*, 47.

[37] See Aristotle's comments on Hippodamus in *The "Politics" of Aristotle*, ed. and trans. Ernest Barker (Oxford: Oxford University Press, 1998), chap. 7.11 (276); also chap. 2.8 (61–66).

[38] The citation is from Rykwert as cited in Sennett, *Conscience of the Eye*, 47. See Joseph Rykwert, *The Idea of a Town: The Anthropology of Urban Form in Rome, Italy and the Ancient World* (Cambridge, Mass.: MIT Press, 1988), 192.

that "the Americans were the first to use it for a different purpose: to deny that complexity and difference existed in the environment":[39]

> The modern grid was meant to be boundless, to extend block after block outwards as the city grew. . . . Just as Americans saw the natural world around them as limitless, they saw their own powers of conquest and habitation as subject to no natural or inherent limitation. The conviction that people can infinitely expand the spaces of human settlement is the first way, geographically, of neutralizing the value of any particular space.[40]

The grid satisfies a reductionist impulse, a desire to render things simple and under rational control. A concomitant denial of the value of particularity occurs with the loss of any clearly identifiable center to a grid plan. Unless deliberately picked out in a way that interrupts the relentless sameness of the streetscape, the center of a grid plan is accidental and of no particular value. Such interruptions are by no means unusual but, as Sennett again points out, "American cities tended more and more to eliminate the public center, as in the plans for Chicago devised in 1833 and those for San Francisco in 1849 and 1856, which provided only a handful of small public spaces within thousands of imagined blocks of building."[41] This is, again, a modern development of the grid plan that departs from the practice of grid-planning in the ancient world. In the design for the rebuilding of Miletus in 479 B.C., for instance, Hippodamus carefully divided the urban territory into sectors with "areas for specific public functions (agora, port, etc.); and provision for the placement of individual public buildings."[42] Classical towns and cities, like the medieval towns and cities of western Europe, gave central architectural definition to the civic and/or religious institutions around which the polis was organized. The temple, the civic administrative buildings, the cathedral, church, and town hall, often fronted by public squares, were accorded an architectural prominence expressive of their role and value in the social order of the polis. Noting this feature of traditional city planning, Philip Bess comments that the architectural prominence given to "civilizing institutions" in traditional cities and towns did not merely symbolize power but aspired "to symbolize legitimate authority in general, and specific (institutionally promoted)

---

[39] Sennett, *Conscience of the Eye*, 48. By way of contrast note Spiro Kostof's observation that "the Hippodamian [grid] system relied on a theoretical formula of geometry . . . [but] that it was carefully adjusted to the specific demands of the site." Kostof, *A History of Architecture: Settings and Rituals*, 2nd ed. (New York: Oxford University Press, 1995), 142.

[40] Sennett, *Conscience of the Eye*, 48.

[41] Sennett, *Conscience of the Eye*, 48.

[42] Kostof, *History of Architecture*, 142.

practices and virtues in particular."[43] Modernity in its worst excesses, however, is marked, as we have seen, by "a relentless homogenising imperative,"[44] one of whose manifestations is the denial of any truth or authority outside of ourselves to which we ought to give allegiance. A "level playing field," though desirable in some respects, may have pernicious accompaniments such as, for instance, the elimination of traditional signifiers of what is true and good and beautiful, and the erosion of community institutions. The Plan Voisin has no place for a church, a synagogue or any other religious building, while space for theatres, community centers, and other venues for social interaction is minimal and architecturally undistinguished.[45]

Although we have continued to build churches, civic buildings, sports stadia, and theatres for public congregation, it seems uncontroversial to suggest that shopping malls, rather than the buildings of religious or civic institutions, are the most prominent emblem now of what Western society holds in common. We are driven by an insatiable consumerism and are encouraged to believe that our discontents can be ameliorated through the acquisition of material goods. It is the shopping mall, therefore, that now constitutes the center or hub of our communities and as each new mall is built, so too is the delusion that the mall will cater to our every need. Shopping malls, almost universally, are places without windows, thus facilitating all the more our disengagement from the world.[46]

A common thread is woven through the foregoing considerations of the Plan Voisin, the Cabrini-Green development, the prevalence of the grid plan, and the replacement of civilizing institutions at the center of traditional cities by the modern shopping mall. Each manifests in different ways the phenomenon of disengagement, claimed by Charles Taylor to be a key feature of modern culture, and so contributes to the "metaphysical homelessness" spoken of at the outset of this chapter. Attempts to ameliorate our homelessness through architectural means have often exacerbated rather than ameliorated the dis-ease. They represent forms of disengagement from what is given, in history and tradition, in nature, and in the landscape. What is given is

---

[43] Bess, *Till We Have Built Jerusalem*, 14. Bess helpfully points out that "authority" is essentially a synonym for trustworthiness, 13.

[44] See, e.g., Gunton, *One, the Three and the Many*, 13.

[45] For further discussion of Le Corbusier's antisocial proposals, see Simon Richards, "The Anti-Social Urbanism of Le Corbusier," *Common Knowledge* 13, no. 1 (2007): 50–66.

[46] For a theological critique of the phenomenon of the shopping mall and other similarly banal places, see John Pahl, *Shopping Malls and Other Sacred Spaces: Putting God in Place* (Grand Rapids: Brazos Press, 2003).

replaced by a new ordering of things constructed "according to the demands of reason's dominance."[47]

Something similar occurs in Immanuel Kant's widely influential account of the knowing process. Established authorities are rejected in favor of the rational deliberations of the individual who dares to think for herself. This process involves the imposition of a new order: "Reason has insight," Kant avers, "only into that which it produces after a plan of its own . . . it must not allow itself to be kept, as it were, in nature's leading-strings, but must itself show the way with principles of judgement based on fixed laws, constraining nature to give answers to questions of reason's own determining."[48] The world is known, on Kant's account, by being assimilated to an order determined by the human mind itself. We are truly "at home," on this account, solely within the confines of our own minds.

I have offered in this section a very selective reading of modern architecture and have concentrated only on some of its worst examples. This section does not offer, therefore, a summary evaluation of all that has gone on in the name of modern architecture. In a fuller treatment, I would, for example, offer a positive appraisal of Le Corbusier's chapel in Ronchamp, Notre Dame du Haut. The intent in this section has merely been to show, through negative example in this case, that our dwelling in the world is inevitably bound up with our efforts to know and to order the world. The examples given are instances, I suggest, of humanity's efforts to establish our own rule, and to foist upon the world an order of our own making. They confirm the diagnosis of our human condition first encountered in Genesis 3. Might there be, however, more positive examples in architecture of the connection between knowing and dwelling that will serve this book's aim of stimulating and enriching our reflection on the subject matter of theology?

Ways of Engagement

It is not unusual to discover in non-Western cultures a much greater respect for the natural order than was exhibited in Le Corbusier's Plan Voisin and in developments like Cabrini-Green. A Christian minister among the Aboriginal people of Australia speaks of their understanding of the relation between knowing and dwelling in the land.

[47] Taylor, *Sources of the Self*, 155.

[48] Immanuel Kant, *Critique of Pure Reason*, trans. Norman Kemp Smith, 2nd ed. (Houndsmill, UK: Macmillan, 1933), pref., ¶B xiii (20).

> To survive, [we] have to know about the land. The land contains our infor-
> mation about our traditional way of life. It's written there. It's like a library
> for our people and children. So we must preserve it. It's very sad when
> mining wipes out our library and there's nothing left for our children to get
> their education from. . . . Land is a breathing place for my people.[49]

The principal virtue in this mode of dwelling is attentiveness, followed by the
readiness to live in obedience to what is given. The knowing and dwelling
evident here, along with the vocabulary of gift, attentiveness, and obedience,
point us in the direction of an architecture and a theology that can speak
more truthfully of what it might take to overcome our alienation from Eden,
from the realm of divine blessing and promise.

The Japanese architect Tadao Ando has designed a church in the city of
Ibaraki in the Osaka prefecture of Japan in which the attitude of attentiveness finds concrete expression. Ando's Church of the Light built in 1989, is
simple in form and unadorned with decoration. It consists of a rectangular
box penetrated on one side by a diagonal wall and features on the front wall
two narrow slits, one horizontal and one vertical. The two slits span the full
breadth and height of the interior space and together create a cross through
which the morning light penetrates the chapel. The lack of adornment along
with the stark concrete walls and ceiling create a sense of profound emptiness
in the interior. The emptiness might evoke for some the empty-handedness
of those who come to worship. The attentiveness in which worship consists
requires that other things be set aside in favor of a readiness to wait upon
God. Worshippers may come to Ando's church at dawn and wait—wait for
the sun's light to strike the exterior wall and to make its way cross-shaped
into the place of worship. The light of God is not at our beck and call. We
must wait upon it, and when it does come, we are reminded, it takes the
form of the suffering and death of Christ. The architect himself has commented, "Light wakens architecture to life." This is a very Johannine theme.
The Gospel of John begins with the confession that the light of the world has
come. And it moves toward the climactic manifestation of God's glory, made
known in the cross of Christ. It is the dawning of this light that brings life to
the world. Ando's chapel reenacts that drama every morning.

A further effect of the dawning light is the enlivening of the interior. The
stark and colorless emptiness of the concrete enclosure is replaced by warmth

---

[49] Rev. Djiniyini, Badaltja, and Rrurrambu, cited in Geoffrey R. Lilburne, *A Sense of
Place: A Christian Theology of the Land* (Nashville: Abingdon, 1989), 35; Lilburne takes the
quote from *My Mother the Land*, ed. Ian R. Yule (Galiwin'ku: Galiwin'ku Literature Production Centre, 1980), 33, 10.

and richness as the light falls upon the natural wood of the furnishings. A theology is being expressed here; the created order, including also the works of our own hands, relies utterly on the gift of God's light, without which it is bereft of life. The prologue to John's Gospel provides appropriate support: "What has come into being in him [the Word] was life, and the life was the light of all people" (John 1:3c-4).

The entrance to the church itself is not straightforward, nor is it easily accessible. The sanctuary is not open for anyone to burst into unprepared but requires, rather, the deliberate negotiation of an entrance turning back on itself, not once but twice, thus requiring of the visitor the patience and persistence exercised on a carefully considered pilgrimage. The interior reveals itself only to those who take time and who are prepared to make the journey. Those who do so, furthermore, are not free to plot their own course, but must follow the lead given by the building itself. Humility is required rather than mastery, receptivity rather than the will to dominate.

FIGURE 6.2
Church of the Light

Here we may draw attention to the contrast between the architecture of Le Corbusier's Plan Voisin and that of Ando's chapel. The first requires the elimination of all that is given in the landscape and of the traditions accumulated through a long history of human habitation of the Marais Quarter in Paris. The second gives opportunity to wait and receive with due care and humility that which is given and cannot be seized. The respective architectural visions may be compared to the contrasting approaches between a theology developed along Feuerbachian lines that regards all talk of God as a human construct with no referent other than itself and a theology that understands itself to have been established on the basis of God's address to his creature. Advocates of the first approach know no authority other than their own, while the second approach involves the confession that God alone is Lord.

Ando's chapel is a building that encourages the disposition commended by Dietrich Bonhoeffer, who advised his students that "teaching about Christ begins in silence."[50] We may extend the point to theology in general, which ought to begin with attentiveness to what is given. The disposition corresponds to a different way of knowing and to a different way of dwelling in the world.

Writing about the sacred in architecture, Philip Bess describes the posture of humility and receptivity that we have seen in Ando's chapel as "sacramental sensibility." The tenor of Bess' discussion is that we cannot suppose ourselves to build sacred space, for the sacredness of space depends always upon the graciousness of God in giving himself to be known in space and time, and through material realities. "The sacred appears on its own terms, wherever it chooses."[51] Those who are called upon to design buildings for human habitation, therefore, may build in *response* to God's initiative in creation and redemption, and in *anticipation* of God's giving himself again. That posture produces an architecture like Ando's that contrasts markedly with much architecture in our modern cities that seems driven by hubris, self-assertion and the will to dominate.

Bess himself suggests that the sacramental sensibility is rarely evident in the contemporary era.

> Late twentieth-century art and architecture seem to aptly display the tenor of our era in works that commonly thematize self-assertion over self-sacrifice; revolt and entitlement over gratitude; the temporary over the durable; transgression over prohibition; autonomy and the pursuit of power over obedience to legitimate authority and the deliberate blurring of distinctions over the desire to understand and order things in clear and right relationships to one another.[52]

A sacramental architecture, by contrast—and, we might say, a sacramental mode of dwelling—will acknowledge the divine ordering of things and will be shaped in response to God's initiative in forming, redeeming, and blessing the creation; it will be marked by self-sacrifice, gratitude, durability, restraint, and obedience to a given order.[53]

---

[50] Dietrich Bonhoeffer, *Christology*, trans. John Bowden (London: Collins, 1966), 27.

[51] Bess, *Till We Have Built Jerusalem*, 73.

[52] Bess, *Till We Have Built Jerusalem*, 72.

[53] Without explicit theological awareness, Edward Casey remarks, "It is time to respect Nature in its own terms, to take our lead from *it* rather than from our own inwrought personal selves and ingrown social structures." See Casey, *Getting Back into Place*, 187 (emphasis in original).

Dwelling/Indwelling

On the east coast of the North Island of New Zealand there is a small sea-side town called Ōhope. It is home to the national *marae* of the Presbyterian Church of Aotearoa New Zealand.[54] A *marae* is the meeting place of a particular Māori tribe or subtribe. It is the focal point of the people's life together and is regarded as a sacred place. It is their *turangawaewae*, their place to stand tall. The church *marae* at Ōhope was established in 1947 to be a focal point for the bicultural partnership between Māori and Pākeha[55] in the Presbyterian Church.

At the center of all *marae* is a meeting house, or *wharenui*, and, among most tribes, the meeting house is regarded as the body of an ancestor. The form of the building is usually a simple rectangle with a dual-pitch roof finished by gables at either end. [56] The elaborately carved barge boards (*maihi*) at the front end of the building represent the arms of the ancestor; the *tāhuhu*, or ridge beam, is the backbone; and the *heke*, or rafters, are the ribs. At the apex of the gable, a *koruru* (carved face) represents the ancestor's head. Beneath the *maihi*, a sheltering porch, *te poho*, represents the breast of the ancestor. "To enter it is to be drawn into his bosom, enfolded in his embrace."[57] The *matapihi*, or window, located to the right of the front door, is the all-seeing eye of the ancestor, watching for the return of his children, while the door itself, the *tatau*, is the mouth kept open as a sign of welcome. Inside the *wharenui*, the *poutokomanawa*, or central column supporting the ridge beam, can be interpreted as the ancestor's beating heart, while the *poupou*, or columns supporting the rafters, represent key figures in the story of the people.

The meeting house at Ōhope, executed by carvers Te Ahinamu Te Hira, Karaka Takao, and John Rua, conforms to this tradition, but it is quite explicitly a Christian *marae*, "founded in Christ and dedicated to Christ."[58]

---

[54] *Aotearoa*, commonly translated "land of the long white cloud," is the Māori name originally given to the North Island but now used for the whole of New Zealand.

[55] *Pākeha* is a term used to describe all non-Māori but is especially applicable to white settlers in New Zealand.

[56] The following account of the meeting house at Ōhope is adapted from the description given in my essay "Architectural Expression of the Body of Christ," in *The Bible and Art, Perspectives from Oceania*, ed. Caroline Blyth and Nāsili Vaka'utu (London: Bloomsbury, 2017), 73–95.

[57] Diane Gilliam-Knight and Loren Robb, eds., *Te Maungarongo: The Ancestral House of the Maori Synod* (Wellington: Presbyterian Church of Aotearoa New Zealand, 1992), 23. The consultants for this volume were Warren Foster, Millie Te Kaawa, Sonny and Mona Riini, and Te Aouru Biddle.

[58] Gilliam-Knight and Robb, *Te Maungarongo*, 21.

Accordingly, the "ancestor" represented in this building is Jesus Christ. The name of the house, *Te Maungarongo*, means "the unifier—the creator of peace and harmony."[59] The people of the *marae* explain that "Christ is the Prince of Peace [who] provides shelter for the children of God."[60] They explain further that "all people, all races, and all creeds, should feel welcome at *Te Maungarongo*, under its outstretched *maihi*—carved as the sheltering and welcoming arms of the *wharenui* and thus of Christ and his church."[61]

FIGURE 6.3
Te Maungarongo, Exterior

FIGURE 6.4
Te Maungarongo, Interior

The carved posts, or *amo*, on either side of the porch would usually be warriors whose task it is to guard the way to the meeting house, but here the "warriors" are, to the right, *nga toa o te aroha*, the guardians of love, and to the left, *nga toa kaitiaki*, those who care for the house and who would lay down their lives in defense of the faith.[62] At *Te Maungarongo*, the *koruru* at the apex of the *maihi* is referred to as the *parata*. While the *koruru* is often a threatening figure who wields a *taiaha*, a weapon of war, the *parata* at *Te Maungarongo* challenges with a cross. The local people explain that it is "a welcoming challenge to turn swords into ploughshares, to take up the cross

[59] Gilliam-Knight and Robb, *Te Maungarongo*, 21.
[60] Gilliam-Knight and Robb, *Te Maungarongo*, 21.
[61] Gilliam-Knight and Robb, *Te Maungarongo*, 9.
[62] Gilliam-Knight and Robb, *Te Maungarongo*, 22.

and follow Christ's example in life."[63] I have explained more fully elsewhere that within Māori understanding, to enter this building is to enter the body of Christ.[64] This requires that all enmity be set aside. To engage in conflict within the walls of the meeting house is unthinkable to Māori. To dwell within the body of Christ is to dwell in peace. Paul adopts the same stance in respect of the body of Christ when, in Ephesians 2:11-22, he speaks at length of the walls of hostility having been broken down, precisely because those to whom he writes have been unified in one body. The architecture of *Te Maungarongo* establishes quite literally the space in which that reality is enacted.

The interior walls of the meeting house are lined with carvings and woven reed panels, while the exposed ridge board and rafters are decorated with *kowhaiwhai*, the scroll paintings traditionally used to record tribal genealogies. All of the decorative elements are highly symbolic. The carved columns depict tribal ancestors but also, in this case, characters from the biblical narratives. They are arranged in pairs on opposite sides of the building. For example, the fourth pair are Whiro and Taane, "two ancestral brothers who fought between themselves for recognition and supremacy,"[65] but they also represent Cain and Abel, the first brothers of the Bible's primeval history whose relationship was destroyed by enmity (Gen 4:1-8). Neither set of brothers are historical figures but their stories reveal the human rivalries that have been played out again and again through the course of human history. The adjacent pair of columns depict another set of brothers, Tanenuiarangi and Rongomaraeroa. These two are acknowledged "for their part in bringing peace between the children of Ranginui (sky father) and Papatuanuku (mother earth). Like Seth and Enoch [Gen 5:1-24], they found favour with God and in these *poupou*, they symbolise contentment and peace in the gentle lines of the carvings and the attitude of prayer."[66] Twelve sets of columns flank the interior of the meeting house, each depicting key figures in the community's tribal and biblical heritage. On the end wall, further carved columns depict the disciples of Christ and the apostle Paul. The carvings, as do all the decorative elements in the *wharenui*, serve a catechetical purpose. They tell the stories of the people who are gathered in this place as the body of Christ, and they signal the presence still of the communion of saints, a people extended through time and space who are made one in Christ. We cannot properly speak of the building and the people as distinct from one

---

[63] Gilliam-Knight and Robb, *Te Maungarongo*, 22.

[64] See again Rae, "Architectural Expression," in Blyth and Vaka'utu, *Bible and Art*.

[65] Gilliam-Knight and Robb, *Te Maungarongo*, 25.

[66] Gilliam-Knight and Robb, *Te Maungarongo*, 26.

another here; rather, together, they are the body of Christ. Nor is it adequate to regard these elements of the building as merely symbolic. As with the mystery of the sacramental body and blood of Christ, one feels at *Te Maungarongo* that, while not requiring any definitive account of how it should be so, Christ has nevertheless honored his promise to be present in the midst of his people.

The *kowhaiwhai* patterns painted on each of the exposed rafters employ swirling motifs drawn from the natural world and so depict the richness of the creation and the dynamic movement of life. Meanwhile, the woven *tukutuku* panels that line the internal walls tell the story of the people and again combine biblical and Maori traditions:

> The *poutama* (stepped pattern) found in some of these *tukutuku* panels signifies the lifting and leading of the people to Christ. The *purapurawhetu* design, meanwhile, denotes a myriad of stars, representing the immense variety and number of the peoples in the world. And the fish pattern (*Te ika*) recalls the traditional Christian symbol that refers to Christ and to the Christian identity of those who display the symbol. The *roimata toroa*—tears of an albatross—is another symbol used frequently throughout the panels.[67] These tears recall the tears of Christ.[68]

The Reverend Warren Foster was one of the key figures overseeing the design and construction of *Te Maungarongo*. Foster says of the meeting house: "You see Te Maungarongo with all his art, as a story that lives . . . in all concepts a place where you can behold, meditate, and feel, the story of Christ; a story that never grows old, a story that is completely woven around you, a story that is completely dedicated to the glory of God."[69] By dwelling together within this house, the local people, along with those who visit, come to know the love and the hospitality of Christ.[70]

---

[67] The Ngāti Porou tribe tell the story of their ancestor Pourangahua bringing *kūmara* (sweet potato) to New Zealand. So enamored was he of his beautiful wife waiting to greet him, he forgot to offer prayers of thanksgiving to the two sacred albatrosses that had accompanied him on the journey. Having made love with his wife, Pourangahua looked back and saw the tears of the albatrosses. This story, according to Ngāti Porou, is the source of the *roimata toroa* design. The story is recalled in Te Ahukaramū Charles Royal, "Papatūanuku—the Land—Whakapapa and Kaupapa," in *Te Ara—the Encyclopedia of New Zealand*, accessed February 18, 2016.

[68] Rae, "Architectural Expression," in Blyth and Vaka'utu, *Bible and Art*, 81.

[69] Gilliam-Knight and Robb, *Te Maungarongo*, 38.

[70] The local people do not dwell permanently within *Te Maungarongo*, but it does become the dwelling place for locals and visitors alike when any communal event takes place. Such events, especially funerals and tribal meetings, typically last for several days. At these

It would be a travesty to describe this house as "a machine for living in," unencumbered by association with the past and indifferent to the surrounding world. That was Le Corbusier's ideal, but at *Te Maungarongo* we encounter a very different mode of knowing and of dwelling. To "live" here is to be immersed in a long tradition through which one's own identity is established and defined. It is to be part of a community—a communion of saints—that extends back through tribal and biblical history and is ever ready to welcome new members into its midst. The detached, objective, rationalistic mode of knowing and dwelling favored by Western epistemologists in the modern era can provide no access to the reality of *Te Maungarongo*. The touristic gaze will not suffice either. Its reality is accessible only to those who remove their shoes and enter its sheltering embrace.[71] This is a building that must be indwelt with patience and respectful attentiveness.[72] Buildings require of us a certain form of seeing and of knowing:

> Buildings, unlike pictures, are not designed to be enjoyed in the looking; the relevant experience by which a building's quality must be judged is the experience of being in it, staying in it, passing through and by it, as a whole sentient and intelligent being. Any insistence on basing an aesthetic judgement entirely on the visual image of the building is an insistence on the impoverishment of experience.[73]

A further feature of the kind of dwelling appropriate to *Te Maungarongo*, again to be contrasted with the ideal of detached objectivity, is that one should expect to be changed in the process. *Te Maungarongo* is built with pedagogical intent. Its representation of the body of Christ and of the communion of saints constitutive of Christ's ecclesial body establishes a realm within which a people are formed. Much like the Passover liturgy through which, year by year, the Jewish people recall and confirm their identity as a people delivered

---

times the house will be used for sleeping, for worship, and for the discussions and storytelling that are an integral part of communal gatherings.

[71] The removal of shoes is mandatory for those entering *Te Maungarongo*. The requirement calls to mind the instruction to Moses to remove his sandals as he entered upon holy ground (Gen 3:5). It is a gesture of humility and respect.

[72] Edward Casey makes the same point: "To dwell," he writes, "is to exercise patience-of-place; it requires willingness to cultivate, often seemingly endlessly, the inhabitational possibilities of a particular residence. Such willingness shows that we care about *how* we live in that residence and that we care about it as a place for living well, not merely as a 'machine for living.'" Casey, *Getting Back into Place*, 174 (emphasis in original).

[73] Francis Sparshott, "The Aesthetics of Architecture and the Politics of Space," in *Philosophy and Architecture*, ed. Michael H. Mitias (Amsterdam: Rodopi, 1994), 3–20, 11–12.

from bondage in Egypt, *Te Maungarongo* recalls and confirms the identity of the people called in this location to be the body of Christ. The built form, along with carved, woven, and painted internal elements, provide a material counterpart to the genealogies recited, the histories retold, and the liturgies enacted whenever the people gather within its four walls. In this way the building contributes to the process of each new generation learning who they are, and so also to the cultivation of a particular form of life.

Remy Kwant thinks that the principle embodied in *Te Maungarongo* is widely applicable. "To inhabit a room or a house or a city," Kwant writes, "means that our familiarity with these environments forms part of our very conduct. . . . All aspects of our dwelling space demand a certain conduct. . . . This space has become part of who we are."[74] Dwelling, then, becomes the proper basis for knowing:

> We inhabit the earth. This is the primordial given. It is only on the basis of this inhabiting that reality becomes accessible to us, that it becomes *for-us*. All sciences, all disciplines, all philosophies and anthropologies grow out of dwelling. No knowledge can place itself above or beyond the sphere of dwelling.[75]

The point is worth repeating: no knowledge can place itself above or beyond the sphere of dwelling. With this observation I return, as promised, to the biblical story of humanity's displacement.

To Know Christ and Him Crucified

One of the symptoms of the homeless condition that afflicts humanity is the presumption of sovereignty. According to Genesis 3, humanity's displacement is a direct consequence of that presumption. The temptation to "be like God" is endlessly alluring. The presumption takes many forms, one of which is an epistemology that equates knowledge with mastery. According to this view, "the thinking subject is dominative in the act of knowing."[76] Mastery is attained, allegedly, by standing aloof, by resisting personal engagement, by adopting a detached and objective stance in relation to the object. Postmodern critiques of this presumption notwithstanding, the notion of knowledge

---

[74] Remy Kwant, "We Inhabit the World," *Humanitas* 12, no. 3 (1976): 299–309, 300.

[75] Kwant, "We Inhabit the World," 309 (emphasis in original).

[76] Francis Martin, "The Word at Prayer: Epistemology in the Psalms," in *The Bible and Epistemology: Biblical Soundings on the Knowledge of God*, ed. Mary Healey and Robin Parry (Milton Keynes: Paternoster, 2007), 43–64, 43.

as mastery retains a strong hold over the academy, not least in theology and biblical studies, where too much personal involvement or confessional commitment can be regarded as problematic. Detachment is regarded still as an academic virtue.

This conception of how knowledge may be attained is rarely, if ever, adequate. I have attempted to demonstrate the point with reference to *Te Maungarongo*, a particularly rich example of a building that cannot be known except by dwelling within it and by taking part in the forms of life that it was built to nourish and sustain. It is generally true of buildings that they cannot be adequately known except by dwelling within them. Recall Sparshott's contention that "any insistence on basing an aesthetic judgement entirely on the visual image of the building is an insistence on the impoverishment of experience."[77] Remy Kwant confirms the point:

> It would appear that the space in which we dwell is of an order different from the space we approach as spectacle. For the spectator things become ob-jects to which he places himself in opposition. . . . He approaches such objects as entities requiring his special attention, his scrutiny. The one who dwells is aware of his surroundings in different manner. He finds himself *with* the things that make up his environment.[78]

Recognition of the need to dwell with and sometimes within the object that we seek to understand edges us back toward a biblical conception of the knowing process, especially, but by no means exclusively, to that found in John's Gospel. Although a good deal is said about Jesus in the opening verses of John's Gospel, it is not until verse 38 that Jesus himself becomes involved in the story. The occasion is an encounter with the disciples of John the Baptist. Prompted by John's testimony concerning Jesus, two of his disciples follow Jesus. Noticing their presence, Jesus turns and says to them, " 'What are you looking for?' They said to him, 'Rabbi' (which translated means Teacher), 'where are you staying?' He said to them, 'Come and see' " (John 1:38-39). The King James version translates the disciple's query, "Rabbi, where dwellest thou?" The Greek verb *menō* used here is appropriately translated "remain," "abide," or "dwell." Although this appears to be a relatively innocent exchange, John introduces here a theme of profound importance in his Gospel. Note first the form of address: "Rabbi." This signifies that Jesus is one from whom the disciples expect to learn. It is precisely with learning in view that they inquire about Jesus' dwelling place. They recognize that if

---

[77] Sparshott, "Aesthetics of Architecture," in Mitias, *Philosophy and Architecture*, 11–12.
[78] Kwant, "We Inhabit the World," 299.

they are to learn from Jesus, then they will need to dwell with him. As the Gospel unfolds, the correctness of this view is confirmed. *Menō* is a verb used repeatedly in John's Gospel—thirty-four times—and in the Johannine epistles, where it is used a further nineteen times. John uses it especially of Jesus' relationship with the Father (e.g., John 14:10), and of Jesus' relationship with those who would learn from him. "Dwelling" or "abiding" in Christ becomes, for John, a favored way of speaking of discipleship (e.g., John 6:56, 8:31, 15:4, 15:7, 15:10; 1 John 2:24, 2:27; 2:28; 2 John 1:9). Jesus is presented as the one in whom we may live.

Knowing and dwelling are inseparably bound up together in the Johannine account. We can know Jesus, and also the Father, only as we dwell with him. 2 John 1:9 connects dwelling explicitly with the knowledge that comes through teaching: "Everyone who does not abide in the teaching of Christ, but goes beyond it, does not have God; whoever abides in the teaching has both the Father and the Son." Here, too, is the evangelist's response to the problem of our homelessness. Originally, in Genesis 3, humanity's displacement was attributed to our defiance of God and of God's good ordering of the world. Now in the Johannine literature, reconciliation with God comes about through the provision of a new dwelling place—in Christ and in his teaching.

John is aware, however, that dwelling with and in Christ requires the assistance of the Spirit. In 1 John 4:13 he advises: "By this we know that we abide in him and he in us, because he has given us of his Spirit." It is on account of this same recognition of our need, that Jesus promises to send the Spirit (John 16:5-15). The matter of dwelling with Christ requires a trinitarian exposition. Through the power of the Spirit, we are taken by the Son into the Father's house (cf. John 14:2-3). Indeed, this is the great news of the gospel, that the life of the triune God is open to others. This recognition encourages Robert Jenson to speak of God's "roominess." God accommodates other persons in his own life.[79] Utilizing an Irenaean manner of speaking, and returning for a moment to *Te Maungarongo*, we might say that the two barge boards on the gable end, the two arms of the ancestor that offer shelter and extend in welcome, are the arms of the Son and the Spirit who gather us into their embrace. It is, to be sure, the body of Christ that is represented in *Te Maungarongo*, but the Irenaean metaphor reminds us that Christ acts always

---

[79] See Robert W. Jenson, *Systematic Theology*, vol. 1, *The Triune God* (Oxford: Oxford University Press, 1997), 226.

in concert with the Spirit. The body of Christ, we might say, is enlivened by the Spirit.

When the Church is spoken of as the body of Christ, Westerners are inclined to think of it in abstract terms, as though it were merely a metaphor. Western theologians have also been inclined to idealize the Church to the point of invisibility, the result being that many despair at the great distance they perceive between the church in its idealized form and the concrete reality they encounter in their own neighborhood. At *Te Maungarongo* we are relieved of that disjunction. The body of Christ is there a concrete reality that visitors are able to enter, quite literally. Within that body, there is to be no enmity, no conflict, no behavior that dishonors Christ or that dishonors others. Whatever may go on outside, within *Te Maungarongo*, no one violates the rule. Within this dwelling place, a people are being formed into the likeness of Christ.

FIGURE 6.5
Cardboard Church *by Paul Hebblethwaite*

When, in John's Gospel, the disciples of John the Baptist ask where Jesus dwells, Jesus responds, "Come and see." That is an invitation to discipleship. As the Gospel unfolds, those who follow Jesus discover that the dwelling place of Christ is with the least and the lowly. Paul Hebblethwaite's installation *Cardboard Church: Communion on the Los Angeles River* offers an apt witness to the dwelling place of Christ. Hebblethwaite constructed the church in one of the large concrete drains running through Los Angeles, which he discovered to be the dwelling place of a "pregnant lady and her AIDS-ridden boyfriend." Hebblethwaite utilizes basic symbolic elements commonly found in church architecture to remind us that "God lives here too."[80] A stain of red wine extends over the floor of the concrete drain. The blood of the new covenant, the blood that facilitates our homecoming, flows to the place where the

---

[80] Paul Hebblethwaite's installation was entered in an exhibition titled "Space and Spirit" hosted at Calvin College in Grand Rapids in January 2005. The citations in the description above are taken from Hebblethwaite's artist's statement about the work.

lowly and the afflicted ones dwell. The truth and order and beauty revealed through the self-presentation of God in the person of Jesus Christ is not available as an abstract formulation or through detached, rational speculation. It is given rather to those who take up the invitation Jesus extends, the invitation to follow him, to come and see where he dwells.

7

Presence and Absence
Discerning the Transcendent in the Realm of the Immanent

The world lives now in a time between the times. It lives in the time between creation and consummation, between the beginning of all things and their true "end" in reconciled communion with the one by whom the world was made. It lives, too, in the time between the reconciliation accomplished once and for all through the life, death, and resurrection of Jesus Christ, and the full realization of that reconciliation in the age to come. The world lives in a time that, as Karl Barth has put it, is "no longer and not yet the time of the 'beholding of [Christ's] glory' (John 1:14; cf. 2 Cor 5:7). It is the time *between* the times—namely, the time of revelation and the time, announced in and with revelation, of seeing face to face (1 Cor 13:12), which will also be the end of time."[1] The liminal reality in which the world now lives may be expressed in spatial as well as in temporal terms. We live in a realm between the dark and formless void (Gen 1:2) and the coming of a new heaven and a new earth, in which a holy city will be established and God will dwell among his people (Rev 21:1-3). We live in a land "east of Eden" (Gen 4:16) that now groans in travail as, with us, it awaits the promised redemption (Rom 8:22).

The world lives in a realm of presence and of absence, a realm of "strange contrast" between Christ's declaration that we will not always have him

---

[1] Karl Barth, *Credo*, trans. J. Strathearn McNabb (London: Hodder & Stoughton, 1936), 114.

with us (Matt 26:11) and his reassuring promise, "remember, I am with you always, to the end of the age" (Matt 28:20).[2] The "strange contrast" between presence and absence appears repeatedly in the Bible. It appears, for instance, in the disjunction between the psalmist's anguished cry, "Why O LORD do you stand far off? Why do you hide yourself in times of trouble?" (Ps 10:1), and the assurance offered elsewhere that "God is our refuge and strength, a very present help in trouble" (46:1). Job, likewise, is in one moment confident that God is present and active, albeit in ways that are incomprehensible to Job—"Your hands fashioned and made me; and now you turn and destroy me" (Job 10:8)—while in the next he complains of God's absence: "Oh that I knew where I might find him, that I might come even to his dwelling! . . . If I go forward, he is not there; or backward, I cannot perceive him; on the left he hides, and I cannot behold him; I turn to the right but I cannot see him" (23:3, 8).

Notification of the Lord's absence often appears in the cry of those who suffer, as we have heard in the anguished lament of the psalmist and of Job; but it is not always so. Giving notice to the disciples of his forthcoming departure, Jesus, according to the report of John's Gospel, sets his own absence in a different context. He explains that, while the disciples cannot follow him now, his departure is to their own benefit. Jesus goes to "prepare a place" for them (John 13:33; 14:2). A little later he says, "it is to your advantage that I go away, for if I do not go away, the Advocate will not come to you; but if I go, I will send him to you" (16:7). In the foreground of this pronouncement lies Jesus' impending death—Jesus is speaking at the supper shared with his disciples before his arrest and crucifixion—but, especially in John's Gospel, Jesus presents his departure from the disciples as his ascension "to the Father," after which his disciples will see him no more (16:16-17). Ascension entails absence. While there is the promise of return (16:16; Acts 1:11), in the meantime—in this time between the times—Jesus is taken from the disciples' sight (Acts 1:9).

Reckoning with the absence of Christ marks this time between the times as an era of hope. That which is promised, that Christ will return and the kingdom of God will be complete, is not yet fulfilled. Therefore the church waits in hope for the coming of its Lord and Savior (1 Cor 4:5; Jas 5:7-8; Titus 2:13). It waits and works (Col 4:11) in hope and in prayerful anticipation of the coming kingdom of God. Here again it lives in that "strange contrast"

---

[2] It is again Karl Barth who speaks of the "strange contrast" between these texts. See *Credo*, 113.

between presence and absence, between a kingdom declared to be present already (Luke 11:20; 17:21) and one that is yet to come (Luke 11:2; 22:18). The New Testament's dual presentation of the kingdom of God as both a present reality and one still to come led the Princeton theologian Gerhardus Vos to coin the now-common expression, "already, but not yet."[3] While there has been much debate on the matter of the kingdom's present and/or future reality, there is no denying N. T. Wright's observation that "both elements are strongly present through the various strands of gospel tradition."[4] Wright himself repeatedly speaks of the future reality of the kingdom "breaking in" to the present.[5] The question asked of Jesus by the emissaries of John the Baptist, along with the answer given by Jesus, provides support for this conception of the relation between the future and the present.

> John summoned two of his disciples and sent them to the Lord to ask, "Are you the one who is to come, or are we to wait for another?" When the men had come to him they said, "John the Baptist has sent us to you to ask, 'Are you the one who is to come, or are we to wait for another?'" Jesus had just then cured many people of diseases, plagues and evil spirits, and had given sight to many who were blind. And he answered them, "Go and tell John what you have seen and heard: the blind receive their sight, the lame walk, the lepers are cleansed, the deaf hear, the dead are raised, the poor have good news brought to them. And blessed is anyone who takes no offense at me." (Luke 7:18-22; cf. Matt 11:2-5)

The form of John's question is the first point of interest here: "Are you [now present among us] the one who is to come?" John inquires about the possibility that a still-future eschatological reality—the coming of the Messiah who will usher in the kingdom of God—is happening already.[6] Jesus in reply invites John's disciples to consider the signs that are before them: the lame

---

[3] See Geerhardus Vos, *The Pauline Eschatology* (Grand Rapids: Eerdmans, 1952), 38–39.

[4] Wright, *Jesus and the Victory of God*, 467.

[5] See, e.g., Wright, *Jesus and the Victory of God*, 468, and, for another instance, Marcus J. Borg and N. T. Wright, *The Meaning of Jesus: Two Visions* (New York: HarperSanFrancisco, 1999), 37.

[6] There is some debate among New Testament scholars about precisely what is meant by the phrase "the one who is to come," but Matthew's immediately preceding reference to Jesus as the Messiah in his report of the episode (Matt 11:2) is sufficient basis for the point I am making here. W. G. Kümmel's suggestion with respect to the Lukan version of the episode, that "the Baptist appears here in no way as a witness to Christ, but as an uncertain questioner, which contradicts the tendency of the early Church to make him such a witness," appears to be rather too skeptical to me, especially in light of Matthew's gloss. See Kümmel,

walk, the blind see, and so on. These features of the longed-for *future* reign of God are indeed "breaking in" to the present. Here and elsewhere the gospels proclaim that "the eschaton announced by the prophets is not about to dawn; in the actions of Jesus it *has* dawned."[7] This "inauguration" of the eschatological reality remains, however, a foretaste of the coming kingdom, and not its full realization.[8]

Beyond the life-giving miracles that were taking place through the ministry of Jesus, the resurrection of Jesus from the dead presented a yet more compelling claim that the future eschatological reality had begun. Wolfhart Pannenberg has in recent years been the most prominent advocate of this view. "For Jesus' Jewish contemporaries," Pannenberg writes, "insofar as they shared the apocalyptic expectation, the occurrence of the resurrection did not first need to be interpreted, but for them it spoke meaningfully in itself: If such a thing had happened, one could no longer doubt what it meant."[9] "If Jesus had been raised," Pannenberg goes on to explain, "then the end of the world had begun."[10] Pannenberg resists, however, a fully realized eschatology. He writes:

> Only at the end of all events can God be revealed in his divinity, that is, as the one who works in all things, who has power over everything. Only because in Jesus' resurrection the end of all things, *which for us has not yet happened*, has already occurred can it be said of Jesus that the ultimate already is present in him, and so also that God himself, his glory, has made its appearance in Jesus in a way that cannot be surpassed.[11]

In his three-volume *Systematic Theology*, Pannenberg, who by the time of its publication between 1988 and 1993 had established his reputation even more firmly as an "eschatological theologian,"[12] repeats his assertion that the still-future reality of the kingdom of God has broken in to the present.

Promise and Fulfilment: The Eschatological Message of Jesus, Studies in Biblical Theology 23 (Naperville, Ill.: Allenson, 1957), 110.

[7] Eduard Schweizer, *The Good News according to Matthew* (London: SPCK, 1976), 256 (emphasis in original).

[8] There was a great deal of debate during the twentieth century about whether the New Testament presents a fully realized eschatology, an inaugurated eschatology, or an imminent eschatology. The second view guides the explorations of the present chapter.

[9] Wolfhart Pannenberg, *Jesus—God and Man*, trans. Lewis L. Wilkins and Duane A. Priebe (London: SCM Press, 1968), 67.

[10] Pannenberg, *Jesus—God and Man*, 67.

[11] Pannenberg, *Jesus—God and Man*, 69 (emphasis added).

[12] On which, see Iain Taylor, *Pannenberg on the Triune God* (London: T&T Clark, 2007), 164.

As already in his earthly proclamation Jesus prepared the way for the Lordship of God, so at his return the lordship of the risen Lord and its consummation will have as its only goal the definitive establishment of the kingdom of God. The kingdom of the Father whose imminence Jesus proclaimed on earth, and which broke in already in his work on earth, is indissolubly bound up with the Son and his work and will thus find its consummation when Jesus Christ returns in glory.[13]

Anticipation of the coming of Christ is a feature not just of Christian faith but also of Israel's hope. We will return below to the distinctively Jewish contention that the unredeemed appearance of the world confirms that the Messiah has not yet come. For the moment, though, I simply draw attention to John Calvin's conviction that the "ancient sacraments" of Israel, by which he meant circumcision, ablutions, sacrifices, and other rites, "referred to the same object towards which our [sacraments] are now directed, their design being to point and lead to Christ, or rather, as images, to represent and make him known."[14] "There is only one difference between those sacraments and ours," Calvin further explains: "they prefigured Christ as promised and still expected; ours represent him as already come and manifested."[15] By the same logic, "the shadows and types of the law, such as the daily sacrifices and the yearly festivals, combined in themselves this dialectic of presence and absence, as they offered to the faithful communion with the One who was not yet present among them."[16] Calvin recognizes, of course, that this dialectic of presence and absence continues in the celebration of the Christian sacraments.[17] Through the elements of the Eucharist, Calvin says, Christ is "in a manner present and in a manner absent."[18]

These brief forays into theological tradition will be sufficient, I hope, to show that within the traditions of Christian faith, those who venture to speak of God have commonly felt compelled to speak not only of divine presence but also of absence, not only of the manifestation of the reign of God in and through the person and work of Jesus, but also of a kingdom yet to

---

[13] Pannenberg, *Systematic Theology*, 3:608.

[14] John Calvin, *Institutes of the Christian Religion*, trans. John Allen (Philadelphia: Presbyterian Board of Christian Education, 1936), 4.14.20 (575–76).

[15] Calvin, *Institutes*, 4.14.20 (575–76).

[16] Randall Zachman, "Communio cum Christo," in *The Calvin Handbook*, ed. Herman J. Selderhuis (Grand Rapids: Eerdmans, 2009), 365–71, 368.

[17] On which, see Zachman, "Communio cum Christo," 368–69.

[18] The phrase is attributed to Calvin by James B. Torrance but without reference. See Torrance, *Worship, Community and the Triune God of Grace* (Downers Grove, Ill.: InterVarsity, 1996), 93.

come. It is this dialectic between presence and absence, between the already and the not yet, that constitutes the theme of this chapter.

Theology, Music, and Time

We may take a lead here from the work of Jeremy Begbie, who, in his remarkable book *Theology, Music and Time*, has already demonstrated that engagement with art can open up new ways of thinking about the subject matter of theology. Of particular interest is Begbie's discussion of the relation between present and future time. The difficulty of articulating precisely what time is has long been recognized, certainly since Augustine famously confessed that as long as no one asks him to define it, he knows what time is, but as soon as he is asked to explain it, he knows not.[19] With more confidence, however, Augustine declares that "the past now is not and the future is not as yet."[20] This conception of the relation among past, present, and future in which the past no longer exists and the future does not yet exist, leaving as real merely a fleeting present, seems unavoidable when one turns one's mind to the problem of time. Begbie shows that when music is considered it becomes possible to conceive time in such a way that "the present is no longer the 'saddle' between the two abysses of past and future, but rather that 'in which "now," "not yet," and "no more" are given together, in the most intimate penetration.'"[21]

Begbie illustrates this musical interpenetration of past, present, and future with numerous examples. Beethoven's last string quartet, opus 135, is one example, in which a dramatic cadence, normally to be interpreted as a "grand closing gesture," appears very early in the first movement. It is the very same cadence that will "(with minor modifications) bring the movement to completion."[22] The ending is here present almost at the beginning of the movement. The future is not merely anticipated but *is* now. In similar fashion, Begbie explains, "Christ's resurrection *concretely* anticipates *the* (final) resurrection of the new creation. Easter speaks of the establishment of a reality which is not simply anticipatory in the sense of shadow to substance, reflection to reality, but is a genuine instantiation of that which is to come."[23]

---

[19] See Augustine, *The "Confessions" of Saint Augustin*, 11.14.17 (*NPNF*, 1:168).

[20] Augustine, *Confessions*, 11.14.17 (*NPNF*, 1:168).

[21] Begbie, *Theology, Music and Time*, 63. The citation within the passage quoted here comes from Victor Zuckerkandl, *Sound and Symbol: Music and the External World*, trans. Willard R. Trask (London: Routledge & Kegan Paul, 1956), 227–28.

[22] Begbie, *Theology, Music and Time*, 115.

[23] Begbie, *Theology, Music and Time*, 115 (emphasis in original).

Begbie's illustrations of the interpenetration in music of past, present, and future render more intelligible the kinds of theological claims seen above, which speak of the future breaking in to the present and open up ways of thinking about God's involvement in history that are not easily conceivable within an Augustinian model of time in which the future is not yet real and the present is constantly slipping into the no-longer-existent past. Begbie's explorations of the fruitfulness of theological engagement with the phenomenon of music, both in *Theology, Music and Time* and through numerous others of his published works, are, of course, much richer and more extensive than I have been able to indicate here, but this brief excursion into Begbie's work provides an impetus to explore whether through engagement with the spatial arts, too, there might emerge new ways of thinking about the relation between presence and absence, the already and the not yet.

Acknowledging God

The arts involved in the shaping of our built environment are adept at negotiating the dialectic between presence and absence. Especially in buildings designed for worship, they have been called upon to give expression to the mystery of the God who is both immanent and yet also transcendent. There are, of course, inept ways to speak through the spatial arts of the presence of God. The Mosaic law warns against one such inept way by prohibiting the making of graven images (Exod 20:4, Deut 5:8). Although there are some difficulties in determining the reasons for the prohibition, the presumption, evident in the fashioning of the golden calf (Exod 32:1), that we are able to "make gods" worthy of worship is clearly rebuked by the divine command. It is idolatrous to "worship" (Exod 32:8) before something that we have made rather than in grateful praise of the Creator who has made us.[24] The making of graven images misconstrues the nature of divine presence precisely by attempting to set bounds upon it and thereby making God available on our terms rather than his own.[25] To adapt Heidegger slightly but preserve his insight, idols also represent the failure both to recognize the signs of God's absence and to wait for intimations of his coming.[26] God rebukes all such

---

[24] Brevard Childs has detailed these difficulties in his fine work *Exodus* (London: SCM Press, 1974), 404–9.

[25] Martin Noth suggests that the making of images could be construed as an attempt to gain power over God. See Noth, *Exodus*, trans. J. S. Bowden (London: SCM Press, 1962), 162–63.

[26] See Heidegger, "Building, Dwelling, Thinking," in *Poetry, Language, Thought*, 150.

efforts, and we return emptyhanded from all endeavors to grasp at the divine. A Mosaic instruction in Deuteronomy provides a further reminder that the genuine presence of God, as apprehended by Israel, provides no warrant for the making of images: "You heard the sound of words but saw no form; there was only a voice" (Deut 4:12). "Since you saw no form," Moses continues, "take care and watch yourselves closely, so that you do not act corruptly by making an idol for yourselves" (Deut 4:15).

While the making of graven images denies the transcendence of God by striving to *capture* the mystery of divine being in artifacts, artisans are called to participate nevertheless, along with all the endeavors of human culture, in the grateful *acknowledgment* of divine presence. Failure to acknowledge the presence of God is, on David Bentley Hart's telling, the defining failure of modernity. In insisting upon "the absolute liberty of personal volition,"[27] modernity nihilistically asserts

> the unreality of any "value" higher than choice, or of any transcendent Good ordering desire toward a higher end. Desire is free to propose, seize, accept or reject, want or not want—but not to obey. Thus society must be secured against the intrusions of the Good, or of God, so that its citizens may determine their own lives by the choices they make from a universe of morally indifferent but variably desirable ends unencumbered by any prior grammar of obligation or value.[28]

Contrary to the idolatry that cannot tolerate divine absence and to the nihilism that cannot live with divine presence, Christian faith seeks obediently to acknowledge the God who is both immanent and transcendent, present yet beyond our grasp, already but not yet. How then might this obedient acknowledgement be expressed through the spatial arts, and in what ways might they help us to expound theological truth?

Beyond Chaos

The first of the biblical creation stories, from Genesis 1:1 to 2:4, "is commonly assigned to the Priestly tradition, which means," as Walter Brueggemann explains, "that it is addressed to a community of exiles."[29] It is addressed,

---

[27] David Bentley Hart, "God or Nothingness," in *I Am the Lord Your God: Christian Reflections on the Ten Commandments*, ed. Carl E. Braaten and Christopher R. Seitz (Grand Rapids: Eerdmans, 2005), 56–76, 55.

[28] Hart, "God or Nothingness," in Braaten and Seitz, *I Am the Lord Your God*, 55–56.

[29] Brueggemann, *Genesis*, 22.

that is, to a people who have been battered and scattered by conquest and whose world is in utter disarray. First in 597 B.C. and then more extensively in 586 B.C., the military forces of the Babylonian king Nebuchadnezzar had rampaged through Judah leaving a trail of destruction and scattering the people, many of whom had been forced into exile in Babylon. The crisis was political and social, but it was also theological. Jerusalem, too, had been destroyed and with it the temple, the place above all where Israel acknowledged and celebrated God's good ordering of things and his covenant love for the world. Israel's defeat brought with it a crisis of faith. Where is God in the face of this devastation? The evidence speaks only of God's absence.

The story of Genesis 1:1—2:4 is a proclamation, a confession, within the midst of this chaos that there is an order established by God, an order that in the best of times is seen and understood only in part and in the worst of times seems to be obscured altogether. According to the opening chapters of Genesis, God's good ordering of creation and God's benevolent rule over all things is present even in the midst of Israel's devastation and holds within it the promise that God's rule throughout creation will bring peace and restoration in the end. The text enjoins faith in the God who in the beginning brought order from chaos, who separated night from day, who brought forth dry land from the swirling waters, who called forth from the land plants bearing fruit, and so established a place suitable for human habitation. God saw that it was good—good for his creatures and good for the realization of his purpose that all creatures should flourish and live together in covenant relationship with him and with one another. These are not scientific or historical claims about how things happened at the origins of the universe; they are theological affirmations about the world having being established by God and ordered to God's good purpose. Brueggemann explains further:

> The main theme of the text is this: God and God's creation are bound together in a distinctive and delicate way. This is the presupposition for everything that follows in the Bible. It is the deepest premise from which good news is possible. God and his creation are bound together by the powerful, gracious movement of God towards that creation. The binding which is established by God is inscrutable. It will not be explained or analyzed. It can only be affirmed and confessed. This text announces the deepest mystery: God wills and will have a faithful relation with the earth. The text invites the listening community to celebrate that reality.[30]

[30] Brueggemann, *Genesis*, 23–24.

The story with which the Bible begins, and with which it continues, is an acknowledgement and also a proclamation that, all evidence to the contrary notwithstanding, the world has an order and an intelligibility that is divinely bestowed and divinely upheld. Despite the disruptions of human sin, despite the disruptions caused by humanity's efforts to foist upon the world an order of its own making,[31] God upholds the order of the world, keeps it in being, and remains faithful to his promise that in the end all the families of the earth will be blessed (Gen 12:2).

The acknowledgement of order manifest in the biblical narrative is not unique to the Jewish and Christian traditions, of course, although there are certainly unique and profoundly important aspects to the biblical construal of the matter. I have suggested in chapter 2 that the building of altars by Abraham and his descendants was a means of marking in the landscape the coordinates of an emerging conception of divine order and purpose; likewise in other cultures spatial means were developed of recognizing and marking an order that was given in the nature of things rather than imposed. Axial systems have played an especially important role in testifying to such an order. Cynthia Jara explains:

> For thousands of years, crossed axes have served to symbolize the understanding that men and women have of their relationship to nature and the universe. In ancient Egypt, for example, where the Nile river, coinciding with the north-south direction, was daily crossed by the east-west path of the sun, axial planning permeated building design. But it was the Romans who institutionalized the cosmic significance of crossed axes by assigning them roles that were explicitly sacred. The Romans considered the north-south axis, which they called the *cardo*, to be the primary axis. The *cardo* was designated the axis of the world. The east-west axis naturally represented the passage of the sun; it was called the *decumanus* Roman building sites were always consecrated by a priest who identified the *cardo* and *decumanus* as crossing at the center, or focal point, of the site.[32]

---

[31] These efforts of humanity to foist upon the world an order of its own making are evident in myriad ways, especially in environmental degradation, political unrest, racial prejudice, and economic inequality, to name just a few, and in the many ill effects these manifestations of sin inflict upon God's creatures.

[32] Cynthia Jara, "Adolf Loos's 'Raumplan' Theory," *Journal of Architectural Education* 48, no. 3 (1995): 185–201, 187. Jara cites Norberg-Schulz as her authority for these claims, particularly Norberg-Schulz's *Intentions in Architecture* (Oslo: Oslo University Press, 1963), and *Existence, Space and Architecture* (New York: Praeger, 1971).

The priest who consecrated the building sites of ancient Rome and identified the crossing point of the *cardo* and *decumanus* was not identifying some tangible object that marked the center or focal point of the site. There was nothing noteworthy there. Rather, the priestly function of establishing a center and marking the spot expresses the conviction that the world itself is ordered in such a way as to require acknowledgement and obedience. That which has no location as such, and in that respect is absent, has nevertheless to be acknowledged, for it gives order and intelligibility to the world and renders it suitable for human habitation. The building to be erected in a particular location testifies and is oriented to that which has no particular location but undergirds and sustains all things.

Cardinal relationships have been, arguably, the single most important consideration in the generation of architectural form, isolated attempts to escape them notwithstanding. The importance of cardinal relationships in architecture is evident in the widely adopted cruciform plan of churches, beginning with the addition of transepts to the ancient Roman basilica and then transferred through the Middle Ages to the Gothic form. Modern churches frequently repeat the well-established axial plan. The two axes, north-south and east-west, create a crossing over which, especially in the basilica form, a dome representing the heavenly realm is often raised. St Paul's Cathedral in London exemplifies the form. The cruciform plan, most evident at ground level, reminds the Christian worshipper of the immanence of God in the person of Christ and of his or her call to participate in the cruciform pattern of Christ's life. The vertical scale of the architecture, meanwhile, especially of the dome, dwarfs the human figure at ground level, encourages those within the church building to lift their eyes heavenward, and so reminds them of the transcendence of God.

The generative and symbolic power of axial relationships is evident not only in the architecture of churches and other public buildings but also in domestic architecture. Cynthia Jara points to the example of the Rufer House designed by Viennese architect Adolf Loos and built in 1922. Loos had formulated a theory of design that became known as *raumplan*. Sometimes translated as "spatial planning," Loos' *raumplan* theory allegedly emphasized spatial planning in three dimensions rather than allowing the volume of architectural form to be determined merely by the vertical extrusion of a two dimensional plan.[33] Jara modifies this proposal, however, through appeal

---

[33] I take the point from Paul Vonberg's post "adolf loos's villa müller, prague," in the architecture blog, February 23, 2014.

to Martin Heidegger's ruminations in "Building, Dwelling Thinking," and especially to Heidegger's notion of "presencing," which, according to Jara, Heidegger uses to describe "the process through which reality is both recognised and understood."[34] Presencing requires "a place of refuge that allows for clearing, reflection and rebuilding."[35] Heidegger himself speaks of "setting something free within its own presencing." This combination of ideas leads Jara to propose an interpretive key for Loos' *raumplan* houses; namely, that of "setting free, or unfolding, within a boundary."[36]

Loos himself never produced a treatise explaining the principles of his spatial planning, so we are left to identify those principles, partially from the writings of his disciples but more importantly, from the buildings themselves.[37] It is through extensive study of the buildings themselves that Jara has identified "a striking feature of all Loos' *raumplan* projects: the pair of orthogonally disposed axes that characterise the underlying order of the houses."[38] The earlier expositors of *raumplan*, Ludwig Münz and Gustav Künstler, had recognized that "there must be a meaningful center of the house, around which individual rooms must be grouped,"[39] but, says Jara, "the idea of a focal point within the house is accepted here only as a useful given; the modernist interpretation does not question the origin of centering in *raumplan*."[40] Jara, however, considers that there is more to it than that.

The center of Loos' Rufer House—and here we speak of the generative "center" of the architecture rather than the geometrical center of the floor plan—is marked by a square column. Although it has a structural function, "as a paradigm, it lacks the technical force of, for example, Le Corbusier's *Dom-ino* scheme.[41] . . . Neither does Rufer's column have the experiential impact of centering which, by contrast, Frank Lloyd Wright achieves when

[34] Jara, "Adolf Loos's 'Raumplan' Theory," 190.

[35] Jara, "Adolf Loos's 'Raumplan' Theory," 191.

[36] Jara, "Adolf Loos's 'Raumplan' Theory," 192.

[37] Jara identifies two "followers" in particular who attempted to explain the principles of *raumplan*: Heinrich Kulka and Ludwig Münz. Gustav Künstler's 1964 monograph on Loos provided further explanation based on extensive archival research. For the details, see Jara, "Adolf Loos's 'Raumplan' Theory," 185. Jara herself contests the interpretations provided by these early expositors.

[38] Jara, "Adolf Loos's 'Raumplan' Theory," 186.

[39] Ludwig Münz and Gustav Künstler, *Adolf Loos: A Pioneer of Modern Architecture* (New York: Praeger, 1966), 140. Cited in Jara, "Adolf Loos's 'Raumplan' Theory," 187.

[40] Jara, "Adolf Loos's 'Raumplan' Theory," 187.

[41] The Maison Dom-Ino was designed by Le Corbusier in 1914 and was intended as a prototype for mass-produced housing. Its defining elements were a series of horizontal slabs supported by a series of slender columns and connected by a zigzagging stair.

he focuses on the hearth as the center of the house."[42] Failing to impress as a vital structural element or as a center, the Rufer column, placed at the intersection of the two axes around which the house is planned, serves as "a particularly effective grounding mechanism."[43] There is here a resemblance to the vertical axis in the Pantheon:

> Speaking about the oculus in the dome of this ancient Roman temple, Norberg-Schulz argues convincingly that the vertical axis bears spiritual connotations because the imagery it generates connects the idea of human standing on the earth with the idea of heavenly aspiration.[44]

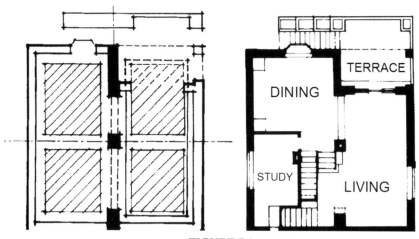

FIGURE 7.1

Rufer House, showing the development of the first floor plan from the quadripartite structure established by the crossed axes and the central column.

Where is the theological interest in all of this? Reference to the "heavenly aspiration" expressed in architecture is not the main point here. Such aspiration is commonplace and commonly understood. More important, first of all, is the representation in architecture of an order that has no concrete presence. It is not available to us as an object in the room. Second, however, and here is the key point, we may observe in the Rufer House the ways in which what actually *takes place* through the architectural form is obedient to that order. As in architecture, so in theology, the order—or let us say now, with more theological resonance, the *Logos*—that has no concrete presence among

[42] Jara, "Adolf Loos's 'Raumplan' Theory," 187.

[43] Jara, "Adolf Loos's 'Raumplan' Theory," 187.

[44] Jara, "Adolf Loos's 'Raumplan' Theory," 187. The source referred to here is Christian Norberg-Schulz, *Meaning in Western Architecture* (New York: Rizzoli, 1980), 51–52.

us in this time between ascension and parousia is revealed in the world just insofar as what takes place in worship, in mission, and in loving service is obedient to the Logos who calls us to abide in him.

Cynthia Jara explains that the ordering principle of the Rufer House is determined by the establishment of a square perimeter: "A quadripartite division of this square is implied through the placement of the central column."[45] The planning proceeds first to the placement of the living room, the most important room in the house. The living room occupies two of the quadrants but retracts slightly at one end to allow an exterior terrace and stair to connect the living room to the garden.

> The next room to emerge out of the *raumplan* is the dining room, second in importance only to the living room. Based on the link between communal living and the social rituals associated with eating, it makes sense that the dining room would be closely related to the living room. In fact, Loos literally draws space out of the larger room, pulling it back around the column . . . The remaining quadrant—the fourth—is reserved for the owner's private study . . . Due to the relatively modest square-footage requirements of this private room, however, the quadrant is amenable to retraction and erosion when, for example, the stairs from below require access to the public rooms on the main floor or when a foyerlike space, negotiating transit to the dining room and ultimately the bedrooms above is needed adjacent to the living room.[46]

Jara explains how the ordering principle established by the crossed axes and central column generates further aspects of the plan. She also notes how the central column itself participates in a number of distinct assemblies.

> From the front half of the living room, the column acts as one jamb of the entry portal, whereas from the back half of the living room it completes a frame that brackets the flow of space into the dining room. Within the living room, the column anchors an enclosing perimeter that serves a unifying function. From the area immediately outside the living room, at the head of the stairs coming up from the floor below, the column engages with a short run of steps and the adjacent ledge to form an entry into the dining room.[47]

---

[45] Jara, "Adolf Loos's 'Raumplan' Theory," 191. The illustration used here was drawn by Julie Oseid and is reproduced in Jara, "Adolf Loos's 'Raumplan' Theory," 196. The copyright is held by Cynthia Jara who, has kindly granted permission to reproduce the drawing in this volume. I have added the text to identify the rooms, again with permission.

[46] Jara, "Adolf Loos's 'Raumplan' Theory," 192.

[47] Jara, "Adolf Loos's 'Raumplan' Theory," 196.

We noted earlier Jara's contention that the central column in the Rufer House may be interpreted according to the well-established pattern of vertical axes having "spiritual connotations" because they generate an imagery that "connects the idea of human standing on the earth with the idea of heavenly aspiration." The location of the column at the crossing point of intersecting axes further recalls the once-conventional practice of a priest determining the cardinal relationships on a building site so that the building to be constructed there could follow the order established by the axes and so conform to and reveal the sacred order established in the universe. I observed further that in theology as in architecture, the Logos through whom all things came to be (John 1:3) is made known in the world just insofar as what takes place in the world is obedient to that Logos. To follow this analogy further, Jara's demonstration of the ways in which the central column in the Rufer House participates in a number of distinct assemblies viewed from different perspectives reminds us that in theology, too, we must attend to the multiple ways in which the divine Logos is revealed in the world. The Logos may be apprehended, but is never fully comprehended, from a vast range of viewing points. The divine Logos made flesh, upon whom the order and intelligibility of the world originally and finally depends, resists assimilation to any singular theological assembly. That is plainly evident in the New Testament itself; four gospels, numerous christological titles, multiple ways of speaking about the atonement, the multifaceted employment of Old Testament reference pressed into the service of bearing witness to the coming of Christ—all confirm the inadequacy of any singular perspective, or any single way of speaking. They remind us that our theological speech, along with our comprehension of the reality with which we are concerned in theology, is incomplete on its own, and is therefore in need of enrichment and expansion by the insights afforded by other points of view. Yet the possibilities for true apprehension of the reality with which we are concerned are not limitless or unconstrained. They constitute a faithful witness only insofar as they are obedient to what is given—obedient, that is, to the Logos in and through whom all things have been created and in whom all things hold together (Col 1:15-16). Further comparison may be made here with the ways in which architecture reveals an ordering principle. As Jara observes, "Even though a design scheme can become tangible only through the gathering of things, the mere assembly of elements is meaningless unless directed by the scheme."[48]

---

[48] Jara, "Adolf Loos's 'Raumplan' Theory," 199.

One more observation may be made, prompted by the way in which Adolf Loos' *raumplan* theory finds expression in the architecture of the Rufer House. In and of itself, the *raumplan* theory is an abstract notion that, as noted earlier, was never actually described by Loos in a formal treatise. It is an idea not available to us except as it becomes incarnate in the built form. Wherever the logic of the *raumplan* does take concrete form, however, a *lebensraum* is created, a hospitable and a joyous place for the living of human life. John's Gospel likewise attributes both the possibility of life and our recognition of its goodness and order not to some abstract philosophical speculation but to the incarnation, to the becoming flesh, of the Logos. "What has come into being in him was life," John declares (John 1:4). God establishes in Christ a *lebensraum* for the creature. The life given by God can be lived in its fullness, John's Gospel explains, only as we learn to dwell in Christ (John 15:4-5). Conformity to the reality established in Christ is our Christian calling. It is properly understood not as a call to create for ourselves a new place to dwell, but rather as a call to live in obedience to the reality already given. Gerhard Sauter thus speaks of our having been "inserted into the hidden history of Jesus Christ in the world. That *is* the living space in which our human history is 'located' and 'takes place.' "[49]

Present and Yet Still to Come

Our explorations above call for the existence of a community that will bear witness through the form and content of its own life to the risen and ascended Christ. It is of course the people gathered into the community of Christ's body who seek to be obedient to the divine Word once made flesh among them; who attend to that Word through their reading of Scripture, preaching, and prayer; who remember his death in eucharistic celebration; who acknowledge through baptism the life given in Christ; and who look forward to Christ's coming again. Precisely through these actions, enabled by the Spirit, the Church seeks to be a witness to Christ's rule over and his upholding of all things. Yet the anticipatory character of Christian existence is not the full story. Even as it looks forward to his coming again, the people seeking to be obedient to the rule of Christ speak of his presence in the world even now. This "time between the times" is an era in which the Church feels bound to speak of absence and yet also of presence. It feels bound to speak not only of the Christ whose return is still awaited and of a kingdom yet

---

[49] Gerhard Sauter, *Eschatological Rationality: Theological Issues in Focus* (Grand Rapids: Baker, 1996), 197 (emphasis in original).

to come but also of that same Christ being present already and exercising already his kingly rule among us.[50] What sense can be made of this dual witness to the presence and the absence of Christ?

The braided tradition of Christian theological reflection reveals two basic ways of getting this wrong, the first involving such stress upon the presence of Christ and his already-present kingdom that the reality of Christ's absence and the as yet unfulfilled nature of the kingdom is obscured. The second misconstrual consists in placing such stress upon the absence of Christ and his kingly rule that the intimations Christ himself gave of a kingdom begun in and through his own ministry are not taken seriously enough. The former tendency appears in a number of variants. We may detect it, for instance, in triumphal ecclesiologies that suppose the kingly rule of Christ is concentrated wholly in the hands of the church on earth. *Unam Sanctam*, the papal bull issued in 1302 by Pope Boniface, veers toward this extreme in its assertion of the superiority of ecclesial over secular rule and its enjoining of total obedience to the pope. The Second Vatican Council of the Roman Catholic Church moderated this triumphalist ecclesiology and instead portrayed the church as a pilgrim people of God, still journeying toward its God-appointed goal.[51] Whereas *Unam Sanctam* had referred to the "Church without blemish or wrinkle,"[52] the Second Vatican Council spoke of "a certain though imperfect communion."[53] The overstatement of Christ's presence and kingly rule evident in *Unam Sanctam* is not the preserve of the Catholic Church, however. The tendency has appeared in Protestant traditions, too. The Lutheran tradition, for example, has been inclined at times to identify the risen and ascended Christ wholly with the church. Dietrich Bonhoeffer's promotion of the claim that the church is "Christ existing as community" and that "Christ himself 'is' the church,"[54] is a notable instance. This Lutheran tendency runs the risk of obscuring the proper distinction between Christ and his church

---

[50] It should be noted here that, as G. C. Berkouwer has put it, "The church's expectation of the return of Jesus Christ has always been closely associated with the second petition of the Lord's prayer—'Thy Kingdom come.'" Berkouwer, *Studies in Dogmatics: The Return of Christ*, trans. James van Oosterom (Grand Rapids: Eerdmans, 1972), 424.

[51] I take the point from Paul Avis, *Reshaping Ecumenical Theology: The Church Made Whole* (London: T&T Clark, 2010), 46.

[52] Cited in Heiko Oberman, *The Reformation: Roots and Ramifications* (London: T&T Clark, 2004), 134.

[53] W. M. Abbott, ed., *The Documents of Vatican II* (London: Geoffrey Chapman, 1966), 345. Cited in Avis, *Reshaping Ecumenical Theology*, 46.

[54] Dietrich Bonhoeffer, *Sanctorum Communio: A Theological Study of the Sociology of the Church* (London: Collins, 1963), 115 and passim.

and underplaying, thereby, Christ's absence. Among Lutheran theologians who defend the notion of the identity of Christ with his church, Robert Jenson recognizes the danger: "If we only say that the church is personally identical with Christ, it may seem that the church can never need reform or be open to it."[55] We need not pursue here the question of whether Jenson's account of the ontological identity between the church and Christ's risen human body successfully avoids the danger to which he alerts us.[56] It is sufficient to note again the danger of so stressing Christ's presence that the reality of his absence is obscured. On the Catholic side, Rudolf Schnackenberg encourages a renewed appreciation of the difference between the church and the kingdom,[57] while Hans Küng warns against "the idealization of the church" and advises that "the people of God, the Church, is not the same as the community of the elect in the consummated kingdom of God."[58] Again from a Catholic perspective, Douglas Farrow advises of the need to recognize the absence as well as the presence of Christ in and with his church:

> Without adequate recognition of the real absence of Christ, the church itself has no real absence; knowledge of his presence renders it prone to self-glorifying and to illusions of worldly power, to making martyrs of others rather than walking the path of martyrdom itself. Without the real presence of Christ, on the other hand, the church has no real presence either. It is not sufficiently potent in or against the world; it falls prey first to sectarianism, then to Erastianism.[59]

A further variant upon the tendency to stress the presence of Christ and his kingdom while paying insufficient attention to their absence is the "realised eschatology" evident in, for instance, the English New Testament scholar C. H. Dodd (1884–1973). While acknowledging that Israel considered the kingdom of God to be a future reality and that this future orientation still appears in places in the New Testament, Dodd contends that those sayings of Jesus that declare the kingdom to have already come are "the

[55] Robert W. Jenson, *Systematic Theology*, vol. 2, *The Works of God* (New York: Oxford University Press, 1999), 213.

[56] For discussion of this question, see Colin E. Gunton, *Father, Son and Holy Spirit: Toward a Fully Trinitarian Theology* (London: T&T Clark, 2003), 219–21.

[57] I owe the point to Pannenberg, *Systematic Theology*, 3:35–36. Pannenberg refers us to Rudolf Schnackenburg's *God's Rule and Kingdom* (New York: Herder & Herder, 1963).

[58] Hans Küng, *The Church*, trans. Ray Ockenden and Rosaleen Ockenden (London: SCM Press, 1968), 131.

[59] Douglas Farrow, *Ascension Theology* (London: T&T Clark, 2011), 70.

most characteristic and distinctive of the Gospel sayings on the subject."[60] Accordingly, Dodd continues, Jesus' declaration "that the Kingdom of God has already come dislocates the whole eschatological scheme in which its expected coming closes the long vista of the future. The *eschaton* has moved from the future to the present, from the sphere of expectation into that of realized experience."[61] What remains to be fulfilled is simply the universal recognition of God's rule. This is the content of Christian hope.

Against this confidence that the kingdom of God has already come, the Jewish objection remains strong. Martin Buber puts it thus:

> We know more deeply, more truly, that world history has not been turned upside down to its very foundations—that the world is not yet redeemed. We *sense* its unredeemedness. The church can, or indeed must, understand this sense of ours as the awareness that *we* are not redeemed. But we know that that is not it. The redemption of the world is for us indivisibly one with the perfecting of creation, with the establishment of the unity which nothing more prevents, the unity which is no longer controverted, and which is realized in all the protean variety of the world. Redemption is one with the kingdom of God in its fulfillment. An anticipation of any single part of the *completed* redemption of the world . . . is something we cannot grasp, although even for us in our mortal hours redeeming and redemption are heralded. . . . We are aware of no centre in history—only its goal, the goal of the way taken by the God who does not linger on his way.[62]

One cannot responsibly contend, Buber argues on behalf of his fellow Jews, that the redemptive rule of God's Messiah has already come when all about us the victims of genocide cry out from the grave. The gas chambers of Nazi Germany, among many other examples, testify that the world still suffers under the rule of powers that are hostile to the purposes of God. It is evident that the redeemer has not yet come, Buber contends, because the world is not yet redeemed. To say otherwise is an offense to the brutally murdered and the gassed whether in the concentration camps of the Third Reich or in the

---

[60] C. H. Dodd, *The Parables of the Kingdom*, rev. ed. (London: Nisbet, 1936), 49.

[61] Dodd, *Parables*, 50.

[62] Martin Buber, *Der Jude und sein Judentum: Gesammelte Aufsätze und Reden* (Cologne: L. Schneider, 1963), 562, cited in Jürgen Moltmann, *The Way of Jesus Christ: Christology in Messianic Dimensions*, trans. Margaret Kohl (London: SCM Press, 1990), 28–29 (emphasis in original). See also Martin Buber, "The Two Foci of the Jewish Soul," in Buber, *Israel and the World: Essays in a Time of Crisis* (New York: Schocken Books, 1963), 28–40. For an informed discussion of Buber's view by a contemporary Jewish theologian, see Michael Kogan, *Opening the Covenant: A Jewish Theology of Christianity* (Oxford: Oxford University Press, 2007), 90–95.

numerous "killing fields" that continue to leave deep scars on human history. According to this evidence, the kingly rule of the redeemer is not present with us yet.

The conviction that the kingdom of God is entirely a future reality is also to be found in the Christian tradition. It was propounded in the late nineteenth century by Johannes Weiss and then taken up by Albert Schweitzer; both rejected the claim made by such as Albrecht Ritschl that the kingdom of God was essentially a moral program already being worked out through human endeavor. Weiss insisted that Jesus proclaimed an apocalyptic kingdom that was still to come.[63] Schweitzer agreed but also contended that Jesus' expectation was not realized; his expectation that such a kingdom was imminent went unfulfilled.[64] The insistence within the Christian tradition that the kingdom is entirely a future reality with no trace yet to be found among us is represented most prominently today by those holding a dispensationalist view of history. Dispensationalists contend that there are seven distinct periods of God's dealings with humanity and that "the seventh dispensation, the millennium, will be inaugurated by the return of Christ in two stages: first, a secret rapture which removes the church before the great tribulation devastates the earth, and second, Christ's coming with the church to establish the kingdom."[65] Such a view of the coming kingdom entails that we live in the meantime in a period of unremitting absence. Christ has not returned and the kingdom is not yet. Another variant of this total stress upon the absence of Christ appears in the medieval church's sometimes Platonic construal of the risen and ascended Christ's presence with the Father where he is at work "building up the heavenly Church, the earthly Church being merely a reflection of heavenly realities."[66]

Between the "realized" eschatology that stresses the presence of the kingdom of God and the "futurist" eschatology that stresses its absence, advocates of "inaugurated" eschatology seek to do justice to those sayings of Jesus that indicate the present reality of the kingdom "around and within you," while also respecting those New Testament texts that present the return of Christ

---

[63] See Johannes Weiss, *Jesus' Proclamation of the Kingdom of God* (Philadelphia: Fortress, 1971)

[64] See Albert Schweitzer, *The Quest of the Historical Jesus*, trans. W. Montgomery, 3rd ed. (London: SCM Press, 1981), 356–57.

[65] Robert C. Clouse, "Fundamentalist Theology," in *The Oxford Handbook of Eschatology*, ed. Jerry L. Walls (Oxford: Oxford University Press, 2008), 263–79, 264. Dispensationalist theology has been popularized by authors such as Hal Lindsay and Tim LaHaye.

[66] I take the point from Dietrich Ritschl, *Memory and Hope: An Enquiry Concerning the Presence of Christ* (New York: Macmillan, 1967), 21.

and the kingdom of God as realities yet to come. Inaugurated eschatology, as indicated in the opening pages of this chapter, is the view that the kingdom of God has "broken in" to the present in and through the life, death, and resurrection of Jesus Christ but that its full realization remains a matter of Christian hope.

While we are accustomed to thinking about the Christian hope in terms of time, there is merit in considering the "nearness" of the kingdom of God, which Jesus announces in Mark 1:15 also in spatial terms. Paul Fiddes has pointed out that the future that is hoped for in Christian imagination is a future characterized by the "fullness of divine presence, expressed in Christian tradition as the 'beatific vision,' in biblical terms as the 'dwelling' of God with his people, and in rabbinic texts as the Shekinah-presence of God."[67] The book of Revelation looks forward to a new heaven and a new earth and declares that "the home of God is among mortals" (Rev 21:3). Fiddes contends that this "human desire for fullness of presence takes symbolic form . . . in the desire for a 'place' or a 'space' to be."[68] This spatial representation of God's coming rule is evident, for example, in Martin Luther King's final speech before his death:

> Well, I don't know what will happen now. We've got some difficult days ahead. But it doesn't matter with me now. Because I've been to the mountaintop. And I don't mind. Like anybody, I would like to live a long life. Longevity has its place. But I'm not concerned about that now. I just want to do God's will. And He's allowed me to go up to the mountain. And I've looked over. And I've seen the promised land. I may not get there with you. But I want you to know tonight, that we, as a people, will get to the promised land. And I'm happy, tonight. I'm not worried about anything. I'm not fearing any man. Mine eyes have seen the glory of the coming of the Lord![69]

The "promised land" represents a political vision that King powerfully articulated on many occasions, but the vision of a promised land is clearly theological as well as political; the hope that one day there will be a place to flourish, a place in which the abundant life intended by God from the beginning will be realized in full, is associated explicitly in King's speech with "the coming of the Lord."

---

[67] Paul Fiddes, *The Promised End: Eschatology in Theology and Literature* (Oxford: Blackwell, 2000), 220.

[68] Fiddes, *Promised End*, 221.

[69] Martin Luther King, speech delivered in Memphis on April 3, 1968, reproduced in Keith D. Miller, *Martin Luther King's Biblical Epic: His Final, Great Speech* (Jackson: University Press of Mississippi, 2012), 182.

Fiddes finds a parallel to this spatial representation of Christian hope in secular visions of Utopia:

> The social world imagined in a Utopia provides a critique of the status quo in current society, and disturbs existing structures with what Bloch called a "real-possible." . . . The Utopia [which] is—literally—a "No-Place" because it is a "not-yet-place" . . . pictures a place in which the self is fully present to itself (knowing itself) and to its environment (being at home in the world). . . . As Karl Mannheim puts it, a Utopia is the projection of human yearnings into space.[70]

There are, of course, some very important differences between secular visions of Utopia and biblical visions of the kingdom of God, not least in the characteristic tendency of the biblical visions to challenge and transform the desires of the human heart, but they have in common nevertheless the desire, or the hope, for "a place or a space to be," as Fiddes has put it. Because that desire is also the central concern of architecture, let us see whether architecture can help us once more to explore the theological dialectic between presence and absence, between present reality and future hope. The proposal to be explored here is that the three-dimensional topography of space provides opportunities within the spatial arts to recognize the interpenetration of our present reality with that which remains distant from us as yet. This three-dimensional topography can generate fresh ways of conceiving the relation between presence and absence.

A Room with a View

One of the most visited buildings on the tourist trail in New Zealand is a small stone church on the shore of Lake Tekapo. The form of the church is far from unique. It is of a type that can be seen in numerous places throughout the world, especially in Great Britain, from which church architecture in New Zealand has most often taken its inspiration. The external form of the church, built from local stone and set in a dramatic alpine landscape, is certainly photogenic, but the particular renown of the church is due to the view from within. From their position in the pews, conventionally arranged to face an altar at the front of the church, the congregation looks outward through a plate glass window to the lake and mountains beyond. A simple cross standing on the window sill appears in silhouette at the center of the scene.

---

[70] Fiddes, *Promised End*, 223.

FIGURE 7.2
Church of the Good Shepherd, Lake Tekapo

FIGURE 7.3
Church of the Good Shepherd, Interior

The Church of the Good Shepherd provides a particularly dramatic instance of what is common in architecture: it draws attention to a relation between the immanent and the transcendent while also distinguishing between them. George Steiner in his book *Real Presences* contends that "it is the enterprise and privilege of the aesthetic to quicken into lit presence the continuum between temporality and eternity, between matter and spirit, between man and the 'other.'"[71] The "other" is not fully comprehended, but

---

[71] George Steiner, *Real Presences* (London: Faber & Faber, 1989), 227.

neither is it absent. In the case of the reality seen through the window at the Church of the Good Shepherd, the viewer knows that the distant reality is neither captured nor confined by the window frame, but the architecture enables a unique apprehension of the reality beyond.

We see as well in this example one way in which the character of a place can be determined in no small measure by that which lies beyond it. That which is remote, beyond the bounds of our present location, is brought near by the architectural framing of the view and has a powerful impact upon one's experience of the present location. Those who testify to the sacredness of the church at Lake Tekapo are prompted to do so, I suggest, because the architecture fosters a sense of interpenetration between here and there, between that which is present and that which is at a distance. The small cross, a symbol of Christ, stands at the intersection of the viewers' imma-nent reality and that which lies beyond. Christ is in his own person the intersection of the temporal and the eternal, of that which is immediate and that which yet remains at a distance. The point of particular importance, however, is the impact made upon the place presently inhabited by a reality that remains at a distance. The character of the location described by the four walls of the church is profoundly transformed by its relation to that which lies beyond. Douglas Farrow considers such interpenetration to be a feature of John's Gospel. John tells the story of Christ's ministry as though the effects of his ascension are retroactive. "In John," Farrow writes, "the one who will ascend speaks and acts as if he has already done so; his descending and ascending somehow interpenetrate, so that the latter recapitulates and lends power to the former."[72] That which is yet to come has begun already to transform the present.

The capacity of architecture to express the interpenetration of the imme-diate and the remote, in a way that is suggestive of the presence among us of the God who is above and beyond all things, is likewise apparent in the following conversation between the American architect Louis Kahn (1901–1974) and Mexican architect Luis Barragan (1902–1988). Kahn writes:

> Once we had breakfast in Mexico City. We talked about a commission he [Barragan] was just offered to design a religious place in the heart of a large

---

[72] Douglas Farrow, *Ascension and Ecclesia: On the Significance of the Doctrine of Ascen-sion for Ecclesiology and Christian Cosmology* (Edinburgh: T&T Clark, 1999), 37. Farrow offers as examples of this interpenetration John 1:18, 3:13, and 13:3; and he cites in support of the point Karl-Joseph Kuschel, who refers to a "fusion" of the times. See Kuschel, *Born before All Time?: The Dispute over Christ's Origin*, trans. John Bowden (London: SCM Press, 1992), 384–86.

city in Texas. He explained how happy it made him to be offered such a trust, but also how let down he was when he saw the site surrounded by uninspired buildings. "I cannot," said he, "find a beginning. I am afraid that I must refuse." I reminded him of Independence Square which gained its significance from all structures around by simply being four feet above the level of the street and then asked, "If you were able to tear down the buildings on one side, revealing to the religious place a mountain range in the distance, would their silence inspire in you a beginning?"[73]

FIGURE 7.4
Jonas Salk Institute for Biological Studies

Barragan agreed that the opening up of such a horizon would indeed provide the basis for a building that could serve as a "religious place." The two architects recognize here that "religion" involves the interpenetration of the immanent and the transcendent, of the immediately present and that which is beyond. It is not simply in places intended to be religious, however, that Barragan and Kahn deemed acknowledgement of the transcendent to be appropriate. At Barragan's suggestion, Kahn left open the dramatic vista to the ocean and to the sky at the Jonas Salk Institute for Biological Studies in La Jolla, California, one of Kahn's most renowned works, rather than articulating the space as an inward-looking garden court. Kahn recalls Barragan's visit to the Salk Institute:

[73] Louis I. Kahn, *Writings, Lectures, Interviews*, ed. Alessandra Latour (New York: Rizzoli, 1991), 233.

> I asked Barragan to come to La Jolla and help me in the choice of planting
> for the garden to the Studies of the Salk Laboratory. When he entered the
> space he went to the concrete walls and touched them and expressed his love
> for them, and then said as he looked across the space and towards the sea,
> "I would not put a tree or blade of grass in this space. This should be a plaza
> of stone, not a garden." I looked at Dr. Salk and he at me and we both felt
> this was deeply right. Feeling our approval, he added joyously, "If you make
> this a plaza, you will gain a façade—a façade to the sky."[74]

As in the church at Lake Tekapo, the plaza at the Salk Institute calls
attention to the interpenetration of proximate and distant space such that the
character of the immediate vicinity is dramatically determined by that which
lies beyond it. Christian theology makes this same claim with respect to
Christ's Parousia and the coming kingdom of God. The essential character of
our present reality is already altered by the future realization of the kingdom
that, in the words of N. T. Wright and others, is "breaking in" to the present.
"The blind receive their sight, the lame walk, the lepers are cleansed, the deaf
hear, the dead are raised, the poor have good news brought to them" (Luke
7:22; cf. Matt 11:2-5). As we have noted earlier, these signs of the irruption
of the kingdom were offered by Jesus in confirmation of the fact that he is
indeed the one who is to come. His coming is beginning already to transform
the reality of those who encounter him.

Louis Kahn intended originally that the space between the two labora-
tory buildings of the Salk Institute should be developed as a garden. Kahn
conceives of gardens in general as places of enclosure and describes them as
"a very private thing."[75] He conceived the space initially as a place to which
the scientists working in the institute could retreat for refreshment and contemplation—in an enclosed realm. It was not to be a place open to a broader
horizon. It is possible that in his original plan for the space between the
buildings Kahn succumbed momentarily, and against his own better judgement, to the modernist distrust of transcendence, and to the belief accompanying a common caricature of science, that the truth of things is to be found
entirely within the realm of immanence.

It was Barragan who recognized the potential of the space formed
between the laboratories and studies of the Salk Institute to direct attention
to a reality that transcends the bounds of human comprehension. The vista
toward the ocean and the sky beyond has a certain symbolic power in the

---

[74] Kahn, *Writings, Lectures, Interviews*, 232–33.
[75] Kahn, *Writings, Lectures, Interviews*, 239.

context of the scientific work to which the institute is dedicated. It invites consideration of the broader context in which the work of science is situated and of the proper limits under which science conducts its extraordinary work. Louis Kahn had his own view on that. Science, he contends, gives attention to things that are measureable, but it does so for the sake of that which is unmeasurable. "The measure," he says, "is only a servant of the unmeasurable."[76] The vista toward the ocean and the sky draws attention to the scientific institute's location in a wider landscape, provides a broader context for the scientific endeavor, and relates it to a world beyond the immediacy of the scientists' intellectual location. The paved terrace and the channel of water running down the center of the plaza establish an axis and a trajectory, but they do not themselves reach the horizon to which they direct attention. Sea and sky lie beyond the place within which the viewer, for the time being, is located. They belong to a realm accessible to the eye but not, at present, to the body.

Here, too, we may draw a parallel in theology. The "one who is to come" is beyond us. He has "ascended into heaven and is seated on the right hand of God the Father Almighty; *from thence he shall come . . .*" as the Apostles' Creed has it.[77] The creed, following the proclamation of Christ in the New Testament, opens up a theological vista. It invites us to look beyond our present reality and locates us within a wider landscape. Just as the scientist, having spent time in the plaza, may return to her lab with a renewed sense of the wider context in which her work is undertaken, so those who gather to worship, who hear the gospel proclaimed, who share bread and wine in memory and in hope, who say the creed together and pray, "your kingdom come," may return to their work having shared in a reality not present yet in its fullness nor wholly accessible for now, but that defines nevertheless the nature of the work to be done and the purpose to which it is directed. The immediate context of one's daily life and the responsibilities to be exercised within it are envisaged in the light of a broader horizon.

The parallel corresponds to an inaugurated rather than to a realized eschatology. There is distance yet between our present reality and the coming kingdom, but that which is at a distance can be apprehended already, and it determines already the character of the space we now inhabit.

---

[76] Kahn, *Writings, Lectures, Interviews*, 235.
[77] The Nicene and the Athanasian Creeds include the same confession.

Mediated Presence

Any claim such as we have made, that things absent or at a distance can be apprehended here and now and that they can transform our present reality, requires an account of mediation. The sacred but invisible order of the cosmos marked in ancient times by the priestly identification of axes on a building site is mediated through the orientation and form of the building itself. The material of building, stone and timber arranged to form a temple, was the medium through which the hidden order and the intelligibility of things was presented. Again in Adolf Loos' Rufer House, the central column, along with the surrounding elements of the built form, is the medium through which an axial logic and order is revealed. Cynthia Jara comments: "Even though a design scheme can become tangible only through the gathering of things, the mere assembly of elements is meaningless unless directed by the scheme."[78] That the logic and meaning of the scheme becomes tangible through the gathering of things is the point of interest here. The "things" mediate the otherwise hidden and intangible meaning.

The built form plays a mediating role also in the framing of vistas to a distant horizon such as we have seen in the Church of the Good Shepherd at Lake Tekapo and again in Louis Kahn's Salk Institute project. Crucial, too, in these schemes is the medium of light. As evening falls and the sun sets day after day, the respective spaces are closed down into darkness and the distant horizon disappears from view. With the waning of the light, the character of each space is transformed. Louis Kahn says of light that it is "the giver of all presences,"[79] while Le Corbusier claims that "light for me is the fundamental basis of architecture. I compose with light."[80] These propositions are neither rare nor merely recent. The Pantheon provides ancient testimony to the ways in which light enlivens and transforms architectural space, while numerous treatises through the course of architectural history refer to the fundamental importance of light in determining the character of architectural space. Equally longstanding has been the association of light with the divine and with revelation. In their mutual recognition of the symbolic power of light, architecture and theology have frequently converged. This was especially apparent in the development of Gothic architecture in the late medieval era. Gothic transparency brought light to the interior of church buildings,

---

[78] Jara, "Adolf Loos's 'Raumplan' Theory," 199.

[79] Kahn, *Writings, Lectures, Interviews*, 248.

[80] Cited in Danièle Pauly, *Le Courbusier: The Chapel at Ronchamp* (Basel: Birkhaüser, 1997), 113.

"and the stained glass transformed it so that it became a mysterious medium that communicated the immanent presence of a transcendent God."[81] John Lewis observes that "the perception of light itself in medieval thought can scarcely be appreciated without attention to the source, God who is light, who 'endures no deprivation of light.'"[82] Karsten Harries supports the point:

> The spiritual perspective of the Middle Ages made it seem obvious that the light that makes things visible here on earth bears an analogical relationship to the true divine light. . . . For the Medieval artist . . . light was more than just another natural phenomenon: it seemed to bridge the gulf separating this world from the sacred beyond.[83]

The capacity of light more generally to bridge the gulf between proximate and distant reality needs no special metaphysical pleading. It is through the medium of light that we know of distant galaxies, while even in our own galaxy our daily lives are illumined by a source 150 million kilometers distant. The power of light to bring near that which is otherwise utterly inaccessible renders it an obvious symbol for the work God does in presenting himself to us.

The divine presence is mediated through the Son and the Spirit. While the Son is frequently referred to in Scripture and in the Christian tradition as the "light of the world," the Spirit, too, is occasionally referred to this way. Saint Symeon the New Theologian (949–1022) repeatedly refers to the Spirit as "light." He devotes a discourse to the matter,[84] and one of his hymns addressed to the Holy Spirit begins, "Come true light."[85] Before Symeon, Gregory Nazianzen (329–390) had likewise spoken of the Spirit, who, along with the Father and the Son, is the "True Light."[86] References such as these suggest a fitting analogy between the mediation of light in the architectural examples given above and the mediation of the Spirit in uniting us to things

---

[81] R. Kevin Seasoltz, *A Sense of the Sacred: Theological Foundations of Christian Architecture and Art* (London: Continuum, 2005), 137.

[82] John Lewis, "The Influence on Medieval Church Architecture of Love for God: A Theological Approach" (Ph.D. diss., University of Otago, 2009), 235. Lewis here cites Pseudo-Dionysius, *De mystica theologia*, in *Pseudo-Dionysius: The Complete Works*, trans. Colm Luibheid (London: SPCK, 1987), chap. 4 (141).

[83] Karsten Harries, *The Ethical Function of Architecture* (Cambridge, Mass.: MIT Press, 1997), 109.

[84] See, e.g., *Symeon the New Theologian: The Discourses*, trans. C. J. Catanzaro (New York: Paulist, 1980), discourse 33.

[85] Cited in John McGuckin, "Symeon the New Theologian's *Hymns of Divine Eros*: A Neglected Masterpiece of the Christian Mystical Tradition," *Spiritus* 5 (2005): 182–202, 189.

[86] Gregory Nazianzen, "On the Holy Spirit," 3 (*NPNF₂* 7:318).

that are absent as yet, namely, the ascended Christ seated at the right hand of the Father, and the kingdom of God, which is yet to be realized in full. The unifying power of the Spirit is prominent in Wolfhart Pannenberg's eschatology. The Spirit, Pannenberg claims, is "an end-time gift [who] already governs the historical present of believers."[87] It is the Spirit who brings God's future into the present.

The pneumatological mediation between presence and absence provided John Calvin with a means of conceiving Christ's presence in the Eucharist. Calvin contends that "the Spirit really unites things separated by local distance."[88] Calvin repeats the point in his commentary on 1 Corinthians. There he writes:

> The sharing of the Lord's body, which, I maintain, is offered to us in the Supper, demands neither a local presence, nor the descent of Christ, nor an infinite extension of His body, nor anything of that sort; for in view of the fact that the Supper is a heavenly act, there is nothing absurd about saying that Christ remains in heaven, and is yet received by us. For the way in which he imparts Himself to us is by the secret power of the Holy Spirit, a power which is able not only to bring together, but also to join together, things which are separated by distance, and by a great distance at that.[89]

Commenting upon Calvin, Douglas Farrow explains,

> The ascended Lord is not everywhere, that is, ubiquitous and hence atopic, but he *is* everywhere accessible. The "infinite spaces" that we cannot leap are effectively compressed for us by the Spirit. In other words, Calvin's insistence on keeping the human Jesus sharply in focus forced him to seek a pneumatological solution to the problem of the presence and the absence.[90]

This spatial way of conceiving the matter is of course analogical. Talk of Christ's ascension "into heaven" does mean that he is not here in the space we inhabit, but it does not entail that he is located someplace else in our space-time continuum. The question of Christ's whereabouts cannot be answered by imagining some spatial location relative to our own, for our own order of space and time is set to be transformed in a new heavens and a new earth

---

[87] Pannenberg, *Systematic Theology*, 3:553. For a helpful commentary on this aspect of Pannenberg's theology, see again Taylor, *Pannenberg on the Triune God*, 168–74.

[88] Calvin, *Institutes*, 4.17.10 (651).

[89] John Calvin, Commentary on 1 Cor 11:24. Cited in I. John Hesselink, "Pneumatology," in *The Calvin Handbook*, ed. J. Selderhuis (Grand Rapids: Eerdmans, 2009), 299–312, 310.

[90] Farrow, *Ascension and Ecclesia*, 178 (emphasis in original).

already inhabited by the one who goes before us to prepare the way. The ascended Christ is no longer to be found in or subject to our space and time. Rather, the whole of our space and time is destined to be subjected to him. When that reordering of our reality is complete, it will finally be true to say that the Lord dwells with his people and God will be all in all (see Rev 21:3, 1 Cor 15:28).

Conclusion

The spatial analogy provided by the vistas at Lake Tekapo and at the Salk Institute, while limited in some respects, serves to illustrate nevertheless the possibility of our present circumstance, our *Sitz im Leben*, we might say, being radically transformed by a reality that lies beyond the space we currently inhabit. Here is a way of rendering the dialectic between the present and yet ascended Christ, or the present and yet still future kingdom of God, that allows for the profound transformation of our present reality by that which is yet to come. That the transformation of architectural space depends upon the medium of light, which comes and goes and presents itself in dramatically variable ways, suggests a further analogy with the mediation of the Spirit who bears witness to Christ, opens up vistas to the coming kingdom, and so is about the task of drawing his people into the presence of Christ.

8

Places Full of Time
Marking Time through the Medium of Place

The title of this chapter, "Places Full of Time," is not original. I have borrowed it from Richard Sennett, who coins the phrase in order to challenge the erasure of the past in Modernity, especially in modernist architecture, and to call for a "more humane urban design."[1] Such design will pay more attention to the historical nature of human existence and thus also to the succession of incidents, some of them centuries old, that form communities and give shape and meaning to human life. Modernity has resisted this claim of historical formation, has interpreted it as limitation, and has therefore sought a timeless truth (and a timeless architecture) accessible through the exercise of reason alone. Abstract ideas, rather than the story of God's involvement in human history, became the source of meaning and truth. In the purposive timelessness of modernity,

> philosophers turned their back to the intuited gathering of things that belong together in the clearing of life as lived, and began to make logical distinctions between object and subject or fact and value. They abstracted being into opposed concepts, and proclaimed the dialectic of abstract ideas and ideals as the source of meaning. Their exclusive concern for the timeless and the eternal destroyed the awareness of human historicity. And so they began the history of philosophical thought, a history that was nothing more

---

[1] Sennett, *Conscience of the Eye*, 190.

than a long descent of misrepresentations that claimed to reveal the truth about beings, but estranged the people from being as such.[2]

Modernity's discomfort with the historical nature of human existence, its "readiness to rupture continuity between past and present," has been evident in theology, too.[3] G. E. Lessing's despairing observation that there exists "an ugly, broad ditch" between himself and the events of Jesus narrated in the gospels, provides an early instance of Modernity's malaise.[4] The passing of time, Lessing supposed, renders the Christ proclaimed in the gospels inaccessible to us because we are no longer able to confirm that what is said of him is true. Thus, for Lessing, our alienation from the God said to be present with us in Christ is construed as an epistemological problem in essence, and is brought about by the passing of time. Lessing himself, who genuinely sought to retain the Christian identity in which he had been reared, took refuge in the "timeless truths" represented in Jesus' ethical teaching. The essence of Christianity could be summed up in the command to love one another and could be affirmed by human reason even if all the historical claims about Jesus turned out to be false.[5]

Two generations after Lessing, the Danish writer Søren Kierkegaard, writing under the pseudonym Johannes Climacus, observed that this account of Christianity, now widely accepted by Kierkegaard's contemporaries, rendered history of no account. "Any point of departure in time," Climacus observes, "is *eo ipso* something accidental, a vanishing point, an occasion."[6] History has no essential bearing on human identity, or upon our discovery of the truth. Although this disparagement of history is characteristic of

---

[2] Robert Jan van Pelt, "Apocalyptic Abjection," in Robert Jan van Pelt and Carroll William Westfall, *Architectural Principles in an Age of Historicism* (New Haven: Yale University Press, 1991), 317–81, 320. Van Pelt thinks that "the advent of Christianity had reinforced this renunciation of being for the sake of some recondite theological truths" (320). I claim, however, that wherever Christian theology has fallen into this way of thinking, it has betrayed its biblical roots.

[3] Jialing Luo, "Imagining Modernity: Memory, Space and Symbolism in The Hague," in *Cities Full of Symbols: A Theory of Urban Space and Culture*, ed. Peter J. M. Nars (Leiden: Leiden University Press, 2011), 173–85, 183.

[4] Gotthold Ephraim Lessing, "On the Proof of the Spirit and of Power," in *Lessing's Theological Writings*, selected and trans. by Henry Chadwick (London: A&C Black, 1956), 51–56, 55.

[5] I will refer repeatedly below to "Lessing's view of time," not because he is uniquely guilty of the problem I am concerned with in this chapter, but rather because he provides a notably clear statement of an attitude that is widely shared.

[6] Søren Kierkegaard, *Philosophical Fragments*, ed. and trans. Howard V. Hong and Edna H. Hong (Princeton: Princeton University Press, 1985), 11.

Modernity, it did not originate with the modern age. As Kierkegaard saw clearly, his contemporaries were merely saying what Socrates had said many centuries earlier, only they said it "not nearly so well."[7] The doctrine of recollection, as set out in the *Meno*,[8] reveals the accidental character of history in Socratic (and Platonic) thought. One learns the truth, Socrates explains, by recollecting the eternal truths divinely implanted in the immortal soul. The historical circumstances under which such recollection takes place are of no account. They are merely incidental, a vanishing point, as Kierkegaard observes, because every individual possesses the truth from eternity and has only to recollect it through the exercise of reason. History effects no alteration to one's store of knowledge, or to one's condition. Modernity's disparagement of history has, therefore, an ancient and venerable pedigree. But that same disparagement of history also sets Modernity in opposition to the Bible. For, according to the biblical record, it is precisely through history that God is at work, making himself known and drawing first Israel, and then Gentiles, too, into covenant relationship with himself. Nowhere is this more distinctly expressed than in the Johannine confession that the eternal Word of God, who was "in the beginning with God . . . has become flesh and lived among us"; John proclaims further that this Word made flesh, the historical figure of Jesus, no less, is "full of grace and truth" (John 1:2, 1:14). That claim—that the truth is given to be known in and through the particularities of history—is said by the apostle Paul to be "foolishness to the Greeks."[9]

We noted in chapter 7 the trouble that St. Augustine had with time. Augustine did not doubt that God was active in history, but he was troubled by the elusiveness of time. Time keeps slipping through our fingers: the present dissolves relentlessly into the past while the future is not yet. Augustine is unsure what to make of this passing of time, for it raises doubts about what in history can be taken as real. This again is an anxiety of the Greek philosophical tradition within which Augustine had been schooled, but it contrasts markedly with the biblical view. The biblical record shows that whenever Israel, troubled by present experience, expressed doubt about the faithfulness of God, it was enjoined to remember. Above all, Israel is enjoined to "remember the Lord your God who brought you out of the land

---

[7] Kierkegaard, *Philosophical Fragments*, 111.

[8] See Plato, *"Protagoras" and "Meno,"* trans. W. K. C. Guthrie (Harmondsworth: Penguin Books, 1956).

[9] Cf. 1 Cor 1:23. Paul refers here specifically to the *crucified* Christ, which, to the Greek mind, heightens the foolishness of the biblical claim all the more.

of Egypt."[10] This injunction to remember establishes a pattern that recurs again and again throughout Israel's scriptures; God is identified through reference to what he has done in history.[11] Yosef Yerushalmi reminds us that "it was ancient Israel that first assigned a decisive significance to history."[12] He continues:

> Only in Israel and nowhere else is the injunction to remember felt as a religious imperative to an entire people. Its reverberations are everywhere, but they reach a crescendo in the Deuteronomic history and in the prophets. "Remember the days of old, consider the years of ages past" (Deut. 32:7). "Remember what Amalek did to you" (Deut. 25:17). "O My people, remember now what Balak king of Moab plotted against you" (Micah 6:5). And with a hammering insistence: "Remember that you were a slave in Egypt."[13]

However much the stories may have been embellished over time, and whatever mythic elements they may have accrued, the principle remains clear that the identity of Israel as God's covenant partner takes shape through the course of history, and it is precisely through that history that Israel learns who God is.

The point especially to be noticed here is that within Israel's theological conceptuality it is simply not true that the events of the past slip relentlessly into oblivion. They are and remain decisive, precisely in their determination of present reality. The Passover haggadah insists:

> In every generation let each man look on himself as if *he* came forth out of Egypt.
> As it is said: "And thou shalt tell thy son in that day, saying: It is because of that which the Lord did for me when I came forth out of Egypt" [Exod 13:8].
> It was not only our fathers that the Holy One, blessed be he, redeemed, but us as well did he redeem along with them.
> As it is said: "And He brought us out from thence, that he might bring us in, to give us the land which He swore to our fathers" [Deut 6:23].[14]

---

[10] See, e.g., Deut 5:15, 8:2; Ps 81:10.

[11] See, e.g., Exod 20:2.

[12] Yosef Hayim Yerushalmi, *Zakhor: Jewish History and Jewish Memory*, rev. ed. (Seattle: University of Washington Press, 1996), 8.

[13] Yerushalmi, *Zakhor*, 9–10.

[14] *The Passover Haggadah*, ed. Nahum N. Glatzer (New York: Schocken Books, 1989), 59 (emphasis added). Some more recent versions of the haggadah apparently employ inclusive

When thinking of time abstractly, however, as Augustine did in his *Confessions*—recall his declaration that "the past now is not and the future is not as yet"[15]—it is difficult to escape the impression that the past has slipped from our grasp and cannot be recovered. The spatial arts, however, offer us an opportunity to think less abstractly about time and to *see* the past quite concretely "before our eyes." Taking a little further the consideration given to time in chapter 7, let us explore how that might be.

Seeing Time

One of the notable characteristics of architecture is that it endures—not indefinitely, but often for a very long time. Architecture is one means, therefore, by which the past remains available to us. A simple example may serve as an initial illustration of the point. When visiting cathedrals, centuries old, in the United Kingdom or elsewhere in Europe, I am struck repeatedly by the flagstones, especially those laid as treads in a set of steps or stairs. Take, for instance, the stair leading to the chapter house at Wells Cathedral as shown in figure 8.1. The stones have been scalloped and worn smooth by the footsteps of thousands, perhaps millions, of those who have come before us to worship in this place. Always I am reminded of the communion of saints stretching back over centuries and in whose company we belong. The past is not lost. It presents itself to us, in this case through the medium of architecture. Interestingly, this example also presents us with the future, although somewhat more symbolically. Sharing the perspective of the photographer, we stand at the foot of a stair which, let us suppose, we are about to ascend. The course of our immediate future is thus laid out before our eyes, while the well-lit space partially visible through the portal at the top promises a further unfolding of that future as we undertake the ascent. This is a stock-in-trade architectural strategy. An inviting vista along a colonnade, across a piazza, through a loggia, or down a corridor presents us quite deliberately with a view of our possible future location and encourages us to take the journey. The architectural vista makes the future available to us, at least in part.

The architectural device of presenting the future as open to view is very commonly used, not least in church architecture. The journey from baptism toward the future, eschatological reconciliation with God is represented in every church in which the baptismal font is sited somewhere close to the

---

language, thus indicating that the masculine language used here is not intended to be gender exclusive.

[15] Augustine, *Confessions*, 11.14.17 (*NPNF*, 1:168).

entrance and at the start of the long central aisle. The aisle is an invitation to pilgrimage that leads to the sanctuary and to the altar where the meeting of God with humanity is celebrated in the Eucharist. The Eucharist recalls Jesus' death, but it also looks forward to the eschatological consummation of the kingdom of God. We will return below to the temporal dimensions of the eucharistic celebration. In the meantime, we note simply the architectural rendering of time. The architecture sets before the Christian pilgrim the future goal of final reconciliation with God and invites her participation in that journey.[16] Karsten Harries confirms the point: "Our experience of recession, and more generally of distance, is inseparable from

FIGURE 8.1
Wells Cathedral

anticipations; the walk down a church aisle thus offers itself as a natural metaphor for the journey of life from birth to death, as the Christian church also holds out the promise that death will not be allowed to triumph."[17]

---

[16] Robert Jenson is critical of this kind of church architecture, in which our relation to God is expressed in spatial terms. "In Gothic churches," he writes, "the structure itself draws us through God's distance to his presence. Gothic architecture synthesizes all the means we have discussed for providing spatially for the God of religion; it is the perfect religious architecture, and our hankering for it in religious moments is a sound, if reprehensible, intuition." Robert W. Jenson, "God, Space and Architecture," in Jenson, *Essays in Theology of Culture* (Grand Rapids: Eerdmans, 1995), 9–15, 12. Jenson contends that relation to the God of the gospel cannot be conceived in spatial terms, as though God were a "Presence out or up there" (13). Rather, "it is a relation to the future. The overcoming of the separation from God that occurs in prayer and praise is not an appeal to a distant one but to a coming one" (13). Jenson rightly resists the suggestion that God might be conceived as one of the things arrayed in space, but he appears to have overlooked the temporal signification at work in Gothic church architecture. Richard Kieckhefer likewise points out that the spatial arrangements serve to mark successive *moments* in the liturgy as worshippers move toward sacramental communion with God. See Kieckhefer, *Theology in Stone: Church Architecture from Byzantium to Berkeley* (Oxford: Oxford University Press, 2004), 27–28.

[17] Harries, *Ethical Function of Architecture*, 218. Harries respects this tradition of church architecture but contends as well that we can no longer believe in what it stands for.

FIGURE 8.2
Cloister at the University of Milan

Alongside the architectural representations of time seen here, architecture presents us with the spread of time in other ways, too. Consider, for example, the time taken to build. Dorita Hannah describes building as "slow theatre."[18] Building takes time, but the time it takes is not lost. Thomas Markus says of all buildings that they are "a developing story, traces of which are always present."[19] Such was the conviction of the cathedral builders of the Middle Ages who knew when they set out that they would not see the completed building. The building of a cathedral commonly took decades, even centuries in some cases, and yet those who worked on the cathedrals presumably thought that the time they invested would be preserved—in the building itself. And so it has been. The stone crafted and placed, the finial carved and installed, the tracery carefully fashioned: each remains just as it was, giving itself to our attention just as it has done for hundreds of years.[20] Lessing need not despair that its essential quality has slipped from our grasp just in virtue of its having been set there hundreds of years ago.[21]

[18] Cited in Tony Watkins, *The Human House: Sustainable Design* (Auckland: Karaka Bay Press, 2009), 214.

[19] Thomas A. Markus, *Buildings and Power: Freedom and Control in Modern Building Types* (New York: Routledge, 1993), 5. Cited in Roger Connah, *Grace and Architecture* (Helsinki: Finnish Building Centre, 1998), 19.

[20] There are, of course, many examples of cathedrals whose stonework has been adjusted and replaced over the years so that the stones we now see are not original, but the fact that the vast majority of stones in such buildings remain just as they were in placement and form is sufficient to secure my point.

[21] I do not pretend that this comment resolves Lessing's entire concern, but it is a first indication of how time might be conceived differently than in Lessing's schema. I will return to the matter below.

Taking Time

The most widely renowned contemporary example of a building taking time is Antonio Gaudí's extraordinary Basílica i Temple Expiatori de la Sagrada Família (hereafter La Sagrada Família) in Barcelona, begun in 1882 and still under construction 135 years later. Construction of the church commenced under the direction of the diocesan architect Francesca de Paula del Villar, but the building had not proceeded very far before differences between the initiators of the project and the architect prompted del Villar's resignation and led to the appointment of Gaudí to take over the design.[22] While Gaudí retained what had been begun at the level of the apse crypt, the church above ground is wholly the result of Gaudí's architectural vision. Gaudí's inheritance of the commission from del Villar set a pattern that has continued throughout the course of the church's construction. While Gaudí remains the generative architectural genius long after his own death, responsibility for the realization of his vision has been entrusted, of necessity, to a succession of supervising architects since and to thousands of artisans, builders, and laborers who have worked on the building but who, on account of their own passing, will not see it finished. Gaudí himself accepted this with equanimity: "It is not a disappointment that I will not be able to finish the temple," he said. "I will grow old, but others will come after me. What must be always preserved is the spirit of the work; its life will depend on the generations that transmit this spirit and bring it to life."[23] I do not share the view of commentators like Ignasi de Solà-Morales who, for all his appreciation of Gaudí's creative genius, nevertheless contends that "the sudden cutting off of Gaudí's life [he died in 1926 after being run over by a tram] is . . . a symbol of the fate of all his work, and in a very particular way of that unfinished work that is the Sagrada Família."[24] De Solà-Morales regards "the disappearance of the architect of the building as an irremediable loss"[25] and appears to suggest that Gaudí's work in its "declining grandeur"[26] has no future other than that of a relic. The consecration of the church in 2010 by Pope Benedict XVI, including the celebration of the Mass with a congregation of seven thousand and the glorious choral singing of massed choirs, suggests instead that its

---

[22] See Jordi Bonet i Armengol, *Temple Sagrada Família*, 3rd ed. (Barcelona: Editorial Escudo de Oro, 1997), 5.

[23] Cited on the website of the Basilica de la Sagrada Família, accessed December 10, 2016.

[24] Ignasi de Solà-Morales, *Antoni Gaudí* (New York: Harry N. Abrams, 2003), 40.

[25] Solà-Morales, *Antoni Gaudí*, 40.

[26] Solà-Morales, *Antoni Gaudí*, 41.

intended purpose as a temple dedicated to the praise of God's glory is indeed being fulfilled.

The construction of La Sagrada Família has become a tradition handed on from one generation to the next. There is a resemblance here to N. T. Wright's suggestion that the drama of salvation is like a five-act play, the plot for which has been established through the first four acts of creation, fall, God's covenant with Israel, and the life, death and resurrection of Jesus, but for which the fifth act has not been written. The church, like actors called upon to improvise a fifth act, is now involved in working out the content of act 5. It is called to be faithful to the plot line established in the first four acts, but its lines are not written for it. Wright explains,

> The "authority" of the first four acts would not consist in an implicit command that the actors should repeat the earlier parts of the play over and over again. It would consist in the fact of an as yet unfinished drama, which contained its own impetus, its own forward movement, which demanded to be concluded in the proper manner but which required of the actors a responsible entering in to the story as it stood, in order first to understand how the threads could appropriately be drawn together, and then to put that understanding into effect by speaking and acting with both *innovation* and *consistency*.[27]

In like manner, Gaudí had not provided detailed design of the complete building, but his vision for the whole provides the basis upon which subsequent architects, builders, and sculptors have been able responsibly to take up Gaudí's vision and to continue the construction with innovation and consistency. The angular figures of the passion façade that comprise Josep Subirach's rendition of Christ's betrayal, suffering, and death are clearly different in style from those of the nativity façade, which were overseen by Gaudí himself; and yet Subirach's more contemporary style may be seen as a faithful expression of Gaudí's vision. There is progression, development, and alteration here, but the progression is faithful rather than indifferent to all that has been done before. As the building continues to develop toward its final completion, the work of the past is not past in the sense of being no longer present. The physical artifact remains present, of course, but, more

---

[27] N. T. Wright, "How Can the Bible Be Authoritative?" *Vox Evangelica* 21 (1991): 7–32, 19 (emphasis in original). Others have suggested amendments to the structure of Wright's five-act play; I am particularly sympathetic to that proposed by Samuel Wells, but Wright's basic idea remains helpful and fruitful. For Wells' suggested amendments, see Samuel Wells, *Improvisation: The Drama of Christian Ethics* (Grand Rapids: Brazos Press, 2004), 51–57.

than that, the vision of the architect himself remains as a present challenge to our own ways of seeing the world. Finnish architect Juhani Pallasmaa states, "Architectural works create frames and horizons of perception, experience and meaning, and ultimately, I confront myself through the work of the other."[28] Pallasmaa explains further that,

> as we encounter a building . . . we encounter the architect's architectural metaphor of his existential world and this imagery inspires, frames and strengthens our own existential encounter with our own world. In architectural generosity the designer donates his existential sense, his life experience and existential wisdom, to the occupant.[29]

Time in this scenario is not an enemy; it poses no threat to human endeavor nor consigns to oblivion what has happened in the past. Rather, time is precisely the condition that allows for the full realization of the reality upon which so many hands have worked. Time may be conceived here as "spacious." Contra Augustine, it is not an infinitesimally small sliver of presence rushing away into nonbeing but the capacious arena of human endeavor. And not just human endeavor, of course. Time may be conceived, more fundamentally, as the capacious realm of divine grace in which nothing is lost, and in which all things are brought to their true end as objects of God's creative and loving purpose.

Those who have worked on the building of La Sagrada Família have invested their time precisely because they have had confidence that their work will be preserved and enhanced through the course of time. That confidence appears to be justified by Mark Burry, an architect who has worked on La Sagrada Família and who says of the sculptures completed decades ago that "the general composition is as *vital* today as it was at the beginning of this [twentieth] century."[30] We may say, comparatively, that God gives time to his creation not so much because he *has confidence* that the work of creation will be preserved and enhanced and brought to glorious completion,

---

[28] Juhani Pallasmaa, "Artistic Generosity, Humility and Expression: Architecture as Lived Metaphor, Collaboration, Faith and Compassion," in Bergmann, *Theology in Built Environments*, 23–38, 28.

[29] Pallasmaa, "Artistic Generosity, Humility and Expression," in Bergmann, *Theology in Built Environments*, 27–38.

[30] Mark Burry, *Expiatory Church of the Sagrada Família* (London: Phaidon, 1993), emphasis added. Absent page numbers in Burry's publication, I indicate the location of the above quotation by noting its position in the text beneath figure 22. The same means of identifying the location of quoted text will also be used for subsequent citations.

but because *he determines* that it shall be so. Time is therefore to be conceived as God's good gift to creation that allows creation to flourish.

The time given to creation is also, of course, an arena of death and decay. Some of creation's death and decay may simply be a necessary part of the mechanism by which creation is enabled to flourish. If this is the case we may be confident that nothing is lost but that all things made and loved by God will be gathered into that reconciled relationship that is the promise of the kingdom. Other things are subjected to death and decay on account of humanity not making good use of the time that has been given us. We have turned against the divine command to be fruitful and multiply and to exercise proper dominion (Gen 1:28). Dominion (lordship) properly exercised is seen in the one who is the world's true Lord. It is he who restores creation to its proper purpose and who exercises his lordship not through domination but through loving service.[31] Insofar as our misuse of the time given us by God leads to death and decay, we stand in need of forgiveness and redemption. Time is not to be blamed for this death and decay; rather, we are at fault. Were it the case that past time was lost, we, too, would be lost and the damage we had done through the course of human history would remain our final legacy. The damage could not be repaired. But the eternal God, who lets no sparrow fall to the ground apart from his loving care (Matt 10:29), recovers and redeems the things damaged on account of our misuse of time. On the basis of Christ's inauguration of a new creation, in which the brokenhearted are healed, the lame walk, the blind receive their sight, the poor receive good news, and so on, we have good grounds for hope that nothing intended by God for good is finally excluded from his promise that in the fullness of time, all things shall have life, and have it abundantly. Time itself does not heal, but God can heal all the wounds of time and wipe every tear from our eye (Rev 21:4).[32] The damage we have done can in the end be undone; the supposed tyranny of time can exert no final power. While time conceived in Lessing's terms is an arena of relentless loss, conceived theologically—in the light of Christ, that is—time is not excluded from the redemptive work of God but will be brought, entire, into the kingdom of God.[33]

---

[31] I have written more fully on this theme in "To Render Praise: Humanity in God's World," in *Environmental Stewardship: Critical Perspectives Past and Present*, ed. R. J. Berry (London: T&T Clark, 2006), 291–311.

[32] Revelation 21:4 goes on to assert that "the former things will pass away." The context suggests that "the former things" refers to all that keeps us from God, notably death and mourning and pain.

[33] I take the point from Paul McPartlan, *The Eucharist Makes the Church: Henri de Lubac and John Zizioulas in Dialogue* (Edinburgh: T&T Clark, 1993), 47.

It is something of an aside here, but Gaudí's own architectural project suffered the setback of sinful human endeavor. During the Spanish Civil War, the workshops of Sagrada Famlia were ransacked and burned. A plot to blow up the four completed towers of the church was fortunately averted. Nevertheless, all the castings of sculptures, and the archives containing Gaudí's models and drawings, were destroyed. Some photographs were salvaged, however—sufficient to allow the work to go on. Those who sought to destroy an enterprise dedicated to the praise and glory of God have not been allowed the final word.

The Convergence of Past, Present, and Future

Just as remembrance of the exodus constitutes for Jewish people a convergence of past and present whereby each participant in the Passover meal should look upon herself as if she came forth out of Egypt, so in Christianity, the nature of our present reality is thought to be determined by a convergence of past events and the coming realization of God's purposes as they are anticipated in the resurrection of Jesus from the dead. The convergence of past, present, and future is represented in La Sagrada Família in at least two ways. I have spoken already of the way in which the work of laborers, builders, and artisans long since completed continues to present itself to our attention. The past is in this way not lost but preserved, and continues to determine the character of our present reality. Yet La Sagrada Família also evokes a powerful sense of the future, precisely because of its incompleteness. Mark Burry observes that "the emotions which it awakes by virtue of its incompleteness are tempered or heightened by an inevitable sense of anticipation."[34] It is difficult to imagine that one could visit the building under construction without being drawn toward a vision of its finished glory and, more importantly, toward a vision of all things gathered in praise of God. In my own case, if I may speak personally, visiting the construction site well before the church's consecration in 2010 felt, ahead of time, as though I were participating in an act of worship. The building itself, even in its partially finished state, gives fitting expression to the doxology proclaimed in the mosaics of its soaring towers: "Hosanna in Excelsis."

The convergence of past, present, and future is evident, too, in the themes of the three façades that represent, successively, the progression of the divine economy. The nativity façade was completed first. The nativity refers, of course, to the birth of Christ, but under Gaudí's direction the nativity

---

[34] Burry, *Sagrada Família*, beside figure 1.

FIGURE 8.3
La Sagrada Família Towers

façade presents us as well with the birth and flourishing of creation. The façade is teeming with the flora and fauna of creation, sculpted in stone and joining in adoration of the Christ child. Creation and incarnation are linked here, appropriately so, for the Christ who comes among us is indeed the one in whom all things were created and hold together and through whom God was pleased to reconcile all things (cf. Col 1:16-19). His coming among us is, as well, the beginning of the new creation.

The second façade to be constructed was the passion façade, undertaken after Gaudí's death and featuring the sculptures by Josep Subirachs. Here in the passion of Christ is Christianity's own Exodus, Christianity's own account of God's saving work, intensified and extended now to embrace the whole creation, to set it free from its bondage to death and decay. This past event, the event of Christ's passion, is the decisive determinant of the world's present reality. In virtue of Christ's passion, the world has been reconciled to God and lives now in the

FIGURE 8.4
Nativity Façade of La Sagrada Família

FIGURE 8.5
Passion Façade of La Sagrada Família

time of grace, the time given by God for faith and repentance, given so that humanity may offer, uncoerced, its grateful and joyous "amen."[35]

The third façade, as yet incomplete, is the glory façade. It is dedicated to the celestial glory of the ascended Christ and testifies to the eschatological consummation of God's purposes for the world. This will complete the temporal sweep of the building's imagery, from creation to final consummation and, along with the other elements of the building, will fulfill Gaudí's intention "to make the whole church both a literal and allegorical representation of the catechism."[36] To be presented thus with the drama of the divine economy, whether through architectural form as here in La Sagrada Família, through music—in Handel's *Messiah*, for example—through Scripture, or through the liturgy of the Church, enables us to experience time not as an ever-dissolving moment that continually slips from our grasp but as the capacious realm of divine grace. Repeating the point made earlier, time conceived thus does not present a threat to our humanity but is the very thing that enables us to be truly human, to be creatures participant in the ongoing drama of God's creative and redemptive purposes for the world.

Living Tradition

Anxiety about the passing of time, along with the mistaken view that time past is time lost, often finds expression in humanity's attempts to freeze time, to capture and retain the moment. Something of this sort appears to have motivated Peter's ill-conceived offer to make dwellings in which to house the transfigured Jesus, along with Moses and Elijah (Matt 17:4). W. F. Albright and C. S. Mann comment that "Peter's desire is to extend the time."[37] To my mind, the desire to extend the time entails here the refusal, albeit unwitting on Peter's part, to *go on* in time toward death and resurrection. Immediately before the story of the transfiguration in Matthew's Gospel we read of Jesus foretelling his death and resurrection, and of Peter's resistant response to the news that Jesus will be crucified (Matt 16:21-22).

In the case of La Sagrada Família, there have been many who have wanted the construction to be stopped. Some have taken the view that the possibility of realizing the vision died with Gaudí himself, while others have suggested

---

[35] I take the point from Karl Barth, *Church Dogmatics*, IV.1, trans. G. W. Bromiley (Edinburgh: T&T Clark, 1956), 737.

[36] Burry, *Sagrada Família*, above figure 16.

[37] W. F. Albright and C. S. Mann, *Matthew: A New Translation with Introduction and Commentary*, Anchor Bible (New York: Doubleday, 1971), 203.

that the building should have been preserved in its unfinished state as a permanent memorial to Gaudí's genius. To this suggestion, Mark Burry replies:

> By continuing the works (and the objective is, above all else, to provide a completed building for the purposes of spiritual congregation rather than fulfil any wider cultural interest through "freezing" the incomplete work) the very least that could be said about the unfinished building today is that the visitor sees something alive rather than merely a curio.[38]

Two points of theological interest emerge from this assessment. The first is the distinction made between "something alive" and a mere curio. The vitality of the building is a function of Gaudí's successors—the architects, the builders, the financial donors, and the church officials—receiving and developing Gaudí's vision. We see here a tradition properly respected as something to be received and *lived* and passed on with renewed vitality to future generations. This is the vocation of those to whom the gospel has been preached and to whom the apostolic faith has been gifted. Vitality is of course the Spirit's gift. It is not the church's calling to preserve and protect a static deposit of theological truth—a curio—but, under the guidance and the enlivening power of the Spirit, to *live* what it has received. This living is to be done in the time given for it by God.

The second point concerns Burry's recognition that the proper end to which the building of La Sagrada Família is directed is "spiritual congregation." For all its monumental significations and proportions, the building is not merely a monument to Gaudí or even to God. A monument—the term comes from the Latin *moneo*—serves to remind, to advise, and to warn, which La Sagrada Família undoubtedly does; but a church building also provides a place for the liturgy, for the "work of the people." Just as thousands of builders and artisans have worked for well over a century on La Sagrada Família, so too the people who gather now in "spiritual congregation" have work to do: the work of confession, the work of intercession, the work of reconciliation, and the work of praise. They are summonsed to this work by Christ himself, who also leads them in it. It is important to recognize as well that the liturgy enacted within the walls of the church establishes the pattern

---

[38] Burry, *Sagrada Família*, beside figure 29. It is important to note that the cessation of construction under the pretext that the unfinished building should serve as a memorial to Gaudí himself would have been a flagrant betrayal of Gaudí's own intent that the building was to glorify God. In accordance with this concern, Gaudí declared "that his death must in no way interrupt the construction of the Sagrada Família." Philippe Thiébaut, *Gaudí: Builder of Visions*, trans. Harry N. Abrams (London: Thames & Hudson, 2002), 95.

for the whole of Christian life. Christians are called to live their whole lives in liturgical time, in the time given for the work of confession, intercession, reconciliation, and praise.

History as God's Project

This chapter began by noting the problem of time and history as it has commonly been conceived in Western thought. As seen in the philosophy of Socrates and Plato and again in modern thinkers like Descartes, Spinoza, and Lessing, time and history are disparaged. That is to say, the Western mind has often denied that the truth and meaning of life might be revealed through the particularities of history. To put the matter again in Kierkegaardian terms, the moment in time cannot be decisive; it is accidental, a vanishing point, and finally of no account. This attitude is exacerbated by the suspicion that time itself slips relentlessly from our grasp and so subjects all things to decay and to the nothingness of death. In the discussion above, however, I have attempted to show that the phenomenon of architecture, through the process of construction and with respect to the endurance of buildings themselves, offers a different way of conceiving time. The church of La Sagrada Família, still under construction in Barcelona, provides a paradigm according to which time and history may be seen as a realm of productivity and formation, the fruits of which are not lost but determine the character of our present reality. This view of time, I have suggested, accords more closely with the biblical conception of history as the terrain within which God is about the business of forming a people and drawing them into that covenant relationality in which the fullness of creaturely life may be realized.

This theological conception of time presents us with the challenge of how we are to inhabit the temporal realm given us by God. Consideration of that matter in anything like the scope and depth that is required lies well beyond the confines of this book and is of course a task to which theology as a whole is endlessly devoted. But we may give some attention to the Bible's own exploration of the matter in architectural terms. At the end of the exilic period, when the people of Israel returned from Babylon and were allowed to inhabit their own land once more, the question arose, as it always does: What was to be done with their time? Cyrus, king of Persia, whose conquest of Babylon had enabled Israel's return home, had ordered that the temple in Jerusalem be rebuilt (see Ezra 6:3), but in the early years of Israel's restoration, little progress was made. That is the context in which the prophet Haggai appears on the scene and challenges Israel to attend to the building of the temple. Haggai observes that the people had succeeded in building "paneled houses" for themselves, but otherwise their lives bear the marks of futility:

> Now therefore thus says the LORD of hosts: Consider how you have fared. You have sown much, and harvested little; you eat but you never have enough; you drink, but you never have your fill; you clothe yourselves, but no one is warm; and you that earn wages earn wages to put them into a bag with holes. (Hag 1:5-6)

The antidote to this futility, Haggai goes on to explain, is the rebuilding of the temple. Through much of Israel's history, God has done perfectly well without temples, but the point of the building program now commended is to draw Israel back to worship. We have here again an interesting convergence of past, present, and future. Israel is drawn *back* to worship. In order to recover its identity,[39] in order to participate once more in God's project of forming a people, in order to escape the futility of its present activity and move again toward God's promised future, Israel has to revisit the past, gather up the fragments of its history, and rebuild the ruins of the temple.[40] Only by this means may Israel participate again in the proper work of the people, in that liturgy of life lived in responsive obedience to God. The work of the people is indeed "responsive." Haggai stresses, three times in 1:14, that it is because God "stirred up their spirits" that the people "came and worked on the house of the LORD of hosts, their God." Time and history are thus shown to be of value; they count for something, rather than being futile, just to the extent that the people of Israel are engaged in God's project and are responsive to his call. We may observe as well, again following Van Pelt, that this connection of past, present, and future makes "history into a unified story of redemption."[41]

---

[39] Marcus Dods notes a hint of reproach in Hag 1:2 when the Lord says, "These people say the time has not yet come to rebuild the LORD's house." The reference to "these people" rather than "my people" suggests that Israel's neglect of worship has undermined their identity as God's people. See Dods, *Haggai, Zechariah, Malachi* (Edinburgh: T&T Clark, 1956), 48. Gerhard von Rad confirms the point, noting with respect to the same verse that "Israel is no longer Israel if she does not seek first the kingdom of God." Gerhard von Rad, *The Message of the Prophets*, trans. D. M. G. Stalker (London: SCM Press, 1968), 248. The people's claim that "the time has not yet come," moreover, accentuates their failure to make proper use of their time.

[40] I take this point from Robert Jan van Pelt, "Prophetic Remembrance," in Van Pelt and Westfall, *Architectural Principles*, 75–137, 82–83.

[41] Van Pelt, "Prophetic Remembrance," in Van Pelt and Westfall, *Architectural Principles*, 78.

Beyond Egocentric Conceptions of Time

A further feature of the trouble that the Western mind has with time is its propensity to think of time egocentrically. Albert Einstein's theory of relativity notwithstanding, we are inclined to absolutize our own present moment and to doubt the reality of past and future time. Jean-Luc Marion explains that "we, who privilege the point of view of the *here and now* as the preeminent dimension of time and hence of (the) Being (of being), can hardly attribute reality but to an available and permanent thing. Or rather, we can hardly conceive that a reality should unfold outside of the available and permanent *here and now*."[42] This has serious consequences in multiple spheres of human understanding, not least in theology, as Lessing has demonstrated. Doubting the reality of all things past and future, we demand that God be available immediately. The demand is evident in Lessing's claim that if only he could see with his own eyes the miracles said to have been performed by Christ, then "I would have gained so much confidence that I would willingly have submitted my intellect to his, and I would have believed him in all things in which equally indisputable experiences did not tell against him."[43] Bereft of the epistemic warrant allegedly provided by immediate experience, Lessing is unable to accept that he should stake his own life on things purported to have happened many centuries ago. The offense Lessing takes at the proclamation of Christ is a version of "the scandal of particularity." Put simply, he is unable to accept that the life, death, and resurrection of Jesus are somehow decisive for salvation, precisely because the "passing of time" has rendered those events, and Christ himself, unavailable to him. Their reality, so far as Lessing is concerned, is lost in time.

Among several features of Lessing's deliberations that can and should be contested, I remain concerned especially here with his conception of time. Lessing succumbs to the view that the moment is forever vanishing and so cannot be decisive. We cannot stake our lives on what takes place in history nor rest any claims to truth on the ever-shifting sands of historical occurrence. This puts Lessing at odds, as we have seen, with the Christian proclamation of Jesus Christ. But need we think of time in this way? I have been arguing, through an engagement with architecture, that time might better be understood as a capacious realm of existence established by God for the living of creaturely life. Architecture makes available to us time's extent and

---

[42] Jean-Luc Marion, *God without Being*, trans. Thomas A. Carlson (Chicago: University of Chicago Press, 1991), 180 (emphasis in original).

[43] Lessing, "On the Proof," In *Lessing's Theological Writings*, 52.

does so in at least three ways: first by presenting us with time past in the form of stones carved and laid many years ago but that determine still the character of our present reality; and second, by involving us in projects that are temporally expansive. I have attempted to show that both ways are evident in the building[44] of La Sagrada Família; indeed all buildings may be regarded, to some greater or lesser extent, as places full of time.

A third way, not yet discussed, in which architecture—indeed, space more generally—presents us with time's extent is revealed in studies done on the nature of memory:

> For Maurice Halbwachs, founder of memory theory, there is no collective memory without a spatial framework, that is, the spatial dimension has a central meaning for remembering. . . . On the one hand, the social frames, on which the individual memory and the act of remembering depend, always draw on spatial frames (*cadre spatial*), without which remembering would not be possible. On the other hand, in order to develop a collective memory, a group, especially a religious group, needs concrete spaces where memory can become concrete, materialise and thus contribute to the group's identity. . . . Space might evoke certain categories of memory, and at the same time cause a stabilising effect by conveying a notion of continuity.[45]

We might say, therefore, that places are stewards of the past. They keep time for us by withstanding the constant erosion of time, as it seems to us when time is conceived egocentrically and abstractly. Halbwachs provides further explanation of the important role played here by the material environment: "Comte remarked that mental equilibrium was, first and foremost, due to the fact that the physical objects of our daily contact change little or not at all, providing us with an image of permanence and stability."[46]

The possibility notwithstanding that buildings may fall into ruin, be demolished, or be destroyed by calamitous events, they are, for the most part, stable and permanent features of our experience. They provide historical continuity and offer what Karen Till has called a "spatial 'fix' to time."[47]

---

[44] Read "building" here as both noun and participle.

[45] Wolfgang Grünberg and Anna Körs, "'Symbolkirchen' as Bridges or Boundary Stones in a Merging Europe?" in Bergmann, *Theology in Built Environments*, 69–107, 84–85.

[46] Maurice Halbwachs, *On Collective Memory*, trans. Lewis A. Coser (Chicago: University of Chicago Press, 1992), 168.

[47] Karen E. Till, *The New Berlin: Memory, Politics, Place* (Minneapolis: University of Minnesota Press, 2005), 9. Cited in Luo, "Imagining Modernity," in Nars, *Cities Full of Symbols*, 175.

Commenting on the desire to build memorials in recognition of deeds done and tragedies having occurred in the past, Edward Casey observes,

> *Places hold memories.* Memories do not float freely in minds or brains—nor do they reside properly in texts or technologies—though they leave their mark in all of these. They are anchored in particular places, which harbor them, keeping them in trust as it were. If public memories survive, this is due in large part to possessing what the Romans called *stabilitas loci*, a "stability of place" in which to arise and last. . . .
>
> The most lasting foundations for public memories are precisely those provided by place.[48]

The relative permanence of architecture serves as a challenge, I suggest, to the assumption that the passing of time severs the past from the present. Although Lessing is correct in his observation that with respect to our knowing of the contingent order, we can never achieve absolute certainty, our hold upon time and history is not as precarious as he supposes. Architecture provides confirmation of that.

Time as the Realm of Divine Action

But let us now think theologically about the matter and return once more to the problem of time and history with which this chapter began. The Jewish and Christian traditions, as we have seen, conceive of time and history (along with space—thus, space-time) as the realm in which God is at work forming a people and drawing all things into reconciled communion with one another and with himself. On Lessing's view, widely shared within the Western intellectual tradition,[49] time and history cannot be the locus of divine action. They are simply too ephemeral for that. Rather than attending to

---

[48] Edward S. Casey, "Public Memory in the Making: Ethics and Place in the Wake of 9/11," in G. Caicco, *Architecture, Ethics and the Personhood of Place* (Hanover, N.H.: University Press of New England, 2007), 69–90, 80–81. Philip Sheldrake observes that cathedrals—we might say church buildings in general—have played a particularly important role in this regard. "The cathedral," Sheldrake writes, "was . . . a repository for the cumulative memory and constantly renewed aspirations of the community. Even today, to enter such a building is to engage with centuries of human pain, achievements, hopes and ideals. This 'memory palace' is a constant reminder that *remembering* is vital to a healthy sense of identity." Sheldrake, "Spiritual City," in Bergmann, *Theology in Built Environments*, 157–58 (emphasis in original).

[49] Although it is especially prominent in Western thought, the disparagement of time and history is evident in other cultures, too, especially among those that share a common heritage in the Indo-European tradition of thought.

what has taken place through the course of Israel's history, culminating, as Christians believe, in the life, death, and resurrection of Jesus, those who seek to know God should devote their energy and their powers of reason to the discernment of necessary and *timeless* truth. According to this view, the events of history have no impact upon the essential nature of things, including our own essential natures. What happens in time is merely incidental. What matters, in the dualistic framework dividing the *cosmos aisthētos*, the spatio-temporal world of appearances, from the *cosmos noētos*, the intelligible world of eternal ideas, is the participation of one's immortal and immaterial soul in that eternal realm.

This, however, is not the biblical view. According to the biblical witness, "the moment," as Søren Kierkegaard liked to call it, is decisive. It is decisive precisely because, as noted above, history is the realm of God's creative, redemptive, and transformative engagement with his creatures. Kierkegaard has another, biblical, term for the moment; he refers to it as "the fullness of time" and has in mind especially here God's own participation in time through the person of Jesus Christ. It is this "moment"—the moment Lessing despairs of knowing—that is decisive for our salvation. One of Kierkegaard's pseudonyms, Vigilius Haufniensis, writes in *The Concept of Anxiety* that "the moment is that ambiguity when time and eternity touch each other."[50] The "moment" refers also in Kierkegaard's thought to the individual's participation in the coming-together of eternity and time. Kierkegaard offers various ways of speaking of this participation. He sometimes calls it "faith," at other times "discipleship," and sometimes "contemporaneity with Christ." However he may refer to it, our participation in the reality established through the life, death, and resurrection of Jesus is essential, Kierkegaard contends, to the realization of our true humanity. The reality in question is the redemption and the reconciliation of a world that has been disrupted and disfigured by humanity's defiance of God.

An important, and tragic, corollary of Lessing's view of time is that he cannot accept what has been done for us. Perhaps it is this resistance that lies at the heart of our modern malaise. Our insatiable thirst for the novel may be at root an effort to overcome all that we sense may be wrong with our lives by severing our connection to the past. We are intent on justifying ourselves, while refusing the news that the work of justification has already been done. That is the tragedy of our modern view that the past is forever lost to us. In

---

[50] Søren Kierkegaard, *The Concept of Anxiety*, ed. and trans. Reidar Thomte (Princeton: Princeton University Press, 1980), 89.

consequence of this, Kierkegaard again observes, the specifically theological means for dealing with the failures of the past, "conversion, atonement and redemption, are [also] lost."[51] Likewise, he continues, "the concepts of resurrection and judgement are destroyed."[52] Christianly conceived, it is through the intersection of time and eternity, and through the presence in time of the eternal God who comes in servant form and who through his own death and resurrection releases us from the grip of death, that a new creation comes to birth. According to Kierkegaard, that is why, for Christianity, "it is precisely the historical that is essential."[53]

Time and the Eucharist

At the focal center of Antonio Gaudí's La Sagrada Família, there stands an altar, already installed and consecrated despite the building's incompletion. The altar is a place for the celebration of the Eucharist, for the celebration of that sacrament in which past, present, and future converge. Jean-Luc Marion observes that the Eucharist is the memorial of a past event that remains "less a past fact than a pledge given in the past in order, today still, to appeal to a future—an advent, that of the Messiah—that does not cease to govern *this* today from beginning to end."[54] The Eucharist, corresponding to the Passover meal of Israel, is the specifically Christian witness to the temporal extent of the divine economy. Paul's instruction in 1 Corinthians 11:26 makes the point: "For as often as you eat this bread and drink the cup, you proclaim the Lord's death until he comes." That which is done now—the sharing of bread and wine—is, simultaneously, a proclamation of what has already been accomplished and the anticipation of what is yet to come. Both the past and the future converge upon the present and determine its true character. The present, on this account, is the space and time given to creation to take up God's invitation to participate through the Spirit in what has been accomplished once and for all in Christ and will be fulfilled in the age to come.

The consecration of La Sagrada Família's altar in a church that remains incomplete has a profound, though probably unintentional, theological appropriateness, for the celebration hosted there looks forward to a reality whose completion is yet to come—namely, the kingdom of God. It is for

---

[51] Kierkegaard, *Concept of Anxiety*, 90.

[52] Kierkegaard, *Concept of Anxiety*, 90.

[53] Søren Kierkegaard, *Journals and Papers*, vol. 2, ed. and trans. Howard V. Hong and Edna H. Hong (Bloomington: Indiana University Press, 1970), entry 1635, IV C 35 (233).

[54] Marion, *God without Being*, 172–73 (emphasis in original).

this reason that Louis Bouyer insists: "The fact that the eucharistic celebration has an eschatological orientation, that it is not a final step but that it looks toward a further consummation, needs certainly to be emphasized in some way where Christians gather for the eucharist."[55] Yet, as I have suggested above, the future and coming kingdom of God, inaugurated through Christ's incarnate life among us, is not solely future but appears already in history—specifically in those places where Christ and the Spirit are at work releasing creation from its travail. This work is the work of transformation; it is God's redemptive reordering of things so that they might be conformed to Christ and so to the coming kingdom. The Christian celebration of the Eucharist is, at once, the remembrance, the enactment, and the prophetic proclamation of this reconciling work of God.

Conclusion

I have attempted in this chapter to address the problematic conception of time that has repeatedly plagued Western thought. Time is regarded as an enemy relentlessly consigning to nonbeing all that takes place in the world. I have taken Gotthold Lessing as an exemplar of this view. Its adverse consequences, by no means limited to theology, include the disparagement of the created world of space and time; a defective soteriology according to which salvation is achieved by escaping the spatio-temporal conditions of created existence; and the refusal to believe that God is at work in history. Time conceived abstractly and egocentrically certainly leads us to such conclusions. To repeat the point made above, we are inclined to absolutize our own moment in time and to doubt the reality of past and future time. We are quick to become anxious, then, when we perceive from this perspective that the moment is constantly slipping from our grasp.

Through consideration of the ways in which architecture takes place in time, I have argued that a different conception of time is possible. It is a conception that safeguards time's extent and that enables us to recognize time as the capacious realm of God's creative, redemptive, and formative economy. God uses time to bring the creature to God's own end in reconciled

---

[55] Louis Bouyer, *Liturgy and Architecture* (Notre Dame: University of Notre Dame Press, 1967), 94–95. The point is cited by George Hunsinger, who adds the comment that "an eschatological liturgy needs to be facilitated by the architecture." Hunsinger, *The Eucharist and Ecumenism: Let Us Keep the Feast* (Cambridge: Cambridge University Press, 2008), 328.

communion with himself.[56] We can be sure, therefore, that no time is lost. The Christian hope, grounded in the resurrection of Jesus from the dead, is that all the wounds of history will be healed, that all the tears shed will be wiped from our eyes, and that all that has made our lives worth living will be gathered into creation's final celebration of praise.

While the principal concern of this chapter has been to contest Lessing's conception of time rather than to address questions of epistemology, I observed at the outset that, in Lessing's view, our alienation from the God said to be present with us in Christ is construed as an epistemological problem brought about by the passing of time. What has been said about time permits us, however, a final observation about Lessing's epistemological concern. Lessing's insistence that the passing of time leaves him unable to know whether the things said in the gospels are true can be answered only through the prompting of the Spirit, who enables recognition that the reality to which the gospels testify has not disappeared in our own day. Such recognition commonly occurs, as was discovered once on a journey to Emmaus, when Christ is made known in the breaking of bread.

---

[56] The same point is made and explored at length by Douglas Knight in *The Eschatological Economy: Time and the Hospitality of God* (Grand Rapids: Eerdmans, 2006).

9

Building from the Rubble
Reaching for Redemption through Memory and Hope

The twentieth century, it has often been remarked, was a century of
bloodshed and unspeakable evil. It was a century of brutal regimes, not
perhaps unprecedented in the depths of evil to which they sank, but certainly
unprecedented in the scale of their destruction. Mao, Stalin, and Hitler were
together responsible for the slaughter of more than 100 million people, and
the figure attributed to each alone far exceeded that of any previous regime.
The scale of these leaders' murderous regimes makes them stand out from
all others, but there are of course plenty of recent and current examples—in
Rwanda, Nigeria, Gaza, Ukraine, Syria, and so on—that confront us with
the terrible reality of human sinfulness and leave us pondering whether anything can be said or done to make amends, to heal the wounds, or to give
cause for hope that such evil may one day be overcome.

Christian faith continues to be nourished through roots deeply implanted
in Jewish soil. From Judaism, especially, Christian faith has learned some
things about suffering and evil. It has learned that the reality of evil defies
rational explanation. It has learned that there is no good reason why evil
should exist. Indeed, the efforts sometimes made to justify the reality of
evil—by Job's comforters, for instance—have, according to the book of Job,
been rebuked by the Lord himself. In Judaism and in Christianity, furthermore, the conviction persists that evil will not survive the final unfolding of
God's purposes. And so the tradition conveyed through Jewish and Christian Scripture includes words of protest and lament at the evil that is done.

It also includes words of repentance and remorse, to be used in times when Scripture's readers have themselves been the perpetrators of evil. In this chapter I want to focus particularly upon the responses to atrocity that have been offered by artists and particularly by architects, one of whom has been profoundly shaped by Jewish tradition.

In the aftermath of the Second World War, as Europe and the world slowly learned of the horrors that had taken place at Auschwitz, Dachau, Belsen, and elsewhere, and in which the German people had been at least partially complicit, there were those who argued that on account of such atrocity there could be no more philosophy and no more art. Prominent among them was Theodor Adorno, who famously declared that "to write poetry after Auschwitz is barbaric."[1] Adorno's declaration became a slogan around which expressions of the horror and incomprehensibility of the Holocaust were gathered, a chastening, salutary reminder that the depravity perpetrated under the Nazi regime was perpetrated by our own kind, by fellow human beings. The degree to which ordinary citizens were persuaded by Hitler's rhetoric and went along with his violence, albeit they were only partially aware of its terrible extent, implicated the human race as a whole. *We human beings* are capable of this. One of the central problems confronted in Adorno's philosophy was the question of how it is possible that humankind "instead of entering into a truly human condition, is sinking into a new kind of barbarism."[2] To write poetry or to create art in the aftermath of a horror such as was perpetrated against the victims of the Holocaust would be to conceal the full extent of our inhumanity and to suppose, absurdly, that we could make amends. Adorno's verdict on the propriety of art suggests, rather, that a humanity capable of such evil had squandered irrevocably any claim upon the true, the good, and the beautiful, while the pretension that any sense could be made of what had happened would be an intolerable affront to the victims. As Terry Smith has put it, "All artists can do is contemplate, in immobile silence, the enormity of the devastation that had been wrought."[3]

---

[1] Theodor Adorno, "Cultural Criticism and Society," in Adorno, *Prisms* (Cambridge: MIT Press, 1981), 17–34; reprinted in *The Adorno Reader*, ed. Brian O'Connor (Oxford: Blackwell, 2000), 195–210, 210. The declaration that there could be no more philosophy and no more poetry was directed in fact specifically to speech about the Holocaust and does not represent Adorno's view of the prospects for philosophy or art in general, as his own further contributions to philosophy and aesthetic theory reveal.

[2] Max Horkheimer and Theodor Adorno, *Dialectic of Enlightenment* (New York: Herder & Herder, 1972), xi.

[3] Terry Smith, *The Architecture of Aftermath* (Chicago: University of Chicago Press, 2006), 69.

For a time Adorno rejected even an art that tried to show the horror. Smith again explains that such efforts "risked . . . the danger that their very artistry might provide pleasures, however indirect and inadvertent, to those receiving the political messages, thus blunting the artists' obligation to the victims of the Holocaust: to show that it was, above all, unthinkable, inconceivable."[4]

Adorno did qualify his position in later writings; he acknowledged that the suffering of the victims "has as much right to expression as a tortured man has to scream; hence it may have been wrong to say that after Auschwitz you can no longer write poems."[5] Among efforts to represent the screams of the tortured, Adorno approved especially Samuel Beckett's play *Endgame*, which, he writes, "trains the viewer for a condition where everyone involved expects—upon lifting the lid from the nearest trashcan—to find his own parents . . . Beckett's traschcans are the emblems of culture restored after Auschwitz."[6] It would seem, however, following Adorno's line of thought, that while a culture of sorts may be restored, it cannot be redeemed. We cannot make amends. We cannot be forgiven, and we must not be allowed to forget. That bleak conviction, however, does bestow upon us an ethical responsibility. Adorno came to the view that "a new categorical imperative has been imposed by Hitler upon unfree mankind: to arrange their thoughts and actions so that Auschwitz will not repeat itself, so that nothing similar will happen."[7]

Unfortunately, however, it does not appear to lie within the capacities of humankind to see to it that nothing similar happens again. The common recurrence of murder, of genocide, of war, and of terror testifies to a brutality within our human race that we have not been able to heal. We may say with some justification that human brutality of this nature is abnormal, but we have also to acknowledge that it does occur, *again and again*. The terrorist attacks of September 11, 2001, for recent instance, the murderous rampage on Utøya Island in Norway in 2011, and the destruction of Aleppo in 2016, do not match the horrors of Nazism in their murderous extent, but the hatred leading to their conception and the chilling efficiency of their execution reveal a depth of evil in some human hearts just as shocking and

---

[4] Smith, *Architecture of Aftermath*, 69. Smith takes the point from Adorno's "Commitment," in Adorno, *Notes to Literature*, vol. 2 (New York: Columbia University Press, 1992), 85–86.

[5] Adorno, *Negative Dialectics* (London: Routledge & Kegan Paul, 1973), 362.

[6] Adorno, "Trying to Understand *Endgame*," *New German Critique* 26 (1982): 119–50; also in O'Connor, *Adorno Reader*, 343. I owe these references Smith's discussion of Adorno in *Architecture of Aftermath*, 68–70.

[7] Adorno, *Negative Dialectics*, 365.

incomprehensible as that which conceived the Holocaust. The singularity of the Holocaust pertains to its scale but not to its kind. Nevertheless, and taking up Adorno's new imperative, we cannot simply fall silent in the face of such atrocity. As Robert Jan van Pelt has suggested, "Although [Auschwitz] is impervious to all efforts to make it 'habitable' through discourse, it speaks to us nevertheless. The memory of Auschwitz challenges us not to surrender to its implications of despair, or apathy, or resignation. Auschwitz calls us to resistance."[8] Such resistance is the responsibility of architects, too, especially because, Van Pelt reminds us, "they had a unique responsibility in the creation and the perfection of the death camps: professional architects designed the camps, the barracks and the crematoria."[9]

Almost immediately upon comprehending the scale of the destruction wrought on 9/11, the people of the United States and more broadly in the Western world began to ask how we could make amends. What was to be done in the face of terror? How should we respond? The question was posed first to politicians, and it was the mayor of New York City, Rudy Giuliani, who managed to find some words of reassurance—reassurance that there was a way forward, a way to cope. People went also to the churches, searching for words with which to express their grief and hoping that there might be some solace in God. Beyond that they looked to the military to make amends. Indeed, above all, in the Western world—in the so-called "Christian" West—we looked to the military to make amends.

While, tragically in my view, the military continues to be entrusted with the task of dealing with terrorism and putting things right, we have also from time to time looked to artists for guidance about what should be done in the aftermath of evil. This was soon the case after 9/11 as New Yorkers contemplated Ground Zero and the great hole left in the middle of Manhattan. New Yorkers looked to architects to tell them what should happen next. After the rubble was cleared and meticulous efforts had been made to salvage the remains of the three thousand victims at the World Trade Center site, something had to be done to memorialize, to rebuild, and to express America's response to the terror that had come into its midst. Architects found themselves as key players in America's search for a way forward in response to and beyond the evil that had been done. Rafael Viñoly, one of the architects eventually involved in submitting proposals for the redevelopment of

---

[8] Van Pelt, "Prophetic Remembrance," in Van Pelt and Westfall, *Architectural Principles*, 120.

[9] Van Pelt, "Prophetic Remembrance," in Van Pelt and Westfall, *Architectural Principles*, 120.

Ground Zero, recognized very early the responsibility that artists would be called upon to assume. Viñoly wrote in the *New York Times* just two weeks after 9/11:

> There is a sense of void among us. A void that is charged with the weight of emotion, the fears of risk and the expectation that we can overcome. In a curious parallel, that void is the common territory of art. It is the place where the unexpected power of invention can reach beyond the limits of logic and set a new direction.[10]

Of course, the architects called upon to build something new from the rubble of Ground Zero were dealing only in part with a void. They were dealing, to be sure, with the void left where the twin towers had once stood, with sixteen acres of empty real estate; and they were dealing with the emptiness left among the friends and families of the three thousand people who had died. That had somehow to be acknowledged and respected. But alongside these voids the architects had also to deal with a mass of competing, perhaps irreconcilable demands: the demands of Larry Silverstein, the property developer who held the lease on the World Trade Center site and who wanted his ten million square feet of office space back; the demands and expectations of the Lower Manhattan Development Corporation, appointed by the governor of New York to oversee the rebuilding process and make sure that the interests of the city as a whole were taken into account; the demands of those like Mayor Giuliani who wanted the sixteen acres set aside as a memorial to the victims and for no building, other than a memorial, to be set upon it; the demands of the Port Authority, which still owned the land and which was responsible for the transport infrastructure of New York and for rebuilding the transport hub destroyed when the twin towers collapsed. The architects had also to deal with the demands of those who escaped the crumbling towers, and of those thousands of people who lived and worked nearby, all of whom "felt that they were entitled to some say in what was to be built where the twin towers had stood."[11] One measure of the public demand to have a say in the rebuilding process is the thousands of people who turned up to the numerous forums held around New York to debate the prospects for Ground Zero, including four thousand attendees at a town hall meeting in July 2002 called "Listening to the City." The competing demands and expectations

---

[10] Rafael Viñoly, "Fill the Void with Beauty," *New York Times*, September 23, 2001. Cited in Smith, *Architecture of Aftermath*, v.

[11] I take the point from Paul Goldberger, *Up from Zero: Politics, Architecture and the Rebuilding of New York* (New York: Random House, 2004), xiv.

might have seemed overwhelming and impossible to meet. Suzanne Stephens, however, who writes for the *Architectural Record*, spoke on behalf of her architectural colleagues: "After this cataclysmic event, many architects felt that they must do *something*, and that is to do what they know best—design. Theirs was an optimistic resolve; that innovative architecture may offer a way to heal ourselves as well as Manhattan's mangled downtown."[12] Whether architecture can offer a way to heal us will be a matter for further consideration as this chapter develops, but let us begin by investigating in more detail the initial progress made at Ground Zero.

Two early responses offered markedly contrasting proposals. Mayor Giuliani's plea that the site be left empty except for a memorial to the victims won support from some, particularly from the families of those who had died. In contrast, a good many people, according to poll results, supported former mayor Ed Koch's call, made within hours of the attack, to rebuild the towers just as they had been before—in defiance of the terrorists! Team Twin Towers, an advocacy group led by film and television executive Randy Warner, produced plans for replica buildings with increased structural and security features. But this was the response of those unchastened by what had happened, of those who believed that the most important thing to be done was to reassert American power and the superiority of American values, or at least the values of those powerful political and business interests that had overridden widespread public protest to build the towers in the first place. The proposal to rebuild replica towers was a response of those forgetful of the communities and small businesses that had been erased from the map in order to make way for the twin towers when first constructed and forgetful of the inhospitable, dehumanizing and widely derided features of the original World Trade Center buildings.[13]

The unchastened hubris of Team Twin Towers' proposal was exceeded, however, by the sculptor James Turrell, who claimed,

> I am interested in seeing the working culture of New York continue. People want a memorial now because they're feeling emotional, but emotions pass, all emotion passes, and then the memorial has no meaning. The new

---

[12] Suzanne Stephens, "Fantasy Intersects with Reality at Ground Zero," in *Imagining Ground Zero: Official and Unofficial Proposals for the World Trade Center Competition*, ed. Suzanne Stephens, Ian Luna, and Ron Broadhurst (London: Thames & Hudson, 2004), 12–25, 12.

[13] For an account of the controversy surrounding the building of the World Trade Center, see James Glanz and Eric Lipton, *City in the Sky: The Rise and Fall of the World Trade Center* (New York: Henry Holt, 2003), 62–87.

buildings should be higher than the old ones, and there should be three of them.[14]

What does it take to mend the world? What does it take to salvage our humanity in the face of human atrocity? First of all, I suggest, it requires that we see and understand clearly both our limitations and the nature of our brokenness. That acquisitive materialism is fragile both as an economic system and as the occasion and design spirit of the original World Trade Center[15] would be one lesson with which to begin. Another lesson might be that building things that are higher and bigger and stronger than those of our rivals is no way to secure our identity as human beings, or to preserve our humanity. A third lesson would be that reconciliation, Christianly conceived, is the work of one who did not strive for glory but emptied himself and took the form of a servant (Phil 2:7). Learning such lessons is something that Team Twin Towers and James Turrell signally failed to do. While they did have supporters, many others involved in the debate recognized that those responsible for doing something with the space at Ground Zero could not proceed as if there were nothing to be learned about our own participation in and contribution to the brokenness of our world.

In the years immediately following 9/11, literally hundreds of architectural visions were put forward, some solicited under the terms of several design competitions and others volunteered by architects and planners apparently sharing Suzanne Stephens' confidence that innovative architecture, if not able to offer a means to heal ourselves, could at least provide an appropriate memorial to the dead and give voice to America's, or New York's, indomitable spirit.

The official design competition, staged jointly by the Lower Manhattan Development Corporation and the Port Authority, eventually narrowed the field of entrants to seven design teams who presented nine schemes. The principal guidelines offered to the architects were that the proposals should include "respect for the footprint of the two World Trade Center towers; space for a memorial (to be designed later); 6.5–10 million square feet of office space; one million square feet of retail; and a major transit hub serving the region."[16] On December 18, 2002, the nine schemes were unveiled at the

---

[14] Cited in Smith, *Architecture of Aftermath*, 162. Smith's source is the citation in Deborah Solomon, "From the Rubble, Ideas for Rebirth," *New York Times*, September 30, 2001, B37.

[15] I have adapted the point from Smith, *Architecture of Aftermath*, 150.

[16] Peter Marcuse, "The Ground Zero Architectural Competition: Designing without a Plan," *Progressive Planning Magazine*, Winter 2003, accessed July 20, 2014.

Winter Garden adjacent to Ground Zero. It is important to understand that these schemes were not well-developed proposals for actual buildings. The competition brief called for innovative design studies expressive of a vision for the site that could then be developed at a later date through actual building designs.

After a couple of weeks of deliberation, the panel of judges announced that the renowned Polish-born, Jewish American architect Daniel Libeskind had presented the winning scheme. Libeskind had been invited to join the advisory panel charged with assessing the entries but had been unable to attend the preliminary meetings. As an afterthought, apparently, he decided to enter the competition himself.[17] At the Winter Garden on December 18, Libeskind was the first to present his scheme:

> Libeskind went up to the lectern. His first words were not about architecture at all. "I believe this is about a day that altered all of our lives," he said. And then he went on to describe his own arrival in the United States forty-three years earlier. "I arrived by ship to New York as a teenager, an immigrant, and like millions of others before me, my first sight was the Statue of Liberty and the amazing skyline of Manhattan," Libeskind said. "I have never forgotten that sight or what it stands for."[18]

Libeskind continued:

> When I first began this project, New Yorkers were divided as to whether to keep the site of the World Trade Center empty or to fill the site completely and build upon it. I meditated many days on this seemingly impossible dichotomy. To acknowledge the terrible deaths which occurred on this site, while looking to the future with hope, seemed like two moments which could not be joined. I sought to find a solution which would bring these seemingly contradictory viewpoints into unexpected unity. So, I went to look at the site, to stand within it, to see people walking around it, to feel its power and to listen to its voices. And this is what I heard, felt and saw.
>
> The great slurry walls are the most dramatic elements which survived the attack, an engineering wonder constructed on bedrock foundations and designed to hold back the Hudson River. The foundations withstood the unimaginable trauma of the destruction and stand as eloquent as the Constitution itself asserting the durability of Democracy and the value of individual life.[19]

---

[17] So reports Goldberger, *Up from Zero*, 7.
[18] As cited in Goldberger, *Up from Zero*, 8.
[19] Cited in Smith, *Architecture of Aftermath*, 180.

I have quoted Libeskind at length because it is this speech, as much as his architectural scheme, that won Libeskind the competition. He managed to convince the judges and indeed the gathered audience that he, better than any of the other entrants, understood the problem and the challenges that lay before all who had an interest in what happened at Ground Zero. "Libeskind did not talk about square footage or economics, and he barely used an architectural term in his presentation. He talked about commemoration, memory, mourning, and renewal, and he did it with the zeal of a preacher. 'Life victorious,' were his final words, to sustained applause."[20]

One of the first tasks of an artist, I suggest, is to help us to see and to understand better the reality that lies before us and around us. Whether or not one agrees with Daniel Libeskind in every particular of his analysis, he provided more convincing evidence than any other architect that he understood the memories, the anguish, and the hope that required expression in whatever was to be done at Ground Zero. He understood that if there is to be healing we have first to understand the nature and extent of our brokenness.

There are reasons why this Polish-born, Jewish immigrant to America managed to present a better understanding of the situation than any of his rivals in the competition. Libeskind's most notable work to that point had been the Jewish Museum in Berlin. In that building Libeskind had shown himself capable of breaking Adorno's silence. This Jewish architect had given Germany a building, a work of art, that upheld the memory of the Holocaust, gave voice to the victim's screams and yet could say as well that light and hope are not extinguished.

The museum itself consists of two buildings: a baroque building called the Kollegienhaus that was first a courthouse, and beside it, the new building designed by Libeskind and completed in 1999. The two buildings are joined by a passage below ground but have no visible connection above ground. One can enter the Libeskind Building only by passing through the baroque building. The history memorialized here is represented not merely in the artifacts that are exhibited in the museum, but also in the journey visitors must make through the buildings themselves. The museum is encountered first of all as an arrangement of streets and passageways. Three different axes connect the various parts of the building, each expressing a specific theme. Ricardo Bianchini explains:

> The "Axis of Continuity," leading to the exhibition galleries, symbolizes the continuum of history. The "Axis of Emigration," representing who was

---

[20] Goldberger, *Up from Zero*, 9.

forced to leave Germany, leads both to daylight and to the Garden of Exile and Emigration. . . . The third axis leads to a dark dead-end where the Holocaust tower lies; along the path, glass cases containing objects belonging to some of the persons killed by the Nazis are placed. These three divergent axes intersect; thus expressing the connection between these three different stories of the German Jews.[21]

Libeskind himself describes "three basic ideas that formed the foundation for the Jewish Museum design":

First, the impossibility of understanding the history of Berlin without understanding the enormous intellectual, economic, and cultural contribution made by its Jewish citizens. Second, the necessity to integrate physically and spiritually the meaning of the Holocaust into the consciousness and memory of the city of Berlin. Third, that only through the acknowledgement and incorporation of this erasure and void of Jewish life in Berlin, can the history of Berlin and Europe have a human future.[22]

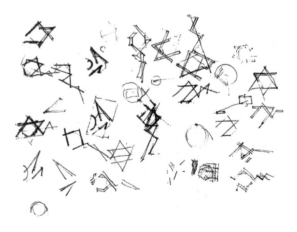

FIGURE 9.1
Star of David Concept Drawing

Libeskind's initial concept drawings for the museum take up the motif of the Star of David, but the star is broken, contorted, deformed. Eventually, in the architecture itself, the star is unfolded; the form is disrupted but not lost.[23]

---

[21] Riccardo Bianchini, "The Jewish Museum Berlin by Daniel Libeskind—Part 2," accessed February 27, 2017.

[22] Daniel Libeskind, *The Space of Encounter* (New York: Universe, 2000), 23.

[23] The zigzag contours of the building derive also from Libeskind's sketch of imaginary lines on a Berlin city map connecting the site with the street addresses of prominent members

Libeskind further explains that the museum "is a project about two lines of thinking, organization and relationship. One is a straight line, but broken into many fragments; the other is a tortuous line, but continuing indefinitely."[24] The straight line, representing perhaps the unwavering determination of genocidal logic, intersects the broken but infinite line of the Star of David, and where it does so it forms a series of voids running the full height of the museum's layered galleries. The voids speak of the fate of those six million Jews who became victims of a logic that was itself nihilistic, empty, and utterly bereft. Libeskind says of the voids that they represent "that which can never be exhibited when it comes to Jewish Berlin history: Humanity reduced to ashes."[25]

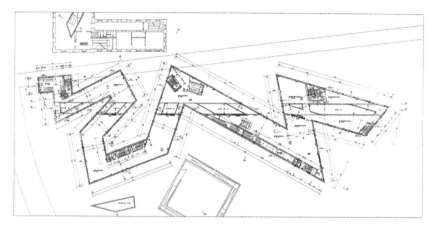

FIGURE 9.2
Museum Plan

Although this reduction of our humanity remains incomprehensible, a witness to it can be offered nevertheless, thus providing a memorial and an occasion for penitence. Such a witness is provided by an installation in one of the voids by the Israeli artist Menashe Kadishman. Ten thousand faces punched out of steel are distributed on the ground of the "Memory Void," the only "voided" space of the Libeskind Building that can be entered. The

---

of Berlin's Jewish history—Henrich von Kleist, Heinrich Heine, Mies van der Rohe, Rahel Varnhagen, Walter Benjamin, and Arnold Schönberg. See the explanation in, for example, Bernhard Schneider, *Daniel Libeskind: Jewish Museum Berlin*, 3rd ed. (1999; Munich: Prestel, 2004), 36.

[24] Libeskind, *Space of Encounter*, 23.

[25] Cited by Riccardo Bianchini in "Daniel Libeskind—Jewish Museum."

work, titled "Shalechet," or "Fallen Leaves," is dedicated not only to Jews killed during the Shoah, but to all victims of violence and war. Visitors are invited to walk on the faces and listen to the sounds created by the metal sheets as they clang and rattle against one another. The clanging metal recalls the sounds of death camps—the chains and the metal doors bolted against the victims of the gas chambers. I cannot imagine wanting to walk on these faces. But perhaps the artists' instruction that we should do so encourages us to recognize our complicity in at least some of the world's suffering. Lying there untouched and silent, however, the sculpted faces remind us simultaneously both of the humanity of every single victim, and of the dehumanizing effects of evil and sin.

FIGURE 9.3
Jewish Museum Void

I noted above that the museum is encountered first of all as an arrangement of streets and passageways; these constitute the various exhibition spaces. Terry Smith explains that on entering the building the visitor is confronted with a steep stair leading down into an abyss. On reaching the foot of the stairs, one is faced with the entrances to the three axes, or underground streets. No directions are offered, no clues make any sense of what lies before, although each street does have a single destination. "Turning right up a short passage, the Holocaust void is entered only through a heavy concrete door, which is then closed. The unheated, uncooled space inside is shaped into a large wedge by twenty-seven-foot-high unadorned concrete walls. You can just make out the sounds of the city outside as it goes about its business. Above, a thin strip of white light, reflected from some unseeable source, rims the top of one wall."[26] Explaining the symbolism of the light, Libeskind cites an interview with a survivor of the Holocaust:

[26] Smith, *Architecture of Aftermath*, 81–82.

"What do you suppose that white light in the sky that you saw from the crack in the cattle car on your way to Stutthof really was?" the interviewer asked Elaine some thirty years later in her Brooklyn home. [Elaine answered:] "You see, in order to survive you must believe in something, you need a source of inspiration, of courage, something bigger than yourself, something to overcome reality. The line was my source of inspiration, my sign from heaven. Many years later, after liberation, when my children were growing up, I realized that the white light might have been fumes from a passing airplane's exhaust pipe, but does it really matter?"[27]

From the basement entry point, the visitor ascends through the labyrinthine exhibition spaces, themselves windowless except for the top floor where one looks out upon the city of Berlin. The lower galleries are punctuated, however, by shards of glass and light, reminiscent of Kristallnacht, during which flames engulfed Berlin's synagogues and left the streets littered with shattered glass. These gouges and slashes are also tears in the fabric of the building evoking a violence that defaced the Jewish community of Germany. But, as is evident from the façade of the building, the shards of light appear through lines that, if pieced together, would form the Star of David. Light, hope, and a reminder of divine election are given, even in the midst of brokenness.

FIGURE 9.4
Holocaust Tower

Light has long been a symbol of beginnings, of hope, and of possibilities remaining open even in the midst of suffering and struggle. The motif of light is used again in the Garden of Exile, which recalls the exiles endured throughout Israel's history and especially the exile of Jews who fled or who were forced to leave Berlin during the Nazi regime. The garden is comprised of forty-nine vertical concrete shafts, each having a willow oak

[27] Yaffa Eliach, *Hasidic Tales of the Holocaust* (New York: Oxford University Press, 1982). Cited in Libeskind, *Space of Encounter*, 49.

FIGURE 9.5
Jewish Museum next to the Original Baroque Building

growing from its apex. Every shaft is tilted twelve degrees from the vertical, so recreating the sense of disorientation and instability felt by those who were exiled. Together, the forty-nine shafts create a feeling of entrapment. But the light above and the growing trees indicate the possibility of release.

A Jewish museum in Berlin is a memorial to be sure. It gathers up and recalls a history. But it is also a testament to an improbable new birth, to continuity in spite of rupture; it offers an eloquent gesture of hope even as it commemorates loss.[28] Libeskind has managed in this context to provide through his architecture an expression of our human need to go on, not forgetting the atrocity, but neither letting it be wholly determinative of our future.

Let us return now to the site in Manhattan and to Libeskind's attempts there to commemorate loss while again offering a gesture of hope. Recall first the narrow downward stair by which one enters the Jewish Museum. Descent as the motif of grief, particularly the grief occasioned by terror, was utilized again in Libeskind's scheme for the memorial at Ground Zero. In his presentation at the Winter Garden in 2002, Libeskind explained, "We have to be able to enter this hallowed, sacred ground while creating a quiet, meditative and spiritual space. We need to journey down, some 70 feet into

---

[28] I have rephrased this point taken from Howard Jacobson's review of the museum, "An Afterthought of Violence," *Guardian*, October 11, 2007.

Ground Zero, onto the bedrock foundation, a procession with deliberation into the deep indelible footprints of Tower One and Tower Two."[29]

That vision has been only partially realized in the memorial designed by Michael Arad with assistance from the landscape architect Peter Walker. Two great voids occupying the exact footprints of the twin towers descend thirty feet below ground level, and on each side cascades of water fall into the pools below. At ground level the names of the victims of the 9/11 attacks are etched in long bronze strips running around the rim of each pool. In a large paved plaza surrounding the two memorial pools, there is a plantation of trees symbolizing that life goes on. The trees are a more humble and chastened expression of the continuance of life than the rebuilding of replica towers would have been. Trees are not our own creation. Our power to sustain life and to make amends in the face of evil is strictly limited. But life anew might be received as a gift—a gift not of our own making.

There is a further expression of human limitation in the dominant feature of the memorial; namely, the cascading waterfalls marking the perimeters of the former towers. Arad's original proposal called for visitors to walk beside screens of falling water down into the voids left by the twin towers' below-ground structure. In the memorial as built, however, it is just the water that descends, first into a collecting pool and then further into a central chasm, giving the impression that it disappears deep within the bedrock of New York. Arad explains that the disappearance of the water into an abyss "gives the sense of something being torn apart and not mending."[30] The title of the work, "Reflecting Absence," reveals Arad's intent to portray the irreparable loss of life that took place on 9/11. In a review of the memorial published in the *Huffington Post*, C. Roger Denson observes: "Had Arad installed fountains instead of waterfalls, he would have embodied willful defiance—as in water being made by humans to defy gravity. Fountains embody the human will to overwhelm and dominate nature—not the kind of sentiment that embodies the healing of traumatized spirits."[31] The water falling under the force of gravity irrecoverably into the abyss reveals, by contrast, humanity's necessary subjection to forces beyond our control and so also our limitations.

---

[29] Daniel Libeskind, presentation at the Winter Garden, December 18, 2002, accessed July 27, 2011.

[30] Cited on the website of the 9/11 Memorial and Museum.

[31] G. Roger Denson, "Michael Arad's 9/11 Memorial 'Reflecting Absence': More Than a Metaphor or a Monument," *Huffington Post*, September 9, 2011 (updated May 27, 2016).

FIGURE 9.6
Reflecting Absence Memorial

Descent is the movement of grief; it is also the movement of chastening, of humility, and perhaps of repentance. The same motif is used in the Vietnam memorial in Washington, D.C. designed by architect Maya Lin. A long, gradually descending path takes the visitor past the names of tens of thousands of soldiers who died in Vietnam, which are etched into black marble panels in which visitors see their own faces reflected. Following the slow descent, the path bends back towards the Washington Monument and leads slowly upward to reach ground level, where the visitor apprehends the world again, perhaps in a new light. Paul Goldberger suggests, correctly in my view, that the descent takes the visitor "deeper into the abyss of war," but I am not persuaded by his contention that in "the move slowly back upward again, toward the light, the sun, and the city . . . you realize that, metaphorically at least, you have undergone a passage toward redemption."[32] Redemption does not come that easily. The dead are not raised by the visitor's ascent, nor are the wounds of war healed. Redemption involves forgiveness, repentance, and a new life, rather than a return to life as normal. Maya Lin's monument provides opportunity for remembrance, and penitence perhaps, but it does not presume to offer redemption. Andreas Huyssen, also wary of claims of redemption, warns of a too-easy absolution, secured through the building of memorials. "The more monuments there are," Huyssen suggests, "the more the past becomes invisible, the easier it is to forget: redemption,

---

[32] Goldberger's observations appear in his book *Why Architecture Matters* (New Haven: Yale University Press, 2009), 21.

FIGURE 9.7
Vietnam War Memorial

thus, through forgetting."[33] It is as if, having built (or visited) a memorial, we have fulfilled our duty to the past and are now entitled to forget.

The lack of triumphalism in the Vietnam memorial and its sobering effect on those who visit initially caused outrage. Some public officials voiced their displeasure, calling the wall "a black gash of shame."[34] They were not ready for any suggestion of penitence or remorse. Others, however, will listen sympathetically to the words of Vincent Scully, who writes that Maya Lin was "able to find a visual equivalent of the sense of sorrow, the fundamental sorrow which is the basic fact of war."[35] The architecture of the wall honors those who lost their lives, but it also invites contemplation of a wider tragedy, that of humanity's persistent recourse to war itself and the gouges war leaves in the landscape.

Recall here Adorno's conviction that all of us are implicated in the Holocaust. It is our race that has done this, the human race. Accordingly, therefore, the memorials of war and of conflict should remind us that we are all

---

[33] Andreas Huyssen, "Monumental Seduction," *New German Critique* 69 (1996): 181–200, 184.

[34] Cited in Kent Garber, "A Milestone for a Memorial That Has Touched Millions," *U.S. News and World Report*, November 3, 2007, accessed April 11, 2017.

[35] Cited in Nicholas Capasso, "Vietnam Veterans Memorial," in *The Critical Edge: Controversy in Recent American Architecture*, ed. Tod A. Marder (Cambridge, Mass.: MIT Press, 1985), 189–99, 189.

caught up in the fallenness of our world and that we are all responsible. Triumphalism has no place. Thus at Ground Zero, rebuilding the towers as they were before, only higher, and this time building three of them[36] would have shown only that we had learned nothing. It is salutary that the modifications to the replica towers proposed by Team Twin Towers were an increase in structural strength and increased security. The recommendation in the face of terror was to brace ourselves for more attacks but to make ourselves more impregnable, more unassailable.

Writing just two days after 9/11, Nicolai Ouroussoff, a columnist for the *Los Angeles Times*, offered a contrasting view of what should be done:

> America is now faced with two fundamentally divergent choices. The first, a natural impulse, would be to lash out at our enemies while barricading ourselves in an impregnable fortress. After the devastation caused by the Oklahoma City bombing in 1995, for example, the U.S. Government Services Administration issued strict new security guidelines for the design of new government buildings. Dozens of new courthouses have been built since then. Often, the results were imposing concrete structures, grim symbols of a society under siege.
>
> The other option requires more courage. It would call for creating an urban landscape shaped by qualities of openness and empathy, not paranoia.[37]

As the redevelopment of Ground Zero and the surrounding neighborhood proceeded, Ourousoff's plea for an "urban landscape shaped by qualities of openness and empathy, not paranoia" came in the form of the question whether there would be space for a mosque in the vicinity of Ground Zero. The proposal to build a multi-faith Community Center including a mosque two blocks from the World Trade Center site prompted vociferous opposition from some. At the time of writing, a makeshift center with accessible community facilities and a memorial to the victims of 9/11 has been established in the nineteenth-century industrial building on the site set aside for the new center, but plans for a new building incorporating a mosque have so far been frustrated.[38] The gestures of openness and empathy that could be represented

---

[36] We noted above that this was proposed by James Turrell; something similar was proposed by Team Twin Towers.

[37] Nicolai Ouroussof, "Towers' Symbolic Image," *Los Angeles Times*, September 13, 2001, A3. I owe the reference to Smith, *Architecture of Aftermath*.

[38] For a fuller account of the controversy, see Jacob N. Kinnard, *Places in Motion: The Fluid Identities of Temples, Images, and Pilgrims* (New York: Oxford University Press, 2014), chap. 2.

in the building of a multi-faith center have not so far been embraced by the surrounding community.

What of the site at Ground Zero itself? Two features dominated Libeskind's original vision for the site, a memorial utilizing the voids left by the twin towers, and a series of four new towers, the most prominent of which Libeskind called the Freedom Tower. Speaking at the 2012 convention of the American Institute of Architects, Libeskind spoke of his vision for the site. It should be a site of memory combined with the values of America: "freedom, liberty, a participatory society, and tolerance."

> The memorials should reach all the way deep down to the bedrock of New York where this tragedy, where those people were lost, and show us through the slurry wall, through these great foundations, how New York rises from its depths to the very skyline, to the very top of the skyline with the freedom tower. . . . It is important that when we look at the sky of New York, we remember that this is about independence, about the declaration of human rights.[39]

Libeskind's proposal for the Freedom Tower included an asymmetrical spire that echoed the outstretched arm and torch of the Statue of Liberty and reached a symbolic height of 1,776 feet—a reference, of course, to the date of the Declaration of Independence. A garden cascading down the outstretched arm utilized plants once more as a sign of regeneration and new life, but their suspension at 1,000 feet above ground level without any connection to the soil represented, to my mind, a somewhat hubristic effort to defy the way creation itself is ordered. In the tower eventually built, designed by David Childs of Skidmore Owings and Merrill, this symbolic height of 1,776 feet is almost all that survives from Libeskind's proposal.

Despite the protestations of George Pataki, former governor of New York, that the tower as built is "a symbol of our freedom and independence," it is not notably distinguishable from numerous skyscrapers around the world whose architectural form is largely determined by utilitarian concerns. The tower is in this respect an opportunity lost. The memorial pools, however, and the plaza that surrounds them, while not realizing in full the vision offered by Libeskind, provide an opportunity to remember the tragedy of

---

[39] See Irina Vinnitskaya, "Ground Zero Master Plan / Studio Daniel Libeskind," *Arch Daily*, September 23, 2012. The article includes a link to the speech Libeskind gave to the AIA convention. The video is entitled "AIA Architects of Healing: Daniel Libeskind, AIA," and can be viewed at https://youtu.be/r7hSBSujK3U.

9/11, to contemplate our vulnerability, and perhaps to recognize the fragility of even our grandest schemes.

When John Whitehead, chairman of the Lower Manhattan Development Corporation, opened the proceedings at the 2002 Winter Garden presentation of the original design schemes for Ground Zero, he began with the following remarks:

> The original World Trade Center was more than a set of buildings. It stood for global commerce over global conflict. These teams have produced world-class work that embraces and extends the ethos of the World Trade Center. Underlying these diverse plans is the common theme of rebirth. Beyond the powerful aesthetic statement that these designs make, they also convey powerful messages—they must speak to our children and our children's children about who we are and what we stand for.[40]

Architecture has had this role for as long as we can remember, ever since human beings began building temples and pyramids, ever since Abraham pitched his tent near Bethel and built an altar there to the Lord (Gen 12:8). "As for me and my household," that altar made clear to Abraham's offspring, "we will serve the LORD" (Josh 24:15).

I suggested earlier that mending the world depends on our coming to see and understand the nature of the world's brokenness. It depends on our coming to see and understand our need of healing, to understand who we really are. I have tried to illustrate the ways in which the work of architects, if it is to contribute to the mending of our world, has also to begin with a proper understanding of ourselves and of our brokenness.

Libeskind's Jewish Museum in Berlin provides us with a good example of this, I think, whereas the architecture taking shape at Ground Zero does so with only partial success. Architecture itself, of course, cannot heal our brokenness. But what we build and how we build it can reveal the extent to which the Spirit is at work within us, nudging us toward forgiveness and reconciliation and a true mending of the world.

---

[40] Cited in Goldberger, *Up from Zero*, 6.

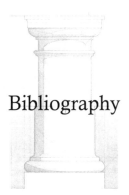

Bibliography

Abbott, W. M., ed. *The Documents of Vatican II*. London: Geoffrey Chapman, 1966.

Ackerman, James S. "The Tuscan/Rustic Order: A Study in the Metaphorical Language of Architecture." *Journal of the Society of Architectural Historians* 42, no. 1 (1983): 15–34.

Adorno, Theodor. *The Adorno Reader*. Edited by Brian O'Connor. Oxford: Blackwell, 2000.

———. "Cultural Criticism and Society." In Adorno, *Prisms*, 17–34. Cambridge: MIT Press, 1981. Reprinted in O'Connor, *Adorno Reader*, 195–210.

———. *Negative Dialectics*. London: Routledge & Kegan Paul, 1973.

———. *Notes to Literature*. Vol. 2. New York: Columbia University Press, 1992.

———. "Trying to Understand *Endgame*." *New German Critique* 26 (1982): 119–50.

Alberti, Leon Battista. *L'architettura (De re aedificatoria)*. Edited and translated by G. Orlandi and P. Portoghesi. Vol. 1. Milan: Il Polifilo, 1966.

Albright, W. F., and C. S. Mann. *Matthew: A New Translation with Introduction and Commentary*. Anchor Bible. New York: Doubleday, 1971.

Alighieri, Dante. *Paradiso: A Verse Translation*. Edited and translated by Robert and Jean Hollander. New York: Doubleday, 2007.

Allsop, Bruce. *A History of Classical Architecture*. London: Sir Isaac Pitman & Sons, 1965.

Althaus, Paul. *Die letzten Dinge: Entwurf einer christlichen Eschatologie*. 1st ed. Gütersloh: C. Bertlesmann, 1922.

Aquinas, Thomas. *The treatise "De regimine principum" or "De regno,"* in *Aquinas: Political Writings*, edited by R. W. Dyson, 5–51. Cambridge: Cambridge University Press, 2002.

Aristotle. *The "Politics" of Aristotle*. Edited and translated by Ernest Barker. Oxford: Oxford University Press, 1998.

Augustine. *The City of God against the Pagans*. Translated by R. W. Dyson. Cambridge: Cambridge University Press, 1998.

―――. *The "Confessions" of Saint Augustin*. In vol. 1 of *The Nicene and Post-Nicene Fathers*, Series 1, edited by Philip Schaff. Reprint, Peabody, Mass.: Hendrickson, 1994.

Avis, Paul. *Reshaping Ecumenical Theology: The Church Made Whole*. London: T&T Clark, 2010.

Baldasso, Renzo. "Function and Epidemiology in Filarete's Ospedale Maggiore." In *The Medieval Hospital and Medical Practice*, edited by Barbara S. Bowers, 107–20. Aldershot: Ashgate, 2007.

Barrie, Thomas. "A Home in the World: The Ontological Significance of Home." In *Architecture, Culture and Spirituality*, edited by Thomas Barrie, Julio Bermudez, and Phillip James Tabb, 93–108. Farnham: Ashgate, 2015.

Barth, Karl. *Church Dogmatics*. Edited by G. W. Bromiley and T. F. Torrance. 13 vols. Edinburgh: T&T Clark, 1956–1969.

―――. *Credo*. Translated by J. Strathearn McNabb. London: Hodder & Stoughton, 1936.

Bartholomew, Craig G. *Where Mortals Dwell: A Christian View of Place for Today*. Grand Rapids: Baker Academic, 2011.

Basil. *De Spiritu Sancto*. In vol. 8 of the *Nicene and Post-Nicene Fathers*, Series 2. Edited by Philip Schaff and Henry Wace. Reprint, Peabody, Mass.: Hendrickson, 1994.

Bauckham, Richard. *God and the Crisis of Freedom*. Louisville, Ky.: Westminster John Knox, 2002.

―――. *The Theology of the Book of Revelation*. Cambridge: Cambridge University Press, 1993.

Beale, G. K. *The Temple and the Church's Mission: A Biblical Theology of the Dwelling Place of God*. Downers Grove, Ill.: InterVarsity, 2004.

Beattie, Tina. *Eve's Pilgrimage: A Woman's Quest for the City of God*. London: Burns & Oates, 2002.

Begbie, Jeremy S. Introduction to *Sounding the Depths: Theology through the Arts*, edited by Jeremy S. Begbie, 1–13. London: SCM Press, 2002.

―――. *Music, Modernity and God: Essays in Listening*. Oxford: Oxford University Press, 2013.

―――. *Resounding Truth: Christian Wisdom in the World of Music*. Grand Rapids: Baker, 2007.

―――. *Theology, Music and Time*. Cambridge: Cambridge University Press, 2000.

―――. "Theology through the Arts." Oral presentation at the Theology and the Built Environment colloquium. Calvin College, Grand Rapids, September 2002.

―――. "Theology through the Arts." Unpublished Rationale Document for the Music and Theology colloquium, December 2001.

Bell, Allan. "Interpreting the Bible on Language: Babel and Ricoeur's Interpretive Arc." In *Ears That Hear: Explorations in Theological Interpretation of the Bible*, edited by Joel B. Green and Tim Meadowcroft, 70–93. Sheffield: Sheffield Phoenix Press, 2013.

Benson, Bruce Ellis. "Improvising Texts, Improvising Communities." In *Resonant Witness: Conversations between Music and Theology*, edited by Jeremy S. Begbie and Steven R. Guthrie, 295–322. Grand Rapids: Eerdmans, 2011.

Benson, C. David. "The Dead and the Living: Some Medieval Descriptions of the Ruins and Relics of Rome Known to the English." In Classen and Sandidge, *Urban Space*, 147–82.

Berger, Peter, Brigitte Berger, and Hansfried Kellner. *The Homeless Mind: Modernization and Consciousness*. New York: Random House, 1973.

Bergmann, Sigurd. "God's Here and Now in Built Environments." In Bergmann, *Theology in Built Environments*, 9–22.

———, ed. *Theology in Built Environments: Exploring Religion, Architecture, and Design*. New Brunswick: Transaction, 2009.

Berkouwer, G. C. *Studies in Dogmatics: The Return of Christ*. Translated by James van Oosterom. Grand Rapids: Eerdmans, 1972.

Berry, W. *Way of Ignorance*. Emeryville, Calif.: Shoemaker & Hoard, 2005.

Bess, Philip. *Till We Have Built Jerusalem: Architecture, Urbanism and the Sacred*. Wilmington, Del.: ISI Books, 2006.

Bianchini, Riccardo. "The Jewish Museum Berlin by Daniel Libeskind—Part 2." Accessed February 27, 2017. http://www.inexhibit.com/case-studies/daniel-libeskind-jewish-museum-part2/.

Birch, Debra J. *Pilgrimage to Rome in the Middle Ages: Continuity and Change*. Woodbridge, UK: Boydell Press, 1998.

Blowers, Paul M. "The *Regula Fidei* and the Narrative Character of Early Christian Faith." *Pro Ecclesia* 6, no. 2 (1998): 199–228.

Bonet i Armengol, Jordi. *Temple Sagrada Família*. 3rd ed. Barcelona: Editorial Escudo de Oro, 1997.

Bonhoeffer, Dietrich. *Christology*. Translated by John Bowden. London: Collins, 1966.

———. *Sanctorum Communio: A Theological Study of the Sociology of the Church*. London: Collins, 1963.

Borg, Marcus J., and N. T. Wright. *The Meaning of Jesus: Two Visions*. New York: HarperSanFrancisco, 1999.

Bouma-Prediger, Steven, and Brian J. Walsh. *Beyond Homelessness: Christian Faith in a Culture of Displacement*. Grand Rapids: Eerdmans, 2008.

Bouyer, Louis. *Liturgy and Architecture*. Notre Dame, Ind.: University of Notre Dame Press, 1967.

Brandenburg, Hugo. "The Use of Older Elements in the Architecture of Fourth- and Fifth-Century Rome: A Contribution to the Evaluation of Spolia." In Brilliant and Kinney, *Reuse Value*, 53–73.

Brenk, Beat. "Spolia from Constantine to Charlemagne: Aesthetics versus Ideology." *Dumbarton Oaks Papers* 41 [*Studies on Art and Archeology in Honor of Ernst Kitzinger on His Seventy-Fifth Birthday*] (1987): 103–9.

Brilliant, Richard, and Dale Kinney, eds. *Reuse Value: Spolia and Appropriation in Art and Architecture from Constantine to Sherrie Levine*. Farnham: Ashgate, 2011.

Brodman, James W. "Religion and Discipline in the Hospitals of Thirteenth-Century France." In *The Medieval Hospital and Medical Practice*, edited by Barbara S. Bowers, 123–32. Aldershot: Ashgate, 2007.

Brueggemann, Walter. *The Land: Place as Gift, Promise and Challenge in Biblical Faith*. London: SPCK, 1978.

———. *Genesis*. Interpretation Commentary. Atlanta: John Knox, 1982.

Bruschi, Arnaldo. *Bramante*. London: Thames & Hudson, 1973.

Buber, Martin. *Der Jude und sein Judentum: Gesammelte Aufsätze und Reden*. Cologne: L. Schneider, 1963.

———. "The Two Foci of the Jewish Soul." In Buber, *Israel and the World: Essays in a Time of Crisis*, 28–40. New York: Schocken Books, 1963.

Bultmann, Rudolf. *The Presence of Eternity: History and Eschatology*. New York: Harper, 1957.

Burnaby, John. *Amor Dei: A Study of the Religion of St. Augustine*. London: Hodder & Stoughton, 1938.

Burry, Mark. *Expiatory Church of the Sagrada Família*. London: Phaidon, 1993.

Calvin, John. *Institutes of the Christian Religion*. Translated by John Allen. Philadelphia: Presbyterian Board of Christian Education, 1936.

Capasso, Nicholas. "Vietnam Veterans Memorial." In *The Critical Edge: Controversy in Recent American Architecture*, edited by Tod A. Marder, 188–99. Cambridge, Mass.: MIT Press, 1985.

Casey, Edward S. *Getting Back into Place: Toward a Renewed Understanding of the Place-World*. Bloomington: Indiana University Press, 1993.

———. "Public Memory in the Making: Ethics and Place in the Wake of 9/11." In *Architecture, Ethics and the Personhood of Place*, edited by Gregory Caicco, 69–90. Hanover, N.H.: University Press of New England, 2007.

Castello, Lineau. *Rethinking the Meaning of Place: Conceiving Place in Architecture-Urbanism*. Farnham: Ashgate, 2010.

Cate, James Jeffrey. "How Green Was John's World? Ecology and Revelation." In *Essays on Revelation: Appropriating Yesterday's Apocalypse in Today's World*, edited by Gerald L. Stevens, 145–55. Eugene, Oreg.: Wipf & Stock, 2010.

Charles, Robert H. *A Critical and Exegetical Commentary on the Revelation of St. John*. 2 vols. International Critical Commentary. Edinburgh: T&T Clark, 1920.

Childs, Brevard. *Exodus*. London: SCM Press, 1974.

Classen, Albrecht. "Urban Space in the Middle Ages and the Early Modern Age: Historical, Mental, Cultural and Social Economic Investigations." In Classen and Sandidge, *Urban Space*, 1–146.

Classen, Albrecht, and Marilyn Sandidge, eds. *Urban Space in the Middle Ages and Early Modern Age*. Berlin: Walter de Gruyter, 2009.

Clement of Alexandria. *Stromateis*. In vol. 2 of *The Ante-Nicene Fathers*. Edited by Alexander Roberts and James Donaldson. 10 vols. Reprint, Peabody, Mass.: Hendrickson, 1994.

Cloag, John. *The Architectural Interpretation of History*. London: A&C Black, 1975.

Clouse, Robert C. "Fundamentalist Theology." In *The Oxford Handbook of Eschatology*, edited by Jerry L. Walls, 263–79. Oxford: Oxford University Press, 2008.

Cochrane, Charles N. *Christianity and Classical Culture*. 2nd ed. Oxford: Oxford University Press, 1944.

Cohon, Samuel S. *Essays in Jewish Theology*. Cincinnati: Hebrew Union College Press, 1987.

Connah, Roger. *Grace and Architecture*. Helsinki: Finnish Building Centre, 1998.

Costas, Orlando E. *Liberating News: A Theology of Contextual Evangelization*. Grand Rapids: Eerdmans, 1989.

Crippa, Maria Antonietta. "A Dwelling for Man within the Harmony of the Cosmos." In *Living Gaudí: The Architect's Complete Vision*, edited by Maria Antonietta Crippa, 11–38. New York: Rizzoli, 2006.

Davies, John G. *The Secular Use of Church Buildings*. London: SCM Press, 1968.

De Botton, Alain. *The Architecture of Happiness*. London: Penguin Books, 2006.

De Lange, Nicholas. *Judaism*. Oxford: Oxford University Press, 1986.

Denson, G. Roger. "Michael Arad's 9/11 Memorial 'Reflecting Absence': More Than a Metaphor or a Monument." *Huffington Post*, September 9, 2011. Updated May 27, 2016. http://www.huffingtonpost.com/g-roger-denson/michael-arads-911-memoria_b_955454.html.

Descartes, René. *"Discourse on Method" and "The Meditations."* Translated by F. E. Sutcliffe. Harmondsworth: Penguin Books, 1968.

Dodd, C. H. *The Parables of the Kingdom*. Rev. ed. London: Nisbet, 1936.

Dods, Marcus. *Haggai, Zechariah, Malachi*. Edinburgh: T&T Clark, 1956.

Dovey, K. "Home and Homelessness." In *Home Environments*, edited by I. Altman and C. M. Werner, 33–64. Human Behavior and Environment 8. New York: Plenum, 1985.

Dripps, R. D. *The First House: Myth, Paradigm and the Task of Architecture*. Cambridge, Mass.: MIT Press, 1997.

Dyer, Joseph. "Roman Processions of the Major Litany (*litaniae maiores*) from the Sixth to the Twelfth Century." In Ó Carragain and Neuman de Vegvar, *Roma Felix*, 112–37.

Eliach, Yaffa. *Hasidic Tales of the Holocaust*. New York: Oxford University Press, 1982.

Eliade, Mircea. *The Sacred and the Profane: The Nature of Religion*. Translated by Willard R. Trask. New York: Harcourt, Brace & World, 1959.

Ellul, Jacques. *The Meaning of the City*. Translated by Dennis Pardee. Grand Rapids: Eerdmans, 1970.

Emerson, Mary. *Greek Sanctuaries: An Introduction*. London: Bristol Classical Press, 2007.

Ennen, Edith. *The Medieval Town*. Translated by Natalie Fryde. Europe in the Middle Ages. Amsterdam: North-Holland, 1979.

Esch, Arnold. "On the Reuse of Antiquity: The Perspectives of the Archaeologist and the Historian." In Brilliant and Kinney, *Reuse Value*, 13–31.

———. "Spolien: Zur Wiederverwendung antiker Baustücke und Skulpturen in mittelalterlichen Italien." *Archiv für Kulturgeschichte* 51 (1969): 1–64.

Farrow, Douglas. *Acension and Ecclesia: On the Significance of the Doctrine of Ascension for Ecclesiology and Christian Cosmology*. Edinburgh: T&T Clark, 1999.

———. *Ascension Theology*. London: T&T Clark, 2011.

Fiddes, Paul. *The Promised End: Eschatology in Theology and Literature*. Oxford: Blackwell, 2000.

Filarete [Antonio di Piero Averlino]. *Antonio Averlino detto il Filarete, Trattato di architettura*. Edited by Maria Finoli and Liliana Grassi. 2 vols. Milan: Edizioni il Polifilo, 1972. English translation by John R. Spenser, *Treatise on Architecture: Being the Treatise by Antonio di Piero Averlino, Known as Filarete*. 2 vols. New Haven, Conn.: Yale University Press, 1965.

Freyne, Sean. *Jesus, a Jewish Galilean: A New Reading of the Jesus Story*. London: T&T Clark, 2004.

Fromm, Erich. *The Forgotten Language: An Introduction to the Understanding of Dreams, Fairy Tales and Myths*. New York: Rinehart, 1951.

Frugoni, Arsenio. Introduction to C. Frugoni, *A Day in a Medieval City*, 1–13. Chicago: University of Chicago Press, 2005.

Frugoni, Chiara. *A Day in a Medieval City*. Chicago: University of Chicago Press, 2005.

Garber, Kent. "A Milestone for a Memorial That Has Touched Millions," *U.S. News and World Report*, November 3, 2007. https://www.usnews.com/news/articles/2007/11/03/milestone-for-a-memorial-that-has-touched.

Giedion, Sigfried. *Space, Time and Architecture: The Growth of a New Tradition*. Cambridge, Mass.: Harvard University Press, 1967.

Gilliam-Knight, Diane, and Loren Robb, eds. *Te Maungarongo: The Ancestral House of the Maori Synod*. Wellington: Presbyterian Church of Aotearoa New Zealand, 1992.

Girouard, Mark. *Cities and People: A Social and Architectural History*. New Haven: Yale University Press, 1985.

Glanz, James, and Eric Lipton. *City in the Sky: The Rise and Fall of the World Trade Center*. New York: Henry Holt, 2003.

Glatzer, Nahum N., ed. *The Passover Haggadah*. New York: Schocken Books, 1989.

Goldberger, Paul. *Up from Zero: Politics, Architecture and the Rebuilding of New York*. New York: Random House, 2004.

———. *Why Architecture Matters*. New Haven: Yale University Press, 2009.

Goldingay, John. *Old Testament Theology*. Vol. 2, *Israel's Faith*. Downers Grove, Ill.: InterVarsity, 2006.

Gorringe, T. J. *A Theology of the Built Environment: Justice, Empowerment, Redemption*. Cambridge: Cambridge University Press, 2002.

Greene-McCreight, Kathryn. "Rule of Faith." In *Dictionary for Theological Interpretation of the Bible*, edited by Kevin J. Vanhoozer, 703–4. Grand Rapids: Baker Academic, 2005.

Greenstein, Howard R. *Judaism—an Eternal Covenant*. Philadelphia: Fortress, 1983.

Gregory Nazianzus (Gregory Nazianzen). "On the Holy Spirit," in vol. 7 of *The Nicene and Post-Nicene Fathers*, Series 2. Edited by Philip Schaff and Henry Wace. Reprint, Peabody, Mass.: Hendrickson, 1994.

———. *Orations*. In vol. 7 of the *The Nicene and Post-Nicene Fathers*, Series 2. Edited by Philip Schaff and Henry Wace. Reprint, Peabody, Mass.: Hendrickson, 1994.

Grünberg, Wolfgang, and Anna Körs. "'Symbolkirchen' as Bridges or Boundary Stones in a Merging Europe?" In Bergmann, *Theology in Built Environments*, 69–107.

Grundmann, Stefan, ed. *The Architecture of Rome*. Stuttgart: Axel Menges, 1998.

Gunton, Colin E. *Christ and Creation*. Carlisle, UK: Paternoster, 1992.

———. *Father, Son and Holy Spirit: Toward a Fully Trinitarian Theology*. London: T&T Clark, 2003.

———. "God, Grace and Freedom." In *God and Freedom: Essays in Historical and Systematic Theology*, edited by Colin E. Gunton, 119–33. Edinburgh: T&T Clark, 1995.

———. *The One, the Three and the Many: God, Creation and the Culture of Modernity*. Cambridge: Cambridge University Press, 1993.

———. *The Triune Creator: A Historical and Systematic Study*. Edinburgh: Edinburgh University Press, 1998.

Halbwachs, Maurice. *On Collective Memory*. Translated by Lewis A. Coser. Chicago: University of Chicago Press, 1992.

Harries, Karsten. *The Ethical Function of Architecture*. Cambridge: Mass.: MIT Press, 1997.

Hart, David Bentley. "God or Nothingness." In *I Am the Lord Your God: Christian Reflections on the Ten Commandments*, edited by Carl E. Braaten and Christopher R. Seitz, 56–76. Grand Rapids: Eerdmans, 2005.

Havel, Václav. "It Always Makes Sense to Tell the Truth." In *Open Letters: Selected Writings, 1965–1990*, ed. Paul Wilson, 84–101. London: Faber & Faber, 1991.

Heidegger, Martin. "Building, Dwelling, Thinking." In Heidegger, *Poetry, Language, Thought*, translated by Albert Hofstadter, 145–61. New York: Harper & Row, 1971.

Heschel, Abraham. "Law and Life." In *Between God and Man: An Interpretation of Judaism: From the Writings of Abraham J. Heschel*, edited by Fritz A. Rothschild, 161–64. New York: Harper & Brothers, 1959.

————. "Religion and Law." In *Between God and Man: An Interpretation of Judaism. From the Writings of Abraham J. Heschel*, edited by Fritz A. Rothschild, 155–61. New York: Harper & Brothers, 1959.

Hesselink, I. John. "Pneumatology." In *The Calvin Handbook*, edited by J. Selderhuis, 299–312. Grand Rapids: Eerdmans, 2009.

Holt, Elizabeth Gilmore, ed. *A Documentary History of Art*. Vol. 1, *The Middle Ages and the Renaissance*. Princeton: Princeton University Press, 1947.

Hood, Renate Viveen. "Pure or Defiled? A Sociological Analysis of John's Apocalypse." In *Essays on Revelation: Appropriating Yesterday's Apocalypse in Today's World*, edited by Gerald L. Stevens, 87–99. Eugene, Oreg.: Wipf & Stock, 2010.

Horkheimer, Max, and Theodor Adorno. *Dialectic of Enlightenment*. New York: Herder & Herder, 1972.

Hunsinger, George. *The Eucharist and Ecumenism: Let Us Keep the Feast*. Cambridge: Cambridge University Press, 2008.

Hunter, Shennan. "Women, Men and Markets: The Gendering of Market Space in LateMedieval Ghent." In Classen and Sandidge, *Urban Space*, 409–31.

Huyssen, Andreas. "Monumental Seduction." *New German Critique* 69 (1996): 181–200.

Inge, John. *A Christian Theology of Place*. Aldershot: Ashgate, 2003.

Inwood, William Henry. *The Erechtheion at Athens*. London: James Carpenter & Son, 1827.

Irenaeus. *Against the Heresies*. In vol. 1 of *The Ante-Nicene Fathers*, edited by Alexander Roberts and James Donaldson. Reprint, Peabody, Mass.: Hendrickson, 1994.

Isidore of Seville. *The Etymologies of Isidore of Seville*. Translated by Stephen A. Barney, W. J. Lewis, J. A. Beach, and Oliver Berghof. Cambridge: Cambridge University Press, 2006.

Jacobson, Howard. "An Afterthought of Violence." *Guardian*, October 11, 2007.

Jara, Cynthia. "Adolf Loos's 'Raumplan' Theory." *Journal of Architectural Education* 48, no. 3 (1995): 185–201.

Jenson, Robert W. "God, Space and Architecture." In Jenson, *Essays in Theology of Culture*, 9–15. Grand Rapids: Eerdmans, 1995.

————. *Systematic Theology*. 2 vols. Oxford: Oxford University Press, 1997–1999.

Jerome. "Letter 123." In vol. 6 of *The Nicene and Post-Nicene Fathers*, Series 2. Edited by Philip Schaff and Henry Wace. Reprint, Peabody, Mass.: Hendrickson, 1994.

Johnson, Kristen Deede. *Theology, Political Theory and Pluralism: Beyond Tolerance and Difference*. Cambridge: Cambridge University Press, 2006.

Kahn, Louis I. *Writings, Lectures, Interviews*. Edited by Alessandra Latour. New York: Rizzoli, 1991.

Kant, Immanuel. *Critique of Pure Reason*. Translated by Norman Kemp Smith. 2nd ed. Houndsmill, UK: Macmillan, 1933.

Kessler, Herbert L., and Johanna Zacharias. *Rome 1300: On the Path of a Pilgrim*. New Haven: Yale University Press, 2000.

Kieckhefer, Richard. *Theology in Stone: Church Architecture from Byzantium to Berkeley*. Oxford: Oxford University Press, 2004.

Kierkegaard, Søren. *The Concept of Anxiety*. Edited and translated by Reidar Thomte. Princeton: Princeton University Press, 1980.

———. *Journals and Papers*. Vol. 2. Edited and translated by Howard V. Hong and Edna H. Hong. Bloomington: Indiana University Press, 1970.

———. *Philosophical Fragments*. Edited and translated by Howard V. Hong and Edna H. Hong. Princeton: Princeton University Press, 1985.

———. *Upbuilding Discourses in Various Spirits*. Edited and translated by Howard V. Hong and Edna H. Hong. Princeton: Princeton University Press, 1993.

———. *Works of Love*. Edited and translated by Howard V. Hong and Edna H. Hong. Princeton: Princeton University Press, 1995.

Kinnard, Jacob N. *Places in Motion: The Fluid Identities of Temples, Images, and Pilgrims*. New York: Oxford University Press, 2014.

Kinney, Dale. Introduction to Brilliant and Kinney, *Reuse Value*, 1–11.

Knight, Douglas. *The Eschatological Economy: Time and the Hospitality of God*. Grand Rapids: Eerdmans, 2006.

Kogan, Michael. *Opening the Covenant: A Jewish Theology of Christianity*. Oxford: Oxford University Press, 2007.

Kostof, Spiro. *A History of Architecture: Settings and Rituals*. 2nd ed. New York: Oxford University Press, 1995.

Kovacs, Judith, and Christopher Rowland. *Revelation: The Apocalypse of Jesus Christ*. Blackwell Bible Commentaries. Oxford: Blackwell, 2004.

Kraus, Rosalind. "Grids." *October* 9 (1979): 50–64.

Kuhn, Thomas. *The Structure of Scientific Revolutions*. 2nd ed. Chicago: University of Chicago Press, 1970.

Kümmel, W. G. *Promise and Fulfilment: The Eschatological Message of Jesus*. Studies in Biblical Theology 23. Naperville, Ill.: Allenson, 1957.

Küng, Hans. *The Church*. Translated by Ray Ockenden and Rosaleen Ockenden. London: SCM Press, 1968.

Kunstler, James Howard. *The Rise and Decline of America's Man-Made Landscape*. New York: Touchstone, 1994.

Kuschel, Karl-Joseph. *Born before All Time?: The Dispute over Christ's Origin*. Translated by John Bowden. London: SCM Press, 1992.

Kwant, Remy. "We Inhabit the World." *Humanitas* 12, no. 3 (1976): 299–309.

Lane, William. *The Gospel of Mark*. Grand Rapids: Eerdmans, 1974.

Laugier, Marc-Antoine. *An Essay on Architecture*. Translated by Wolfgang Hermann and Annie Hermann. Los Angeles: Hennessey & Ingalls, 1977.

Le Corbusier. *The City of Tomorrow*. Translated by F. Etchells. New York: Dover, 1987.

―――. *Towards an Architecture.* 2nd ed. 1928. Reprint, London: Frances Lincoln, 2008.

LeFebvre, Henri. "Reflections on the Politics of Space." Translated by Michael J. Enders. *Antipode* 8 (1976): 30–36.

Le Gates, Richard T., and Frederic Stout, eds. *The City Reader.* London: Routledge, 1996.

Lesk, Alexandra L. "A Diachronic Examination of the Erechtheion and Its Reception." Ph.D. diss., University of Cincinnati, 2004.

Lessing, Gotthold Ephraim. "On the Proof of the Spirit and of Power." In *Lessing's Theological Writings,* selected and translated by Henry Chadwick, 51–56. London: A&C Black, 1956.

Lewis, John. "The Influence on Medieval Church Architecture of Love for God: A Theological Approach." Ph.D. diss., University of Otago, 2009.

Libeskind, Daniel. Presentation at the Winter Garden. December 18, 2002. http://www.renewnyc.com/plan%5Fdes%5Fdev/wtc%5Fsite/new%5Fdesign%5Fplans/firm_d/default.asp.

―――. *The Space of Encounter.* New York: Universe, 2000.

Lightfoot, R. H. *Locality and Doctrine in the Gospels.* London: Hodder & Stoughton, 1938.

Lilburne, Geoffrey R. *A Sense of Place: A Christian Theology of the Land.* Nashville: Abingdon, 1989.

Liverani, Paolo. "Reading *Spolia* in Late Antiquity and Contemporary Perception." In Brilliant and Kinney, *Reuse Value,* 33–51.

Luo, Jialing. "Imagining Modernity: Memory, Space and Symbolism in The Hague." In *Cities Full of Symbols: A Theory of Urban Space and Culture,* edited by Peter J. M. Nars, 173–85. Leiden: Leiden University Press, 2011.

Luther, Martin. "Lectures on Galatians." In *Luther's Works,* vol. 26, edited by Jaroslav Pelikan. Saint Louis: Concordia, 1963.

MacIntyre, Alasdair. *After Virtue.* Notre Dame, Ind.: University of Notre Dame Press, 1981.

Malina, Bruce J. *The New Jerusalem in the Revelation of John: The City as Symbol of Life with God.* Collegeville, Minn.: Liturgical Press, 1995.

Malpas, Jeff. *Heidegger's Topology: Being, Place, World.* Cambridge, Mass.: MIT Press, 2006.

Marcuse, Peter. "The Ground Zero Architectural Competition: Designing without a Plan." *Progressive Planning Magazine,* Winter 2003, http://www.plannersnetwork.org/2003/01/the-ground-zero-architectural-competition-designing-without-a-plan/.

Marion, Jean Luc. *God without Being.* Translated by Thomas A. Carlson. Chicago: University of Chicago Press, 1991.

Markus, R. A. *The End of Ancient Christianity.* Cambridge: Cambridge University Press, 1990.

Markus, Thomas A. *Buildings and Power: Freedom and Control in Modern Building Types*. New York: Routledge, 1993.

Martin, Francis. "The Word at Prayer: Epistemology in the Psalms." In *The Bible and Epistemology: Biblical Soundings on the Knowledge of God*, edited by Mary Healey and Robin Parry, 43–64. Milton Keynes: Paternoster, 2007.

Mayernik, David. *Timeless Cities: An Architect's Reflections on Renaissance Italy*. Boulder, Colo.: Westview Press, 2003.

McGuckin, John. "Symeon the New Theologian's *Hymns of Divine Eros*: A Neglected Masterpiece of the Christian Mystical Tradition." *Spiritus* 5 (2005): 182–202.

McPartlan, Paul. *The Eucharist Makes the Church: Henri de Lubac and John Zizioulas in Dialogue*. Edinburgh: T&T Clark, 1993.

Merton, Thomas. Introduction to Augustine, *The City of God*, translated by Marcus Dods, xv–xx. New York: Random House, 1950.

Middleton, J. Richard. *A New Heaven and a New Earth: Reclaiming Biblical Eschatology*. Grand Rapids: Baker, 2014.

Miles, Malcolm. *Art, Space and the City: Public Art and Urban Futures*. London: Routledge, 1989.

Mill, John Stuart. "On Liberty." In Mill, *Three Essays: "On Liberty"; "Representative Government"; "The Subjection of Women,"* 5–141. Oxford: Oxford University Press, 1975.

Miller, Keith D. *Martin Luther King's Biblical Epic: His Final, Great Speech*. Jackson: University Press of Mississippi, 2012.

Mollat, Michael. *The Poor in the Middle Ages: An Essay in Social History*. Translated by Arthur Goldhammer. New Haven: Yale University Press, 1986.

Moltmann, Jürgen. *The Coming of God*. Translated by Margaret Kohl. Minneapolis: Fortress, 1996.

———. *The Way of Jesus Christ: Christology in Messianic Dimensions*. Translated by Margaret Kohl. London: SCM Press, 1990.

Montaigne, Michel. *Travel Journal*. Translated by Donald M. Frame. New York: North Point, 1983.

Mostert, Christiaan. "The Kingdom Anticipated: The Church and Eschatology." *International Journal of Systematic Theology* 13, no. 1 (2011): 25–37.

Mumford, Lewis. *The City in History: Its Origins, Its Transformations, and Its Prospects*. New York: Harcourt, Brace & World, 1961.

Münz, Ludwig, and Gustav Künstler. *Adolf Loos: A Pioneer of Modern Architecture*. New York: Praeger, 1966.

Norberg-Schulz, Christian. *L'abitare: L'insediamento, lo spazio urbano, la casa*. Milan: Electa, 1995.

———. *Architecture: Meaning and Place*. New York: Rizzoli, 1988.

———. *The Concept of Dwelling: On the Way to Figurative Architecture*. New York: Rizzoli, 1985.

———. *Existence, Space and Architecture*. New York: Praeger, 1971.

———. *Intentions in Architecture*. Oslo: University Press, 1963.

————. *Meaning in Western Architecture.* New York: Rizzoli, 1980.

Noreen, Kirstin. "Sacred Memory and Confraternal Space: The Insignia of theConfraternity of the Santissimo Salvatore (Rome)." In Ó Carragain and Neuman de Vegvar, *Roma Felix*, 159–87.

Noth, Martin. *Exodus.* Translated by J. S. Bowden. London: SCM Press, 1962.

Oberman, Heiko. *The Reformation: Roots and Ramifications.* London: T&T Clark, 2004.

Ó Carragain, Éamonn, and Carol Neuman de Vegvar, eds. *Roma Felix: Formation and Reflections of Medieval Rome.* Aldershot: Ashgate, 2007.

O'Daly, Gerard. *Augustine's "City of God": A Reader's Guide.* Oxford: Clarendon, 1999.

Oppenheimer, Helen. "Making God Findable." In *The Parish Church: Explorations in the Relationship of the Church and the World*, 65–78, edited by Giles Ecclestone. London: Mowbray, 1988.

Ouroussof, Nicolai. "Towers' Symbolic Image." *Los Angeles Times*, September 13, 2001, A32. http://articles.latimes.com/2001/sep/13/news/mn-45326.

Pahl, John. *Shopping Malls and Other Sacred Spaces: Putting God in Place.* Grand Rapids: Brazos Press, 2003.

Pallasmaa, Juhani. "Artistic Generosity, Humility and Expression: Architecture as Lived Metaphor, Collaboration, Faith and Compassion." In Bergmann, *Theology in Built Environments*, 23–38.

————. *The Embodied Image: Imagination and Imagery in Architecture.* Chichester: John Wiley & Sons, 2011.

Pannenberg, Wolfhart. *Jesus—God and Man.* Translated by Lewis L. Wilkins and Duane A. Priebe. London: SCM Press, 1968.

————. *Systematic Theology.* Translated by Geoffrey W. Bromiley. Vol. 3. Grand Rapids: Eerdmans, 1998.

————. *Theology and the Kingdom of God.* Edited by R. J. Neuhaus. Philadelphia: Westminster, 1969.

Park, K., and J. Henderson. " 'The First Hospital among Christians': The Ospedale di Santa Maria Nuova in Early Sixteenth-Century Florence." *Medical History* 35, no. 2 (1991): 164–88.

Pastor, Ludwig, Freiherr von. *Sisto V: Il Creatore della Nuova Roma.* Rome: Tipografia Poliglotta Vaticana, 1922.

Pauly, Danièle. *Le Courbusier: The Chapel at Ronchamp.* Basel: Birkhaüser, 1997.

Peterson, Eugene H. *The Pastor.* New York: HarperCollins, 2011.

Pirenne, Henri. *Medieval Cities.* Princeton: Princeton University Press, 1925.

Plato. *"Protagoras" and "Meno."* Translated by W. K. C. Guthrie. Harmondsworth: Penguin Books, 1956.

————. *Timaeus.* Translated by Francis M. Cornford. Indianapolis: Liberal Arts, 1959.

Pseudo-Dionysius. *De mystica theologia.* In *Pseudo-Dionysius: The Complete Works*, translated by Colm Luibheid, 133–42. London: SPCK, 1987.

Rae, Murray. "Architectural Expression of the Body of Christ." In *The Bible and Art, Perspectives from Oceania*, edited by Caroline Blyth and Nāsili Vaka'utu, 73–95. London: Bloomsbury, 2017.

―――. "To Render Praise: Humanity in God's World." In *Environmental Stewardship: Critical Perspectives Past and Present*, edited by R. J. Berry, 291–311. London: T&T Clark, 2006.

Richards, Simon. "The Anti-Social Urbanism of Le Corbusier." *Common Knowledge* 13, no. 1 (2007): 50–66.

Ritschl, Dietrich. *Memory and Hope: An Enquiry Concerning the Presence of Christ.* New York: Macmillan, 1967.

Rogers, Richard. *Cities for a Small Planet.* London: Faber & Faber, 1997.

Rowe, C. Kavin. *World Upside Down: Reading Acts in the Graeco-Roman Age.* Oxford: Oxford University Press, 2009.

Rowe, Peter G. *Civic Realism.* Cambridge, Mass.: MIT Press, 1997.

Royal, Te Ahukaramū Charles. "Papatūanuku—the Land—Whakapapa and Kaupapa." In *Te Ara—the Encyclopedia of New Zealand.* Accessed February 18, 2016. http://www.TeAra.govt.nz/en/speech/11470/roimata-toroa-pattern.

Ruskin, John. *The Stones of Venice.* Vol. 3, *The Fall.* 4th ed. Orpington, UK: George Allen, 1886.

Russell, David M. *The "New Heavens and the New Earth": Hope for the Creation in Jewish Apocalyptic and the New Testament.* Studies in Biblical Apocalyptic Literature 1. Philadelphia: Visionary Press, 1996.

Rykwert, Joseph. *The Idea of a Town: The Anthropology of Urban Form in Rome, Italy and the Ancient World.* Cambridge, Mass.: MIT Press, 1988.

―――. *On Adam's House in Paradise: The Idea of the Primitive Hut in Architectural History.* 2nd ed. Cambridge, Mass.: MIT Press, 1981.

Sanders, E. P. *Paul and Palestinian Judaism.* Philadelphia: Fortress, 1977.

Sauter, Gerhard. *Eschatological Rationality: Theological Issues in Focus.* Grand Rapids: Baker, 1996.

Saxer, Victor. "L'utilisation par le liturgie de l'éspace urbain et suburbain: L'exemple de Rome dans l'antiquité et le haut Moyen-Âge." In *Actes du XIe Congrès International d'Archéologie Chrétienne: Lyon, Vienne, Grenoble, Genève et Aoste (21–28 septembre 1986)*, edited by Noël Duval, 2:917–1033. 2 vols. Studi di Antichità Cristiana 41—Collection de l'École française de Rome 123. Rome: École française de Rome, 1989.

Schnackenburg, Rudolf. *God's Rule and Kingdom.* New York: Herder & Herder, 1963.

Schneider, Bernhard. *Daniel Libeskind: Jewish Museum Berlin.* 1999. 3rd ed. Munich: Prestel, 2004.

Schoeps, H. J. *Paul: The Theology of the Apostle in the Light of Jewish Religious History.* Philadelphia: Westminster, 1961.

Schweitzer, Albert. *The Quest of the Historical Jesus.* Translated by W. Montgomery. 3rd ed. London: SCM Press, 1981.

Schweizer, Eduard. *The Good News according to Matthew*. London: SPCK, 1976.

Scruton, Roger. *The Aesthetics of Architecture*. London: Methuen, 1979.

Seasoltz, R. Kevin. *A Sense of the Sacred: Theological Foundations of Christian Architecture and Art*. London: Continuum, 2005.

Sennett, Richard. *The Conscience of the Eye: The Design and Social Life of Cities*. New York: W. W. Norton, 1990.

Serlio, Sebastiano. *Tutte l'opere d'architettura et prospettiva di Sebastiano Serlio Bolognese*. Venice, 1619.

Seymour, M. C., ed. *The Metrical Version of Mandeville's Travels*. Early English Society, o.s. 269. London: Oxford University Press, 1973.

Sheldrake, Philip. *Spaces for the Sacred: Place, Memory and Identity*. London: SCM Press, 2001.

———. "A Spiritual City? Place, Memory and City Making." In *Architecture, Ethics and the Personhood of Place*, edited by Gregory Caicco, 50–68. Hanover, N.H.: University Press New England, 2007.

———. *The Spiritual City: Theology, Spirituality, and the Urban*. Oxford: Wiley Blackwell, 2014.

———. "A Spiritual City: Urban Vision and the Christian Tradition." In Bergmann, *Theology in Built Environments*, 151–69.

Smith, P. D. *City: A Guidebook for the Urban Age*. London: Bloomsbury, 2012.

Smith, Terry. *The Architecture of Aftermath*. Chicago: University of Chicago Press, 2006.

Smith, Thomas Gordon. *Classical Architecture: Rule and Invention*. Layton, Utah: Gibbs M. Smith, 1988.

Solà-Morales, Ignasi de. *Antoni Gaudí*. New York: Harry N. Abrams, 2003.

Solomon, Deborah. "From the Rubble, Ideas for Rebirth." *New York Times*, September 30, 2001, B37.

Sovik, E. A. *Architecture for Worship*. Minneapolis: Augsburg, 1973.

Sparshott, Francis. "The Aesthetics of Architecture and the Politics of Space." In *Philosophy and Architecture*, edited by Michael H. Mitias, 3–20. Amsterdam: Rodopi, 1994.

Steiner, George. *Real Presences*. London: Faber & Faber, 1989.

Stephens, Mark B. *Annihilation or Renewal? The Meaning and Function of New Creation in the Book of Revelation*. Tübingen: Mohr Siebeck, 2011.

Stephens, Suzanne. "Fantasy Intersects with Reality at Ground Zero." In *Imagining Ground Zero: Official and Unofficial Proposals for the World Trade Center Competition*, edited by Suzanne Stephens, Ian Luna, and Ron Broadhurst, 12–25. London: Thames & Hudson, 2004.

Summerson, John. *The Classical Language of Architecture*. London: Thames & Hudson, 1980.

Symeon. *Symeon the New Theologian: The Discourses*. Translated by C. J. Catanzaro. New York: Paulist, 1980.

Taylor, Charles. *The Ethics of Authenticity*. Cambridge, Mass.: Harvard University Press, 1991.

———. *Hegel and Modern Society*. Cambridge: Cambridge University Press, 1979.

———. *Sources of the Self: The Making of Modern Identity*. Cambridge, Mass.: Harvard University Press, 1989.

Taylor, Iain. *Pannenberg on the Triune God*. London: T&T Clark, 2007.

Tertullian. *The Prescription against Heretics*. In vol. 3 of *The Ante-Nicene Fathers*. Edited by Alexander Roberts and James Donaldson. Reprint, Peabody, Mass.: Hendrickson, 1994.

Thacker, Alan. "Rome of the Martyrs: Saints, Cults and Relics, Fourth to Seventh Centuries." In Ó Carragain and Neuman de Vegvar, *Roma Felix*, 13–49.

Thiébaut, Philippe. *Gaudí: Builder of Visions*. Translated by Harry N. Abrams. London: Thames & Hudson, 2002.

Till, Karen E. *The New Berlin: Memory, Politics, Place*. Minneapolis: University of Minnesota Press, 2005.

Torrance, James B. *Worship, Community and the Triune God of Grace*. Downers Grove, Ill.: InterVarsity, 1996.

Torrance, Thomas F. *Space, Time and Incarnation*. Oxford: Oxford University Press, 1969.

Tuan, Yi-Fu. *Space and Place: The Perspective of Experience*. Minneapolis: University of Minnesota Press, 1977.

Turner, Harold W. *From Temple to Meeting House*. The Hague: Mouton, 1979.

Tzonis, Alexander, and Liane Lefaivre. *Classical Architecture: The Poetics of Order*. Cambridge, Mass.: MIT Press, 1986.

Van Pelt, Robert Jan. "Apocalyptic Abjection" and "Prophetic Remembrance." In van Pelt and Carroll William Westfall, *Architectural Principles in an Age of Historicism*, 317–81 and 75–137. New Haven: Yale University Press, 1991.

Vinnitskaya, Irina. "Ground Zero Master Plan / Studio Daniel Libeskind." *Arch Daily*, September 23, 2012. www.archdaily.com/272280/ground-zero -master-plan-studio-daniel-libeskind/.

Viñoly, Rafael. "Fill the Void with Beauty." *New York Times*, September 23, 2001.

Vitruvius. *On Architecture*. Translated by Frank Granger. 2 vols. Loeb Classical Library. London: William Heinemann, 1931.

———. *The Ten Books on Architecture*. Translated by Morris Hicky Morgan. New York: Dover, 1960.

Von Rad, Gerhard, *The Message of the Prophets*. Translated by D. M. G. Stalker. London: SCM Press, 1968.

Vos, Geerhardus. *The Pauline Eschatology*. Grand Rapids: Eerdmans, 1952.

Ward, Graham. *Cities of God*. London: Routledge, 2000.

Watkins, Tony. *The Human House: Sustainable Design*. Auckland: Karaka Bay Press, 2009.

Webster, John. *Barth's Moral Theology*. Edinburgh: T&T Clark, 1985.

Weiss, Johannes. *Jesus' Proclamation of the Kingdom of God*. Philadelphia: Fortress, 1971.

Wells, Samuel. *Improvisation: The Drama of Christian Ethics*. Grand Rapids: Brazos Press, 2004.

Westerholm, Stephen. *Israel's Law and the Church's Faith: Paul and His Recent Interpreters*. Grand Rapids: Eerdmans, 1988.

White, Lynn. "The Historical Roots of Our Ecological Crisis." *Science* 155, no. 3767 (1967): 1203–12.

Wilken, Robert L. "Augustine's City of God Today." In *The Two Cities of God*, edited by Carl E. Braaten and Robert W. Jenson, 28–41. Grand Rapids: Eerdmans, 1997.

Williams, Rowan. "Making It Strange: Theology in Other(s') Words." In *Sounding the Depths: Theology through the Arts*, edited by Jeremy S. Begbie, 19–38. London: SCM Press, 2002.

Wolin, Sheldon. *Politics and Visions: Continuity and Innovation in Western Political Thought*. Boston: Little, Brown, 1960.

Wright, N. T. "How Can the Bible Be Authoritative?" *Vox Evangelica* 21 (1991): 7–32.

———. *Jesus and the Victory of God*. London: SPCK, 1996.

Yeoman, Selwyn. "Is Anyone in Charge Here? A Christological Evaluation of the Idea of Human Dominion over Creation." Ph.D. diss., University of Otago, 2011.

Yerushalmi, Yosef Hayim. *Zakhor: Jewish History and Jewish Memory*. Rev. ed. Seattle: University of Washington Press, 1996.

Yule, Ian R., ed. *My Mother the Land*. Galiwin'ku: Galiwin'ku Literature Production Centre, 1980.

Zachman, Randall. "Communio cum Christo." In *The Calvin Handbook*, edited by Herman J. Selderhuis, 365–71. Grand Rapids: Eerdmans, 2009.

Zizioulas, John. *Lectures in Christian Dogmatics*. Edited by Douglas H. Knight. London: T&T Clark, 2008.

Zuckerkandl, Victor. *Sound and Symbol: Music and the External World*. Translated by Willard R. Trask. London: Routledge & Kegan Paul, 1956.

Credits

Figure 1.1 The Mall, Washington, D.C. Photo © Dreamstime.com/Laryn Kragt Bakker.

Figure 2.1 St Paul's Cathedral. Photo by Author.

Figure 2.2 Library of Admont Abbey. © Photographer Jorge Royan, under a Creative Commons license. http://www.royan.com.ar.

Figure 3.1 Tuscan Order. Watercolor by Crystal Filep. Used with permission.

Figure 3.2 Ionic Order. Watercolor by Crystal Filep. Used with permission.

Figure 3.3 Corinthian Order. Watercolor by Crystal Filep. Used with permission.

Figure 3.4 Doric Temple. Watercolor by Crystal Filep. Used with permission.

Figure 3.5 The Tempietto. Photo by Author.

Figure 3.6 Metopes of the Tempietto. Photo by Author.

Figure 3.7 San Carlo alle Quattro Fontane. Photo by Author.

Figure 3.8 The Erechtheion. © Dreamstime.com/Evgeniy Fesenko.

Figure 4.1 Porphyry Columns in the Baptistery of St. John Lateran, Rome. Photo by Author.

Figure 4.2 Apse Mosaic, Santa Pudenziana. Photo by Author.

Figure 4.3 The Pantheon. Photo by Author.

Figure 4.4 The Colosseum. Photo by Author.

Figure 4.5 The Colosseum Cross. Photo by Author.

Figure 5.1   *The Virgin commends Siena to Jesus*, tablet by Biccherna, painted by Neroccio di Bartolomeo, 1480 (High Renaissance). Exhibited at the State Archives of Siena. Reproduced with the permission of the Ministero per i Beni e le Attività Culturali / Alinari Archives, Florence. Photograph by George Tatge for Alinari.

Figure 5.2   The Arch of Titus. Photo by Author.

Figure 5.3   Trident Street Pattern, in *La nuova topografia di Roma Comasco*, by Giambattista Nolli, ca. 1692–1756. Public domain.

Figure 5.4   The Borgo District, Public domain.

Figure 5.5   Piazza del Campo. Photo by Author.

Figure 5.6   Ospedale degli Innocenti. Photo by Author.

Figure 5.7   Roundels of the Ospedale degli Innocenti. Photo by Author.

Figure 5.8   Hospital of the Holy Spirit, Rome. Photo by Otellodian, 2011. Creative Commons.

Figure 5.9   San Clemente Atrium. Photo by Author.

Figure 5.10   San Clemente Interior. Photo by Author.

Figure 6.1   Plan Voisin. Photo by SiefkinDR. Creative Commons.

Figure 6.2   Church of the Light. Photo © Dreamstime.com/Siraanamwong.

Figure 6.3   *Te Maungarongo*, Exterior. Photo by Author.

Figure 6.4   *Te Maungarongo*, Interior. Photo by Author.

Figure 6.5   *Cardboard Church*, by Paul Hebblethwaite. Photo by Paul Hebblethwaite. Used with permission of the artist.

Figure 7.1   Rufer House, showing the development of the first floor plan from the quadripartite structure established by the crossed axes and the central column. Drawings by Julie Oseid. © Cynthia Jara. Used with permission.

Figure 7.2   Church of the Good Shepherd, Lake Tekapo. Photo by Author.

Figure 7.3   Church of the Good Shepherd, Interior. Photo by Denis Wilford. © Denis Wilford 2001–2016. Creative Commons Attribution 4.0 International License.

Figure 7.4   Salk Institute for Biological Studies. Photo by Thomas Bögl. Used with permission.

Figure 8.1   Wells Cathedral. Photo © Holly Hayes/EdStockPhoto. Used with permission.

Figure 8.2   Cloister at the University of Milan. Photo by Author.

Figure 8.3   La Sagrada Família Towers. Photo © Dreamstime.com/Carlos Sanchez Pereyra.

Figure 8.4   Nativity Façade of La Sagrada Família. Photo by author.

Figure 8.5   Passion façade of La Sagrada Família. Photo © Dreamstime
.com/Veniamin Kraskov.

Figure 9.1   Star of David Concept Drawing, by Daniel Libeskind. Courtesy Studio Daniel Libeskind.

Figure 9.2   Museum Plan. Drawing by Daniel Libeskind. © SDL. Courtesy Studio Daniel Libeskind.

Figure 9.3   Jewish Museum Void. Photo by Torsten Seidel. © Torsten Seidel. Courtesy Studio Daniel Libeskind.

Figure 9.4   Holocaust Tower. Photo by Bitter Bredt. © Bitter Bredt. Courtesy Studio Daniel Libeskind.

Figure 9.5   Jewish Museum next to the Original Baroque Building. Photo by Bitter Bredt. © Bitter Bredt. Courtesy Studio Daniel Libeskind.

Figure 9.6   Reflecting Absence Memorial, by Michael Arad. Photo by Carolyn Cole (AP Photo/Carolyn Cole, Pool). Used with permission. © 2017 The Associated Press.

Figure 9.7   Vietnam War Memorial, by Maya Lin. Photo © Dreamstime
.com/Matthew Brown.

Scripture Index

Genesis		
1:1–2:4	149, 188, 189	
1–11	24	
1:2	181	
1:27	105, 149	
1:28	223	
1:29	149	
1:31	23	
2	22, 150	
2:9-10	142	
2:16	23	
2:17	151	
2:18	105	
2:18-25	149	
3	150, 167, 176	
3:5	151, 175n71	
3:8	23	
3:23	151	
4:1-8	173	
4:8	151	
4:12	23, 151	
4:16	23, 181	
4:17	23	
5:1-24	173	
9:11	78, 100	
12:1	24	

	22, 150
	149, 188, 189
	24

12:2	190
12:3	127
12:7	25
12:8	256
22	27
Exodus	
3:5	27, 140
4:22	33
13:8	216
15:17	28
20:2	216n11
20:4	187
32:1, 8	187
Deuteronomy	
4:12, 15	188
5:8	187
5:15	216n10
6:23	216
8:2	216n10
25:17	216
32:7	216
Joshua	
24:15	256
2 Samuel	
7	29
7:5-7	29

1 Kings
1:8-9   6
8   143
8:10, 11   143
8:12, 13   144
8:27   143
8:28-29   143, 144
Ezra
6:3   228
Job
10:8   182
23:3, 8   182
Psalms
3:3   112
8   24
8:3-6   15
10:1   182
18:1   112
22:3   29
33   106
46:1   182
48:8   108
81:10   216n10
87:5   108
132:13   28
137:4   108
139:5-10   139n85
147   127
Isaiah
1:11-17   116
6:1   143
6:1b-3   143
24:12-13   107
37:15   29
38:17   96
43:35   96n52
61:1, 4   103
65:21   103
66:1-2   29
Jeremiah
29:4-7   117
Lamentations
3:22   106
Ezekiel
40–48   108, 113
Haggai
1:2   229n39
1:5-6   229

Micah
4:3   81
6:5   216
1:14   229
Matthew
1:13   33
2:1-7   32
3:6   33
5   63
5:17-18   63
5:18   65
5:21-22   63n68
5:43-44   63n69
7:28-29   64n70
10:29   223
11:2   183n6
11:2-5   183, 206
11:4   103
11:4-5   146
12   63
12:2   63
12:9-14   63
13:2   30
13:24-30   92
16:21-22   226
17:4   30, 226
18:23-35   62
22:34-40   60n63
22:37-39   56
22:40   56, 65
23:27   60n63
23:37   79
26:11   182
26:32   31
28:10   31
28:16   32
28:20   182
Mark
1:5, 9   33
1:15   201
2:27   64
9:5-6   30
13:2   30
16:7   31
17:19   60n63
Luke
7:18-22   183
7:22   103, 146, 206

9:33	30	8:21	112
11:2	183	8:22	181
11:20	183	8:22-23	104
17:21	183	8:23	100
22:18	183	8:37-39	139n85
24:13-27	34	10:4	60, 61
John		11:16	27n47
1:2	215	12:19, 20	62n67
1:3	195	12–15	62
1:3c-4	169	13:9	62n67
1:4	196	13:9-10	62
1:14	139, 181, 215	14:11	62n67
1:18	204n72	15:3, 11, 12, 21	62n67
1:38-39	177	1 Corinthians	
1:46	32	1:23	215n9
3:13	204n72	3:16	31
5:2-17	106	4:5	182
6:56	178	8:4-10	92
7:52	32	11:24	210n89
8:31	178	11:26	234
8:32	21	13:12	181
9:12	89	15	104n69
13:3	204n72	15:28	211
13:33	182	15:51-53	100
14:2	182	2 Corinthians	
14:2-3	178	5:7	181
14:10	178	5:19	97, 112
15:4	178	Galatians	
15:4-5	196	3:17	59
15:7, 10	178	3:21	61
16:5-15	178	Ephesians	
16:7	182	1:20	100
16:16-17	182	2:11-22	173
18:36	88	Philippians	
19:12	89	2:7	243
Acts		Colossians	
1:9, 11	182	1:15-16	195
2	130	1:15-17	61
2:44	119n38	1:16-17	99
2:46	130	1:16-19	225
11:9	99	1:20	61, 91, 99, 112
14:17	73	1:22	61
17:7	89	4:11	182
Romans		Titus	
3:20	61	2:13	182
3:31	61	Hebrews	
6:15	61	8:12	96n52
8:18-27	104n69	10:17	96n52

11:10, 16	108	18	75
12:22	108	18:1-24	78
13:12	34	18:2-5	76
13:14	108	18:11-13	78
James		20–21	113
5:7-8	182	21	104n69, 106. 108
1 John		21:1	76, 103
2:24, 27, 28	178	21:1-3	181
4:13	178	21:2	76, 82
2 John		21:3	93, 116, 138, 201, 211
1:9	178	21:4	223
Revelation		21:5	91, 100, 106
4	78	21:9–22:9	108
4:3	78	21:12-13	122
5	78	21:22	122, 145
11:1-2	108	22	108
11:15	82	22:1	82
11:18	86	22:1-2	142
17:1–19:10	108	22:3-6	144
17:9	75		

General Index

Abelard, 106n1
Abraham, 5, 24–29, 120, 139, 190, 256
Acheropita, 93–94
Ackerman, James S., 41n9
Admont Abbey, 16–17
Adorno, Theodore, 238–40, 245, 253
Alberti, Leon Battista, 40n8, 47, 64, 133
Albright, W.F., 226
Allsop, Bruce, 52n36
altar, 5, 8, 24–28, 234
Althaus, Paul, 100
Ando, Tadao, 168–70
Aquinas, Thomas, 100, 106n1, 128
Arad, Michael, 251
Arch of Constantine, 94, 121
Arch of Titus, 94, 123
Aristotle, 106n1, 154–55, 158, 164
Armengol, Jordi Bonet i, 220n22
art, 2–4, 8, 53, 238–39, 241
Augustine, St., 92, 97, 100, 107, 109–14,
    118–19, 126–27, 130–31, 137, 144–46,
    186, 215, 217, 222
authority, 65–66, 166, 169–70; of Christ,
    62–64; of Scripture, 65; of the individual,
    37, 57
Avis, Paul, 197n51

axis, 164, 190, 193, 207, 245–46

Babel, tower of, 28, 35, 163n31
Babylon, 75–76, 78, 108, 111, 115–16, 189,
    228
Baldasso, Renzo, 134n73
Banksy, 8
baptism, 69–70, 82, 196, 217; of Jesus, 33
baptistery (of St John Lateran), 82, 84, 89
Barragan, Luis, 204–6
Barrie, Thomas, 152n9, 153, 157
Barth, Karl, 127, 139, 143, 181, 182n2,
    226n35
Bartholomew, Craig, 12, 23n40, 30n54,
    151n3
Basil, St., 98
basilica, 81–82, 101, 191
Baths of Diocletian, 52, 90
Bauckham, Richard, 38, 75n2, 108, 138
Beale, G. K., 6n15
Beattie, Tina, 90, 91n42, 106n1
Beckett, Samuel, 239
Begbie, Jeremy, 2–4, 8, 186–87
Bell, Allan, 163n31
Benson, Bruce Ellis, 45, 75n86
Benson, C. David, 87

Berger, Brigitte, 151–52
Berger, Peter, 151–52
Bergmann, Sigurd, 5, 11n1
Berkouwer, G. C., 197n50
Bernadine, St., 129
Bernini, Gian Lorenzo, 94, 125
Berry, Wendell, 12n7
Bess, Philip, 113, 158–59, 165–66, 170
Bianchini, Ricardo, 245, 246n21, 247n25
Biddle, Te Aouru, 171n57
Birch, Debra J., 133n67
Blowers, Paul, 67–68, 69n81
Bonhoeffer, Dietrich, 169–70, 197
Borg, Marcus J., 183n5
Borgo District, 93, 125, 145
Borromini, Francesco, 51
Boumer-Prediger, Steven, 151n4
Bouyer, Louis, 235
Bramante, Donato, 48–50
Brandenburg, Hugo, 84n26, 85n28
Brenk, Beat, 83n24
Brilliant, Richard, 85n27, 87
Brodman, James W., 134
Brueggemann, Walter, 25, 26n44, 149n1,
    188–89
Brunelleschi, Filippo, 131–32
Bruschi, Arnaldo, 49–50
Buber, Martin, 199
Bultmann, Rudolf, 77
Burnaby, John, 130–31
Burry, Mark, 222, 224, 226n36, 227

Cabrini-Green housing, 161–63, 166–67
Callicrates, 64
Calvin, John, 185, 210
Canonicus, Benedictus, 120
Capasso, Nicholas, 253n35
Casey, Edward S., 24, 152, 170n53, 175n72,
    232
Castel Sant'Angelo, 80, 93
Castello, Lineau, 11–12
Castiglione, Baldassare, 85n29
Cate, James Jeffrey, 77–78
chaos, 188–89
charity, 112, 136–37
Charles, Robert H., 77
Childs, Brevard, 187n24
Childs, David, 255

Christ, 50, 60–62, 65, 68–71, 81–83, 88–
    91, 94, 99–101, 111–12, 131, 142–44,
    180, 196–98, 204, 214, 225, 227, 230,
    233–36; absence of, 182, 185, 197–98,
    200; ascension of, 182, 204, 210–11;
    body of, 70, 125–26, 131, 145, 171–76,
    178–79; coming of, 185, 195; dwelling
    in, 178, 196; faith in, 61; place of, 30–31,
    179; presence of, 93, 126, 197–98, 211;
    return of, 182, 185, 197n50, 200; risen,
    31, 33, 67, 196; victory of, 108; see also
    Jesus
Church of Saint John, Lateran, 75, 80, 84,
    99, 120–21, 133
Church of Sant'Adriano, 89
Church of Santi Cosma e Damiano, 89–90,
    91n62
Church of the Good Shepherd, 203–4, 208
city, 6, 75–76, 80–81, 90, 104, 106–10,
    115, 118, 120, 131, 138, 147, 165; earthly,
    76, 79, 92, 107–8, 112–13, 126, 146;
    eternal, 110, 115; heavenly, 8, 93, 96–97,
    99, 108–10, 113–16, 122–23, 126, 130–
    31, 137, 144–46; holy, 76, 79, 80, 100,
    107, 112, 114, 123–24, 137, 140, 145,
    181; medieval, 116, 119, 127, 129, 134,
    146; of God, 110–13, 119, 127, 130, 136,
    144; sanctification of, 93–94, 100, 138;
    welfare of, 116–17, 131
Classen, Albrecht, 101, 129n56
Clement of Alexandria, 31
Cloag, John, 82n20
Clouse, Robert C., 200n65
Cochrane, Charles, 136
Cohon, Samuel, S., 62n67
Colosseum, 85, 87, 94–97, 101
Columbus Platform, 54–55, 61n66
communion of saints, 115, 121–22, 173,
    175, 217
community, 105, 107–8, 110, 114–16, 127,
    131, 196–98
Comte, Auguste, 231
Connah, Roger, 219n19
Connors, Joseph, 79
Constantine, 75, 79–81, 83, 90, 92n45, 111,
    115
consumerism, 70, 78, 166

cosmos, 14–16, 30, 39, 77, 153–56, 162, 233

Costas, Orlando E., 32n59, 33

creation, 8, 29, 66–67, 78, 98, 104, 105, 112, 149–50, 170, 188–89, 222; annihilation of, 86; flourishing of, 5, 66, 142, 223, 225; goodness of 63, 99, 102, 137; new, 7, 69–70, 76–77, 81–83, 99–100, 103, 115, 147, 186, 223, 234; old, 7, 76–77, 81–82, 99; renewal of, 81, 99–100, 103; restoration of, 89, 223; transformation of, 81–82, 84, 101

Crippa, Maria Antonietta, 16n21, 22n36

Da Vinci, Leonardo, 40n6

Dante Aligheri, 128

Davies, John G., 57n31

Day, Dorothy, 71

De Botton, Alain, 2, 57

De Lange, Nicholas, 54–55, 61n66

De Montaigne, Michel, 129

De Quincy, Quatremére, 154, 155, 158

decalogue, 60, 62, 69

Del Villar, Francesca de Paula, 220

Denson, C. Roger, 251

Descartes, René, 156–58, 160n27, 162, 228

disengagement, 156–57, 161–63, 166

displacement, 23–24, 151–52, 176, 178

Dodd, C. H., 198–99

Dods, Marcus, 229n39

Douglass, Frederick, 71

Dovey, K., 152n8

Dripps, Robert D., 5, 14–15, 18–22, 28

dwelling, 19, 35, 126, 149–50, 152, 167–68, 170–71, 174–79; of Christ, 93; of God, 143, 201

Dyer, Joseph, 118

economy, 40, 43–44; divine, 79, 87, 98–102, 126, 136–37, 224, 226, 234–35

Eden, 23, 112, 142, 151, 168, 181

Einstein, Albert, 230

Eliach, Yaffa, 249n27

Eliade, Mircea, 15n14, 16n19, 27

Ellul, Jacques, 23

Emerson, Mary, 46, 47n23, 53n37

emplacement, 23, 151n3

Enlightenment, 37, 66, 113, 158

Erechtheion, 52–53, 58, 72n87

Esch, Arnold, 83–84

eschatology, 106, 113, 210; annihilationist, 7, 100; futurist, 200; inaugurated, 200–201; realized, 184, 198, 200, 207; transformative, 7, 98, 100

eucharist, 69–70, 129, 131, 143, 147, 185,196, 210, 218, 234–35

Eusebius, 111

Farrow, Douglas, 198, 204, 210

Fiddes, Paul, 201–2

Filarete, Antonio, 134

forgiveness, 69–70, 96, 106, 136, 223, 252, 256

Foster, Warren, 171n57, 174

freedom, 20–21, 37–39, 50–55, 57, 60, 62, 64, 66–67, 69–70, 73, 105–6, 255

Freedom Tower, 2, 255

Freyne, Sean, 34n63

Fromm, Erich, 3

Frugoni, Arsenio, 128

Frugoni, Chiara, 117n30

Galilee, 31–34

Garber, Kent, 253n34

Gaudí, Antonio, 220–21, 224–27, 234

Gerhard, Johann, 100

Giedion, Sigfried, 145n97

Girouard, Mark, 134–35

Giuliani, Rudy, 240–42

Glanz, James, 242n13

God, 6, 23, 24–35, 50, 58–61, 73, 99–100, 102, 105–8, 112, 126–27, 136–38, 149–52, 170, 178, 184–85, 187, 189, 199, 213–16, 223, 228–30, 233–35; absence of, 7, 182, 187, 189; action of, 69; freedom of, 139–40; glory of, 22, 73, 92, 98, 104, 168–69, 174, 231, 224–25; grace of, 70, 136; immanence of, 191; people of, 59, 61–62, 65, 69, 111, 120, 197–98, 229n39; presence of, 7, 23, 27, 28, 116, 122, 138–40, 143–44, 188, 201, 204, 218n16; providence of, 73; purposes of, 5, 33, 64, 66–67, 69–70, 87, 89, 92, 96, 103–4, 106, 108, 110–11, 136, 149, 199, 222, 224, 226, 237; self-disclosure of, 4, 25, 28, transcendence of, 188, 191; will

of, 57, 60, 201, 209; Word of, 30, 72, 103, 215; work of, 33, 70, 72, 78
Goethe, Johan von, 157–58
Goldberger, Paul, 241n11, 244n17, 244n18, 245n20, 252, 256n40
Goldingay, John, 86
Gorringe, Timothy J., 5, 11n1, 106n1, 109n11, 129n59
Gothic, 51n33, 191, 208, 218n16
grace, 48, 59–60, 70, 91, 97, 106, 131, 136, 144, 215, 222, 226
Greene-McCreight, Kathryn, 66n72
Greenstein, Howard R., 54n42
Gregory Nazianzen, 69, 209
Gregory of Nyssa, 126
grid, 160, 162–66
Gromaticus, Hyginus, 164
Ground Zero, 6, 240–43, 245, 250–51, 254–56
Grünberg, Wolfgang, 231n45
Grundmann, Stefan, 81n18
Gunton, Colin E., 30n53, 69–70, 136, 156–57, 166n44, 198n56

Halbwachs, Maurice, 231
Hannah, Dorita, 219
Harries, Karsten, 209, 218
Hart, David Bentley, 188
Havel, Václav, 24
Hayberger, Gotthard, 16n20
Hebblethwaite, Paul, 179
Heidegger, Martin, 21–22, 187, 192
Heim, Karl, 11n1
Helena, Empress, 122
Henderson, J., 133n69
Heraclitus, 155
Heschel, Abraham J., 55n46, 56–58
Hesselink, I. John, 210n89
Hippodamus, 164–65
history, 28n49, 97, 120, 163, 187, 196, 199–200, 214–16, 228–30, 232–33, 235–36
Hood, Renate Viveen, 76n4
hope, 110, 182, 201–2, 236, 244–45, 249–50
Horkheimer, Max, 238n2
hospital, 84–85, 94, 98, 131, 133–36; of the Holy Spirit, 135; see also Ospedale
Hotel-Dieu, 134

Hunsinger, George, 235n55
Hunter, Shennan, 129n59
Huyssen, Andreas, 252–53

Ictinus, 64
identity, 23, 25, 54, 99, 175–76; of Christ, 198; Christian, 61, 68, 174, 214; human, 214, 243; of Israel, 216, 229; national, 7
Ignatius, 66n72
incarnation, 136, 196, 225
individualism, 70, 115, 157–58
Inge, John, 11n1, 26n44, 28n49
invention, 45, 48, 50–55, 64–66, 71, 73, 158, 241
inventiveness, 46–49, 51, 53, 56, 62–63, 65, 69, 72
Inwood, Henry William, 53
Irenaeus, 66n72, 68–69, 71, 100
Isidore of Seville, 109
Israel, 24, 26–30, 33–34, 54–55, 58–61, 65, 149–50, 185, 188–89, 215–16, 228–29

Jacobson, Howard, 250n28
Jara, Cynthia, 190–95, 208
Jenson, Robert W., 178, 198, 218n16
Jerome, 111
Jerusalem, 103, 107, 111, 114, 123; heavenly, 6, 88, 101, 113–16, 122; new, 76, 79–81, 92–93, 98–99, 106, 108, 113, 115–16, 138, 145
Jesus, 30–35, 55–56, 60, 62–65, 67–68, 117, 119, 125, 146–47, 172, 177–80, 181–85, 198–201, 214–15; as king, 88–89; authority of, 63; birth of, 32; crucifixion of, 95; death of, 32, 103, 147, 181–82, 218; ministry of, 30–34, 102, 136; resurrection of, 67, 99, 103, 147, 181, 184, 224, 233, 236; transfiguration of, 226; see also Christ
Jewish Museum, Berlin, 6, 245–48, 250, 256
Johnson, Kirsten Deede, 131
Jonas Salk Institute, 205–6, 208, 211
Judaism, 28, 33, 54–55, 57–59, 77, 123n45, 237

Kadishman, Menashe, 247
Kahn, Louis, 6, 204–8

Kant, Immanuel, 56–57, 167
Kellner, Hansfried, 151
Kessler, Herbert, 75, 81–82, 90n40, 93n47,
  94n49, 115n27, 121–22, 133n66, 141n90,
  142, 143n94
Kieckhefer, Richard, 218n16
Kierkegaard, Søren, 96, 214–15, 228,
  233–34
King, Martin Luther, 201
kingdom of God, 7, 72, 84, 88, 99, 111,
  131, 137, 182–85, 198–202, 206, 210–11,
  218, 223, 229n48, 234–35
Kinnard, Jacob N., 254n38
Kinney, Dale, 83n25, 85n27, 87n34, 97n57
Knight, Douglas H., 236n56
Koch, Ed, 242
Kogan, Michael, 199n62
Körs, Anna, 231n45
Kostof, Spiro, 165n39, 165n42
Kovacs, Judith, 76n3
Kraus, Rosalind, 164
Kuhn, Thomas, 19–20
Kulka, Heinrich, 192n37
Kümmel, W. G., 183n6
Küng, Hans, 198
Kunstler, Gustav, 192
Kunstler, James Howard, 107
Kuschel, Karl-Joseph, 204n72
Kwant, Remy, 176–77

La Sagrada Família, 220–22, 224–28, 231,
  234
Lane, William, 33
Laugier, Marc-Antoine, 50–51, 64, 72n87
law, 7, 37–39, 44, 54–65, 69, 73, 142, 159,
  167, 185, 187
Le Corbusier, 21, 102n65, 159–63, 166n45,
  167, 169, 175, 192, 208
Lefaivre, Liane, 42n11
Lefebvre, Henri, 4
Lesk, Alexandra, 53
Lessing, G. E., 214, 219, 223, 228, 230,
  232–33, 235–36
Lewis, John, 209
Libeskind, Daniel, 6, 244–51, 255–56
light, 168–69, 208–9, 211, 248–50
Lightfoot, R. H., 32
Lilburne, Geoffrey R., 168n49

Lin, Maya, 252–53
Lincoln, Abraham, 71
Lipton, Eric, 242n13
Liverani, Paolo, 83n23
Logos, 143, 193–96
Loos, Adolf, 6, 191–92, 194, 196, 208
Luo, Jialing, 214n3, 231n47
Luther, Martin, 59, 66, 71–72
Lutheran, 100, 197–98

MacIntyre, Alasdair, 159
Malevich, Kazimir, 164
Malina, Bruce J., 110
Malpas, Jeff, 12
Mandeville's Travels, 87
Mann, C. S., 226
Mannheim, Karl, 202
Marcuse, Peter, 243n16
Marion, Jean-Luc, 230, 234
Markus, R. A., 146n101
Markus, Thomas A., 219
Martin, Francis, 176n76
Mayernik, David, 50, 79, 102, 109n8, 113,
  120n40, 120n41, 121n42, 124, 125n47,
  128–29, 131–32
McGuckin, John, 209n85
McPartlan, Paul, 223n33
meaning, 2, 4, 12, 16, 18, 20, 208, 213,
  222, 228
mediation, 208–11
memorial, 25, 54, 87, 96–97, 232, 234,
  241–43, 247, 250–55
memory, 2, 50, 96–97, 113, 121, 231,
  232n48, 245–46, 255
Merton, Thomas, 112, 118, 137n81
Michelangelo, 125
Middleton, J. Richard, 100
Miles, Malcolm, 129n59
Miletus, 164–65
Mill, John Stuart, 38
Modernism, 107, 159
modernist, 102, 159, 192, 206, 213
Modernity, 37, 127, 151, 156, 158, 160, 166,
  188, 213–15
Mollat, Michael, 133n68
Moltmann, Jürgen, 100, 199n62
monasteries, 131–33
Mondrian, Piet, 164

monument, 7, 22, 87, 114, 227, 252
Mostert, Christiaan, 147
Mumford, Lewis, 89, 106n2, 110, 115, 120,
    129n59, 133, 134n71, 145–46
Münz, Ludwig, 192
music, 3, 8, 45, 186–87, 226

Nazianzen, Gregory, 69, 209
Nietzsche, Friedrich, 159
Norberg-Schulz, Christian, 3, 16, 152,
    190n32, 193
Noreen, Kirstin, 94n50
Noth, Martin, 187n25
Notre Dame du Haut, 167

Oberman, Heiko, 197n52
O'Daly, Gerard, 88, 111
Oppenheimer, Helen, 27n48
order, 14–16, 18, 21, 25, 28, 38–39, 40, 43–
    44, 47–48, 51, 54; Composite, 40, 51,
    132; Corinthian, 41, 43; Doric, 41–42,
    46, 49; Ionic, 41–42, 57; Tuscan, 41
Oseid, Julie, 194
Ospedale degli Innocenti, 131–33
Ospedale Maggiore, 134
Ouroussoff, Nicolai, 254
Ovid, 111n18

Pahl, John, 166n46
Pallasmaa, Juhani, 152n10, 222
Pannenberg, Wolfhart, 60, 147, 184–85,
    198n57, 210
Pantheon, 90–92, 193, 208
paradigm, 16, 18–21, 192, 228; theological,
    25–28, 32–34
Parihaka, 71
Park, K., 133n69
Parks, Rosa, 71
Parmenides, 155
Parthenon, 1, 42, 46, 47, 53, 62, 64
Pataki, George, 255
Pauly, Danièle, 208
Perrault, Claude, 47
Peterson, Eugene, 1, 2
Phideias, 64
Piazza del Campo, 128–31
Piazza del Popolo, 124, 145
Piazza San Marco, 128

Piazza San Pietro, 125
pilgrimage, 35, 81, 138n83, 140, 145–46,
    169, 218
Pirenne, Henri, 146n100
Plan Voisin, 159–63, 166–67, 169
Plato, 154–56, 158, 162, 228
Plaza de Mayo, 7
Polycarp, 66n72
Pope: Alexander VI, 93; Benedict XIV,
    95; Benedict XVI, 220; Boniface IV,
    90; Boniface VIII, 197; Clement X, 95;
    Damasus, 138n83; Felix IV, 89; Innocent
    III, 135; Innocent VIII, 94; Leo X,
    85n29; Miltiades, 75; Nicholas V, 124;
    Paschal 1, 93n47; Paschal II, 133; Sixtus
    IV, 135; Sixtus V, 95, 145; Sylvester, 87
Porta Flaminia, 124
Porta Praenestina, 122
postmodernity, 158, 160
proportion, 15–16, 20, 43, 64, 153

Quarton, Enguerrand, 80

Raphael, 85n29
rationalism, 158–59
raumplan, 191–96
reason, 48, 56–57, 155–56, 158, 162–63,
    167, 213–15, 233
reconciliation, 59, 96, 99, 101–2, 106, 112,
    122, 178, 181, 217–18, 227–28, 233, 243,
    256
redemption, 24, 68–69, 79–80, 90–91, 94,
    97, 100–101, 106n1, 111, 181, 199, 223,
    229, 233–34, 252
relics, 93, 121–22, 138
Renaissance, 6, 40, 47–48, 50–51, 58, 64,
    66, 95, 98, 102, 109, 113, 115, 124–26,
    145, 147, 158–59
representation, 21–22, 25, 27, 125, 193,
    201–2, 226
resurrection, 100, 103, 135, 184, 186; *see
    also* Jesus
Riini, Mona, 171n57
Riini, Sonny, 171n57
Ritschl, Albrecht, 200
Ritschl, Dietrich, 200n66
Rogers, Richard, 107

Rome, 6, 75–76, 79–95, 98–102, 104, 107–8, 111, 115–16, 118, 120–24, 126–27, 132, 135, 138, 140, 145
Rowe, C. Kavin, 89
Rowe, Peter G., 129, 130n60
Rowland, Christopher, 76n3
Royal, Te Ahukarumū Charles, 174n67
Rua, John, 171
Rufer House, 191–96, 208
rule, 7, 20, 37, 39, 43–50, 52–54, 56–57, 60, 62, 64–68, 73, 105, 154; monastic, 70; of Christ, 81–82, 196–97; of faith, 60, 65–69, 71–73; of God, 189, 199, 201
Ruskin, John, 44
Russell, David M., 78n12
Rykwert, Joseph, 48, 155n16, 164n38

sacred, 94, 118, 124, 138, 170, 195, 208–9; place, 29–30, 134, 139, 171; space, 30, 90, 143–45, 170
Saint Paul's Cathedral (London), 16–17, 191
Saint Peter's Basilica, 93, 121, 125
salvation, 1, 33, 61–62, 67, 70, 116, 147, 221, 230, 233, 235
San Carlo alle Quattro Fontane, 51
San Clemente, church of, 91–92, 140–41, 143–44
Sanders, E. P., 59n59
Santa Croce, 121–22
Santa Maria Antiqua, 89
Santa Maria dei Miracoli, 125
Santa Maria di Montesanto, 125
Santa Maria Maggiore, 121
Santa Prassede, 93n47, 121
Santa Pudenziana, 88
Sauter, Gerhard, 196
Saxer, Victor, 118
Schnackenberg, Rudolf, 198
Schneider, Bernhard, 247n23
Schoeps, H. J., 58n58
Schweitzer, Albert, 200
Schweizer, Eduard, 184n7
science, 2, 28, 37, 53, 206–7
Scully, Vincent, 253
Seasoltz, R. Kevin, 209n81
Sennett, Richard, 117–19, 157n22, 160n29, 163n32, 164–65, 213
Serlio, Sebastiano, 15n16, 41–42, 47, 64

Sheldrake, Philip, 5, 11, 109, 118n33, 120n40, 122n43, 137, 232n48
Silverstein, Larry, 241
sin, 57, 69–70, 72–73, 96, 98–99, 102, 104, 108, 131, 190
Smith, P. D., 92n44, 145
Smith, Terry, 238–39, 241n10, 243n14, 244n19, 248, 254n37
Smith, Thomas Gordon, 45, 48, 51–52, 65, 68
Socrates, 158, 215, 228
Sojourner Truth, 71
Solà-Morales, Ignasi, 220
Sovik, E. A., 30–31
Sparshott, Francis, 175n73, 177
Spindler, M., 11n1
Spinoza, Benedict, 228
Spirit, 209–11, 227, 234–36, 256
spolia, 82–85, 87, 89, 101
Steiner, George, 203
Stephens, Mark B., 77–78, 82n18, 86, 102–3
Stephens, Suzanne, 242–43
Subirachs, Josep, 221, 225
Summerson, John, 15n16, 40n8, 45–48
Symeon, St., 209
symmetry, 15–16, 40, 43, 52, 64, 15–54

Takao, Karaka, 171
Taylor, Charles, 26, 37–38, 119n37, 156, 161, 166–67
Taylor, Iain, 184n12, 210n87
Te Hira, Te Ahinamu, 171
Te Kaawa, Millie, 171n57
Te Maungarongo, 171–79
Te Whiti o Rongomai, 71
Tempietto, 48–50
temple, 6, 15–16, 27–31, 34–35, 41–43, 45–50, 92, 122–23, 130, 143–45, 229
Tertullian, 66n72, 69
Thacker, Alan, 138n83
Thiébaut, Philippe, 227n38
Tibullus, 111n18
Till, Karen E., 231
time, 163, 181–82, 186–87, 196, 210–11, 213–36
Tohu Kākahi, 71
Torah, 54–58, 61–62

Torrance, Alan, 59
Torrance, James B., 185n18
Torrance, T. F., 11n1, 31n58
tradition, 19, 44–45, 50, 55–57, 66, 157–59, 162, 166, 175, 221, 226–27
Trafalgar Square, 7
triglyphs, 41–43, 46–47
Trinity, 67, 80, 124–26, 137, 145, 178
Tuan, Yi-Fu, 12
Turner, Harold, 11n1, 16n19, 26n44, 28n51, 29, 31
Turrell, James, 242–43, 254n36
Tzonis, Alexander, 42n11

Unwin, Raymond, 119n37
Utopia, 103, 159, 163, 202

Van Pelt, Robert Jan, 214n2, 229, 240
Vietnam Memorial, 252–53
Vinnitskaya, Irina, 255n39
Viñoly, Rafael, 240–41
Virgil, 111n18
Vitruvius, 5, 11, 13–16, 18, 19, 21, 24, 35, 39–45, 47–48, 50, 52–54, 57n53, 60, 64, 69, 80, 98, 153–54, 156, 158
Vonberg, Paul, 191n33
Von Rad, Gerhard, 229n48
Vos, Gerhardus, 183

Walker, Peter, 251
Walsh, Brian, 151n4
Ward, Graham, 106n1, 126
Warner, Randy, 242

Watkins, Tony, 219n18
Webster, John, 38, 67n73
Weiss, Johannes, 200
Wells Cathedral, 217–18
Wells, Samuel, 221n27
Westerholm, Stephen, 58n58
Westminster Abbey, 1
White, Lyn, 39n5
Whitehead, John, 256
Wilberforce, William, 71
Wilken, Robert L., 110n13, 127–28
Williams, Rowan, 4
wisdom, 8, 37, 44, 47–48, 50, 55–57, 60, 65, 72, 105, 158–59, 222
Wolin, Sheldon, 114
World Trade Center, 240–44, 256
worship, 15, 24, 28, 30–32, 44, 59, 61–62, 65, 69–70, 73, 78, 81–82, 91, 115–16, 144–46, 168, 187, 194, 207, 229
Wright, Frank Lloyd, 192
Wright, N. T., 104n69, 183, 206, 221

Yeoman, Selwyn, 39n5
Yerushalmi, Yosef, 216
Young, Gayle, 96

Zacharias, Johanna, 75, 81–82, 90n40, 93n47, 94n49, 115n27, 121–22, 133n66, 141n90, 142, 143n94
Zachman, Randall, 185n16
Zizioulas, John, 147
Zuckerkandl, Victor, 186n21